the Unofficial Guide™ to Earning What You Deserve

Jason Rich

Macmillan • USA

Macmillan General Reference
A Simon & Schuster Macmillan Company
1633 Broadway
New York, New York 10019-6785

Macmillan Publishing books may be purchased for business or sales
promotional use. For information please write: Special Markets
Department, Macmillan Publishing USA, 1633 Broadway, New York,
NY 10019.

ISBN: 0-02-862716-4

Manufactured in the United States of America

10 9 8 7 6 5 4 3 2 1

First edition

This book is dedicated to my two closest and dearest friends, Mark and Ellen, who constantly challenge and motivate me to achieve success in whatever it is I set out to do. It's also dedicated to my family for providing me with the advantages growing up that eventually allowed me to pursue and achieve my own career goals and dreams.

Acknowledgments

I'd like to thank Nancy Mikhail, Jennifer Farthing, and Alexander Goldman at Macmillan for making this book possible and offering me guidance as the manuscript was created. Thanks also to Jeff Herman, my agent, for making this deal happen, which led to my writing this book.

I'd also like to thank you, the reader, for picking up this book. It's my greatest hope that the information you're about to read will be useful in pursuing your own career goals and objectives. If you'd like to share your thoughts or experiences, please drop by my web site (http://www.jasonrich.com) or e-mail me at jr7777@aol.com.

Contents

The *Unofficial Guide* Reader's Bill of Rights

We Give You More Than the Official Line

Welcome to the *Unofficial Guide* series of Lifestyles titles—books that deliver critical, unbiased information that other books can't or won't reveal—*the inside scoop*. Our goal is to provide you with the *most accessible, useful* information and advice possible. The recommendations we offer in these pages are not influenced by the corporate line of any organization or industry; we give you the hard facts, whether those institutions like them or not. If something is ill-advised or will cause a loss of time and/or money, we'll give you ample warning. And if it is a worthwhile option, we'll let you know that, too.

Armed and Ready

Our hand-picked authors confidently and critically report on a wide range of topics that matter to smart readers like you. Our authors are passionate about their subjects, but have distanced themselves enough from them to help you be armed and protected, and help you make educated decisions as you go through your process. It is our intent that, from having read this book, you will avoid the pitfalls everyone else falls into and get it right the first time.

Don't be fooled by cheap imitations; this is the *genuine article Unofficial Guide* series from Macmillan Publishing. You may be familiar with our proven track record of the travel *Unofficial Guides*, which have more than two million copies in print. Each year thousands of travelers—new and old—are armed with a brand new, fully updated edition of the flagship *Unofficial Guide to Walt Disney World*, by Bob Sehlinger. It is our intention here to provide you with the same level of objective authority that Mr. Sehlinger does in his brainchild.

The Unofficial Panel of Experts

Every work in the Lifestyle *Unofficial Guides* is intensively inspected by a team of three top professionals in their fields. These experts review the manuscript for factual accuracy, comprehensiveness, and an insider's determination as to whether the manuscript fulfills the credo in this Reader's Bill of Rights. In other words, our Panel ensures that you are, in fact, getting "the inside scoop."

Our Pledge

The authors, the editorial staff, and the Unofficial Panel of Experts assembled for *Unofficial Guides* are determined to lay out the most valuable alternatives available for our readers. This dictum means that our writers must be explicit, prescriptive, and above all, direct. We strive to be thorough and complete, but our goal is not necessarily to have the "most" or "all" of the information on a topic; this is not, after all, an encyclopedia. Our objective is to help you narrow down your options to the best of what is available, unbiased by affiliation with any industry or organization.

In each *Unofficial Guide* we give you:

- Comprehensive coverage of necessary and vital information

- Authoritative, rigidly fact-checked data

- The most up-to-date insights into trends

- Savvy, sophisticated writing that's also readable

- Sensible, applicable facts and secrets that only an insider knows

Special Features

Every book in our series offers the following six special sidebars in the margins that were devised to help you get things done cheaply, efficiently, and smartly.

1. "Timesaver"—tips and shortcuts that save you time.

2. "Moneysaver"—tips and shortcuts that save you money.

3. "Watch Out!"—more serious cautions and warnings.

4. "Bright Idea"—general tips and shortcuts to help you find an easier or smarter way to do something.

5. "Quote"—statements from real people that are intended to be prescriptive and valuable to you.

6. "Unofficially..."—an insider's fact or anecdote.

We also recognize your need to have quick information at your fingertips, and have thus provided the following comprehensive sections at the back of the book:

1. **Glossary:** Definitions of complicated terminology and jargon.

2. **Resource Guide:** Lists of relevant agencies, associations, institutions, web sites, etc.

3. **Recommended Reading List:** Suggested titles that can help you get more in-depth information on related topics.

4. **Index.**

Letters, Comments, and Questions from Readers

We strive to continually improve the *Unofficial* series, and input from our readers is a valuable way for us to do that.

Many of those who have used the *Unofficial Guide* travel books write to the authors to ask questions, make comments, or share their own discoveries and lessons. For lifestyle *Unofficial Guides*, we would also appreciate all such correspondence, both positive and critical, and we will make best efforts to incorporate appropriate readers' feedback and comments in revised editions of this work.

How to write to us:

Unofficial Guides
Macmillan Lifestyle Guides
Macmillan Publishing
1633 Broadway
New York, NY 10019

Attention: Reader's Comments

The *Unofficial Guide* Panel of Experts

The *Unofficial* editorial team recognizes that you've purchased this book with the expectation of getting the most authoritative, carefully inspected information currently available. Toward that end, on each and every title in this series, we have selected a minimum of three "official" experts comprising the "Unofficial Panel" who painstakingly review the manuscripts to ensure: factual accuracy of all data; inclusion of the most up-to-date and relevant information; and that, from an insider's perspective, the authors have armed you with all the necessary facts you need—but the institutions don't want you to know.

For *The Unofficial Guide to Earning What You Deserve,* we are proud to introduce the following panel of experts:

Robert Melendes is a recruiter for Lynne Palmer Executive Recruitment. He has held several managerial positions in publishing.

Hilary J. Bland is a Senior Human Resources Representative at Macmillan Publishing USA in New York, NY. Prior to joining Macmillan she was an executive recruiter and a training & development consultant in the financial services industry. Hilary is a graduate of Mount Holyoke College and holds an MA in Organizational Psychology from Columbia University.

H. Anthony Medley received his B.S. in Finance from UCLA, and his J.D. from the University of Virginia School of Law. He has negotiated billions of dollars worth of contracts of all sorts. As counsel for Litton Industries, he negotiated the contract for the design and construction of the Spruance Class Destroyer, the largest contract the U.S. Navy had signed to that date. He is the author of several books, including *Sweaty Palms: The Neglected Art of Being Interviewed.*

Introduction

A s the title of this book suggests, *The Unofficial Guide to Earning What You Deserve* was written to help you ultimately achieve your maximum earning potential right now in your current job (or the job you'll soon be landing), as well as in the future, wherever your career path may lead.

Having written two other career-related books—*First Job, Great Job: America's Hottest Business Leaders Share Their Secrets* (Macmillan) and *Job Hunting for the Utterly Confused* (McGraw-Hill), as well as articles for *National Business Employment Weekly* and *The Wall Street Journal's Managing Your Career,* and an ongoing (weekly) career column for the *Boston Herald* newspaper, over the years I have spoken with countless job seekers, headhunters, HR professionals, and executives from companies of all sizes and in many different industries. What you're about to read in the next 17 chapters reflects some of the more important information you'll need in order to earn what you deserve.

What I have discovered is the majority of people who are currently employed dislike their job and/or feel like they're overworked and underpaid. Some people have fallen into the trap of accepting a dead-end job, and after working in that job anywhere from six months to two years, they realize that they've made bad career decisions, yet don't know how to fix their mistakes. Far too many people are totally disenchanted with their job or career. Too many people dread waking up in the morning and showing up for work, and they often feel depressed, stressed out, frustrated, or totally bored with their job. You don't have to be one of these people!

On the other hand, some of the luckier people I've spoken with absolutely love their job or career. They have a true passion for the work they do, and enjoy the challenges they face each day, as well as the environment they work in, and the people they work with. Often, these are the people who are highly career driven and have a great deal of ambition. You can be one of these people!

While these people may appear lucky, in reality, luck had little to do with their success. What allowed these people to achieve their career goals and dreams was hard work, dedication, careful planning, a good education, and the ability to analyze their likes, dislikes, skills and weaknesses, and use this information in a way that continuously allows them to set and achieve goals for themselves.

What sets the lucky people apart from those who hate their jobs? The answer is very little, which means that there is probably little holding you back from achieving your own career related goals and dreams. What's that, you don't have any well-defined career goals? Well, that's one of the first things you'll need to change. This book will show you why setting goals is critical for achieving career related success, and will explain how to go about achieving your career-related goals, whatever they might be.

Just because you don't have an Ivy League education, you can still most likely work your way up the corporate ladder at whatever company you choose to work for (assuming you're not in a dead-end job). Likewise, if you have an Ivy League education, you can't expect high-paying, executive-level jobs to be handed to you, just because you have a fancy diploma. In today's business world, having a good education is important, but having a marketable skill set and proven work experience is even more critical for landing the best jobs.

As long as you're willing to work hard, seek out additional training and education (when needed), and spend the time and energy needed to develop an understanding for yourself and the types of work you're interested and capable of doing, there's little holding you back from earning what you deserve.

This book was written for:

People either about to graduate (or who are recent graduates) and who are entering the work force for the first time. From this book, you'll learn how to define your interests and skills, showcase your talents, determine what type of work environment you're best suited to work in, and find (and ultimately land) the best job opportunities for you. After learning how to analyze your wants, needs, strengths, weaknesses, and interests, this book will explain how to find the best job opportunities (many of which are never advertised), and the help you create a resume and cover letter that will best showcase your qualifications for the job you want. The book will walk you through the entire job search process, and ultimately focus on helping you negotiate the best possible salary and compensation package for yourself, based upon your qualifications and earning potential.

People who are currently employed, but feel like their hard work has gone unnoticed by their superiors. It's extremely common for people to accept a job, work extremely hard, yet not receive any recognition from their employer, much less a raise or promotion. If you're in this situation, this book will help you determine why your accomplishments have gone unnoticed and help you change that. If you truly deserve higher pay or a promotion, this book will help you get exactly what you deserve (which may be different from what you want or are currently receiving). From this book, you'll learn how to better showcase your skills and accomplishments, communicate better with your superiors, perform well during employee reviews/ evaluations, and how to seek out and receive a raise and/or promotion.

The days of working for one company (or corporation) for your entire career are gone. It's extremely common for people to switch jobs (and employers) every few years. It's also common for people to decide to pursue other career paths entirely. If you're interested in changing jobs or changing careers, this book will help you make the change as easily as possible, while helping you maximize your earning potential.

For some people, in order to truly earn what they deserve (or be totally satisfied with their career), they can't work for someone else. Thus, they choose to practice their professional as someone who is self-employed, or they choose to start their own small business (or home-based business).

If you believe you have an entrepreneurial spirit and an incredible will to succeed as your own boss, than this book will help you get started, and help you avoid the common mistakes associated with working for yourself and/or starting your own business.

The Unofficial Guide to Earning What You Deserve offers a lot of information, resources, tips and strategies to help you advance your career forward and negotiate the best possible salary for yourself. However, there are no shortcuts to achieving career-related success. Nothing can take the place of hard work. If you want to land a job that pays well, you must be able to prove to a potential employer that you'll be a valuable asset and that you have the qualifications necessary to fill the responsibilities of the job you're applying for. An employer isn't going to pay you a high salary because they like you. You'll receive a high salary because it's something that you've earned. The same holds true for obtaining a raise or promotion. These are rewards for employees who have proven their value to their employers.

Just because you deserve a fair salary doesn't necessary mean you'll get one. This is another area where this book will come in handy. Companies are in business to make money. Their goal is to pay employees as little as possible, yet get the most value out of them. Ultimately, it will be your ability to negotiate and your willingness to work hard and prove yourself to be a valuable asset to a company that will allow you to earn the salary you deserve. This salary will be based upon a variety of criteria, including your qualifications (your skills, education, work experience, and ability to perform the job you're hired to do).

In addition to having the core skills needed to fill a specific job, to be a highly marketable applicant, or to vastly improve your chances of earning raise or promotion, you'll need to focus on your personal skill set. It will also be necessary to develop the core personality traits that virtually all employers look for in applicants or employees.

Your personal skill set incorporates all of the skills you have that can somehow make you a more valuable and useful employee. Everyone has their own unique personal skill set that sets them apart from other applicants or co-workers. How you develop and showcase this skill set on an ongoing basis throughout your career will have a major impact on your success.

Likewise, having the personality traits that employers believe to be valuable will also make your chances of landing a new job or obtaining a raise/promotion a bit easier. While every employer looks for a different set of personality traits and puts stronger importance on some traits over others, just a few of the more common things that employers look for are employees who are:

Able and willing to learn and adapt to an ever changing work environment

Career-driven

Competent

Decision-makers

Dedicated

Friendly

Goal-oriented

Hard working

Honest

Motivated

Respectful

Responsible

Self-reliant

Team-oriented

Well organized

Always striving to enhance your personal skill set and improve upon the personality traits that employers believe are important is something that should be an ongoing goal and something that you constantly work toward, whether you're looking for a job or you're happily employed. As you'll learn from this book, there are many ways you can immediately begin enhancing your personal skill set and developing the personality traits employers look for.

Every employer considers its employees an asset. In business, every asset has a specific financial value, whether it's an employee, piece of equipment, or an office building. As someone who works for a company, based on your work, you have a value to that employer. Your perceived value is reflected in terms of dollars and cents, and is paid to you in the form of a salary (and benefits package). This is the price a company is willing to pay for your services.

By making yourself more valuable to an employer, your earning potential increases. This sometimes requires that you develop new skills or take on more responsibilities. Learning how to better showcase your value to an employer will help you earn the salary that you want and deserve.

The Unofficial Guide to Earning What You Deserve is divided into sections that target different aspects of the job search and career management process. Depending on your circumstances, you may want to read only those sections that apply to your immediate needs, however, you'll be best served by reading this entire book, from cover-to-cover, and then going back and focusing on those chapters or sections that relate to your particular situation.

As you read this book, keep a pad and pen handy, because you'll be asked many questions to which you should actually take the time to write out answers. This will help you prepare for a job search, better position yourself to earn a raise or promotion, or help to prepare you for a salary negotiation with your (potential) employer. Throughout this book, you'll also be provided with hundreds of resources that will help you gather more information or obtain the answers to your personal career-related questions. Since many people now have access to the Internet's World Wide Web, many useful web site addresses have been listed. These are online resources (often free of charge to use) where you can go to learn more information about a specific company, topic, or product.

Today's business world is highly competitive. While you must work hard to meet the ever growing expectations of employers, you must always keep your own personal and professional best interests in mind, and at times, make decisions that will impact your career and lifestyle. Before pursuing any career or job opportunities, think about all of the ramifications involved and make sure that the opportunities you choose to pursue will somehow help you achieve your long-term career objectives and goals.

As you read this book, keep an open mind. If some of the information you read seems obvious, that's great because it means that you're already at least one step ahead of many of your co-workers or fellow job applicants. Everyone's personal situation is different. This book offers advice that you'll find useful, no matter what type of job or career you choose to pursue, however, the personal and professional decisions you make regarding your career are ultimate your own. You must make decisions that you are comfortable with, and not let anyone or anything interfere with what in your heart you believe to be the right thing for you to do in order to achieve your career goals and dreams, as well as your true earning potential. Don't believe people who tell you that you can't do something or achieve your goals. As long as your dreams and goals are realistic, and you're willing to work hard, they can be achieved! So, to get started, simply turn the page!

What Are You Worth?

GET THE SCOOP ON...
Defining your goals ▪ Learning to love your
work ▪ Marketing yourself as an employee

PART I

Chapter 1

It All Comes Down to Dollars and Good Sense

*T*he *Unofficial Guide to Earning What You Deserve* is designed to provide you with the information and resources you need to seek out the very best job opportunities and to reach your true earning potential. This book will teach you how to enhance your personal skill set and become a highly marketable employee, and also to negotiate the best possible salary for yourself.

If you're already happily employed but believe you deserve a raise or a promotion (but you still need to convince your employer of this fact), this book will provide you with strategies to help you get what you want and deserve. For some people, their true earning potential can only be reached by working for themselves, so this option is explored as well.

By reading this book, you'll discover that wanting to earn a higher salary from your next job, wanting a raise, or wanting a promotion is very different from actually deserving any of these things. An employer isn't going to simply give you a higher

3

salary because you're a nice person. They're going to offer you a higher salary because you deserve it and you have proven you could be a valuable asset to the company based on your qualifications—your personal skill set, work experience, and education. Likewise, an employer isn't going to just give you a raise or a promotion. These are things that must be earned, often through hard work and putting in the time necessary to "pay your dues."

Assuming you're willing to do what's necessary to earn the salary you want, this book will help you capture your employer's attention and negotiate the best possible job opportunity and compensation package for yourself. By reading this book, you'll learn to better understand your employer's expectations so you can showcase yourself as being worthy of receiving the raise, promotion or starting salary you want and deserve.

If you're particularly talented in a particular profession and already have experience and education that puts you in high demand by employers, you may find that your earning potential will be greater if you decide to work for yourself, providing consulting services to other companies for example. You might find it more productive and rewarding (emotionally and financially) to use your knowledge and skills to start your own company, instead of working for a company. These options are also explored later in this book.

Before you can set off on a quest to land the best job opportunity or earn the highest possible salary (based on your earning potential), you first must discover some information about yourself. This chapter will help you:

- Define yourself as a person and determine your likes and dislikes as they apply to your career options.

- Define your personal, professional, and financial goals for the short-term and long-term.

- Understand why it's vital that you truly have a passion for your work.

- Position yourself as a marketable employee by understanding today's job market and determine what you can expect as we enter into the next millennium.

Who are you?

In order to find a job that will allow you to earn what you deserve, and at the same time be emotionally rewarding for you, you'll need to spend some time considering:

- Your own strengths and weaknesses.

- Your most marketable skills.

- How to position your education and previous work experience so that you're in high demand by employers.

- What industry you have the most career advancement and earning potential.

- What type of work environment you personally are most suited to prosper.

As you consider these issues, you need to determine what you personally are looking for out of a job or your career as a whole, and think about these issues as they relate to the long-term. Every job you accept should somehow help you move your career forward and be a step toward helping you achieve your ultimate personal, professional, and financial goals.

For you to be truly outstanding in whatever type of job you choose to accept, it must involve work that you can be passionate about and an employer you can enjoy working for. If you ever wondered why so many people hate their work, it's because they didn't take time to consider what it was they wanted to do with their lives and then properly consider all of the available career opportunities available to them based on their desires, qualifications, and potential. It's too easy to fall into a dead-end job that causes you to dread waking up each morning.

To avoid this situation, simply take the time (while you're looking for a job or career opportunity) to consider:

■ What you want

■ What you enjoy

■ What you need

■ What you're qualified to do

Once you know these things, make every effort to seek out the opportunities that allow you to nicely merge them. Don't simply accept the first opportunity that comes your way or be willing to make too many compromises. If you can't find the absolute perfect job right now, find one that's the next best thing, and at the same time, get whatever additional training, education, or experience you need to land what you'd consider to be your dream job.

Earning what you deserve and being able to enjoy your work is going to take a lot of motivation and hard work, both while you're involved in a job search and after you're employed. Your career is something that will constantly evolve as you gain new experiences, take on new responsibilities, learn new skills, and continue to work your way toward achieving your personal, professional, and financial goals.

The thing about having your own goals is that if you really want to achieve them, you're going to have to take it upon yourself to do so. Chances are, you aren't going to find an employer that will make your goals a reality on your behalf. If you want to receive a high salary, you'll have to work hard to earn it. In order to receive a $75,000 per year salary (plus benefits and perks), for example, you'll have to develop the skill set and expertise so that you provide at least $75,000 per year worth of value to an employer. All companies are in business to make money, and none is going to pay you a salary that you don't deserve or offer you benefits that haven't been earned.

If you have worked hard to develop the skills, obtain the education, and gain the experience that an employer is looking for, with the proper negotiation, you'll be able to earn what you deserve. This becomes easier if you have the skills needed to market yourself properly to an employer and have the ability to create a demand for your services.

Finding the right job or career means figuring out who you are as a person and determining exactly what want and need out of every aspect of your job. For example, if you have been trained as an accountant and have a strong interest in finance, then you need to determine if you want to work for an accounting firm, be part of a company's in-house accounting department, or start your own accounting firm and take on clients. If you choose to work for a company (whether it's an accounting firm or working for a company's in-house accounting department), you need to determine a few things:

> 66
> There are as many ways of breaking into an industry as there are people in it. I am a great believer in hard work. I think that the people who work hard, who are tenacious, and who don't quit are the ones who are going to succeed.
> —Jeri Taylor, Executive Producer, *Star Trek: Voyager* (UPN).
> 99

- What size company you'd most enjoy working for.
- What type of corporate environment you find appealing.
- What industry you want to work in (or what type of clients you'd like to have).

After all, working as an accountant for a small accounting firm that handles its clients' personal income tax returns will provide a very different experience than working for a large accounting firm that handles Fortune 500 companies. The experience will also be different if you're an in-house accountant for a twenty-person company that designs web pages, as opposed to someone working for the in-house accounting department of a corporate giant like Microsoft or The Walt Disney Company.

As you choose what type of work environment you're best suited to prosper in, you also need to consider the career track that's available to you with each employer, and make sure that you never accept a dead-end job. Ideally, you want a job that has an unlimited career track that's based on how hard you work, your dedication to the company and your proven abilities. Can you potentially work your way up an employer's corporate ladder to reach senior vice presidential status (or higher)? If so, what will it take for you to achieve this, if this is in fact your career goal? How long will it take working for a specific employer? Could you potentially reach your goal faster working for another employer?

How much effort are you willing to put into achieving your goals? Are you willing to return to school to get more education or obtain additional on-the-job training? Are you willing to work as much overtime as necessary to gain seniority or capture the attention of your employer? Do you have the motivation necessary to constantly outperform your coworkers and achieve higher productivity in order to earn promotions or pay raises faster?

Knowing as much as possible about yourself, your capabilities, your potential, and your likes and dislikes will help you find the very best career opportunities for yourself. Chapters 2, 3 and 6 will help you to better pinpoint what employers are looking for and help you tap your own creativity in order to find those opportunities that are unadvertised but that will allow you to truly reach your potential.

Define your personal, professional, and financial goals

In order to ensure that you don't fall into a dead-end job or make the wrong career decision(s), you need to have a good understanding of what you're ultimately trying to achieve, so that you have something definitive to work toward. This means setting short-term and long-term goals. Over time, these goals may evolve, but you always want to have a clear picture of what you're striving to accomplish and know what steps you need to take in order to make your goals become reality.

The very best way to achieve your goals is to write them down and study them regularly. Next, take each of your goals (one at a time) and divide them into smaller sub-goals that are more easily attainable. Finally, figure out what you need to do to achieve each of your sub-goals and then develop a timeline or schedule for yourself so that you're always somehow working toward achieving a sub-goal.

One long-term goal may be divided into 10 or 20 (or more) sub-goals, but each time you achieve one of those sub-goals, you'll know that you are that much closer to achieving your ultimate goal. Tracking all of this on paper is an excellent strategy, because you'll always be able to see what you've accomplished, what you should be working on currently, what needs to be done next, and what you're ultimately trying to achieve.

Your goals should be well thought out and well organized. This might mean categorizing them as personal goals, professional goals, and financial goals. Everyone has different values and different dreams, so the definition of success for one person will be very different from someone else's definition. Thus, it's important that the goals you develop for yourself are your own. Your goals should incorporate what's important to you and what you value. A goal might involve:

- Obtaining true happiness
- Earning lots of money
- Having an impressive job title
- Owning a flashy sports car
- Owning a nice home or condo
- Having a close family
- Having children
- Building and maintaining close friendships
- Having a flexible work schedule
- Someday being your own boss and/or starting your own company
- Returning to school to earn an advanced degree
- Breaking a smoking habit

■ Being promoted to Senior Vice President at the company you work for

It really doesn't matter what your goals are, as long as they're what you want and you're willing to do what's necessary to achieve them. As you organize your various goals, classify them as short-term (achievable within six months), mid-term (achievable in between six months and two years), or long-term (achievable in two to five years or longer). You should also list lifetime goals, which are those that may seem almost unattainable now, but that could be achieved in five to 10 years (or more) if you constantly make small steps forward toward achieving them.

For example, if you're just graduating from school, a lifetime goal might be to become the CEO of a specific Fortune 500 company. Right now, you're probably qualified for an entry-level position, but if you work hard and set goals for yourself that slowly allow you to move up the corporate ladder, and over time you earn promotions, there is every chance that your ultimate goal might someday become a reality. After all, the CEOs of today's biggest corporations weren't born CEOs. While some of them were born into a family business, many CEOs of major corporations went to school, worked hard, and slowly climbed the corporate ladder (usually moving to different companies that offered better opportunities along the way).

If you're willing to plan, work hard, obtain additional skills (through education and training), and seek out opportunities, there are no professional or financial goals that you can't achieve.

> 66
> You can't just sit around waiting to get lucky. There's a saying, 'You have to make your own luck,' and I really believe this is true.
> —Howard Lincoln, Chairman, Nintendo of America, Inc.
> 99

66

Dedication is the key to success. Whatever you're involved with, dedication and commitment become so important. You have to put in the necessary time and work hard to accomplish anything, whether you're playing professional sports or working in business. Obviously, you're lucky if you have talent, but the people who actually make it are the people who sacrifice the most, who are the most dedicated, and who work the hardest.
—Wayne Gretzky, New York Rangers

99

Making your goals achievable

In order for a goal to be achievable, it must be well defined and then broken down into more manageable and even more achievable sub-goals. You also must develop a true belief in yourself and develop the motivation to ensure that your goals become a reality, despite what other people say or do. A goal must also be practical. For example, winning the lottery is not a practical goal, because your chances of hitting it big are slim and you have no control over the outcome. A goal must also be something that comes from your heart. A goal can't be dictated to you by someone else, even if that person is a parent, spouse, or someone else close to you.

No matter how old you are, it's never too late to start working toward your goals. Even if you never achieve your ultimate life-long goal(s), your emotional well being will be much more positive if you know in your heart that you've constantly worked toward achieving them. Most people simply let life pass them by, never lifting a finger or making a conscious effort to define their true goals, much less do what's necessary to make their goals a reality.

If you're at a point in your life where you have some goals floating around in the back of your head, but you haven't yet written them down or thought them through, there's no better time than the present to do this. At the same time, you should consider why you haven't yet achieved your goals. Some of the common reasons why people don't achieve their goals:

- Laziness
- They're unfocused
- Lack of motivation
- Lack of confidence and/or self-esteem

- They're afraid of failure
- Lack of resources
- Lack of opportunities
- Lack of organization
- Lack of knowledge regarding how to set and achieve goals

Take some time to analyze you own life and personal situation. Why haven't you achieved your goals (or at least began working toward your goals)? What could you start doing today (*right this minute*) to focus on your goals, break them up into sub-goals and then start achieving those sub-goals, one at a time? In order to achieve your professional goals, for example, what type of job do you need? What needs to change about your current job? What additional training or education must you acquire?

As you consider what needs to be done in order to achieve your goals, write down any and all of the obstacles (or potential obstacles) that you might encounter. Aside from giving up or walking away, what can you do to compensate for or overcome each of these obstacles? Through careful consideration and research, you should be able to determine what obstacles lie ahead and then develop plans, in advance, to overcome them.

One excellent strategy for achieving your goals is to find people who have already achieved similar goals and use them as role models. Study what they've accomplished and what they did to achieve their goals. If possible, make contact with your role model and make him or her your personal mentor. If you've selected someone who is a celebrity, a public figure, or one who is no longer living, learn everything you can about that person through

> **"**
> If you really believe you can do something, you'll somehow find a way. You will overcome all obstacles and challenges.
> —Debbi Fields, founder and President, Mrs. Fields Cookies.
> **"**

Unofficially...
In Barry Farber's *Diamond in the Rough* program, you'll hear insights into the process of success from such high achievers as Tom Peters and Bruce Jenner. This is a six-audiocassette program that includes an Action Planner Workbook ($59.95).

research. Being able to follow in the footsteps of someone you truly admire will not only provide you with guidance, but will be a source of motivation. A mentor (a role model with whom you have contact) often has the ability to help open up opportunities for you or help you network with key people.

If you ask anyone who is happy and successful what actually made them successful, and what allowed them to achieve their goals and dreams, the response you'll hear constantly is hard work, dedication, and being self-motivated. Also, you'll find that the person has a true passion for whatever it is that they do. Whether you discuss this with a successful business person, a professional athlete, an entrepreneur, a homemaker, or some type of artist, the response will be basically the same.

Once you have a basic understanding of what it takes to define a goal and what you'll need to do in order to achieve it, spend some time thinking about what you've been doing wrong up until now that has kept you from properly defining and/or achieving your goals. Next, think about whatever it is that you're doing right and consider ways you can enhance or magnify those efforts.

There are dozens of motivational experts who offer books, tapes, and/or videos designed to help anyone define their goals and transform them into reality. Two excellent programs are *Personal Power 2* by Anthony Robbins and *Diamond in the Rough* by Barry J. Farber. Both of these programs are available from Nightingale Conant (800-323-5552 / http://www.nightingale.com), a mail-order company that specializes in motivational, self-help, and instructional books, videos, and audio programs.

Understanding today's job market and the job market for the next millennium

After you've determined what type of job(s) you're qualified to fill and in what industry you want to work, it's important that you take the necessary time to investigate the job market.

What types of jobs are available now? Is there a high demand among employers for people with your qualifications? What is the job market in your industry expected to be like five to ten years in the future? What impact does technology have on your job opportunities today? What about five or ten years down the road? What career advancement opportunities are or will be available to someone with your qualifications after you've spent anywhere from six months to three years (or more) in one position?

These are all questions that can be answered through research. For example, visit virtually any library and look up your occupation, the industry you hope to work in, or your potential job title in *The Occupational Outlook Handbook, The Career Guide to Industries,* or *The Employment Outlook, 1996-2006: A Summary of BLS Projections.* All three of these reference books are published by the U.S. Department of Labor's Bureau of Labor Statistics.

As you research a particular industry or occupation, determine how you'll fit in, based on your qualifications, i.e., your skills, experience, and education. The U.S. Department of Labor reports, "The number of wage and salary worker jobs in the United States totaled nearly 122 million in 1996 and is projected to reach almost 140 million by 2006. In addition to these workers, the U.S. economy also provided employment for nearly 11 million self-employed workers and about 180,000 unpaid family

Bright Idea
Knowing what types of jobs are available, what level of jobs are available, and what the outlook for a specific industry or occupation is before entering into it, is an excellent career planning strategy.

workers...Fully 87 percent of the Nation's workforce possessed a high school diploma, or its equivalent, in 1996. As the premium placed on education in today's economy increases, workers are responding by pursuing additional training. In 1996, the Nation's workforce that had some college or an associate's degree totaled 29 percent, while an additional 26 percent had continued in their studies and had at attained a bachelor's degree, or higher."

If you choose to pursue a career in agricultural services, for example, you should know that over 30 percent of all workers in this field are employed in California, Florida, and Texas. Also, a large number of the available jobs are considered entry level (with skills that can be acquired in less than a week), meaning that your earning potential will be low. Construction workers, on the other hand, are among the highest hourly wage earners in America, and construction is one of the U.S. economy's largest industries.

Define yourself as an employee

After identifying for yourself what makes you a marketable job candidate, you must find creative ways to convey this information to potential employers, initially using your resume and cover letters, and later through your job interviews. Using your resume as a model, you'll need to develop a sixty-second sales pitch for yourself that you can use on the telephone or in-person with potential employers in order to capture their attention. Your goal is to demonstrate that you have the skills, experience, education, and personality that an employer is looking for, and that you will provide more value to an employer than other applicants. As you define yourself as an employee, you must make an effort to focus on what employers are looking for, and cater to their needs.

If you're currently employed and looking to earn a raise or promotion, you'll need to carefully analyze the wants and needs of your employer, identify the various ways you can use your skills to help the employer better reach its goals, and be able to showcase what you have already accomplished while employed in your current job.

You'll need to answer the question, "Why should an employer make an even bigger investment in me instead of someone else?" Whether or not you will earn a raise or promotion becomes a dollars-and-cents issue for an employer. You must be able to prove that you're worth what you're asking for and that you're capable of taking on greater challenges and responsibilities. The raise and/or promotion you want must be earned, and you must be able to demonstrate to an employer that you are, in fact, deserving of what you're requesting.

Chapters 8 and 9 will help you position yourself to employers and assist you in showcasing your qualifications in the best possible way so that you stand out from other applicants and create the perception that you'll be an extremely valuable asset to a potential employer.

The labor force in America (1996 to 2006)

The labor force is constantly changing and, now more than ever, there are plenty of career opportunities available for older workers, minorities, and females. Current trends, according to the U.S. Department of Labor, demonstrate that "with the aging of the population, coupled with increases in the labor force activity of older workers, older workers will be the fastest growing segment of the labor force [between 1996 and 2006]." During this same period, "women's [versus men's] share of the labor force will continue to grow, rising from 46 to

47 percent...The labor force participation rate for [all] women has risen from 51 percent in 1976 to 55 percent in 1996, and is projected to increase to 61 percent by 2006." In other words, it's projected that by 2006, 61 percent of all working-age women in America will hold paying jobs.

Meanwhile, the U.S. Department of Labor reports, "The labor force growth of Hispanics and Asians and others will be much faster than blacks and white non-Hispanics due to the effects of immigration. Hispanics are the fastest growing group over the 1996 to 2006 period, increasing more than three times as fast as the overall work force, followed closely by the 'Asian and other' group...As a result, the Hispanic labor force will overtake the black labor force in size by 2006."

During the 1996 to 2006 period, over 40 million workers will enter the work force. "Of the over 40 million entrants, 25 million will be an offset to those who left the labor force. The other 15 million people account for the projected growth of the labor force. Over the 1986 to 1996 period, there were 34.6 million entrants and 18.4 million leavers," reports the U.S. Department of Labor. "The majority of the labor force entrants are projected to be white non-Hispanics, 24.2 million between 1996 and 2006, 2 million more than during the 1986 to 1996 period. Black non-Hispanics account for 6.2 million entrants, 300,000 more than Hispanic entrants."

As we proceed into the next millennium, all net job growth will be in the service producing sector. "Service producing industries are projected to account for all of the growth of wage and salary worker employment over the 1996 to 2006 period. These industries include transportation, communications, and utilities; wholesale and retail trade; finance, insurance, and real estate; services, including agricultural services and private households; and government," reports the U.S. Department of Labor.

Of the millions of jobs that will become available between now and 2006 in all industries, the majority of them (a projected 67.7 percent) will require no more than a high school education and/or on-the-job training. Approximately 23.3 of the available jobs will require a bachelor's degree or higher, while the highest paying jobs (about 9.1 percent of the available jobs by 2006) will require post-secondary education.

How will your value as an employee increase or decrease in the next decade?

This question will be different for everyone, based on your occupation, what industry you're working in, and what skills, education, and experience you have to offer to employers. A major factor that will impact your earning potential over the next decade will be how well you keep up with changes in your industry and technological innovations. The best way to ensure that you'll provide value to an employer over the next 10 years is to make sure you're working in a growing (or expanding) industry, that your particular job offers upward mobility, and that you personally pursue additional education and/or on-the-job training that will allow you to stay on the cutting edge as changes take place within your field.

Most employers will not insist that you receive extra on-the-job training or that you have the skills needed to be a useful or marketable employee in the future, as long as you have the necessary skills

"

The days of earning a gold watch for a lifetime's work at a company are gone. If you have the tools, the right skills, the right attitude, and the ability to spot opportunities, then you're probably going to have multiple jobs and careers in your lifetime, and you're going to be successful.
—Jim McCann, President and CEO, 1-800-FLOWERS.

"

and ability to perform the job you're hired to do now. Thus, it becomes *your* responsibility to seek out training opportunities to ensure that you maintain a personal skill that will keep you in high demand and highly marketable in the future. No matter what career, job, or occupation you're looking to pursue, one way to ensure you'll have the skills in demand by employers in the future is to make sure that you become computer literate now, and that you keep up with technological advancements.

Becoming computer literate means becoming familiar with the use of a personal computer or a computer network, and being able to effectively operate popular business applications, such as Microsoft Word, Microsoft Excel, Microsoft Explorer, Lotus 1-2-3, Lotus Notes, WordPerfect, QuickBooks, Act!, or other Windows-based applications. As you'll discover later in this book, computer training is available from a wide range of sources, and obtaining the basic knowledge you need right now requires a relatively small time and financial commitment, yet the long-term advantages to your career will be dramatic.

Making yourself a marketable employee

As you'll learn in Chapter 3, one way to make yourself a marketable employee is to clearly define your personal skill set. You also must be able to promote this skill set (along with your work experience and educational background) to potential employers as you solicit new job opportunities, a pay raise, or a promotion. You also want to make sure that you have the skills and personality traits that are in hot demand by employers.

Based on your qualifications, your ability to earn what you deserve will depend on knowing what your fair market value as an employee is, and your ability to demonstrate your true value and potential to an employer or potential employer. The concept of determining your fair market value is explored in Chapters 2, 3, 4, and 5. This entails pinpointing your most marketable skills and capabilities and then determining what they're worth to an employer based on factors including:

- The industry in which you'll be working.
- Your geographic location.
- The size and financial strength of an employer.
- The size and availability of the labor pool.
- What other people with similar qualifications are earning.

In addition to having the skills and education that are in hot demand by employers, you'll need to develop the right attitude. In today's job market, your attitude is almost as important (if not equally as important) as your aptitude.

Assuming you have the qualifications and attitude an employer is looking for in order to fill a job, then your chances of getting hired are excellent. Your next challenge will be to negotiate the salary and overall compensation package for yourself that you deserve and are capable of earning.

According to the U.S. Department of Labor, "Like other characteristics, earnings differ from industry to industry. These differences are the result of a highly complicated process that relies on a number of factors. For example, wages may vary due to the occupations in the industry, average hours worked, required skills, geographical location, industry profits, union affiliation, and educational requirements."

In Chapter 11, you'll discover how to determine how much you need to earn to cover your living expenses, etc., and how this differs dramatically from earning what you want to earn and earning what you deserve to earn. Earning what you need means receiving a paycheck that allows you to cover your basic living expenses (rent/mortgage, car payments, food, clothing, etc.) Earning what you want refers back to the goals you've set for yourself and the quality of life you'd like to experience. Since most people aspire to have a better quality of life than they currently do (they want to live in a more expensive house, drive a fancier car, eat at nicer restaurants, etc.), this will mean earning considerably more than what you require to cover your current living expenses. To do this, you may have to obtain additional education and/or training, work longer hours, become more productive, or seek out better career/job opportunities.

Earning what you deserve relates to what an employer is willing to pay you based on the value you bring to the company. Every company assigns a financial value to a specific job description. If you meet or exceed the requirements of your job, then you'll be paid what the employer believes you deserve or have earned based on your hard work. When you apply for a raise or promotion, it will not be given to you by an employer. It will most likely be something that you earn and that will be awarded to you based on your hard work and dedication, or for achieving specific work-related goals or objectives.

Maybe you should consider a career change

People in entry-level jobs all the way up to top-level executives sometimes feel the need to change careers, perhaps because their personal goals and interests change, or maybe after working within an industry, they realize that they've made bad career decisions. Some people realize that by making a major career change, their earning potential will increase dramatically or they'd be better able to achieve their life-long dreams.

If you feel the need to change careers, for whatever reason, understand that this can be done successfully, but it will be a bit more difficult than simply finding and landing a new job. A career change refers to going from one occupation to another. You'll be taking on new responsibilities and challenges, because you'll be working in a totally different industry. For example, a career change could involve going from a managerial position at a retail store, to earning a law degree and becoming an attorney, to obtaining a real estate license in order to sell houses, or to earning a teaching license to become an educator.

The first step is to carefully analyze why you want to change careers. What is it about your current career that you don't like? How will your life improve if you change careers? Next, it's important to do some intense research to determine what type of career you ultimately want to have. This might require meeting with a career counselor to help you clearly define your interests and objectives. You should also take full advantage of your networking skills and speak with people currently working in the career you hope to break into.

Before pursuing any new career opportunities, compile a detailed list of all your work-related skills, education, and accomplishments. Once you know what career you're interested in pursuing, compare your skill set and educational background to what the job requirements are for the new career. Your skill set, which might include being computer literate, having good public speaking abilities, and having strong managerial or organizational skills, could be transferable to a new career, even if the actual work experience you have acquired while using these skills isn't directly transferable.

Determine what knowledge and skills you're lacking and decide how you'll go about acquiring the needed education and skills. Chances are, you'll have to obtain additional schooling or training, so consider the amount of time it will take, the cost, and the overall commitment that will be necessary to obtain the needed education. Is returning to school full-time or part-time an option? Are there night or weekend classes you can take that will allow you to remain in your current job so you can continue to earn a paycheck?

By changing careers, you're actually starting again almost from scratch, as if you're first graduating from high school or college, because you have little or no related work experience. It's usually work-related experience that employers are looking for, so while you might have proven skills that can be applied to a new career, your goal is to determine a way to position yourself as a qualified applicant—without stretching the truth or without having work experience in the field you hope to move into.

Upon obtaining the necessary education and licenses (if applicable) that you'll need to land a job in the new career that interests you, choose a "Functional" resumé format (described in Chapter 8) that showcases your skills and accomplishments, while at the same time downplaying your past employment history. The goal of your resumé and cover letter should be to communicate everything about your skills, experience, and education that relate directly to the new career.

Try to obtain related work experience, even if it means doing volunteer work or accepting an unpaid internship. Ideally, you want to show some work-related experience on your resumé when you attempt to change careers. If you have the necessary education and skill set, however, you should be able to sell yourself to a potential employer and successfully change careers.

Be sure to use whatever networking contacts you have to help you find and land a new job. Through a personal introduction to a company, you're more apt to get the attention of employers if you come highly recommended by someone who understands your accomplishments and skills. Also, take full advantage of the services offered by the career placement office at whatever educational institution you return to for the specialized or advanced education you need for the new career.

Finally, don't act too quickly. Before quitting your current job, make sure you have a formulated plan and a complete understanding of what you're getting into. Understand the financial risks involved. If possible, stay at your current job until you have the additional education you need and you've actually found a new job that offers a career change opportunity.

How this book can help you change your life

The purpose of this book is to help you identify and obtain the best possible employment opportunities,

Bright Idea
In terms of job interviews, be prepared to explain honestly why you're changing careers and how your skills fit nicely into the career you're now pursuing. Focus on what you can offer to the potential employer, and be prepared to answer the question, "Why doesn't your past work experience relate to the job you're applying for?"

and to assist you in negotiating the best compensation package based on your qualifications. In order to help you earn what you deserve, this book explores the various types of employment opportunities available to you, including becoming self-employed and the options available to you if you decide to launch your own company.

Two of the central themes that will be repeated several times throughout this book is that to earn what you deserve, it's going to take hard work. Also, earning what you deserve is very different from earning what you want or need.

When it comes to earning a living for yourself, it all comes to down dollars and good sense. You'll need the dollars to pay your bills and cover your cost of living expenses, etc., and the good sense to be able to make positive career decisions that will allow you to earn the salary that you deserve.

Just the facts

- Define yourself and identify your likes and dislikes as they pertain to your professional life.

- You must find a career opportunity based on what you need, what you want, what you enjoy and what you're qualified to do.

- Define your personal, professional, and financial goals, and begin working toward making your larger and more long-term goals a reality by breaking them down into smaller, more manageable, achievable goals.

- It's important to carefully research all of your potential career and job opportunities, as well as the industries you could work in. You also want to develop a general understanding of the job market as a whole in order to discover how and where you fit in.

▪ Make yourself a highly marketable member of the work force by developing the qualifications and personality traits that employers are looking for.

GET THE SCOOP ON...
Determining what you're worth to an employer
■ Discovering current salary ranges for people
with your qualifications ■ How to determine
your own fair market value as
an employee ■ Trends that impact salary ranges

Becoming Salary Savvy

Chapter 2

Before you go out and find yourself a job that allows you to earn what you deserve, or get a raise from your present employer that makes you feel as valuable as you actually are, it's your responsibility to determine exactly what you're worth. Your true value is not based on what you perceive it to be, but instead on a variety of tangible elements that need to be researched and understood by you and ultimately by your employer.

Who decides how much you get paid?

Most people think that an employee's salary is a somewhat arbitrary figure determined by someone's boss. This figure is perceived to be based on how much the boss likes an employee from a personality standpoint. Also figured somewhere in this equation are perhaps the employee's skill level and qualifications.

In reality, the salaries offered by employers are based on a variety of factors that are extremely impersonal and relate more to a company's bottom line. By understanding how an employer decides how much to pay its employees, you'll be in a stronger negotiating position when it comes time to determining your own salary. From an employer's standpoint, the question that's asked when calculating salaries is how much an employee—with a specific educational background, set of skills, and work history—is worth to the company. When someone is hired by a company, that company is making a financial investment in an individual. The value of that investment gets analyzed just like any other investment.

Before someone decides to purchase an expensive appliance or a new car, for example, it's common practice to shop around and determine what features specific models offer and at what price. The more features offered, the higher a consumer is usually willing to pay. The manufacturer's reputation is also considered.

An employer uses a similar process when setting salaries. If an employer is going to make a $30,000, $40,000, or $50,000+ per year investment in an employee, they want to ensure that the person they hire will be worth that investment and that their skills and work experience are better than what other applicants offer. Applicants and employees looking for a raise or promotion are evaluated as assets to a company. Seldom are decisions made based on personal issues. Just as consumers look at the features built into a new appliance or automobile, employers examine and compare the personal skill sets of potential employees. Likewise, just as a consumer is more apt to purchase a dishwasher or television set made by a well-known manufacturer, an employer is more apt to hire someone with proven work experience and a good reputation.

How much of an asset an employee is to a company is just one of the factors that's considered when a company determines compensation packages for its employees.

Take a dip in the talent pool

One of the major factors that's considered by employers when setting salary ranges for specific positions is how large the talent pool of potential employees is. Basically, it's a supply and demand issue. The larger the supply of qualified workers for a specific job description, the less the employers will be willing to pay someone to fill that position. It's much harder to negotiate your salary if you plan on working as a cashier at a retail chain store, for example, because employers consider these positions easy to fill. Thus, they offer a pre-determined, often non-negotiable compensation package. If too few qualified workers are available to employers, they'll pay more to attract the qualified talent, specifically if the job involves specialized skills, an advanced degree, or some sort of special license. It's no secret that in the high-tech field, for example, programmers are in hot demand. There are too few skilled programmers and computer specialists to fill the growing number of programming jobs available.

The competition

Getting back to the supply versus demand issues in the talent pool, if the supply of workers is adequate to meet the demand by employers, the employer's decision about who gets paid the most and who ultimately gets hired will be based even more heavily on someone's skills and qualifications. In this scenario, there's a lot of competition among employees and

Bright Idea
Making yourself qualified to fill one of the jobs that are in hot demand in any industry (by improving your skill set) gives you greater earning potential and makes you more marketable.

job seekers alike, because employers will often hire people who are perhaps too qualified for the job they're being hired to do, simply because they're available at a highly competitive salary.

Competition can also be fierce among employers looking to hire qualified talent from a pool that's too small to meet the demand. In times when the economy is strong and unemployment is low, finding people to work in retail stores at a mall, for example, becomes difficult for employers. This forces the popular retail chain stores to improve their compensation packages, not just by boosting salaries, but also by making their benefits packages more attractive to job seekers. As a job seeker looking to work in retail, especially if you have previous work experience, your opportunity to earn the highest possible salary will be when the majority of the stores in a mall, for example, are understaffed due to a smaller than adequate talent pool.

Similar supply and demand scenarios can happen in virtually any industry, which is why it's important for you, as the job seeker, to understand the strength of the job market and know what types of skills are in the hottest demand by employers.

Geography: Where in the world are the best jobs?

Having the skills needed to fill the hottest jobs is important, but finding the jobs you're qualified for can also become a matter of geography. While some occupations are in demand throughout the country, others are more readily available in major U.S. cities or in specific regions of the country. In some lines of work, those who have the ability to move anywhere when looking for career opportunities can find areas where their particular skills are in hotter demand, and thus negotiate higher salaries for themselves.

The strength of regional economies certainly plays a major role in what employers are willing to pay their employees, at least in some industries. To discover what types of jobs are in hot demand in a specific geographic area requires some research. One source of this information is state employment agencies, which are listed in the telephone book.

Understand industry trends and how they impact your career

Understand the industry you plan on working in (or currently work in). If you're first entering the job market or switching careers, ideally you want to work in an industry that's thriving. If you're currently working in an industry and you're looking for a promotion or career advancement, it's important to understand what's happening within your industry as well as with your employer in order to properly set and ultimately achieve your long-term career goals.

According to the Bureau of Labor Statistics, these are the 10 general industries with the fastest employment growth, between 1996 and 2006:

TABLE 2.1. ESTIMATED GROWTH BETWEEN 1996 AND 2006

Computer and data processing services	108%
Health services	68%
Management and public relations	60%
Miscellaneous transportation services	60%
Residential care	59%
Personnel supply services	53%
Water and sanitation	51%
Individual and miscellaneous social services	50%
Offices of health practitioners	47%
Amusement and recreation services	41%

The Bureau of Labor Statistics also reports that the 10 occupations with the largest job growth between 1996 and 2006 are projected to be:

TABLE 2.2. ESTIMATED GROWTH BETWEEN 1996 AND 2006

Cashiers	17%
Systems analysts	103%
General managers and top executives	15%
Registered nurses	21%
Salespeople (retail)	10%
Truck drivers	15%
Home health aides	76%
Teacher aides and educational assistants	38%
Nursing aides, orderlies and attendants	25%
Receptionists and information clerks	30%

The 10 occupations with the fastest employment growth between 1996 and 2006 include:

TABLE 2.3. ESTIMATED GROWTH BETWEEN 1996 AND 2006

Database administrators, computer support specialists and all other computer scientists	118%
Computer engineers	109%
Systems analysts	103%
Personal and home care aides	85%
Physical and corrective therapy assistants and aides	79%
Home health aides	76%
Medical assistants	74%
Desktop publishing specialists	74%
Physical therapists	71%
Occupational therapy assistants and aides	69%

No matter what industry you plan to work in, you'll be able to uncover reliable information that will help you determine the size of the industry, as well as its overall stability and future potential.

Knowing, for example, that an industry is projecting dramatic growth and will face a shortages of specific types of skilled laborers means that salaries could rise dramatically, especially if the employment pool doesn't expand as quickly as the industry itself.

Just as job seekers rely on industry trends to determine in which industries the best jobs can be found, employers use this information to help them set salary ranges for specific types of jobs. Knowing and understanding the same industry-related information as your employer or potential employer will help you better negotiate a fair salary and overall compensation package.

Size does matter, at least when it comes to employers

As a general rule, if you're applying for an entry-level or middle-management job with a smaller company, you'll have greater salary negotiation strength, especially if you're bringing an excellent set of skills and previous related work experience to the bargaining table. Job seekers have the most flexibility when it comes to salary negotiation if the small- or medium-sized employer can be flexible in terms of the job description you'll be filling. Large companies and corporations tend to have very specific job descriptions and look to hire people at a pre-determined salary who can fill a specific job. There's little room to negotiate, even if you're qualified to fill a job and handle additional responsibilities that fall outside of your job description.

While most companies will have a pre-determined salary range for each position, if you come to the negotiation table with a skill set that allows you to fill a job opening perfectly, you'll be perceived as being even more valuable to the

Unofficially...
For the remainder of this decade and into the next millennium, the job outlook in service-based industries looks extremely bright, while manufacturing jobs based in the U.S. will most likely remain constant or diminish.

employer. In many cases, if you approach the salary negotiation process correctly, you'll be more handsomely compensated for your skills, but only if the company hiring you has flexibility in terms of modifying or customizing job descriptions and responsibilities.

Unfortunately, unless you're applying for (and are qualified to fill) an executive-level position at a large corporation, the job you're being hired to fill will have a well-established set of responsibilities and a job description that is spelled out. The employer will have a pre-determined salary range for available positions, and they usually won't be willing to negotiate too much when it comes to compensation packages.

If you have specialized skills that are ideal for a specific type of position, you're more apt to be able to negotiate a better compensation package if you're willing to take some risk and work for a small, start-up company.

Your experience counts

When it comes to landing a new job, the biggest question on the mind of employers is whether or not you have what it takes to succeed in the job. If you have previous and related work experience, not only will you be more seriously considered for whatever jobs you apply for, you'll also be in a much better bargaining position when it comes to salary negotiations. It's one thing to talk about your potential and what you think you might be able to do for an employer, based on your education. Your claims, however, will be far more powerful if you're able to say that while you were working for a previous employer, you achieved very specific accomplishments and that there's no doubt in your mind you'll

Bright Idea
In order to attract the top talent, start-up companies in virtually all industries are forced to pay more. Small and start-up companies also usually offer greater and more flexible job responsibilities and the ability to earn promotions faster.

be able to repeat or exceed those accomplishments if you're hired.

It's far less of a risk for an employer to hire someone with previous and related work experience to fill a job opening, since you've already proven your capabilities. Thus, it's critical for you to showcase your work experiences within your resumé, during job interviews or during periodic employee evaluations.

Identifying and showcasing your personal skill set

Your previous work experience is critical when applying for a new job, because it's this experience that allows you to demonstrate previous accomplishments. Your personal skill set can be used to market not only past performance, but your future potential. It's this future potential that can really get an employer excited about hiring you. The more excited the employer is, the more they'll be willing to pay in order to get you on their team.

Before your actual job search begins, it's important that you carefully define your skill set and determine what, if anything, you can to do enhance it. The next chapter of this book explores how you can increase your worth to an employer (and your marketability as an applicant), by improving your personal skill set through additional training and/or education.

Everyone has a personal skill set, which includes specific things that they're particularly good at, whether it's managing others, organizing, selling, fluency in the use of specific computer programs, having the ability to write well or communicate verbally in a public speaking situation. Skills can be general or relate to specific tasks needed to fulfil the

Bright Idea
Having previous work experience will allow the employer to justify offering you a salary that's on the higher end of their pre-defined salary range for a specific job.

Unofficially...
Simply saying you have certain skills or listing them on a resumé isn't enough. Employers will want proof that you have specific skills and that you know how to use them. Thus, during your job interview (and during the salary negotiation process) or during an employee evaluation, it's important to describe your skills using specific examples of how you've used them in the past and how you plan to use them in the future.

requirements of a job. The greater your personal skill set, the more valuable you'll be to a potential employer.

The skills you have generally fall into three categories:

Job Related Skills   These are the specific skills you must have in order to succeed in a specific job.

Transferable Skills   These general work-related skills are transferable to various types of jobs and are broader in terms of their scope. One example of a transferable skill is being computer literate and being fluent in popular programs. Having excellent writing or public speaking skills, and/or good "people" skills are also examples of transferable skills that are in demand by virtually all employers.

Personal Skills   These are basic skills that most employers believe are absolutely critical for someone to have in order to be successful in any business or work environment. These skills tend to be more abstract, yet are extremely important. Being friendly, a team player, well-organized, motivated, creative, dependable, honest, hardworking, dedicated, tactful, reliable, and responsible are among the personal skills that employers look for.

Some of the most important skills employers look for include:

- The ability to communicate well with others verbally and in writing
- Computer literacy
- Creativity

- Leadership
- Motivation and determination; being a self-starter
- Problem-solving abilities
- The ability to learn and adapt
- The ability to work with others (teamwork)

Pinpointing your proven ability and perceived value to an employer

When it comes to being taken seriously as an applicant, absolutely nothing can replace the need to create a high value for yourself in the mind of the employer. The more valuable an asset the potential employer perceives you to be, the more he'll want to hire you and the more power you'll have when salary negotiations begin.

Anyone can talk about their potential and how they could use their skills and knowledge to accomplish specific tasks if given the opportunity. Far fewer people are able to clearly describe their actual past work experience in a way that convinces the employer that they're capable of meeting the requirements of a job opening.

Describing your past work experiences in detail and providing very specific examples of your accomplishments is the key to proving to an employer that you're capable of doing the job you're applying for. During your discussions, talk about specific skills you have and how you have used them successful on-the-job in the past.

After all, as the employer, wouldn't you rather hire someone who has already proven they have what it takes to be successful in the job you're hiring them to fill? Don't rely on your resumé to describe your accomplishments and skills to a potential employer. During the job interview, it's your responsibility to showcase your accomplishments and skills in a way that makes you appear totally compatible with the job opening. By doing research and truly understanding the job opening you're applying for, you can custom tailor your job interview presentation so that you position yourself to be a huge asset to the potential employer.

For example, you read a "help wanted" ad for an experienced administrative assistant with the ability to use Microsoft Word. During your job interview, not only must you describe all of your skills that allow you to be a top-notch administrative assistant, it's critical that you provide specific examples showcasing your proficiency with Microsoft Word. How much experience have you had using Word? What training do you have? What did you use this program to accomplish? How competent are you in using this program, not just for word processing but for desktop publishing or creating Web content? These are some of the questions you'd want to answer in order to demonstrate your specific skills using Word, which in this case is what the employer is interested in.

Discovering your worth

Once you've pinpointed your most marketable skills, you've determined in what industry you want to work, and you have a really good understanding of the type of job opening you're hoping to fill, it's necessary to discover exactly what your income potential is, and this takes research. This section will help you determine a salary range for yourself based on a variety of criteria. Knowing what people in your line of work, in your geographic area and in your industry earn is the something that needs to be determined before entering into any type of salary negotiation and before you begin to analyze specific job offers.

Determine your value by analyzing your skills and marketability

The first step in determining a salary range for yourself (your earning potential) is to analyze your personal skill set, education, and experience. Next, pinpoint specific career opportunities in various industries that will take full advantage of what you have to offer to an employer. This information will help you find industries and specific job opportunities you're best suited for and will be happiest in.

The following questionnaire is designed to help you discover your true interests and skills; determine what you like about your current job (and your life); and what you've disliked the most about previous work experiences.

As you answer these questions, be totally honest with yourself. Nobody else needs to see your responses, however, it's important that you write out your answers on a separate sheet of paper so that you can better analyze your own career-related goals.

How would you describe your life right now? Are you emotionally satisfied with your job, relationships, family life, etc.?

If you could change something about your life, what would it be?

List between three and five things you can start doing right now that will help you make the changes in your life that you most desire.

1.

2.

3.

---

continues

4.

5.

How would you describe your present lifestyle?

In five or ten years, how would you like your lifestyle to change?

What is your current financial status?

In the next five and ten years, what changes in your financial status are required in order to meet your personal goals? Are you planning to get married and have kids; buy a house or condo; purchase a new car, yacht, or vacation home; save for your retirement; pay for a child's college education; put yourself through graduate school or obtain an advanced degree; pay off debts or loans; or invest in a new business?

In order to pay your bills and continue living at your current lifestyle, how much money do you need to earn annually?

In order to improve your lifestyle to meet your long-term goals, how much money would you realistically like to earn annually in your next job?

What work-related benefits do you current have that you absolutely need?

What work-related benefits would you like to have?

As an employee, how do you like to be rewarded for a job well done?

What are the things you currently enjoy doing either on-the-job or in your personal life?

1.

2.

3.

4.

5.

What are the things you hate doing either on-the-job or in your personal life?

1.

2.

3.

4.

5.

What are some of your qualities or personality traits that you're the most proud of?

1.

2.

3.

What are some of the qualities and personality traits that you don't like about yourself, you think need improvement, or that you know people don't like about you?

1.

2.

3.

What are some of the things you can start doing today to change the things about yourself that you're not happy with?

After evaluating your current educational background, what areas or skills do you think you still need to obtain or improve upon in order to achieve your personal and professional goals?

Based on your personal skill set, list 10 of your most valuable and marketable skills that you use on-the-job on a separate piece of paper?

continues

How do you currently use each of these 10 skills on-the-job? (Provide specific examples you could list on your resume or bring up during a job interview or during an employee evaluation.)

If given the opportunity, how could you be using your top skills on-the-job?

What are some of your other skills that an employer might be interested in, but that don't necessarily relate directly to your job?

What five skills do you want to acquire or master that you don't yet have?

1.

2.

3.

4.

5.

How could you use each of these skills to advance your career?

What would it take to acquire each of these skills?

What actions could you begin taking right now to improve upon your personal skill set and make you more marketable to potential employers?

If you decided to go back to school and obtain an advanced degree or continue your education, what subject(s) or degree(s) would you pursue and why? How would this additional education help you to achieve your long-term career goals?

Describe five accomplishments from your past work experiences of which you're the most proud. Why did you choose each of these accomplishments?

1.

2.

3.

4.

5.

What was your strongest subject in school? Which were your favorite subjects? Which subjects did you like the least?

As a job applicant, what are five of your biggest strengths?

1.

2.

3.

4.

5.

As a job applicant, what are five of your biggest weaknesses?

1.

2.

3.

4.

5.

What do you need to do to overcome these weaknesses?

What did you hate the most about your last job?

What did you like the most about your last job?

What would you have liked to change about your last job?

What five work-related tasks are you really good at? Which tasks do you enjoy the most?

continues

1.

2.

3.

4.

5.

If you were to write a job description for your ultimate dream job, what would it say?

What type of work environment do you prosper in?

What type of coworkers do you prefer to work with?

How would you define true career success for yourself?

How would you define true personal success for yourself?

What needs to be done in order to achieve this success?

By analyzing your skills, desires, likes, and dislikes, you can compare this information to what's required for specific job or career opportunity to help you determine what career path is ultimately best for you personally. Later, in Chapter 12, you'll discover how to analyze a job offer to determine if it's what you're looking for. Ultimately, you want to land a job that'll be rewarding emotionally and financially, and you want to be doing something that you have a true passion for.

Doing research on salaries

It's one thing to go into the job search process saying you want to earn $50,000 a year for doing your job, such as being a secretary or personal assistant, but realistically, you must determine if that's the salary range being offered to people with your skills and qualifications and who currently hold the type of job you're applying for.

As you kick off your job search and you determine specifically what type of job you're looking to fill, research what the salary range is for that type of position. The remaining portion of this chapter describes some of the resources available to help you determine current salary ranges and your future earning potential based on your personal skills, education, experience and the type of job you want to fill.

Read all about it...in trade journals

No matter what industry you hope to work in, or what occupation you're qualified to fill, there's a trade journal, industry newspaper, or newsletter that will provide ongoing information about the types of jobs available in your field and the salary ranges for those jobs. *Advertising Age*, for example, is the trade journal read by people in the advertising field, while a publication called *GameWeek* is read by people working in the computer and video game industry. Reading trade journals is one of the very best ways to stay on top of the current trends and major events within any industry. You'll find current and back issues of popular industry magazines at libraries or online.

Check with professional organizations and associations

There are over 3,000 different professional organizations and associations in America. *The Encyclopedia of Associations* (Gale Research) and *The National Trade and Professional Associations Directory* (Columbia Books) are two resources available at most libraries that list the names, addresses, phone numbers, and web site URLs for these associations.

Bright Idea
The Associations Database (http://www.marketingsource.com/associtions/) is a searchable directory of 1,500 business-related associations around the world. You may search by title, area code, city, state, zip code, or category. This database is also available on disk and in print. The online version of the directory can be searched for free. To order the disk or printed version, call (800) 575-5369.

Professional organizations and associations often publish magazines or newsletters that contain career-related information. These groups also conduct ongoing research pertaining to salary ranges for specific jobs throughout the country. Becoming involved in a professional organization/association provides excellent networking opportunities that can help you throughout your career, plus can be a valuable resource for job seekers in search of industry or occupation-specific information.

Talk with others in your field

Get the inside scoop about a specific organization or job by talking to people who actually work for the organization you're interested in, or who are employed doing exactly the type of work you're interested in pursuing. Finding people you don't already know can be done through networking, however, talking to people you already have a professional or personal friendship with will provide you with an abundance of reliable information.

As you discuss the type of work you're interested in with people already working in that field, ask questions about salary potential, upward mobility in terms of promotions, and determine specifically what the job/position entails. Ask questions like, "What are some of your daily responsibilities?" While not everyone is willing to openly discuss their own salary or what they like or dislike about a specific employer, you'll be able to learn a lot from people who have first-hand experience doing the type of work you hope to do.

Determine what people in your position are being paid

By determining what people currently working in the position you're applying to fill are earning, and what other employers are paying people with similar jobs, you'll be able to determine in-advance the salary range you could potentially earn if you're hired. This information is one of the key pieces of information you'll want to know before entering into a salary negotiation.

There are multiple ways to determine the salary ranges for the job(s) you're interested in. For starts, check a newspaper's help wanted ads. Many employers list specific salaries or ranges in their ads, plus provide insight into the types of benefits offered. Also, check the job opening listings online. These listings tend to be more verbose and provide more detailed information about specific jobs and related salaries. Online job listings can be found on the specialty career-related web sites (such as The Monster Board or CareerMosaic) and at individual company web sites.

What the government has to say

For over 50 years, the U.S. Government's Bureau of Labor Statistics and U.S. Department of Labor (http://stats.bls.gov/ocohome.htm) have been publishing *The Occupational Outlook Handbook* (OOH), a book designed to help job seekers and employers alike understand the job market.

The 528-page 1998–99 edition of the OOH provides detailed information on about 250 occupations (accounting for over 114 million jobs, or six out of every seven jobs in the United States).

The OOH provides reliable information that can be used to help you determine your own earning potential now and in the future, based on your skills, educational background, and the occupation you plan to pursue.

Information about each occupation highlighted in the OOH includes:

- The nature of the work
- Typical working conditions
- Skill/experience/education requirements
- Opportunities for advancement
- Estimated number of jobs available nationwide
- Projections for employment through 2006
- Information on salary ranges

Simply knowing what industry you want to work in isn't enough. It's important to match your personal skill set, education, and experience to the specific jobs available within an industry. The OOH breaks down dozens of industries and describes specific jobs available within them, allowing job seekers to compare similar opportunities within different industries.

Knowing some basic facts about the projected strength of the economy and what the growth industries will be over the next several years will help you dramatically when it comes to planning your long-term career path and career-related goals. Since most people attempt to plan a career path for themselves that includes a steadily increasing salary over a number of years, choosing to work in an industry that's growing will help to guarantee that the higher paying jobs will be available in the industry you choose to work in.

According to the OOH, manufacturing-related jobs are projected to represent 13 percent of the total wage and salary worker employment base by 2006. This is down two percent, compared to 1996. New construction jobs are expected to be created 25 percent slower than during the previous 10-year period.

Unofficially...
According to the 1998–99 edition of the OOH, "The labor force will grow to 14.9 million between 1996 and 2006. As a result of an increase in the percentage of the population working or looking for work, the labor force will continue to grow faster than the population rate."

The good news is that "employment in service-producing industries will increase faster than average, with growth near 30 percent. Service and retail trade industries will account for 14.8 million out of a total projected growth of 17.5 million wage and salary jobs. Business, health, and education services will account for 70 percent of the growth within the service industry."

For those looking to work in professional specialty occupations (law, engineering, computers, education, health, etc.), these jobs are expected to increase faster and have more job growth than any major occupational group. The 1998–99 OOH reports, "Within professional specialty occupations, computer/high-tech related occupations and teachers will add 2.3 million new jobs, accounting for 15 percent of all new jobs between 1996 and 2006."

The OOH projects a dramatic growth in computer and data processing services-related jobs, with 1.3 million additional jobs being added between 1996 and 2006. Skilled workers will be needed to fill these jobs.

As we progress into the next millennium, education will play an even greater role in a job seeker's ability to land a high paying job with upward mobility. There are, however, a few career exceptions for which a college degree (or higher level of education) is not required, but a higher than average earning potential is possible. Automotive mechanics, carpenters, and blue-collar worker supervisors are examples of these jobs.

The 1998–99 OOH projects, "Almost two-thirds of the projected growth (in the number of jobs) will be in occupations that require less than a college degree. However, these positions generally offer the

Unofficially...
Additional statistics reported in the 1998–99 edition of the OOH state that "The number of self-employed workers is expected to increase to 11.6 million by 2006, while the number of unpaid family workers will decline... Between 1996 and 2006, women's share of the labor force is projected to slowly increase from 46 to 47 percent, continuing a pattern since 1976." Meanwhile, "Workers over the age of 45 will account for a larger share of the labor force as the baby-boom generation ages."

lowest pay and benefits. Jobs requiring the least education and training—those that can be learned on the job—will provide two out of three openings due to growth and replacement needs; three of every four openings will be in occupations that generally require less than a bachelor's degree."

Based on the level of training/education you have, here are some of the jobs that *The 1998–99 Occupational Outlook Handbook* reports will offer the best opportunities through 2006:

First-Professional Degree

- Chiropractors
- Veterinarians and veterinary inspectors
- Physicians
- Lawyers
- Clergy

Doctoral Degree

- Biological scientists
- Medical scientists
- College and university faculty
- Mathematicians and all other mathematical scientists

Master's Degree

- Speech-language pathologists and audiologists
- Counselors
- Curators, archivists, museum technicians
- Psychologists
- Operation research analysts

A closer look: Career opportunities in psychology

Currently, the demand for school psychologists and industrial/organizational (I/O) psychologists is growing rapidly, explained Dr. Frank Farley, a former president of the American Psychological Association (APA), the world's largest association of psychologists, with over 155,000 members.

As the title suggests, school psychologists work in public and private schools, dealing directly with students in need of special services to overcome behavioral disorders, emotional problems, or learning disabilities. I/O psychologists are trained to provide their services in the work place. People with this sub-specialty in psychology are hired by corporations as full-time employees or consultants, and tend to have high income levels. Their responsibilities include studying and implementing ways to improve productivity and the quality of work life.

"Most school psychologists have a master's degree, not a doctorate. People with master's degrees are also finding a tremendous number of career opportunities working for HMOs or managed healthcare programs. Anyone interested in becoming a psychologist can begin by pursuing a bachelor's degree, which is often a stepping stone to a more advanced degree," said Dr. Farley, who has spent over 20 years teaching psychology and is currently affiliated with Temple University in Philadelphia.

Jobs available for psychologists with a bachelor's degree tend to be more entry level and require the supervision of someone with a higher degree. The APA reports that the number of doctoral graduates in psychology has doubled over the past 12 years, yet the jobs available continue to outweigh the supply.

To learn more about the many types of careers available to psychologists, contact the American Psychological Association at (800) 374-2721 (www.apa.org) and request a free copy of *Psychology:*

Careers for the 21st Century. This booklet describes the many subfields in psychology, the job outlook, what psychologists actually do, and specific educational requirements.

Work Experience, plus bachelor's or higher degree

- Engineering, science and computer systems managers
- Marketing, advertising and public relations managers
- Artists and commercial artists
- Management Analysts
- Financial managers

Bachelor's Degree

- Database administrators and computer support specialists
- Computer engineers
- Systems analyst
- Physical therapists
- Occupational therapists

Associate's Degree

- Paralegals
- Health information technicians
- Dental hygienists
- Respiratory therapists
- Cardiology technologists

Post-secondary Vocational Training

- Data processing equipment repairs
- Emergency medical technicians
- Manicurists
- Surgical technologists
- Medical secretaries

Unofficially...
The U.S. Bureau of Labor Statistics reports that the paralegal profession will have the second greatest growth rate of any career in the late-1990's.

Work Experience

- Food service and lodging managers
- Teachers and instructors, vocational education and training
- Lawn service managers
- Instructors, adult education
- Nursery and greenhouse managers

Long-Term Training and Experience

(Requiring more than 12 months of on-the-job training)

- Desktop publishing specialists
- Flight attendants
- Musicians
- Correction officers
- Producers, directors, actors and entertainers

Moderate-Term Training and Experience

(One to 12 months of combined on-the-job training and informal training)

- Physical and corrective therapy assistants and aides
- Medical assistants
- Occupational therapy assistants and aides
- Social and human services assistants
- Instructors and coaches, sports and physical training

Short-Term Training and Experience

(Up to one month of on-the-job experience)

- Personal and home care aides
- Home health aides
- Amusement and recreation attendants

Unofficially...
The OOH is available at most public and school libraries, but it can also be ordered from the Superintendent of Documents, U.S. Government printing Office, Washington, DC 20402, (202) 512-1800. Credit card orders can also be placed by calling (312) 353-1880. Price: $42 soft cover, $46 hard cover, $28 CD-Rom.

■ Adjustment clerks

■ Bill and account collectors

Other useful publications and organizations

To discover more information about specific career opportunities and the salary ranges earned by people in those careers, look for the following publications at your local or school library, favorite bookstore, or online:

Adams Jobs Almanac This annually published directory describes over 7,000 U.S. employers and is broken down by industry. The Career Outlooks section of this directory lists employment growth, educational requirements, average starting salary, career outlook and information about where the jobs are for about 50 popular occupations. Adams Jobs Almanac is published annually by Adams Media Corporation ($15.95) and is available from bookstores.

American Salaries & Wages Survey Published by Gale Research, this directory describes over 42,000 job titles and lists salary ranges for each.

National Association of Older Workers Employment Services (The National Council on the Aging) Career services and information is provided to older members of the work force (202-479-1200).

The American Almanac of Jobs and Salaries Published by Avon Books, this book is similar to *The Occupational Outlook Handbook* and describes hundreds of job descriptions and salary ranges.

The Directory of Occupational Titles (DOT)
This online directory (http://www.wave.net/
upg/immigration/dot_index.html) offers
descriptions of over 12,000 occupations and
career opportunities. A Windows-based software version of this directory is available, or it
can be accessed and searched online. DOT
assists job seekers, employers, educational
and training institutions, researchers, and
others by detailing tasks performed, educational requirements, and skills needed for the
described jobs.

*The President's Committee on Employment
of People with Disabilities*   Learn about
job opportunities and career paths for people
with physical or mental disabilities (202-
376-6200).

The Salary Survey   Published annually by
the National Association of Colleges and
Employers (800-544-5272 or www.jobweb.org)
offers salary ranges for hundreds of entry-
level positions that college graduates will most
likely find themselves applying to fill.

The U.S. Industrial Outlook   Published by
the U.S. Department of Commerce, this
directory offers descriptions of 350 industries
and offers information about current and
future (projected) trends within each industry. *The U.S. Industrial Outlook* (USIO) is comparable to the *Occupational Outlook Handbook*
(OOH) in many respects. The big difference
is the USIO provides up-to-date information
on industries rather than occupations.
Developed by the U.S. Department of
Commerce, it is the source to obtain brief

overviews of U.S. industries and their business prospects. (http://www.owt.com/jobsinfo/outlook.htm)

Veteran's Employment and Training Service (VETS)   Free career services and employment information is provided to veterans of the United States military (202-219-9116).

In chapters 10 through 14, this book describes specific salary negotiation strategies designed to help you reach your maximum potential and earn what you deserve. Before any negotiations can begin, however, you have to have a thorough understanding of what you're worth and what employers are willing to pay someone with your talents.

Just the facts

- By understanding industry trends, you will be better able to predict and negotiate your financial compensation.

- Your personal skill set allows you to position yourself as a highly valuable applicant to the potential employer.

- Use your actual work experience can be used to create a higher perceived value for you as an employee when applying for a job.

- Determine the salary range paid to people currently working in your field by contacting industry associations/organizations; checking the help wanted ads in newspapers and online; using your networking skills; and taking advantage of government reports.

GET THE SCOOP ON...
What employers are looking for ▪ Enhancing
your current skills ▪ Methods for mastering new
skills ▪ Taking advantage of on-the-job training
▪ The benefit(s) of pursuing additional education ▪ Marketing your personal skill set

Increasing Your Worth

Whether you already have a steady job
and you're looking to earn a promotion, take on more responsibility and
ultimately earn a larger pay check, or you're looking
to land a new job with even greater financial
rewards, you must constantly strive to enhance your
skill set. This is a life-long endeavor that never stops
paying off as you pursue your career path.

What skills do employers really look for?

The very best way to land an awesome job or to wow
'em during a periodic employee evaluation is to
offer the employer the specific skills and personal
traits that they're looking for. This is in addition to
having the experience and education needed to succeed in whatever career opportunities you choose to
pursue.

Everyone, whether they've never pursued any
education beyond high school or have been educated at the most prestigious Ivy League universities,
have personal skill sets that incorporate their

natural abilities with the skills they've learned and mastered in school, on-the-job, and in their personal lives. It's this personal skill set that makes every employee and job seeker unique, and it's one of the most marketable tools an employee has when applying for jobs or seeking out a promotion. Your personal skill set is what sets you apart from the competition and makes you stand out from others in your field.

When it comes to evaluating potential or current employees, there are certain skills and personal qualities that are in hot demand. The ideal employee is someone whose skills and personal traits match perfectly with what the employer perceives as being important.

In the previous chapter, you answered questions designed to help you pinpoint your own personal skill set and personality traits. This chapter will help you further refine this information and develop yourself into the ultimate employee or applicant that employers are looking for.

Accentuate the positives

The following is a list of transferable and personal skills that are highly marketable. At this point, pinpoint which skills and personality traits you possess and that you'd feel comfortable offering to an employer:

- Advising/ counseling
- Analyzing
- Arbitrating
- Analytical thinking
- Brainstorming
- Budget management
- Buying
- Coaching
- Computer skills
- Controlling

- Coordinating
- Creating
- Cultivating
- Data entry
- Decision making
- Designing
- Diagnosing
- Drawing
- Editing
- Entertaining
- Fund-raising
- Innovating
- Investigating
- Leading (projects, groups, teams, etc.)
- Listening
- Marketing
- Mediating
- Meeting planning
- Multilingual
- Multitasking
- Negotiating
- Order taking / order processing
- Organizing (people, programs, processes, projects, events, etc.)
- Planning
- Policy making
- Preparing and making presentations
- Problem solving
- Proficiency using popular software packages
- Public relations
- Public speaking
- Researching
- Scheduling
- Selling
- Spreadsheet management
- Strategic planning
- Supervising
- Taking risks / risk assessment
- Telemarketing
- Time management
- Training
- Troubleshooting
- Typing
- Web page design
- Web surfing (online research)
- Writing

The following are personality traits and personal skills in demand by employers. Many of the items listed here aren't taught in school, yet they're extremely valuable in a work environment. If you don't have any or all of these skills or personality traits, you can acquire virtually any of them by making a conscious effort and with practice.

As you review this list, think about which of these skills and personality traits you possess and have already used on-the-job. On a separate sheet of paper, list each applicable skill and how you have used it successfully.

Next, think about which of these skills and personality traits you could begin using on-the-job and in your professional life. No matter who you are, you should be able to apply at least 10 items from the following list directly to your career and lifestyle, and then be able to promote these skills in order to showcase yourself as a valuable asset to your employer.

- Able to follow orders
- Adaptable
- Aggressive
- Alert
- Always on time
- Articulate
- Attentive
- Cheerful
- Clean cut
- Clever
- Competent
- Computer savvy
- Creative
- Deadline oriented
- Dedicated
- Dependable
- Detail oriented
- Dynamic
- Effective
- Efficient
- Enthusiastic
- Excellent follow-through abilities

- Fashionable
- Flexible
- Friendly
- Goal oriented
- Good humored
- Hardworking
- Honest
- Leadership
- Listener
- Motivated
- Multilingual
- Nonsmoking
- Outgoing
- Polite
- Productive
- Professional
- Reliable
- Sincere
- Stable
- Successful
- Superior communication skills (verbal and written)
- Tactful
- Team player
- Trustworthy
- Well traveled (worldly)
- Well organized
- Well-rounded

Don't ignore the negatives

There are also many personality traits that can be detrimental to your career, traits that employers don't like to see. If any of the items on this list describe you, seriously consider what you can do to change for the better. As you review this list, think about how you perceive yourself, but also how your superiors, coworkers, and subordinates think of you. In your professional life, your reputation is important and something that will follow you around for your entire career, whether you stay with the same employer or switch jobs multiple times. Even if you have already developed a poor reputation, it's never too late to make adjustments. How people perceive you will ultimately have a huge impact on your long-term success.

Negative personality traits:

- Annoying
- Arrogant
- Careless
- Childish
- Depressing
- Dishonest
- Disorganized
- Disrespectful
- Inefficient
- Insincere
- Irrational
- Irresponsible
- Mean
- Messy
- Nasty
- Narrow-minded

- Obnoxious
- Outspoken
- Overly emotional
- Poor dresser (unfashionable)
- Pretentious
- Procrastinator
- Rude
- Self-centered
- Selfish
- Short tempered
- Shy
- Tardy
- Uncooperative
- Unprofessional
- Unreliable

Rounding out your skill set with job related skills

Using your responses to the questionnaire from the previous chapter, list at least 10 job-related skills that you possess and provide specific examples of how you have successfully used these skills in the past. Job-related skills are those skills or personal traits that are absolutely required to succeed in a specific job. For example, if you're a secretary, you must have typing and filing skills and be fluent using at least one popular word processing program. You must also be good at dealing with people on the telephone and be very detail oriented.

1.

2.

3.

4.

5.

6.

7.

8.

9.

10.

Read trade journals and participate in professional forums/newsgroups online

An Internet newsgroup is an online "bulletin board" where people can post public messages about a specific topic. Using special software designed to allow computer users to access and read newsgroups (a feature built into most web browser and/or e-mail software), anyone with access to the Internet can access Internet newsgroups and read or post messages. Unlike Internet mailing lists, you must use your newsgroup reader software to read messages posted to a newsgroup. The messages are not automatically sent to the "in box" of your e-mail software. To find a newsgroup that caters to your area of interest, use the keyword search features of Listz's Usenet Directory (www.liszt.com/news) or Deja News (www.dejanews.com).

An Internet mailing list consists of a group of people, usually with a common interest, who share their thoughts and ideas via a virtual conversation by sending public e-mail messages that everyone on the group's mailing list receives. To be able to participate in a mailing list, a computer user must

Bright Idea
One way to help you determine exactly what personal, transferable, and job specific skills can be of use to you in your own career is to read industry or career-specific trade journals and participate with your peers online via professional forums and newsgroups.

"subscribe" to a list, which usually requires that an e-mail message be sent to a specific address requesting that your name be added. Once the request is processed, you'll begin receiving the messages that people participating in the mailing list send. These messages will arrive in your e-mail software's in-box.

How to expand upon your personal skill set

Whether you're starting out in the business world or you're the CEO of a Fortune 500 company, your personal skill set will always be something to build upon and cultivate. Learning new skills can be as easy as reading a book or trade journal, or can involve returning to school (part-time or full-time) to pursue an advanced degree over a several year period. No matter what skills you ultimately acquire, chances are they'll help to make you a more marketable employee and a greater asset to your company.

There's an age-old saying that states, "Knowledge is power." Developing skills and acquiring knowledge will help you perform your job better, make you a suitable candidate for higher paying jobs (with more responsibility), and allow you to successfully perform tasks that are outside of your immediate job responsibilities (which could help lead to career advancement and a higher pay check).

The following are just some of the ways you can acquire new skills and knowledge using the resources currently at your disposal. Truly enhancing your skill set will require a commitment of time and perhaps money, but you'll reap the benefits of your investment in the future.

Based on your personal and professional goals, here are some of the ways you can improve your education and personal skill set:

Adult education classes

Community and state colleges are among the institutions that offer adult education classes. These classes are often taught by experts in their field or professors from well-known colleges or universities, yet the tuition fees are typically extremely low. Adult education programs offer classes in everything from perfecting your golf or tennis game to mastering computer skills or public speaking techniques. The classes are typically offered in the evenings or on weekends and they're designed specifically for busy people.

Attend seminars

Many professional associations offer educational seminars on topics that relate to specific occupations or industries. These are usually one- or two-day events taught by experts in their field. To stay on top of developments in your field, participating in seminars is an ideal way to learn and be able to interact with the instructor to get your questions answered. Some employers encourage their employees to participate in educational seminars taught by an industry association and are willing to the pay tuition.

Correspondence classes

If your long-term career objectives involve earning an advanced degree or acquiring a professional license of some type, but you don't have the time or financial resources to attend classes at a college or university, one alternative is to participate in a correspondence program from an accredited institution.

Correspondence classes, or home-study programs, allow you to learn the required material at your own pace by reading assigned textbooks, watching videos, listening to audiocassettes of lectures, and sometimes participating in conference calls with professors. You'll never have to sit in a classroom and you can learn at your own pace.

To achieve success once you sign up for any type of correspondence course, you must be self-motivated and set aside the time necessary to complete coursework on an ongoing basis. You must set milestones and deadlines for yourself and do everything within your power to achieve them, because there will be no professor to discipline you for not completing assignments on time or for showing up late for class. This type of education isn't for everyone, but it does offer certain financial advantages and the freedom to truly set your own schedule.

Moneysaver
The tuition for correspondence classes is far less than attending a college or university as a full-time or part-time student. Yet, if you're dedicated, self-motivated, and disciplined, the education you acquire (as well as the degree or license you eventually earn) will be equivalent to what you'd achieve by attending a traditional college or university.

Instructional videos

If you don't have the time or financial resources to attend seminars in-person, there are many videocassette-based programs and training videos that allow you to learn by watching TV. Instructional videos are available from a wide range of sources and cover everything from very basic skills to highly advanced and specialized material.

The biggest drawback to using videocassette programs as a method of learning is that they're non-interactive. There's no live professor, and thus you can't ask questions. Many companies use videocassette programs to provide specialized training to employees. If your employer has produced training programs, inquire about how to gain access to them, even if the knowledge offered doesn't fit directly into your job description. Watching your company's training programs is an excellent way to learn specialized skills that your employer believes are important. Mastering these skills will open up additional career opportunities for you.

Thanks to multimedia computer technology, video-based training programs are becoming interactive using CD-ROM, Internet and DVD-ROM technology. These new interactive training programs combine live-action video instruction with computer graphics and programming, so the student can learn at their own pace and be automatically tested on the material being taught, ensuring maximum retention and comprehension. A growing number of companies are producing customized computer-based training programs to help train employees.

Instructional books-on-tape

There are literally thousands of self-help and how-to books available at bookstores. The problem is, few people actually have time to sit down and read these books. Books-on-tape, however, allows you to obtain the same knowledge and insight as you would by reading full-length books, yet all you have to do is sit back and listen to audio cassettes or CDs at home, on a Walkman, or in your car.

Your commute to and from work, driving to and from client appointments, and during down-time or travel time on business trips are all ideal times to listen to self-help or how-to books on tape. From these educational programs, you can learn useful skills from the world's leading experts.

Books-on-tape are available at virtually all major bookstores and from many popular mail-order companies that target business professionals. The skills you can learn from these programs is incredibly

Unofficially...
Vault Report: The Job Seekers Secret Weapon (888-JOB-VAULT or http:// www.vaultreports. com/previews/ internships.html) is one of many companies that offers an online directory, as well as printed directories of internship opportunities available throughout the country. Detailed company profiles are also offered.

diverse. For example, you can learn to enhance your verbal communication skills; memory; time management skills; speed reading; organization; selling skills; business negotiation skills; develop assertiveness; learn a foreign language; discover your ultimate potential and achieve your dreams; or enhance your delegation and management skills.

On-the-job training

When it comes to on-the-job training, there's just one rule: if it's offered, take advantage of it! On-the-job training allows you to learn new skills and almost always get paid at the same time. Not only can on-the-job training teach you the skills you need to master your job, it can also prepare you for a promotion or give you the knowledge needed to take on additional work-related responsibilities that will lead to higher pay. Participating in on-the-job training also makes you more marketable to other employers in your industry should you choose to seek other employment opportunities.

Read self-help books and books about your profession

Reading is an excellent way to learn new skills and obtain additional knowledge at your own pace. There are how-to and self-help books designed to teach you virtually any skill imaginable. After determining what type of skills or knowledge you're interested in learning, visit your local bookstore and start reading. Publications produced internally within your company, such as employee, procedure, or operations manuals are also worthwhile reading materials if you're trying to learn more about how your employer operates.

Return to school for an advanced degree or certification

In many industries, there's only so far up the corporate ladder you can go without an advanced degree. Once you've been out of school for several years, the prospect of going back to school and again becoming a student can be daunting. Combine this with the cost of pursuing an advanced degree, and it becomes a rather large financial commitment, not to mention a huge time commitment.

The good news is that some employers offer education reimbursement as a job benefit, which means they'll pick up some or all of your tuition if you choose to pursue a degree or license that somehow relates to your current career. Some employers will allow you to keep your current job (sometimes with a reduced workload) in order to attend school nights and weekends. This, however, means giving up virtually all of your free time, since during the day you'll be working at your current job, and at night you'll either be in the classroom or studying. In this scenario, the employer will often pay for your education and continue paying your salary.

If your employer doesn't offer tuition reimbursement or you choose to change careers and pursue an education that will prepare you for a new career, you'll have to pay for your own education, and perhaps give up your current job in order to attend school full-time. This means that in addition to paying for your education, you'll be giving up your paycheck, forcing you to rely on your savings or support from a spouse or family member to pay your expenses.

When you earn an advanced degree or license your earning potential should increase dramatically.

Bright Idea
Locating books on highly specialized topics is easy when surfing the Internet. Visit Amazon.Com (www.amazon.com) or Barnes and Noble (www.barnes andnoble.com) and take advantage of the keyword search features these services offer. You can then have any book shipped directly to you when you place an order using a major credit card.

When deciding whether or not to return to school, it's important to do research in order to determine, in advance, what your future earning potential and career options will be. It's necessary to perform a cost/benefit analysis to determine if returning to school is ultimately in your best interest.

When evaluating your options as they relate to obtaining higher education, ask yourself the following questions. To help you make an "educated decision" about your future education, contact the admissions office of several schools you'd consider attending and also seek the guidance of a career counselor. You might also consider seeking advice from your superiors at work.

Questions to ask pertaining to pursuing higher-level education

Answering each of these questions will help you determine the benefits and drawbacks of returning to school when you currently have a full-time job.

- What type of advanced degree or license would you return to school to pursue?
- How would this degree or license help your career move forward?
- What will your earning potential be once you complete your education?
- How easy will it be to land a good job once you've graduated?
- What type of time commitment is involved?
- Would you leave your current job to become a full-time student or take classes part-time?
- If you choose to work part-time, what will your schedule be like? Will you be able to successfully juggle your workload with your academic requirements and personal life?

■ How much will it cost to pursue your education? (Don't forget to factor in lost income while you're in school.) Will your employer pay some or all of your tuition? Will you have to take out student loans and go into debt? How will you pay your living expenses while in school?

■ Will pursuing an advanced degree or license help you achieve your long-term career goals and allow you to land a job you'll be passionate about?

■ What are the five biggest benefits of returning to school?

■ What are the five biggest drawbacks?

■ How will attending classes full-time or part-time impact your personal life? How will your decision impact your spouse and children?

■ What opportunities will you miss out on if you take a sabbatical from your current job to pursue your education?

■ Is your reason for returning to school simply to get away from your current job?

Once you decide that returning to school is in your best interest, you must determine what schools you could attend and which ones you could actually get into. Choosing the right school isn't a decision that should be taken lightly. It's one that will require research.

Factors to consider include: the school's reputation; curriculum options; the academic workload; the size and location of the institution; the size of classes; and the overall cost of attending the school (tuition, living expenses, textbooks, etc.). Investigate scholarship and student loan opportunities, as well as tuition reimbursement plans from your employer, plus other options available to you to help pay for your education.

Figure out, in advance, exactly what you're looking for in an educational institution and then seek the school that best meets your wants and needs. Be prepared to visit individual schools, make appointments to meet with admissions personnel as well as department heads, and carefully evaluate the curriculum and caliber of the faculty.

The two most common grad school degrees awarded are master's and doctorates. A master's program will almost always award an M.A. or an M.S. degree, while a doctoral program will usually award a Ph.D. There are many options available to students based on what type of degree they choose to pursue and in what time frame they plan to pursue it.

Which schools you can actually get admitted into will be impacted by your high school and college GPA, your GRE/GMAT test scores, your work experience, and your ability to pay. Returning to school to earn an advanced degree requires first making many decisions. It's not just a matter of paying tuition and showing up for classes.

Additional information about pursuing an advanced degree can be obtained from The Educational Testing Service (http://www.ets.org/). One of the services offered by the ETS is The SIGI PLUS program, which is a complete, self-directed, interactive system of career guidance. It offers information dedicated to helping you prepare for tomorrow's job market today. The SIGI PLUS program can help you get a clear sense of direction and provide the information you need to develop and implement a new career plan. Contact the career guidance department of any two- or four-year colleges in

Bright Idea
The Yahoo! Internet search engine (http://www.yahoo.com/Regional/Countries/United_States/Education/Colleges_and_Universities/Complete_Listing) also offers a full listing of colleges and universities that have web sites, allowing you to obtain information about advanced education programs online.

your area, or call your local library to obtain access to the program. State employment service offices may also have the software. The SIGI PLUS web site can be reached at http://www.ets.org/sigi/, or for more information, call (800) 257-7444.

Skills that are in demand

When it comes to evaluating your personal skill set, your job-related skills are, of course, absolutely critical, since they are what will allow you to successfully fill the responsibilities of the job you're hired to do. Job-related skills vary greatly, depending on your specific occupation and your employer.

In addition to what's required to fulfill your job responsibilities, all employers look to hire individuals who are well-rounded, team-oriented, enthusiastic, and motivated. Knowing that the business world is changing fast, many employers also look for skills, such as computer literacy and the ability to communicate well (both verbally and in writing), since having these abilities makes virtually anyone a more valuable employee.

Basic computer literacy

For many people who haven't grown up using personal computers, the prospect of learning how to operate one of these gizmos can be very intimidating. Thanks to modern operating systems, using a personal computer has become rather simple and requires a set of skills that virtually anyone can learn in a matter of days with the proper instruction. Of course, there's a very big difference (in terms of the knowledge and computer-related skills required) between using popular programs and becoming a programmer, MIS professional, or systems administrator. What most employers look for is an ability to perform basic tasks on a PC, such as word process-ing, spreadsheet management, using a database, sending/receiving e-mail, and surfing the web.

For beginners, the very best way to learn com-puter skills is by taking classes, since this provides you with a forum to ask questions and interact with an instructor. It's also possible to use videocassette training programs or read instructional books and computer manuals, however, this can be far more frustrating for someone with no computer experi-ence.

Computer classes are taught at computer super-stores (such as CompUSA and Computer City), through adult education programs, Job Corps, at community colleges, at local libraries, and at inde-pendent computer training facilities located throughout the country (check the Yellow Pages under "Computers," "Computer Training," or "Computer Instruction"). The cost of the classes will vary greatly, from a few dollars per session to over $100 per hour.

There's no doubt that as we progress into the next millennium, the need for computer literacy will become an absolute must, and those with at least basic computer skills will have a major advantage in the job market.

Communication skills

With the availability of telephones, fax machines, electronic mail (e-mail), FedEx, video conferencing, cellular telephones, text pagers, U.S. Mail and in-person meetings, communication is a critical aspect of virtually every job. Being able to communicate well with others, get your point across, and consider what others are saying in a timely and efficient man-ner is an absolute must. This means being able to read, write, and speak so that others can easily understand you. The more on-the-job responsibilities you have, the more important it is that you be able to communicate in a highly professional manner so that you can command respect from your coworkers, superiors and subordinates.

There are five primary skills you need to become a good communicator:

- Reading
- Writing
- Speaking
- Public speaking
- Listening

Most high school and college curriculums teach these basic skills, but few teach how these skills should be applied to the business world. This can put you at a disadvantage unless you take it upon yourself to perfect these basic skills so you can apply them successfully on the job. You purchased this book because you're interested in negotiating a salary that you deserve and you want to earn more money. As you'll see, to land a job, negotiate a compensation package, perform well in an annual review, or to earn a promotion, you'll need to take full advantage of your communication skills so that you can convey vital information to your employer or potential employer on a variety of levels.

Reading is a skill that most people learn in elementary school. But if you read hundreds or thousands of pages worth of technical or work-related information, how long would it take? As you read this information, could you easily remember what you read, understand the information and pick out key points? These are the additional skills needed by

Bright Idea
The Evelyn Wood Reading Dynamics course involves participating in an in-person, six-hour seminar that costs under $150. For about $200, you can purchase the course on video-cassette and learn the necessary reading skills and techniques at home, at your own pace. The program is unconditionally guaranteed to vastly improve your reading speed and retention. To learn more about this program, call (800) 447-7323. Other speed reading courses include: Mega Speed Reading (800) 327-8373 and Super Reading (408) 947-6222.

business professionals and those working in many different occupations and industries.

Learning to process vast amounts of information by reading is a skill that takes practice. There are many different speed reading and reading comprehension courses designed to help professionals learn advanced reading skills that simply aren't taught in school. Discovering how to read faster, understand and remember more of what you read, and to pick out important facts and then use that information are the skills taught by various speed reading classes.

If your job involves any amount of reading, you'll see the benefits to taking a speed reading class almost immediately after your instruction begins. Speed reading isn't magic. The concepts taught include innovative ways to use your mind's capacity to process information faster and more efficiently. You'll also learn to use your eyes correctly when you read and better focus your mind.

Mastering the skills taught in any of these classes will help you save time in your daily life, become far more productive, and give you the ability to learn new skills and information faster.

Writing is another extremely valuable skill that hopefully you learned while in high school and/or college. Virtually everyone, however, can benefit from additional training so that they're better able to communicate in writing within a work environment. Can you write business letters, reports, memos, proposals, or faxes in a timely manner? Can you get your point across quickly and succinctly when you create a written document? Do you use proper English grammar and punctuation? Do people always understand what you write? Do you suffer from "writer's block" or find writing to be a labor-intensive chore?

Speaking is, of course, another important method of communication. Whether you're trying to communicate verbally with an individual, a small group of people, or a large crowd, it is important to be able to speak in a manner which people understand. Taking a public speaking class is one way to help you perfect your verbal communication skills: what you say, how you say it, and your use of body language (when dealing with people in-person).

When preparing any type of verbal presentation, whether it's a for a sales call, a one-on-one discussion with your boss, your annual employee review, or an all-out business meeting that will be attended by many people within your company, here are a few steps to help make your verbal communication more effective:

Bright Idea
If your writing skills need polishing, you're not alone. Consider signing up for a business writing class at any college, university, or adult education program. There are also books designed to teach intelligent, well-educated professionals how to enhance their writing skills.

- Prepare your talk in advance and target it specifically to your audience.

- Use stories, specific examples, and anecdotes to illustrate your key points.

- Create notes or an outline for what you plan to say. Avoid writing out your speech word-for-word.

- Practice your speech or presentation so that you're very familiar with it. Practice in front of a mirror or videotape yourself rehearsing the speech in advance.

- Don't memorize a speech word-for-word and avoid reading your speech. If you're familiar with what you want to say and you've practiced how you plan to say it, the words will come naturally.

- Maintain plenty of eye contact with your audience during your one-on-one conversations or in a meeting or presentation situation.

Become a memorable speaker

Learning to be a good speaker takes practice and instruction. Hiring a professional coach to teach you the basics of becoming an excellent speaker is one way to master these skills.

Kay Britten, for example, is a speech coach and motivator. As the founder of Kay Britten Communications, Inc. (810-540-6106 / http://www.kaybritten.com), she has worked with hundreds of professionals, politicians, and business executives from every field. Whether the subject is speaking to groups, meeting the media, voice, personal development, interview or supervisory skills, Britten tunes in to the special abilities and special needs of each individual and inspires them with new understanding, confidence, and renewed motivation.

Executive Communications Group (800-874-8278 / http://www.ecglink.com) is another company that's dedicated to helping business professionals in all industries become better verbal communicators.

Yet another resource available to anyone interested in improving their verbal communication skills is Toastmasters International, which has individual chapters throughout the country. Whatever your goals may be, much of your success in life will depend on your ability to speak. People who can effectively communicate possess one of the skills necessary for successful living.

Toastmasters International provides the tools that enable people to develop this skill. In Toastmasters, you learn by doing—by actually

Unofficially... On her web site, Kay Britten explains, "The quality of your voice has a more powerful effect on others than you may think. A well-resonated voice presents you as a leader, as a person with authority and strength of personality. A well-produced voice is particularly vital for women in the workplace. A thin, nasal, high-pitched or hard-edged voice is a powerful disadvantage."

speaking to groups. You learn in comfortable surroundings, not in a sterile classroom environment.

The Toastmasters program has proven itself around the world. Globally, nearly three million people of all ages and occupations have participated in the program. The Toastmasters experience takes place in a club situation. On average, the gross membership of Toastmasters International increases at a rate of approximately 250 people per day, for a total of more than 170,000 members in more than 8,000 Clubs in more than 50 countries. A typical Toastmasters Club is made up of 20 to 30 people who gather regularly (usually once a week).

The cost of participating in Toastmasters is extremely low, making it affordable to virtually everyone. The program is open to anyone 18 years of age or older. Members come from a variety of occupations and backgrounds. They include doctors, auto mechanics, executives, teachers, homemakers, artists, college students, supervisors, attorneys, engineers, and salespeople. Because members work closely with people whose daily lives are different from their own, they become aware of the community in which they live, and are exposed to different ideas and opinions.

Joining a Toastmasters Club is easy. With more than 8,000 clubs around the world, there is probably at least one near you. You don't need a personal invitation to join. Many clubs are listed with their local Chamber of Commerce, can be located by writing to Toastmasters International, or by checking the "Toastmasters Clubs Around the World" page at the Toastmasters International Home Page (http://www.toastmasters.org). After you receive a listing, simply select the club or clubs that are most convenient for you and attend a meeting.

Shut up and listen!

Bright Idea
To repeat.
Listening is
important.

The final major skill needed to be a superior communicator is good listening skills. This is a skill that's an absolute must when participating in a job search or negotiating your salary, because you need to listen and understand the objections and apprehensions of your potential or current employer. Good listening skills are also needed when it comes to working within group situations, managing or supervising others, or accepting instructions or direction from a superior.

Many self-help or how-to books, videotapes, and instructional audio tapes are available to teach the basics of listening. However, once you've learned the basics, it'll take practice to truly become a good listener, and thus a good communicator. Poor listening can result in lost sales, misunderstandings, and all sorts of time-wasting errors, not to mention lower productivity, and lost earning potential. Later, in Chapter 10, you'll learn the importance of listening in any negotiating session and how to use your listening skills to ultimately get what you want out of your negotiation efforts.

Making yourself a more valuable employee

In addition to mastering a variety of different skills and developing a personal skill set that makes you more marketable as an employee than others in your field, there are other things you can do to make you a more valued asset to any employer.

Overtime work

If you ask any employer what they believe makes a perfect employee, the response is usually that they look for people who are hardworking, dedicated, trustworthy, and enthusiastic. While it's easy to say you possess these qualities, actions always speak louder than words, and working overtime (whether it's paid or unpaid) is an excellent way of demonstrating to an employer that you're a hard worker and dedicated to your job.

Don't wait until a week or so before you plan on hitting your employer up for a raise or promotion to begin spending extra time on the job. Being able to show a track record of staying late at work when your services were needed is a compelling reason for an employer to take your request for a raise or promotion seriously.

Staying late on the job for the sake of staying late won't do much unless you're available to the employer when you're needed the most. On the other hand, having to consistently stay late because you're unable to accurately complete your work in a timely manner is not necessarily something you'll be rewarded for.

Periodically volunteering to take over someone else's shift if they call in sick or have to leave early, and being recognized as someone your employer can count on when they're understaffed or in a bind also makes you valuable.

Recognition and awards

Many employers offer awards, such as "Salesperson of the Week" or "Employee of the Month." While winning these awards won't necessarily translate directly into immediate financial rewards, earning

Bright Idea
Of course, other factors will be taken into account, but being able to prove that you're an extremely hard worker who is dedicated can be worth staying 30 minutes or an hour late one, two or three times per week.

them does help you to develop your reputation for being a dedicated hard worker, which can later translate into a pay raise and/or promotion. Thus, when your employer offers some type of award program, become an active participant and strive to earn as much on-the-job recognition as possible. As you win these awards, keep copies of whatever award certificates or letters of recognition you receive so that you can bring them to the employer's attention again during your annual review or when you begin seeking out new employment opportunities. Winning awards or formal recognition from an employer, boss, or supervisor allows you to show proof of your accomplishments later on.

Volunteering

Let's face it, having to juggle a full-time job, your personal interests, and a family can be a challenge unto itself. Yet, if you have some extra time in your hectic schedule that you want to put to excellent use, consider seeking out opportunities to work as a volunteer. Many employers participate in various charity events throughout the year and seek the support of its employees. By participating in volunteer opportunities through your company, you'll be able to demonstrate once again that you're a team player and someone who is dedicated to their job.

Volunteering could involve coaching the Little League baseball team that your company sponsors, helping to raise money for a charity your company supports, organizing a group of employees to participate in a walkathon for charity, or representing your company at various community events.

Doing volunteer work often means working with other people, which provides you with an opportunity to enhance your communication, presentation, leadership, and teamwork skills. Working for a voluntary organization or a charity can help you develop these skills in a practical way, giving you real life experiences. Volunteering can also provide excellent networking opportunities and give you the satisfaction that what you are doing is worthwhile, such as helping people or solving problems.

If you're interested in doing volunteer work, begin by asking your employer how you might begin participating in efforts that they're already involved in on a corporate level. You might also begin by analyzing your personal skills and interests and determining what type of volunteer work you'd be interested in pursuing. Listing volunteer and charity work on your resumé always looks great.

It's a commitment and investment in your future

Developing your skill set is a lifelong endeavor. As you gain new skills and experience, you become more qualified for a greater number of job opportunities and more valuable to employers. Some skills are easy to acquire and take a minimal investment of time and effort. Other skills, however, require a much bigger commitment. These are often the skills that reap the greatest rewards when it comes to seeking employment opportunities that offer the highest salaries.

Whether or not you're happily employed, you should always be taking an active role in expanding your personal skill set in order to improve yourself. This should be something you want to do for yourself, not simply to pacify or impress an employer.

When given the opportunity to learn a new skill or receive training, ask yourself what short- and

Bright Idea
For ideas on how you can begin volunteering whatever time you have available, visit the Impact Online web site at http://www.impactonline.org orhttp://www.volunteermatch.org.

long-term benefits you'll receive by capitalizing on the opportunity and then evaluate the commitment that's required on your part. Remember, making sacrifices now could offer a huge pay-off later, so evaluate your options carefully and pursue those that will help you achieve your long-term goals and dreams.

Everyone wants to be happy in their job, doing something that they're interested in and that they find emotionally and financially rewarding. In order to achieve your own career-related goals and dreams, it's critical that you develop the personal skill set that will allow you to succeed in whatever career opportunity you choose to pursue.

Just the facts

- To sell yourself as a dedicated employee, it helps to acquire new skills and expand upon your personal skill set.

- An advanced degree or license may help further your career and boost your earning power.

- If you do not have excellent computer or communication skills, consider taking a course to improve yourself in those areas.

Getting What You Deserve...Now

PART II

GET THE SCOOP ON...
Determining if you're being fairly compensated
for your work ▪ Determining if you really
deserve a raise or promotion ▪ Choosing the
best time to request a raise or promotion ▪ The
best way to ask for a raise or promotion

Getting More Money from Your Current Employer

Chapter 4

How would you like to earn what you really deserve, receive the benefits you want, and have the job-related responsibilities you know you're capable of handling? Well, with a bit of hard work and planning, you can have all of this and more!

This chapter provides information for people who are currently employed and who are looking to receive a well-deserved raise or promotion from their employer. Simply wanting more money to show up for work isn't a good reason for your employer to pay you more or give you additional responsibility. Likewise, requesting or demanding a raise because you're experiencing personal financial problems or debt is not an appropriate reason to request a raise from your employer.

Virtually all employers reward employees with raises and/or promotions for one reason—they've earned it through hard work and dedication and through taking on more responsibilities. As you'll discover by reading this chapter, truly deserving a raise or promotion, and being able to prove it, is probably your only chance of actually getting what you want and deserve.

One problem faced by many employees is that, despite their hard work, their efforts and achievements are simply overlooked by their superiors, and their work goes unrewarded. When this happens, it's usually a matter of poor employer/employee communication or poor employee management, not because the employer is cheap or interested in exploiting its employees. If you're faced with a situation where you're overworked and genuinely underpaid, and not earning what you deserve, there are ways of bringing this to an employer's attention. This chapter will show you how. Make no mistake about it, being able to earn what you truly deserve is all about attitude as well as aptitude.

Do you really deserve a raise or promotion?

Everyone believes that they should be paid more money, be required to work fewer hours, receive greater benefits, have more vacation days, and be given fewer work-related responsibilities and more flexible deadlines. Well, this is the real world, so set your expectations to something that's realistic and your chances of getting it will be far greater.

Unfortunately, when it comes to making more money and receiving better benefits, it's not a matter of what you, the employee, wants. It's a matter of what you genuinely deserve, what the industry norms are, and how generous your employer wants to be when it comes to compensating its workers fairly.

If you really want a raise or promotion, it must be earned and well deserved, and even then, it may be something you have to negotiate hard for. After all, the goal of virtually all employers is to get their employees to work as hard a possible for the least amount of money. In order to receive more than what your employer is initially willing to pay, you must stand out from your peers and co-workers, prove yourself to be a valuable asset to the company, and be able to demonstrate specifically why you deserve more money (or a promotion).

Additionally, you must be able to demonstrate exactly what your employer has been getting for its investment in you thus far, and be able to show what your employer can expect from you in the future.

If you've been with a company for over one year and you've worked hard to become a valuable employee, yet you aren't being paid what you truly believe you're worth, it might become necessary to take matters into your own hands and ask for (not demand) a raise.

How often should you be given a raise or promotion?

Most employers evaluate employees every six or twelve months and offer raises and/or promotions as a result of these periodic evaluations. Prior to accepting a job offer, hopefully you asked the employer how often you'd be evaluated and what the employer's evaluation criteria are. Also remember that in some companies, a promotion will only be possible if a job or a position is vacant.

Typically, an employer will be more apt to consider your request for a raise or promotion after you've been on the job at least one year. After this time, most employers will automatically consider rewarding your performance, if it has met or

Unless you're in an entry-level job, don't expect to receive a raise or promotion in your first six months on the job, unless you accomplish something absolutely phenomenal that your employer chooses to reward.

Bright Idea
Chapter 5 offers more details on how to champion an annual review or employee evaluation.

exceeded their expectations. If you've been working in the same position for between 18 months and two years, yet there's been no action on your employer's part to offer you a raise or promotion (aside from a cost of living increase), it's probably time to take matters into your own hands. Request a one-on-one meeting with your superior(s) to discuss your future with the company. Begin by requesting a formal employee evaluation.

Does your employer have a problem with your performance, the quality of your work, or your overall attitude? If something negative is brought to your attention, make every effort to take action and fix the situation quickly before requesting a raise or promotion. If, however, the employer has no negative criticism, take it upon yourself to request a raise, and start by highlighting your accomplishments and contributions to the company, and getting the employer to acknowledge your achievements.

After working in a particular job for between two and three years, chances are you've mastered all of the skills required to successfully fulfill the requirements of that job and you are able to maintain a consistently high-quality level of work. You should also have developed an impressive list of accomplishments while in that position. In an ideal situation, you're taking it upon yourself to seek extra training or additional education to prepare yourself for greater work-related responsibilities.

You genuinely deserve a raise, so prove it!—Getting your employer's attention

The most important thing to understand from this chapter is that wanting a raise and actually deserving a raise are two very different things. How do you know if you truly deserve a raise and/or promotion? Ask yourself the following questions:

- Have you been succeeding at your current job for at least one year, without receiving a raise or promotion?

- Have you met or exceeded all of your employer's expectations?

- Do you consistently complete all of your assigned work in a timely manner?

- Is the work you do always consistent and accurate?

- Do you get along well with the majority of your co-workers and fit in with your company's overall corporate culture?

- Does your employer perceive you to be a motivated and hard worker?

- Have you consistently put in overtime or worked weekends in order to enhance the overall success of your division or company as a whole?

- How does your work rate compared to your coworkers and those with similar responsibilities?

- How does your personal skill set compare to your coworkers and those with similar responsibilities?

- Do you consistently pick up other people's slack or cover for others?

- Have you been in a position to train coworkers or subordinates?

- Have you gone out of your way to take on additional responsibilities that were outside of your job description in order to assist your supervisor or superior(s)?

- While in your current job, have you earned any special awards or received special recognition?

- Have you been directly responsible for any measurable company-wide or division-wide accomplishments, such as boosting overall sales or productivity?

If you've answered "yes" to at least several of these questions, then you probably have the necessary ammunition to approach your employer for a raise and/or promotion. Now, all you have to do is prove it.

The trick to demonstrating your value to an employer is to document everything about yourself that makes you a valuable employee. You want to make the employer realize that they're not taking full advantage of your potential and that you deserve greater responsibilities and financial rewards for your hard work, long-term dedication, and overall efforts. While you want to toot your own horn, so to speak, you don't want to come off as arrogant or desperate, which is why offering proof for your argument that you deserve more responsibility and more money is critical. It's also important that you make your interest in taking on greater responsibilities known to the right people within your organization.

As you prepare for that big meeting with your boss when you plan to request a raise and/or promotion, write down all of your achievements and accomplishments since your last raise, promotion, or employee review. Think in terms of productivity, dollars, or anything else that can be measured. Being able to measure your success in a way that's tangible gives you more ammunition. Think carefully about what your employer needs and wants from you, and how you've measured up to (or exceeded) expectations.

To help you better organize your thoughts and be able to better showcase your value, use a separate sheet of paper to answer the following questions. You can present this information, in writing, to an employer at the end of your in-person meeting (when you request a raise and/or promotion), or simply use it as an outline for preparing your presentation to your employer.

When the employer asks, "Why do you deserve a raise or promotion?" the information you list here should answer that question in a simple and straightforward manner. Remember to provide as many specifics and as much quantitative information as possible. (For example, "I improved the productivity of my division by 20 percent this past year by doing..." or "My sales figures were 15 percent higher than any other salesperson at the company, because....")

Now that you understand the type of information you'll want to bring to your employer's attention when asking for a raise and/or a promotion, the next step is to actually make your request in a highly professional manner.

How to ask for a raise

When it comes to asking for a raise, you always want to take a highly professional approach. Never become overly emotional or confrontational with your employer. You also want to be totally prepared to persuade your employer that you're worth what your asking for, which means taking time, in advance, to carefully plan your strategy.

Delivering an ultimatum is never the tactic to use. You don't want to bully your employer into

Unofficially...
As you demonstrate your value to an employer, use examples, statistics, comparisons, testimonials, cost-benefit analyses, and any other pieces of quantitative information. The more specifics you provide, the stronger your argument will be.

Your Current Job Description:

What Are Your Five Biggest and Proudest Accomplishments in This Position?

1.

2.

3.

4.

5.

Describe Quantitative Results You've Achieved Based on Your Efforts:

Describe the Impact of Your Achievements on Your Superior:

What Impact Have You Had on the Company as a Whole?

Describe Your Current Goals and Objectives:

How Are These Goals Consistent or in Line with Those of Your Employer?

What Responsibilities Have You Taken on Outside Your Job Description?

What Sets You Apart From Your Coworkers
(Skills, Accomplishments, etc.)?

List Five Reasons Why You Deserve a Raise (<u>NOT</u>
why you want one):

1.

2.

3.

4.

5.

If You're Requesting a Promotion, What Job Title
Are You Looking to Fill?

What Would Your Primary Responsibilities Be?

Why Are You Uniquely Qualified to Fill This
Position?

What Specific Skills Do You Have That Will Be
Particularly Useful?

What Specialized Education Do You Have That
Can be Applied to the Job?

What Experience Do You Have That Makes You
Qualified for the Job You Want?

Watch Out!
One of the biggest mistakes people make when asking for a raise is that they deliver an ultimatum, stating something like, "Give me a raise, or I quit." This tactic can be a huge mistake.

doing something they're not comfortable with, and you don't want to leave yourself backed up against a wall if your demands aren't met. Delivering an ultimatum is unprofessional and can create unnecessary tension and hostility between you and your manager.

Before approaching your superior about getting a raise, spend time reviewing your own work history and write down all of your professional accomplishments while working for your current employer. Also, list your most marketable skills that you use continuously use on-the-job, and be prepared to demonstrate to your superior why your particular skill set is valuable. You won't necessarily be showing the employer this list, but it will help dramatically in your preparation.

Include on your list specific examples of how you've become a valuable asset to the company and to your superiors. Consider the following:

- How much new business have you brought to the company?

- How much have you helped to increase productivity?

- What impact have you had on the company's overall success?

- What special projects have you successfully worked on since your past raise or employee evaluation?

- How much unpaid overtime have you put in during the past six months?

- What sets you apart from your coworkers in terms of value to the employer?

Virtually all employers evaluate employees based on their overall track record when it comes to hard work, ongoing dedication, and long-term productivity. The bottom line question the employer will be concerned with is, are you worth the salary you want to be paid? Is it worth it for the company to make an added investment in you, or is it better off from a financial standpoint to invest in another employee? Being able to provide credible arguments in your favor when you meet with the employer will help you land the raise or promotion you're looking for.

Asking for a raise can be very stressful. The best way to eliminate this stress is to be totally prepared. If you don't honestly believe that you deserve a raise, you'll have a very hard time convincing your employer. Remember, if you take a professional approach to your request for a raise or promotion, you have nothing to lose if your request is denied, so go into your meeting with confidence.

At this stage, conducting research is important so that you enter into your negotiation with your employer totally informed. Know exactly what you're asking for based on what you know the employer is able (and willing) to give, and what the company and industry standards are in terms of compensating someone with your particular skills, education, and experience.

After you have developed the list of reasons why you deserve a raise and you've done your research, make a formal appointment with your boss. Don't just walk into his or her office and make your request. Schedule a meeting during a time when you know your boss will be the least stressed and the most open-minded. This should be a private meeting. A raise request should never be brought up during a team meeting or in front of your coworkers.

Your chances for getting a raise will be better if the company is currently doing well and if you were somehow recently involved in a major project, sales effort, or assignment that was successful.

As your meeting begins, outline your accomplishments and contributions to the company. Focus on how much you enjoy working for the company, and how much you believe you'll be able to contribute in the future.

One mistake people make when asking for a raise is that they complain about their personal problems or bring up their personal debts as their reason for needing a raise. While you and you manager may be friendly, and he or she will sympathize with your situation on a personal level, from a professional standpoint, your employer doesn't care about your personal financial problems, credit card bills, or personal debt. Explaining to your boss that you just purchased a new home and you need a raise to make the mortgage payments is not the best approach to take. In fact, this approach can be extremely detrimental, because by explaining your financial problems you demonstrate that you're not a careful or conscientious planner when it comes to financial issues. Knowing this about you, your boss will think twice about giving you additional responsibilities, which ultimately decreases your chances of getting a raise and/or promotion.

During your discussions and negotiations with an employer, never assume they have full knowledge of your accomplishments and contributions to the company. It's your responsibility to accurately document your work and accomplishments and use this information to justify your request.

Be prepared to document everything, just in case your immediate superior or one of your coworkers has attempted to take credit for your hard

Unofficially...
Your best strategy is to focus on why you deserve a raise, not how much you want or need a raise. Make sure your request is consistent with company, industry, and geographic standards. Asking for a large raise that puts you in a much higher income bracket than other people with your qualifications and job description can be detrimental to your efforts, because your request won't be taken seriously.

work without you knowing it. Also, even if your immediate superior is a total incompetent fool, don't bring this up to your boss's boss hoping that he or she will move you into that position.

After reviewing your accomplishments and contributions in detail and getting the employer to acknowledge them, only then should you come right out and ask for a salary increase. Before stating how much of a raise you're looking for, you should do research to determine how much other people in comparable jobs are earning at your company and at other companies in your industry.

Through your research and by speaking with your coworkers (but do be careful when asking coworkers how much they earn—this is a very personal question), determine what type of salary increase your employer typically offers to someone with your level of expertise and seniority at the company (in terms of how long you've been employed).

For example, after one year of employment, your employer may only consider offering a five- or ten-percent salary increase, no matter how good of a job you're doing or how pleased they are with your overall performance. Knowing this, don't waste your efforts trying to land a 15-percent salary increase, because chances are your request won't even be considered, especially if you work for a medium- or large-sized company. Instead, tailor your negotiation and presentation so that you're ultimately offered a raise that's in the upper-range of what they're typically willing to give to someone who truly deserves a raise (based on performance) after one year on the job.

Always avoid arguments or getting yourself into a defensive position. Focus only on your strengths,

Unofficially...
It's critical that you showcase your own merits, not attempt to belittle others in order to get ahead.

without making excuses for weaknesses. The easiest way for an employer to deny your request for a raise is by bringing up your weaknesses or shortcomings. Be prepared for this, and determine in advance a way to turn those negatives into positives. If, however, those negatives are justified and provide the employer with justification for not giving you the raise you want, don't request a raise right now, instead, spend a few months improving your performance and eliminating those objections.

For example, if you know your employer is going to complain about how you show up to work late too often, for two months prior to asking for a raise, make a point to show up for work on-time. So, if your employer uses your tardiness as an objection when you ultimately do ask for a raise, you can point out that your track record has improved over the past 60 days (be prepared to document this). Also, stress that being on time for work (and leaving on time or working late) is something that can be expected of you in the future.

During your meeting, be prepared to negotiate. An employer may consider a proposed ten-percent salary increase out of the question, but might be open to an immediate five-percent raise, with an additional guaranteed five-percent raise within a year if you continue to meet expectations.

Whether or not you receive a raise is almost always a financial issue for the employer, not a personal one, so if you don't receive a raise, don't get angry or over emotional in front of the employer. Remember, many people who ask for a raise do not get one, even if it's deserved. Instead of receiving additional financial compensation, you might still be able to negotiate better benefits or incentives. For example, if the employer agrees that you

Watch Out!
Unfortunately, even if your presentation and request for a raise is flawless, there's always a chance your request will be denied. If your request is denied, ask questions to determine what specifically it would take for you to earn a raise and when the employer would consider evaluating you again. Knowing specifics will help you achieve what the employer requires. Never take this type of rejection personally.

deserve a raise, but states that it's not currently in the budget, ask for extra vacation days or a higher commission rate (if you're in a sales-oriented job). Benefits are worth money, so while negotiating a better benefits package won't put cash in your wallet, it will improve your overall quality of your life.

If your request for a raise is flatly denied, yet you're convinced you are worth significantly more as an employee than what you're being paid, consider looking for a new job, but don't quit your existing job until you've lined up a new one. After receiving new job offers, it may be appropriate to offer your current employer one last opportunity to increase your salary before quitting, but that's a personal decision on your part. Sometimes choosing to pursue a new career opportunity will offer greater financial benefits, but try to maintain a positive professional relationship with the employer you're leaving.

Mistakes to avoid when asking for a raise

Before actually requesting a raise, make sure you have calculated how much of a raise you're looking for, based on your value to the employer, and what the employer typically pays someone with your skills, education, experience, and length of employment with the company. How much of a raise you expect to receive should be reasonable and consistent with company standards.

Also have an idea of what the industry standards are in terms of salary for someone with your qualifications and responsibilities. Failing to research this information will cause you to go into a salary negotiation uninformed, and that's a huge mistake.

The following are some additional strategies for avoiding common mistakes and for obtaining the raise and/or promotion you deserve.

When you're ready to meet with your manager to request a raise and/or promotion, set up a private meeting with your superior. Never broach this subject in front of coworkers or during a staff meeting.

As you embark on the salary negotiation process, be persistent and patient. Don't accept the first offer you're given (unless it meets all your demands), and don't immediately back down if things aren't going your way.

When you meet with your superior, never make an ultimatum or threat. Always act friendly and professional, keeping your positive and negative emotions under control. Remember, whether or not you receive a raise or promotion will be based on your perceived value to the employer. It will be a business decision on the employer's part, not a personal one.

Even if you know that a coworker who is less competent than you are is earning a higher salary, don't use this as your reason for requesting a raise. If someone with similar skills and similar job responsibilities is earning more than you are, you know your employer has a salary range that it's willing to pay and than your current salary isn't at the high end of the range. Your job now is to convince the employer that you deserve to earn a salary that's on the higher end of that range based on your merits. Make sure that you document your accomplishments carefully just in case that coworker who is earning more than you has tried to take credit for your work.

Your objective is to get your employer to see that you are as valuable (or perhaps more valuable) than that coworker who is currently earning more than you. This can be done easily be demonstrating your skills and achievements, and without putting down your coworker or complaining that the employer isn't being fair about how they're compensating you. After outlining all of the reasons why you deserve to be paid more, one way to quickly determine what an employer is thinking in regards to your value is to ask, "Do you believe that I'm being paid what I'm worth based on my accomplishments and contributions to the company?"

If your request for a raise is denied, don't give up. Ask what you could be doing to make yourself more valuable to the employer, and after you've incorporated the employer's suggestions and have results to prove it, go back and ask again for that raise.

Don't forget that every negotiation process involves give and take, and an open line of communication. If the employer agrees that you're worth more, but can't afford to pay what you're looking to earn, consider all of your options before walking away from the negotiation table. If the employer can't increase your salary, perhaps improvements can be made to your benefits package or your commission structure can be adjusted so that it's more favorable. Always be prepared to provide counterproposals and consider counter-offers. Be creative and work with your employer to develop a compensation package that you can be happy with, even if it's not what you originally hoped for.

Many people work for large corporations and are lead to believe that all salaries are predetermined, non-negotiable, and that raises are only awarded at specific times and in pre-determined increments. This may be the case, but it doesn't mean that your earning potential is limited. If you work for a company with a formal salary

Unofficially... Never be a pest, but at the same time, if you're not being compensated fairly for your hard work, keep asking for the raise you deserve until you get it or until it's clear that the only way you'll get what you deserve is to seek employment elsewhere.

structure and well-defined job descriptions, all you have to do to earn more money is learn new skills or obtain additional training so that you become qualified for a higher paying job. Once you have the skills needed for a job that pays more and you've already demonstrated your value to your employer in your current job, request a promotion or transfer to that higher paying position.

While it's an excellent strategy to spend between several weeks and several months prior to requesting a raise positioning yourself as "the perfect employee" by working overtime, taking on additional responsibilities, being extra productive, never let the employer take advantage of you. Make the extra effort with a goal in mind—and if you feel that you are not appreciated, tell your employer politely.

During your salary negotiations, negotiate your salary and benefits separately, starting with your salary first. You'll find that there's more flexibility on your employer's part when it comes to negotiating benefits and perks.

Listen carefully to everything your employer says during a salary negotiation, paying careful attention to objections or concerns. You'll want to address these concerns and develop a true understanding of the employer's point of view. Failing to do this will put you at a disadvantage, because by understanding what the employer's wants and needs are, you'll be in a much better position to meet those needs. Try considering everything from the employer's point of view so that you can develop an understanding about where they're coming from, what their concerns are, and what their objectives are.

Understand the terms of your agreement

Once your employer presents you with an offer, consider it carefully before accepting or rejecting it.

Unofficially...
The salary you'll start off with will most likely determine your future earning potential, since annual or periodic raises will most likely be based on a percentage of your salary. Thus, a higher starting salary will result in higher raises later. Typical raises range between three percent and ten percent of your salary, although this can vary greatly based on your occupation, the industry you work in, and how well your company is doing. If you're looking for a raise that's higher than what's typically given, it'll probably be necessary to obtain a promotion or to change your job description.

Calculate the entire value of your compensation package, including the dollar value of the perks and benefits.

As you're negotiating a new compensation package, make sure both you and your employer are speaking the same language. The wording used to describe a compensation package can have a tremendous impact on what you actually earn. This becomes most obvious when you're dealing with some type of commission structure.

If you're a salesperson, for example, know the lingo that deals with commissions and compensation:

> **Base plus commission** For salespeople, this is a common compensation method. It involves receiving a predetermined base salary plus some type of commission on the sales you actually make. The commission rate you'll be paid will probably be lower than if you were on straight commission, but whether your sales are high or low in a given period, you're guaranteed to receive at least your base pay, which is yours to keep.

> **Draw against commission** This type of compensation plan is totally commission based, however, at the beginning of each pay period, you're given a predetermined draw (a specific amount of money in advance). This draw (advance) is deducted from your commissions at the end of a pay period. If you don't cover your draw during a pay period, you will owe money to the employer, which can often be paid back later when you have a more prosperous period. If you have several poor performance periods, however, you

Watch Out!
It's vital that you and your employer agree on what's expected of you and how you'll be compensated. Miscommunication is one of the most common reasons why people end up being unhappy in the job they accept. Most employers don't intentionally misrepresent a job or its responsibilities. When someone believes a job has been misrepresented to them, it's almost always because of a miscommunication or lack of communication between the employer and the employee. Make sure you get a written description of the job, or write one yourself, then discuss it with the employer, and make sure it gets approved (in writing).

could run into problems. Suppose you are given a $2,000 draw at the start of a month, and by the end of the month you've earned $3,000 in commissions. The result will be that you receive an additional $1,000 commission check. If, however, you only earn $1,500 in commissions, you'll owe the employer $500, and will have to pay the company back from your draw (advance).

Residual commissions   Earning residual commissions is a salesperson's dream, because as long as their accounts are generating revenue for the employer, the salesperson continues to receive a commission. For example, many insurance salespeople receive residual commissions for all of their clients, as long as their clients continue paying their premiums, which could be for many years after the initial sale is made. Through negotiation, you may be able to continue receiving residual commissions owed to you, even after you leave the company you're working for. Many employers are reluctant to offer this type of compensation deal.

Salary plus bonus   If this is the method of compensation you agree upon, you'll receive a predetermined salary each pay period that is not impacted by your performance. At the end of a year (or pre-set amount of time), you'd also receive an added bonus if your performance meets or exceeds specific goals.

Salary plus commission   This is the same as a "base plus commission" compensation structure.

Straight commission   You earn a percentage of your sales. Unless you have proven sales skills and you're positive you'll have immediate success selling a specific product or service, this type of compensation can be a bit risky, since you only get paid based on how much you sell. If you make no sales, you take home no paycheck, even if you put in a 40+ hour work week. For talented sales people, this is an attractive compensation deal, since their income potential is entirely in their control.

Straight salary   As a salesperson, you'll earn a straight salary that is in no way impacted positively or negatively by your sales performance. For a salesperson who is developing their skills, this is a very safe compensation method, although there is no real incentive to excel. Poor performers, however, tend to get fired, since most companies won't continue to carry salespeople or salary-based workers that aren't performing up to expectations.

Variable commission   This type of commission structure is similar to a straight commission, however, the commission rate you're paid goes up or down based on predetermined circumstances. Some salespeople try to negotiate a higher sales commission if they reach or exceed specific monthly goals in order to incorporate an incentive plan into their commission-based compensation package.

How much of a raise should you request?

Knowing what you want or truly believe you deserve to earn and actually sharing that figure with your employer during a salary negotiation are two very different things. You'll be able to determine how much of a raise you should request by researching:

- How much your coworkers, with similar skills are getting paid.

- What your company's salary range is for someone in your position and with your length of employment.

- What the salary range is within your industry and in your geographic area for someone with your skills.

As an employee, you're more apt to receive a higher raise if you're able to demonstrate you've recently obtained new skills or training and you're qualified to take on additional responsibilities within your company. If you're able to do more for your employer, your perceived value goes up, and your employer will be more willing to pay you a higher salary.

For entry level or low paying positions (under $25,000 per year), the employer usually has a pre-determined salary range that's not too negotiable. Your best bet is to understand what the salary range is for this type of job and position yourself so that you're offered a salary that's on the high-end of this range. If you want to earn more money (outside of the pre-defined range), it will be necessary for you to apply for and land a different position—one that pays more and has greater responsibilities.

For positions that pay between $25,000 and $50,000 per year, most employers usually have the ability to negotiate a bit when setting salaries for employees. How much the employer is willing to pay will be based on the applicant's personal skill set, work experience, educational history, and perceived value to the employer.

If you're applying for a high paying job ($50,000+), you have the most salary negotiation potential, since these jobs are skill-based and usually pretty specialized. Thus, the employer is willing to pay more to employees with special skills or abilities. The job descriptions for these high-paying positions are also less defined, allowing employers to hire people with unique skills and abilities, who will become valuable assets to the company.

Are a raise and a promotion the same thing?

In most cases, a raise and a promotion are two different things, although a raise usually accompanies a promotion. When an employee is given a raise, she keeps her same job title and maintains the same job responsibilities. What changes is how much the employee is paid and/or what benefits she's offered. Employers offer raises based on a number of different criteria. Understanding these criteria will help you develop realistic expectations and help you do what it takes to earn the raise you deserve. If you don't already know the answers to the following questions, ask your employer before seeking a raise. Some companies publish employee manuals that will answer most or all of these questions:

- How does the employer determine who is awarded a raise? What criteria is used? Is it based on individual performance, a change in the cost-of-living, or the overall performance of the company (or your division)?

- How often and, specifically, when are employees are evaluated for raises? Can an employee

Unofficially...
Typically, raises are based on cost-of-living increases, an employee's performance, or are awarded as bonuses. Determine in advance what criteria your employer uses, so you can develop realistic expectations.

request an evaluation at any time, or are employee evaluations done automatically every six or twelve months, for example?

- What formula is used for determining how much of a raise an employee gets awarded?

While a raise provides an increase in pay and/or benefits, a promotion usually involves earning a new title and taking on new and/or additional responsibilities. The job description of this new job will probably be somewhat different from your current position, and what the employer expects of you will change. Often (but not always) a promotion is accompanied by a salary increase and/or an improvement in the benefits package offered. There are times when an employer will award a promotion, but no pay increase, in order to reward an employee for a job well done. While this doesn't lead to an immediate pay increase, having a more impressive job title does make you more marketable if you choose to seek employment elsewhere down the road.

Salary, responsibilities and an employer's expectations go hand-in-hand

When you have a job, you're working for some type of business. That business' primary goal is to make money. Thus, the business pays its employees based on their value to the company. A top-level executive makes far more money than someone filling an entry-level position that requires far fewer skills, less education, and experience. With the possible exception of someone being paid on a commission structure, the more responsibilities you have and the more skill-oriented your job is, the higher you'll be paid.

Watch Out!
If you begin a new job and are able to negotiate a higher than average salary for yourself, the employer is going to expect results from you immediately, and in order to keep your job, you'll have to continue performing to meet the employer's high expectations. After all, if you're being paid more than your coworkers and your perceived value is greater, you'd better be able to live up to expectations, starting immediately. Failure to do this could result in your termination, since most employers won't continue paying someone more than they're worth.

Salaries almost always go hand-in-hand with the responsibilities of the job, the difficulty of the job (in terms of the skills needed to fulfill the job responsibilities), and the time you spend on the job. Thus, when an employee takes on greater responsibilities, spends more time on the job, and demonstrates a higher level of overall productivity than their coworkers, it makes sense that those people are rewarded with higher paychecks.

Don't forget about perks and benefits: They do have value

While everyone would prefer to take home a bigger paycheck, the employer is not always willing or able to offer additional compensation to its employees, even if a raise is deserved. If this is the case, before seeking job opportunities with other employers, consider negotiating a better benefits package. Every benefit you receive, whether it's health insurance, dental insurance, long-term disability insurance, child care, free parking, tuition reimbursement, extra paid vacation days, the ability to telecommute one or more days per week, or stock options, each has a financial value.

If there's a benefit you'd like to see improved upon and your best efforts to receive a salary increase have failed, consider negotiations for additional benefits or an improvement to one or more of your existing benefits. For example, instead of a salary increase, perhaps your employer will reward you with a few extra paid vacation days.

Evaluating the raise or promotion you're offered

When an employer offers you a raise or promotion, whether it's voluntary or something you've requested, it's important that you carefully evaluate

Unofficially...
Simply by dividing your annual salary by the number of days you work per year, you can determine how much you earn each work day, and determine the financial value of each paid vacation day. Similar calculations can be made for virtually every type of benefit.

what's being offered to you and how it will impact your career. Any time an employer offers you more money, whether it's in the form of a raise or promotion, with it will come higher expectations. These expectations may not be spelled out, but if you're being paid more than a coworker with a similar job description, the employer is going to expect higher productivity from you. Are you prepared to take on additional responsibilities or meet higher expectations? Is the increased compensation package you're being offered in line with what you currently do or will be doing for your employer? If you were to seek other employment opportunities (with other employers), would you be able to command a higher salary or better benefits package?

The days of employees being totally dedicated and faithful to a single employer for their entire career are gone. If you're not receiving a fair salary for your work, or you have the ability to immediately begin earning more elsewhere, consider seeking other employment opportunities.

Those who take risks stand to reap the greatest rewards

As you've discovered from this chapter, there are many factors that determine how much someone is paid and what benefits they're offered. One additional concept to consider when planning your long-term career goals and negotiating your compensation package is that those who take the biggest risks have the potential for reaping the greatest rewards. For example, if you have a specialized skill set that's in hot demand by employers, you'll be able to command a significantly higher salary and better benefits package if you choose to work for a start-up company. This unto itself can be a risky endeavor,

Timesaver
In Chapters 10 and 11, you'll learn specific negotiation techniques and strategies for earning the highest possible paycheck based on your current skills and abilities, while Chapters 12 and 13 will help you understand specific methods of compensation and how they impact your paycheck.

because that start-up company could go bust, leaving you unemployed, or it could do very well allowing you to earn bonuses or receive stock options that become extremely valuable.

Risk taking comes into play in other circumstances, as well. You could be offered a high paying promotion by your employer, but accepting it will require you to pick up your family and move across the country. After making this major life change, you might discover that you hate your new job, or don't like the city to which you've been transferred. On the other hand, moving across the country for a new job could turn into the best career opportunity of your life, but you'll never know if you're not willing to take some risks as you strive to achieve your career related goals and fulfil your dreams.

From this chapter, you discovered how to get more from your current employer by determining if you in fact deserve a raise or promotion. You also discovered how to go about receiving the raise or promotion you deserve and how to avoid common mistakes made by people in your position.

Just the facts

■ If you really want a raise or promotion, it must be earned and well deserved, and even then, it may be something you have to negotiate hard for.

■ If you've been on-the-job, working in the same position for between 18 months and two years, yet there's been no action on your employer's part to offer you a raise or promotion, it's probably time to take matters into your own hands and request a one-on-one meeting with your superior(s) to discuss your future with the company.

- The trick to demonstrating your value to an employer is to document everything about yourself that makes you a valuable employee. You want to make the employer realize that they're not taking full advantage of your potential and that you deserve greater responsibilities and financial rewards for your hard work, long-term dedication, and overall efforts.

- When it comes to asking for a raise, you always want to take a highly professional approach. Never become overly emotional or confrontational with an employer.

- As you demonstrate your value to an employer, use examples, statistics, comparisons, testimonials, cost-benefit analyses, and any other pieces of quantitative information. The more specifics you provide, the stronger your argument will be.

- Never use an ultimatum when requesting a raise or promotion. If you say something like, "Give me a raise or I quit!" you must be totally willing to quit on the spot, or else you will have lost all of your negotiating strength and credibility. You also run the risk of creating a highly confrontational situation, which can jeopardize your long-term relationship with your employer, even if you're given the raise you request.

GET THE SCOOP ON...
The importance of employee performance
reviews to your long-term career ▪ Positioning
yourself for a promotion or raise ▪ Winning in a
periodic employee review or evaluation

Championing Annual or Periodic Reviews

So, you're currently employed, being paid decently and you're treated well by your employer. Consider yourself lucky, but don't become too content! You have no immediate need to seek employment opportunities elsewhere, but hopefully you're interested in making the most of the job you currently have and in taking full advantage of the potential it offers. This means being able to work your way up the corporate ladder, making it known you're interested in earning promotions, and constantly striving to earn the maximum salary possible by meeting or exceeding your employer's expectations.

Whether you're in a small, medium or large company, your employer will always be interested in your overall performance, in whatever job you're filling. Smaller employers tend to pay close attention to their employees' performance on an ongoing basis, making formal monthly, quarterly, semi-annual, or annual employee reviews or evaluations less important.

117

Unofficially...
Depending on your employer and your relationship with your supervisor, the in-person meeting associated with a performance review or employee evaluation is usually *not* the best time to initiate raise or promotion-related discussions. A better strategy is to complete the review or evaluation, receive excellent feedback and scores, and then set up a separate meeting to discuss your future with the company. Being able to show a recent review that was extremely positive gives you better leverage and negotiating strength later when requesting a raise or promotion.

For medium and large companies with dozens, hundreds, or thousands of employees, regularly scheduled employee reviews or evaluations are an opportunity for an employer to study each individual employee's performance, productivity, and impact on the company as a whole. It's also usually the sole opportunity for an employee to get the attention of top management and an opportunity to ensure your superiors are giving you the credit you deserve for your work-related accomplishments.

This chapter will provide you with what you need to know in order to champion your annual or periodic employee review or evaluation. Of course, your actual performance on the job is a critical component for impressing the employer and developing new opportunities for yourself.

What is a performance review?

In order to ensure an employer and employee are mutually pleased with their relationship, the concept of performance reviews was created to give every employee at a company a chance to be evaluated by their immediate superiors, top-level management, supervisors and/or peers. At the same time, the employee is given an opportunity to discuss their various goals, performance issues, and concerns.

Typically, a performance review has a written and in-person component and ends with the superior giving an employee grades for their work, performance, etc. Every company has a slightly different procedure and set of criteria for employee evaluations and performance reviews. Managers, for example, might be evaluated based upon how well they've demonstrated their communication, managerial, delegation, and leadership skills, as well as their ability to work in a team-oriented situation. The manager's job knowledge, quality of work, overall performance, ethics, adaptability, cost consciousness, and attendance might also be evaluated and graded during a periodic review of evaluation.

The manager's superior(s) would be responsible for grading the employee in each of these categories, either using a numerical or alphabetical system (just like in school), where a 4.0 or an "A" would represent a superior score. They'd also provide a short paragraph describing an employee's strengths or weaknesses in each area. During the in-person portion of the performance review or employee evaluation, this written evaluation is discussed, giving the employer and employee a chance to discuss possible improvements.

In addition to being graded in various categories, a performance review or employee evaluation usually incorporates some type of review of past goals and the setting of new goals for the upcoming year. These goals are typically discussed during the in-person portion of the performance review or employee evaluation.

Based on the performance review or employee evaluation (or a series of them over time), an employer is provided with the information it needs to make educated decisions about raises, promotions, and if necessary, lay-offs. It's true, a performance review or employee evaluation can be very stressful for an employee, especially if the company is facing rough times and downsizing is a much-discussed option for keeping the company profitable. By taking the right approach, you can eliminate much or all of the stress associated with a review or evaluation.

Bright Idea
Well before your scheduled performance review or employee evaluation (preferably when you first land a new job), make a point to determine exactly how you will be evaluated. This information is often described in an employee manual or company policy manual. If you need clarification, however, ask a superior. Knowing this information will help you prepare for your meeting, allowing you to showcase your accomplishments and talents in the best possible light, based on the expectations of the employer.

Unofficially...
Determine if you
will be evaluated
based on your
employer's
expectations,
your actual work,
or compared to
the overall
performance of
your peers.
Determining how
you'll be evalu-
ated and
specifically what
criteria will be
used will help
you better meet
or exceed the
needs of your
employer. This
puts you in a
better position
to request and
ultimately
receive a
raise and/or
promotion.

A performance review or employee evaluation can be turned into an extremely positive situation, assuming you've met your job-related responsibilities throughout the year, and you're able to show a true dedication to your work. Simply by taking the right approach before and during a performance review or employee evaluation, you can transform this meeting into an opportunity to earn yourself a raise or promotion, set yourself up for additional training, or openly discuss grievances that have been making your life miserable.

Depending on the employer, you may be asked to participate in a performance review or employee evaluation every three, four, six or twelve months. As you stay employed at a single company over a period of time, its important that your evaluations demonstrate an increase in your skill level and responsibilities over time, and that your perceived deficiencies in one report are improved upon or eliminated over time in later reports. When a supervisor, manager or member of top management looks at your last several reports, he or she should see that you've been given specific goals and responsibilities, and that you've met those expectations consistently. This is what will help to ensure your long-term employment and open up the possibility of earning a raise or promotion.

Take a few minutes, pretend you are your boss, and fill out the following Performance Review form about yourself. How would you, as an employee, be evaluated (remember, you're completing this form from your employer's point of view)? If you know what your weaknesses are, you can spend some time in advance determining how to best address them and add a positive spin when you meet with your employer. The written portion of a performance review or evaluation that your boss is required to fill out might look something like this:

Performance Review

Name:

Job Title:

Job Code:

Review Period Starting Date:

Review Period Ending Date:

Reviewer:

For each of the following categories (all categories are determined by individual employers and will vary), the reviewer will grade the employee's performance during the recent evaluation period. They'll also provide some type of numeric or alphabetic grade for that performance, and evaluate it based upon criteria such as: "Poor," "Unacceptable," "Does Not Meet Standards," "Needs Improvement," "Satisfactory," "Meets Requirements," "Excellent," or "Exceeds Requirements." A written summary stating the reasoning behind each grade is provided.

Overall Job Knowledge:

Competencies:

Communication:

Managing People:

Leadership Ability:

Teamwork/Cooperation:

Delegation:

Attendance and Punctuality:

In the following section, each defined skill that's needed to successfully meet the requirements of a job are listed. The reviewer then places a check mark next to the appropriate performance level of the employee.

TABLE 5.1. SAMPLE EVALUATION OF REQUIRED SKILLS

Skills Required	Poor	Needs Improve- ment	Meets Require- ments	Very Good	Out- standing

Based on the expectations of the employer and the career goals and past performance of the employee, in this section the reviewer outlines specific skills the employee needs to obtain or improve upon in order to better do their job or be considered for more responsibilities in the future.

TABLE 5.2. A SAMPLE EVALUATION OF SKILLS TO BE DEVELOPED

Skills To Be Developed	Poor	Needs Improve- ment	Meets Require- ments	Very Good	Out- standing

In the following section, the employer lists specific goals or objectives that were given to an employer during the last review period, and then determines to what extent these goals or objectives have been achieved.

TABLE 5.3. ACHIEVED GOALS

Goal	Did Not Achieve	Achieved	Exceeded Expectations

In the following section, the employer lists specific goals and objectives for the immediate future (the upcoming evaluation period) that will be discussed during the in-person portion of the review/evaluation. Many employers encourage their employees to work with the reviewer to develop these goals together. The result of the employee's efforts to achieve these goals will be evaluated during the next performance review/employee evaluation. Try to set goals that you know are achievable and that will produce measurable results.

New Goals / Goals or Objectives To Be Achieved
1.
2.
3.
4.
5.

For Overall Performance, the employer may be encouraged to write a few sentences, or might simply categorize an employee's work as: "Poor," "Needs Improvement," "Meets Requirements, "Very Good" or "Outstanding."

Watch Out!
Any comments (positive or negative) made by the employee or discussed during the review/evaluation will also be incorporated into the written document created by the reviewer and added to your employment record. Since this document becomes part of your permanent record, refrain from saying anything negative about other people or complaining about some aspect of your job you don't like. If you have grievances, bring them up in a professional manner. Never use your performance review or evaluation to complain about your immediate superior or co-workers, or try to blame them for your deficiencies.

Overall Performance:

During the actual in-person portion of the performance review or employee evaluation, the reviewer might discuss the specific career goals of the employee, what the employee plans to do in order to achieve those goals, and what the company will do to assist the employee. What's discussed will also be summarized and included in the written portion of the review or evaluation by the reviewer. This is one way an employer can track an employee's progress over time and determine how career-oriented and motivated someone is.

A performance review or employee evaluation is a meeting that should be taken very seriously, yet it is not something you want to become overly emotional about, especially during the meeting when you're face-to-face with your superior(s). Try to maintain a professional image, maintain control of your nervous habits, use plenty of eye contact (shy people may prefer to look at the interviewer's nose), keep smiling, and participate in the conversation. Don't simply provide "yes" or "no" responses. Feel free to ask questions, always listen carefully to everything that's said, and seriously consider whatever positive or negative feedback is provided to you. As you're given feedback, keep in mind that your work and your productivity are being evaluated, but you as a person are not. By bringing up any negative criticisms, the employer is trying to boost your value as an employee, not insult you or belittle you as a person. Although it is natural to take such criticism personally, in an interview and on the job it is essential to act professionally.

Making a performance review work for you

By understanding exactly what the purpose of a performance review is and knowing what an employer is looking for, you can position yourself to meet or exceed an employer's expectations. This will help you to ace the performance review, and ultimately be perceived as being a valuable employee who deserves greater responsibilities and greater financial rewards.

The time to start preparing for a performance review or employee evaluation is not the night before you're meeting with the employer. At that point, it's pretty much too late to change your reputation or performance record. All you can do on a last-minute basis is put together a list of your accomplishments and strengths, and make the best presentation possible during your face-to-face meeting with your employer.

The very best time to begin your preparation for a review or evaluation is on the day you're hired. By constantly striving to meet or exceed employer expectations and goals, you'll position yourself as someone who is dedicated, loyal, hardworking, and worthy of greater responsibilities. Your employer will be looking at your long-term performance and actions, not at your short-term actions a few days or weeks prior your scheduled review. Don't insult your superior or boss by thinking you can "outsmart" him or her by being on your best behavior for a few days prior to your review. For example, while making a point to show up for work on time every morning for a week or so before your review is scheduled to take place is a nice gesture, it's probably too little too late to make a strong positive impact on the employer's perception of you.

Unofficially...
Treat the in-person aspect of a performance review or employee evaluation just as you would a new job interview. Dress in formal business attire and be on your best and most professional behavior. Check out Chapter 9 for more information on mastering the job interview.

Unofficially...
Some people consider their superior at work to be a close and personal friend. If you're in this situation, it's still important to take a highly professional approach to your review or evaluation. You'll be at an advantage in that you already have an excellent rapport with your superior, however, you both have an agenda that must be adhered to. If there's something negative about your employment record, it is totally inappropriate to ask your superior/friend to cover it up or create a false review.

Assuming you've done your work during a review period and have something to show for it, your next big challenge is demonstrating your accomplishments. Simply by knowing what your employer's expectations are, you can easily work to meet or exceed those expectations and then be able to provide the support materials needed during your review.

As you prepare for your review, spend some time putting together a list of your accomplishments and determine what you think your employer will be most interested in knowing about you and your work. These are the types of questions you can expect from you employer. Start thinking about your responses now, and be prepared to provide specific and quantifiable examples.

- What have you accomplished since your last review?

- What skills have you developed?

- What goals have you achieved?

- What company or division-related problems have you solved?

- What new responsibilities are you capable of taking on?

- What are some of the job-related goals you're interested in pursuing?

- What ideas do you have for improving the way your company or division operates? What can you begin doing to make your ideas a reality?

The Performance Review form found earlier in this chapter will help you determine what type of information your employer is interested in. Also, be sure to think about what you're hoping to get out of the review. In the near future, are you planning to solicit a promotion, or are you simply trying to generate the best possible scores (grades) so you'll be in a better position to earn a raise or keep your job if the company plans to undergo downsizing in the future?

By providing the employer with specific reasons to give you high scores in your review and providing them with the support materials they need to back up their evaluation and scores, the chances of obtaining the positive results you want from the review/evaluation increase dramatically.

Understanding your job description

In order to be successful in your job and meet or exceed your employer's expectations, you must understand your job description and be able to show proficiency in the skills needed to fulfill the job's requirements.

Now that you have compiled a list of your on-the-job accomplishments and the skills you use regularly, separate your list into two categories: 1) what you accomplished that meets your job requirements, and 2) what you accomplished that exceeds your job requirements. Ideally, you want to demonstrate that you've met all of the requirements outlined by the employer for someone in your position, and at the same time, show that you have been able to exceed those requirements by taking on some additional responsibilities. This is what will capture the attention of an employer and result in the most favorable review/evaluation.

Obviously, employers like to see employees performing above and beyond expectations. This is what will separate the people who ultimately earn raises and promotions from those who wind up staying in the same job year after year, receiving nothing

Bright Idea
Prior to a review/evaluation, it's an excellent idea to review the written job description provided to you when you applied for or received your job.

more than occasional cost-of-living increases in their salary.

If you're not sure about the specific requirements of your job, or you need a more detailed written job description for the position you've been hired to fill, consult your employee policy manual or contact your superior. You can also contact someone in the human resources department at your company.

Requesting a performance review

Virtually all medium- and large-sized companies automatically schedule performance reviews or employee evaluations at least once per year (sometimes more frequently). If you're working for a small company or have a supervisor who has been rather lax in meeting his or her responsibilities, and it has been well over one year since you've received any positive or negative feedback from your employer, you have several options.

You could assume everything is okay and stick with the status quo by keeping your mouth shut and by keeping your full attention on your work. Or you could also take it upon yourself to request a performance review/employee evaluation. Here are a few reasons why you might want to do this:

- You believe your work has been superior, yet virtually unnoticed by your employer.

- You deserve a raise or promotion as a reward for your hard work and dedication, yet it has been over one year since you're work has been formally evaluated.

- You have received no formal feedback from your employer, and you're concerned that your superior is not pleased with your work.

- You began working for the employer six months ago and you want to ensure that you're meeting the employer's expectations.

- You're interested in taking on additional responsibilities or receiving additional training, and you want to review your career-related goals with your employer.

Depending on your relationship with your superior, there are many different approaches to take in order to request a performance review/evaluation. The most formal way is to create a memo outlining your recent achievements and requesting that an in-person meeting be scheduled at your supervisor's convenience. Within this memo, mention the reason for your request and what you hope to get out of the meeting.

A less formal approach is to verbally request a one-on-one meeting with your supervisor at his or her convenience. This request should be made privately and in-person at a time when your supervisor isn't under tight deadlines.

When you make your request, be sure that you make it clear that you're interested in receiving the supervisor's feedback regarding your work. By outlining your reason for requesting the review and providing the employer with much of the information they'll be requesting in order to complete a Performance Review form, you'll be helping your superior prepare for the meeting.

Documenting your achievements, skills, and potential

Even if you consider your supervisor or employer to be your best friend, never assume that she's been closely following your daily work or that she's familiar with all of your accomplishments. It's vital that

Bright Idea
If you can't reach your supervisor directly, consider scheduling a formal meeting by contacting his or her secretary/assistant.

you be prepared to provide this information accurately, honestly, and succinctly during your review/evaluation.

Based on the information you provide, at the very least you want to convince your employer that you're worth what you're being paid. If you're interested in pursuing a raise or promotion, the information you provide needs to depict you as someone who has exceeded expectations and who has outperformed your coworkers. You need to demonstrate the ability to take on more responsibilities and show that you're deserving of a raise or promotion. After all, employers offer raises and promotions based on merit, not simply because it's something the employee wants to believes they deserve.

Look back at your preparation for your job interview. Many of the same rules apply in this situation, only instead of showcasing past work experiences with other employers, you want to demonstrate exactly what you've accomplished while working for your current employer, particularly during the most recent review period (the past three, six or twelve months). What are you the most proud of? What skills have you used? What do you plan on doing in the future? What future potential can you offer to the company? Most importantly, if you're hoping to land a raise or promotion based on the review/evaluation, why should an employer make an added investment in you and not someone else?

As you prepare for your review/evaluation, determine what you're doing now that's an improvement over what you were doing at the time of your last review/evaluation. Can you document an improvement in productivity? Has your attendance improved dramatically? Have you been on time for work consistently? Has the accuracy of your work improved? Have you developed or perfected specific skills since your last evaluation? Are you responsible for saving the company money or increasing revenue?

The very best way to ensure that you're able to demonstrate your work-related accomplishments is to keep a work journal on an on-going basis. This journal should be both a dairy and a scrapbook that's updated at least once per week.

Within your work journal, describe all of your on-the-job projects, accomplishments, goals, and special activities. Jot down ideas you have for improving yourself, your division or your organization, and keep copies of documents (such as non-classified sales reports, etc.) that can be used as support materials during your review/evaluations. Make sure you write down dates and details pertaining to your work and the achieved results.

Using a three-ring binder or a daily planner (with plenty of room to write) for your work journal works well, however, you can also maintain the information using a word processor and keep a separate file for support materials. Maintaining a work journal should take no more than 15 or 30 minutes per week, yet the benefits will be dramatic when it comes time to preparing for a performance review, evaluation or a meeting to discuss a raise or promotion.

Your work journal should focus on your results and achievements. Once you have them documented, when you review them with your employer, make sure that your employer acknowledges your work and gives you credit for your achievements. Once you get an employer to acknowledge your

Timesaver
Day Timers, Inc., the company that manufactures daily planners, offers a wide range of planners and organizers that can be used not only to keep track of your daily schedule, but also to maintain a work diary. To request a free catalog from Day Timers, Inc., call (800) 225-5005 or visit the company's web site at http:// www.daytimer. com. You can also take a look at a variety of planners at a local office supplies store such as Staples. Other famous planners are the Filofax and DayRunner.

value, you'll be in a much stronger negotiating position later, when it comes time to requesting a raise or promotion. Remember, most employers don't give raises, employees earn them.

You may think you're entitled to a raise every year (beyond a cost of living increase), however, unless you continuously demonstrate an increase in productivity and added value as an employee, instead of being considered for a raise, you may be considered for a lay-off. (Especially if the company plans to downsize in order to cut costs.) Just because it comes time for your annual review, it doesn't mean you automatically deserve or will receive a raise.

Tooting your own horn

One of the traits that virtually all successful people share is that they're self-promoters. Without coming off as conceited, they're able to toot their own horn and make their coworkers, peers, and superiors understand their accomplishments and develop a sense of respect for them. At the same time, these people never take sole credit for their accomplishments. They promote themselves as being part of a highly effective team.

In a team-oriented situation, everyone has specific responsibilities, and showcasing your unique responsibilities is what will earn the respect of your employer or supervisor. Don't make the mistake of allowing a coworker or superior to take credit for your hard work, simply because you weren't comfortable describing, showcasing and documenting your achievements to your employer.

Being able to successfully talk about yourself in a positive way will probably take some practice, because it makes most people feel uncomfortable.

There's also a fine line between talking about yourself so that you look good and coming off as self-centered and arrogant.

If you're uncomfortable talking about yourself and your accomplishments, one excellent way to handle a performance review is to create a one-page summary of your skills, responsibilities, and work-related achievements. This document would be very similar to the Performance Review form that your employer/supervisor will be filling out, however, it's created by you. By presenting a summary of your work to an employer just before the in-person portion of your review or evaluation, you'll be presenting your employer with the information you need to get across.

The summary of your skills, responsibilities, and achievements should be well written, well organized and use bulleted points to convey important information. It needs to be written in a positive style, just like your resumé. The document should also be typed on printed on white paper. Use "action verbs" to describe accomplishments to add impact to your written statements. The same basic rules apply to creating this document.

After providing a work summary to your boss or supervisor, use your face-to-face meeting to go into additional details and provide specific examples that relate to the information submitted on the page. You still want to discuss your skills, responsibilities, and achievements, but using the one-page summary you create will help you guide the discussion, plus you'll be providing something in writing that your reviewer can refer to later.

Unlike a resumé, there is no pre-defined format you need to follow when creating a summary page

Timesaver
Chapter 8 offers detailed information, and a list of action verbs appears in table 8.1.

to present to your employer prior to a review or evaluation. The following example demonstrates how you might want to format the information on your work summary page. Remember, keep the document short and sweet, but make sure it provides information that demonstrates your value to your employer. You'll use your in-person meeting to elaborate on the facts.

Summary of Accomplishments:

Name:

Job Title:

Job Code/Employee Number:

Review Period Starting Date:

Review Period Ending Date:

Work-Related Achievements:

   (Provide specific examples)

1.

2.

3.

4.

5.

Results of Your Achievements:

   (Include specifics and quantitative information. Examples: You were responsible for a 15-percent improvement in your division's productivity; a 20-percent increase in sales for the quarter; a 10-percent cut in costs.)

1.

2.

3.

4.

5.

Impact of Your Achievements:

Describe the impact of your work on the company as a whole, on your division, and how your success impacts your supervisor.

Use of Skills:

What skills have you perfected or acquired since your last review/evaluation? How are you using these skills on-the-job? What has been the impact?

New Goals/Objectives:

Describe your new goals and objectives and your plans for achieving them in the immediate future and over the long term.

Unofficially...
Unless your employer specifically requests that you summarize your accomplishments and skills in writing, it's not required that you actually submit your version of your work summary to an employer. You should still complete this document, and at the very least, use it as an outline for yourself during the in-person meeting.

Helping your company achieve its goals

You have short- and long-term career goals and objectives. You also have financial responsibilities you must meet and the desire to continuously upgrade your lifestyle. Having your own goals is critical to your personal and professional development over the course of your career, however, when dealing with your employer, it's important to place your focus on the needs and goals of the company (and your superior), not on yourself.

This doesn't mean you should abandon your dreams, goals, and desires. During a review or evaluation, position yourself as a value to your company. To do this, focus on everything you do (and have the potential to do) that helps the employer achieve its corporate goals and objectives. What do you do that makes the job(s) of your superior(s) easier? How does your work and your achievements help your employer? What value do you offer to the employer? How can the employer take better advantage of your personal skill set and experience?

During your review/evaluation, describe your achievements, skills, and experience. Instead of conveying the message that all you're concerned about is your paycheck, job security, and possible raise or promotion, put the focus on meeting the needs of the company and why you're in a unique position to assist the company in achieving its goals. By appearing to put the needs of your company ahead of your own (of course, this isn't actually the case), you'll be able to position yourself as a dedicated employee, which is something all employers look for when evaluating people for raises and promotions. In doing this, never lie or stretch the truth about yourself, your job or your capabilities.

Seeking opportunities—They don't always come to you

Wouldn't it be great if all you needed to do was meet the responsibilities of your job and to be automatically considered for promotions and raises? Well, in the real world, this is seldom how things work.

If you know, for example, a position that's just above yours in seniority is about to open up, it's your job to bring to your employer's attention that you're interested in being considered for that job. It's always a smarter idea for an employer to hire from

Bright Idea
If you have new ideas on how you can better help your employer to achieve its goals and be more productive (these ideas should relate to your job and its related responsibilities), be sure to bring them up during your review.

within, because they already know what they're getting and there's less risk—and it's cheaper for the
employer! Contacting the appropriate people
within your company when a job opens up that
you're interested in filling is one excellent strategy
for moving up the corporate ladder, assuming
you're qualified to fill that position. If you happen
to know the person currently in the job, ask that
person for a recommendation, especially if it's
someone you work with on a regular basis or someone who is familiar with your work.

Another way to be given greater responsibilities
and opportunities and prove that you should be
considered for a raise or promotion is to examine
your company's operations and the work of your
immediate superiors, and look for gaps that need to
be filled. Is there a special project you can participate in that will benefit the company and provide
you with an opportunity to showcase your talents? Is
your immediate superior working on one or more
special projects and appears to be totally stressed
out and overworked? If so, what could you do (as a
favor) to ease their workload? Are there opportunities within your company to receive special attention, such as contests among salespeople to exceed
quotas? If so, participate in these "events" and do
whatever you can to earn awards or recognition.

Some of the best methods for seeking out opportunities include:

Networking   Participate in company-organized events, go out to lunch with groups of
your coworkers, strike up conversations with
your superiors, and tap into your networking
skills of communication with people working
for your company at all levels.

Watch Out
Unless you do
something that's
absolutely
incredible,
chances are your
boss isn't going
to notice how
good of a job
you're doing on a
day-to-day basis.
He also is not
going to read
your mind and
know you're look-
ing to move up
the corporate
ladder. It's your
job to under-
stand how your
company oper-
ates and to seek
big and small
opportunities
that will help
you achieve your
personal career-
related goals.

Assist your boss or supervisor   If your boss is working on a special project or seems overwhelmed with her workload, offer assistance and get involved. Taking on special projects (in addition to your regular workload) is an excellent way to showcase the talents you have that don't necessarily get used to complete your day-to-day work responsibilities.

Building your reputation within your company By participating in company-organized events, assisting your superiors with special projects, being friendly with your coworkers (and making an effort to be a team player), you'll build a very positive reputation within your company. Developing a good reputation will help you achieve your career goals, make it far easier to obtain positive recommendations from your coworkers and superiors, and help you position yourself as someone who others want to work with. Simply by participating in several extremely positive reviews or evaluations, you'll be building up your reputation.

Always be on the lookout for new job opportunities, especially if you're happy with your current job   The best time to seek out new career opportunities is when you're happily employed. Always be a "passive" job seeker—someone open to examining new opportunities that you come across.

Just the facts

- To ultimately earn raises or promotions, you must be constantly proving yourself and your value on the job. After all, employers don't give raises or promotions away; they're earned. A performance review or employee evaluation is an opportunity for you to ensure that your employer truly understands your value and understands the work you've been doing. While the in-person meeting associated with a review or evaluation is probably not the best time to request a raise or promotion, by earning good reviews over time, you'll be in a much better negotiating position when you do request a raise or ask to be considered for a promotion.

- A performance review or employee evaluation is not something to get nervous or overly emotional about, unless you've been slacking off on the job or you're about to get busted for doing something wrong.

- To ensure that you'll receive the biggest benefits from your review/evaluation, plan ahead. Outline your accomplishments and be prepared to show specific quantifiable details that relate to your work.

- Never assume that your employer already knows how hard you work or what your accomplishments are. Be prepared to outline this information for them, both in writing and in-person.

- During your performance review/evaluation, focus on the needs and goals of the company and what you're doing to help the company achieve its short- and long-term goals. Also, be prepared to demonstrate how your work benefits your immediate superiors and your division.

- Spend the necessary amount of time planning for your review/evaluation. This is particularly important if you deserve to receive an excellent evaluation. You must be able to demonstrate your accomplishments to a reviewer who might not be aware of your day-to-day work.

- Use the review/evaluation to make sure that nobody else is taking credit for your accomplishments and hard work. Always document your work and be able to show proof that your accomplishments are your own.

**Don't Settle For Less—
Take Charge!**

PART III

GET THE SCOOP ON...
How to find the best employment opportunities
▪ The importance of staying away from dead-
end jobs (and how to identify them before it's
too late) ▪ The pros and cons of using a head-
hunter ▪ Changing jobs versus changing careers

Seeking New Employment Opportunities

Chapter 6

Those "good old days" when someone was hired right out of school by a major corporation and was expected to work for that company their entire career then retire with a gold watch are gone, probably forever. No longer are employees totally dedicated to their employers, or are employers providing long-term job security to their employees. People tend to change jobs and employers every three to seven years over the course of their career. It's also become extremely common for people to change careers and pursue new areas of interest, sometimes several times before retirement.

As the new millennium approaches, many new job opportunities are being created and the way companies do business is changing rapidly. The world is opening up, creating a global economy, and technology has begun playing a major (and ever growing) role in virtually everyone's lives. Those who become extremely successful will be those who can adapt quickly, easily learn new skills, have the ability to take on new responsibilities, and think outside of the box as they plan their career-related goals.

Now, more than ever, it is critical for someone to always be focused on building and expanding upon their personal skill set, allowing them to adapt to an ever changing work environment and easily move from job to job, taking their skills, knowledge, and experience with them. In each job you fill, you must make the employer believe you're working to fulfill the company's goals and meet the employer's expectations (it's easiest to be actually doing this).

You must always be seeking new opportunities and discovering ways to advance your career, because nobody, including your employer, is going to go out of their way to do what's in your best interest (unless it helps them as well). This chapter will help you seek the best job opportunities when it comes time to graduate from school or leave your current employer and begin working for a new employer.

This chapter is for someone looking for a new job with a new employer. It's for someone about to embark on the sometimes confusing and always stressful job search process. Searching for a job is something that virtually everyone has to do at least once in their lifetime (sometimes, it's required many times during ones career).

Once you embark on your job search, the first step is to define yourself as a job seeker and carefully determine what types of employment opportunities you're interested in, and then to actually find the very best job opportunities available (and that you're qualified to fill).

Bright Idea
If you break down the entire job search into a series of steps, and take a well-organized approach to your job search, you'll find yourself gainfully employed in a job that you love in no time!

What to expect from the job search process

How easy it will be for you to land a job will depend on many things. If you use your networking skills and get hired in a new job as a direct result of having a connection with the new employer, your job search will be relatively stress-free and easy—consider yourself lucky!

When most people kick off a job search, it involves:

- Hunting down job opportunities
- Sending out resumés and cover letters
- Making countless follow-up calls
- Choosing appropriate interview outfits
- Doing company research
- Learning about various industries
- Participating in job interviews
- Sending out "Thank You" notes
- Dealing with the countless details associated with each job search-related task

For most, job searching is time-consuming and can easily become a full-time project. A job search involves effort, careful planning, decision making, negotiating, dealing with positive and negative emotions, and overcoming nervous habits and fears associated with this process.

As you embark on this process, if you do things correctly, you'll learn a lot about yourself; your goals and dreams; and your likes and dislikes. Before you can land a job, however, you must first hunt down the very best job opportunities that are available and put your efforts toward applying for those jobs that you're most qualified to fill.

The first step is to determine exactly what your interests, strengths, skills, weakness, likes and dislikes are. Keeping this information in mind, it's necessary to pinpoint the type of job(s) you're qualified to fill and then determine what jobs are actually available. Accomplishing this is going to take a considerable amount of time, dedication, and research. Unfortunately, if you want to do a good job uncovering all of the best possible job opportunities that you're qualified for, there are few time-saving shortcuts.

If you're confused about the type of career or occupation you're qualified to pursue or that you want to pursue, seriously consider seeking the assistance of a career counselor. Many high schools, colleges, and universities offer free career counseling to students and alumni. Employment agencies also offer career counseling services, plus you can hire the services of an independent career counselor who will help you pinpoint the types of jobs you should pursue, based on your skills, education, work experience, and interests.

Once you know what type of job, occupation, or career you're interested in pursuing, you'll need to use your creativity to pinpoint opportunities that are of interest to you. The remainder of this chapter will help you find those opportunities using all of your available resources.

How and where to find the best job openings

It's believed that upwards of 80 percent of all job openings are never publicly advertised in "help wanted" ads or even on the Internet. This being the case, if you're going to discover all of the opportunities available, it's necessary to explore all of the

Watch Out!
The biggest mistake you can make is being dishonest with yourself. Choosing to pursue job opportunities that don't interest you, that you won't enjoy, and/or that you're not qualified for can be a total waste of your time or result in your landing a dead-end job or remaining unemployed.

job search resources available to you. The following are some of the resources available and how to best use them to find a job you're qualified for and that you'll love.

Newspapers (help wanted ads)

The local or regional newspaper is usually the very first place people look when they begin their job search. Here you'll find an assortment of classified help wanted ads, as well as display ads from employers. Use a newspaper's ads to give you a heads up regarding the types of jobs that are available. Since many ads list a salary range that's being offered, you can also determine from a newspaper an approximate range for what people with similar skills and experiences are earning.

The drawback of newspaper ads is that once the ad breaks, the employer immediately receives dozens or perhaps hundreds of resumés all at once. So, if you respond to the ad, you're immediately stuck in a pile, which means your resumé and cover letter has to work extra hard on your behalf to capture the attention of that employer.

Across the country, a growing number of newspapers offer on-line editions and reproduce their "help wanted" ads on the Internet, allowing visitors to use a powerful search feature that can save the job seeker time and effort.

Trade magazines/newsletters

Virtually every industry and occupation has its own trade magazine, newspaper, newsletter, or web site (and often the web site has the most current information). The content in these publications is highly focused. You'll find news regarding the key players in the industry, and also have access to job

Timesaver
To find a particular newspaper online, visit the Yahoo! Internet search engine (www.yahoo.com) and click on the "Newspapers" option found under the '"News & Media" heading on the main page. You can also visit the Newspapers Online site (www. newspapers.com) or www. careerpath.com, which also offer a listing of URLs for news-papers that can be found on the web.

opportunity listings. Industry- or occupation-oriented publications can be used for research to help you determine which employers within an industry you'd be interested in working for, plus they can help you find specific opportunities or determine specific executives within a company you could contact to learn more about job opportunities available.

Many public libraries (as well as college and university libraries) subscribe to a wide selection of industry-oriented publications. The majority of these publications are available through subscription only. Publications like *Advertising Age* (for the advertising industry) and *Billboard* or *Radio & Records* (for the recording/music industry) are usually available at larger newsstands or at major bookstores (like Barnes & Noble Booksellers) that carry a wide assortment of magazines. A large portion of the industry or occupation-oriented magazines and newsletters can also be found online.

Industry associations/organizations/trade shows

Just as many occupations and industries have their own publications, they also have associations and organizations that people working within a specific field or industry can join. These national organizations often have local chapters in major cities that sponsor regular meetings. This provides excellent networking opportunities. Industry associations also often sponsor semi-annual or annual trade shows or seminars, which also provide excellent networking opportunities and an opportunity to meet in-person with key players in a particular industry. By interacting with people already working in an occupation or industry in which you're interested, your chances of discovering unadvertised job opportunities increases dramatically.

Unofficially...
As part of your job search efforts, track down and read six months' worth of back issues of a trade magazine, newspaper, or newsletter. By comparing the help wanted ads in back issues, you can determine which companies are hiring large numbers of employees (expanding), and which jobs the employers are having trouble filling (because those ads will reappear in several issues of the publication). Companies that are having trouble hiring will often be more flexible about job requirements.

Headhunters/employment agencies

Headhunters and employment agencies help match qualified job seekers with employers that have job openings. Headhunters are typically hired (and paid) by employers. Their job is to track down qualified applicants for specific job openings. Most headhunters deal with mid-level or executive-level jobs only, and their allegiance is usually to the employer.

Employment agencies typically work for both the employers and job seekers (and are paid by either or both parties when they make a match and someone is hired.) Since employment agencies are in the business of matching qualified candidates for specific jobs, they often provide job seekers with career counseling and assistance creating a resumé. Some also provide skill training.

Most headhunters and employment agencies (also called Executive Search Firms) advertise in the Yellow Pages, as well as in the "Employment" sections of newspapers and publications containing help wanted ads. Many also maintain web sites on the Internet. To find them online, use any Internet search engine and enter the keyword search phrase "Employment Agencies," "Headhunters" or "Executive Search Firms." You can also try Kennedy publications' *Directory of Executive Recruiters*, which has indexes for geographical location, industry, and job function.

Temp agencies

While temporary employment agencies operate very much like regular employment agencies, they specialize in placing people in temporary employment situations that could last anywhere from one day to several months. Even if you're definitely looking for a full-time, permanent job, consider contacting at least one or two temporary employment agencies.

If you're having trouble capturing the attention of employers simply by submitting resumés and cover letters, get placed in temporary work assignments (during your job search efforts); not only will you receive a paycheck, you'll also have the opportunity to prove yourself to a potential permanent employer.

Since some people don't know what type of work environment or industry they'd enjoy working in, or they're having trouble pinpointing companies where their skills and experience can be put to their best use, temporary employment is an extremely viable option, at least for the short-term. Working in a series of temp jobs allows you (the job seeker) to experiment and experience several different work environments with different employers in a relatively short period of time. This also provides an excellent networking opportunity.

Consider every temp job you take on as an audition with a potential permanent employer. Thus, to increase your chances of being offered a full-time, permanent position, you must demonstrate your skills and potential by putting forth your absolute best efforts while on the job. Showcasing your skills and giving a potential employer a first-hand opportunity to see you in action is far more powerful than any resumé and cover letter you could submit, and is a far better sales tool than performing well in a job interview situation.

Thus, if there's a specific company you have your heart set on working for, yet you're having trouble getting your foot in the door as a traditional job

Unofficially...
A huge percentage of people who start off working in a temp position wind up getting hired to fill a permanent and full-time position by the employer, or at least getting offered a job.

applicant, consider working with a temporary employment agency and getting yourself placed within that company on a temporary assignment. Once you've done that, do everything within your power to impress the employer and tap your networking skills so that you have a chance to meet and interact with people at that company who are in a position to hire you as a permanent employee.

There are probably dozens of temporary employment agencies in your city or region. Choose one that has a superior reputation, and if you're looking to eventually relocate, select an agency that has branches nationwide. You'll find temporary employment agencies listed in the Yellow Pages and advertised in the "Employment" sections of newspapers.

World Wide Web (Internet)

Using the web can be somewhat scary for people with little or no computer skills, however, the Internet is one of the most powerful job search resources available to any job seeker. The Internet can be used for conducting industry or company research, networking, tracking down career opportunities, and/or distributing your resumé electronically. In terms of finding specific job openings, there are hundreds of specialty career-related sites that allow job seekers to search through hundreds or thousands of potential opportunities in a matter of seconds. Using the powerful search capabilities of computers, a job seeker can pinpoint job opportunities in a specific industry, with a specific company, in a particular city or region, or use virtually any other search criteria.

The following are some of the most popular career-related web sites on the Internet. You'll

Timesaver
One of the nation's leading temporary employment agencies is Kelly Services. To learn more about temping, visit Kelly Services' web site at http://www. kellyservices.com or call (888) GO-KELLY. The company owns and operates more than 1,600 offices in the United States, and 18 other nations.

Timesaver

Are you having trouble determining your true interests and identifying your skills? Visit CareerPro online (http://www. career-pro. com/profile. htm) and take advantage of the site's Personal Profiler. Simply answer 20 questions and let the computer help you define your personality type or pinpoint the types of career opportunities in which you'll prosper. A more elaborate online "Temperament/ Personality Profiler" can be accessed at http://www. keirsey.com/ cgibin/keirsey/ newkts.cgi."

find that each of these sites offers a variety of complimentary services to job seekers, including job listings.

TABLE 6.1. CAREER-RELATED WEB SITES

AltaVista Careers	http://www.altavista.digital.com
America's Job Bank	http://www.ajb.dni.us
Career Builder	http://www.careerbuilder.com
Career City	http://www.careercity.com
Career Exchange	http://www.careerexchange.com
Career Mosaic	http://www.careermosaic.com
CareerMart	http://www.careermart.com
CareerNet	http://www.careernet.com
CareerPath	http://www.careerpath.com
CareerPro	http://www.career-pro.com
CareerWeb	http://www.careerweb.com
E-Span	http://www.espan.com
Job Bank USA	http://www.jobbankusa.com
Jobfind.Com	http://www.jobfind.com
JobLynx	http://www.joblyunx.com
Net-Temps	http://www.net-temps.com
The Monster Board	http://www.monster.com
Yahoo Employment Classifieds	http://classifieds.yahoo.com/ employment.html
ZD Net Job Database	http://www.zdnet.com/ cc/jobs/jobs.html

Aside from these specialty career-related web sites, the Internet features company web pages, Internet newsgroups, and mailing lists can that be excellent job search tools.

Company web sites

These days, a huge number of companies maintain corporate web sites, and additional companies (in all industries) are creating an online presence for themselves daily. Once you've pinpointed a handful of companies you'd be interested in working for, visit each company's corporate web site. From these sites you'll often find:

- Detailed company background information
- Product and service information
- Executive biographies
- Detailed job opening listings

To find the company web page for any Fortune 500 company, visit The Fortune 500 List at: http://www.pathfinder.com/fortune/fortune500/500list.html or The Egregious Fortune 500 Homepage Directory at: http://www.sas.upenn.edu/~alizaidi/directory.html. You can also use any Internet search engine. Enter any company name as the search phrase to locate almost any company online.

Visiting the employment opportunities section of a company's web site is a quick and easy way to determine what companies are hiring. In addition, the job openings listed on these web pages tend to be far more detailed than anything you'd find in a newspaper, magazine or even on the career-related web sites.

Internet newsgroups and mailing lists

Internet Newsgroups are online "bulletin boards" that cater to specific areas of interest. Access to a newsgroup is free, however, you need special software (built into many popular web browsers or e-mail software packages) to access these newsgroups. There are thousands of special interests newsgroups on the Internet. To find the ones that cater to your occupation or industry, use the DejaNews newsgroups search engine (http://www.dejanews.com).

An Internet Mailing List is similar to a newsgroup, however, every time someone posts a message to a mailing list, it automatically gets

Bright Idea
On the Internet, Tripod's Internship Center offers a searchable directory of internship opportunities available across the country. Point your web browser to http://www.tripod.com/jobs_career/intern_visa/.

forwarded to the inbox of your e-mail account. Users must subscribe to a mailing list, which is free of charge. To search through the 80,000+ Internet mailing lists for the ones that cater to your interests, visit the Listz search engine (http://www.listz.com). Both newsgroups and mailing lists provide excellent networking opportunities.

Networking

Word of mouth is how the majority of job openings are filled at companies of all sizes. After all, employers prefer to hire people they know or who come highly recommended to them by current employees. Knowing this, every job seeker must take full advantage of their networking skills in order to find the best job opportunities, especially those that aren't advertised.

When it comes to the job search, networking is an extremely broad term. It involves contacting people you know (friends, family, your friend's parents, coworkers, past employers, associates, customers, clients, past professors, etc.), and also developing and taking advantage of new contacts that you meet by seeking out people who you believe can help you find and land a job.

Instead of approaching a potential employer blindly (e.g., submitting resumé either unsolicited in response to an ad), having someone tell you about a job opportunity and then make an introduction on your behalf to a potential employer gives you a definite advantage over other applicants. It's also a powerful and positive statement when an executive or employee within the company you hope to work for recommends you for a job.

Even if you've never tried formally networking in the past, you already have a base of network contacts you can tap...everyone does! You also have the power to seek out and meet new people who are in a position to assist you in landing a job. If you're looking to meet new contacts or you're having trouble coming up with people you already know who might be able to offer you some assistance in your job search, consider the following options:

- Access the Internet (company web sites, career-related sites, newsgroups and mailing lists).
- Attend career and job fairs.
- Attend social functions sponsored by religious organizations (your church, temple or house of worship).
- Attend trade shows.
- Attend meetings of professional organizations and associations.
- Contact past employers and coworkers.
- Contact past clients and customers.
- Contact past professors, teachers, and fellow-alumni.
- Participate in social gatherings.
- Perform charity work.
- Read industry or occupation-oriented trade publications.
- Talk to members of your health club, golf club or country club.
- Talk to people in your neighborhood that deal regularly with others (e.g., barbers, hairstylists, bank tellers, postal workers, local shopkeepers, etc.).
- Talk to people when traveling.
- Tap the connections of your family and friends.
- Work with a temporary employment agency and get a temp job.

Grab a pen and paper, then sit down and create a list of at least 25 people you know who you could contact to see if they know of any job opportunities available that you're suitable for, or who could possibly make an introduction for you to a potential employer. Write down their names and telephone numbers. Next, pick up the phone and start making calls to the people on your list.

Every time someone says they can't help you directly, make a point to ask them if they know someone who can, and ask them to introduce you to that person. Assuming that each of the 25 people you contact also knows at least 25 people, you have the potential of tapping the resources and knowledge of at least 625 people. Being able to do this is what networking is all about. You'll find that it's more effective to ask about a specific industry, job function, or company than to ask for a job directly.

If you own a computer, start using a contact management program (such as Microsoft Outlook or Act!) and start maintaining a database of your personal and professional contacts. As you meet people throughout your career, add them to your database.

Contacting someone in your personal network can be done in-person, by phone, e-mail, U.S. mail or fax. You'll probably have much better results by contacting someone directly by telephone or in-person (direct and personal contact always work best). When you make contact with someone who you don't consider to be a close friend or relative, always be friendly and professional, and never become a pest. Assume the person you're contacting is very busy and treat him like he's doing you a huge favor by helping you in your job search efforts.

Unofficially...
Networking is a skill that is useful throughout your entire career, so if this isn't something you're currently taking advantage of, it's never too late to start.

As you make contact with people as part of your networking efforts:

- Ask questions.
- Seek guidance.
- See if they know of job opportunities for which you'd be suited.
- Request referrals.

Avoid dead-end jobs

One of the biggest mistakes made by job seekers is that they panic that a "good" job opportunity won't come along, so they wind up taking the very first job that's offered to them, whether or not it's a job they're interested in or will be good at. This leads to feelings of disappointment later, which is a major reason why such a huge portion of the work force hate their jobs.

Another reason why people quickly become dissatisfied with their career or job choice is because they didn't do an adequate amount of research before accepting it to determine if the job was really what they perceived it to be.

A dead-end job is one that doesn't offer you the opportunity to advance in your career without quitting and seeking employment elsewhere. For example, if you're hired to be a telephone receptionist for a company, and there is no chance of receiving additional training or eventually being promoted by the employer, that's a dead-end job. As a job seeker, you want to find employers that want to see you grow and see your career move forward over time. You want an employer that will advance you up the corporate ladder as you obtain additional skills, obtain additional training, and prove yourself to be

Bright Idea
If you don't have access to a personal computer, consider purchasing a personal digital assistant (PDA), or purchase a business card file and start collecting business cards of people you meet at work, at school, through internships or part-time jobs, while traveling, at social events, etc.

worthy of greater responsibilities. In other words, if you're hired for an entry-level position, you want to know that within six months or a year, you'll at least be evaluated for a promotion and given one if it's deserved.

The only way to avoid falling into a dead-end job or one that you hate is to ask plenty of questions as you evaluate each job opportunity, and do plenty of research about the company you're interested in working for. If the company has an employee manual, ask to read it prior to accepting a job offer. Also, ask to speak with the people who will be your coworkers and immediate supervisors, again before accepting a job offer.

Make sure you receive a detailed job description in writing. You want to know exactly what's expected of you, what your employer's expectations are in terms of performance, and you need to know what you can expect from your employer. The more you learn about a company and a specific job opportunity before you accept a job offer, the less chance you'll have of being mislead or falling into a dead-end job that you dislike or quickly become frustrated with.

Once you've spent a considerable amount of time in the position, what will be your options if you want to move up within the company? Using what criteria will you be evaluated? How often will evaluations take place? What additional training or education will you need? Finally, ask yourself if the job is one that you'll enjoy. Will you wake up every morning excited to go to work, or will you fall into an endless cycle of hating your job and dreading the next work day?

Yet another mistake people make when choosing a job, occupation, or career is that they allow their

Timesaver
As you consider a job offer, determine what your daily responsibilities will be and determine if the job will continue to provide challenges for you and still be interesting six months, one year, or three years down the road.

parents, friends, spouse, or someone of authority push them into something they have no interest in. To ultimately be happy and successful in your career, you must pursue work that you enjoy and have a genuine interest in, no matter how much pressure your parents, spouse or anyone else puts on you to do something you don't want to do. Take control of your own life, pursue your own career goals, and carefully evaluate your own options. Of course, you should consider the advice of the people close to you, but never let them push you into a job you know you won't be happy in, even if there's a high salary and great benefits package involved.

Accepting a job you know you won't like simply for the money, or because you know you have a particular skill which makes you suitable for the job are not good reasons for making your life miserable. Having the skill to be an accountant, for example, is great. This is a career that can offer vast financial rewards. If, however, you dislike sitting in front of a computer screen all day crunching numbers on a spreadsheet, then accounting is probably not a profession you should pursue.

The ideal job should combine your skills and interests, be one that you enjoy doing and find extremely rewarding. Obviously, every job will involve performing tasks that you dislike, however, those things you hate should be just a small part of your typical work day or week. When you find a job that meets your criteria, you'll know it, and this should be the job opportunity you strive for throughout your job search effort.

Don't repeat past mistakes
Think carefully about your last job or your last several jobs? What did you hate about those jobs the

most——the working conditions, the office politics, the atmosphere, your coworkers, your boss, the type of work, your daily responsibilities, the lack of challenge, the monotony, the constant threat of being terminated or downsized, or the stress associated with the job? Once you determine exactly what you hated about your past work experiences, next ask yourself specifically what it was about those things that you hated. Make a list for yourself (in writing.)

As you evaluate future job opportunities, compare these opportunities to your list. In this case, you want as few matches as possible. Learn from your past mistakes and do whatever you can to avoid repeating them. If you hated the structured environment related to working for a large corporation, seek employment opportunities with small- or medium-sized companies. If you hated working for a boss who was a back-stabbing tyrant, make sure you spend some time with your future boss (before accepting a new job), and ask current employees about this potential boss. Know exactly what you're getting into before accepting a job offer by asking questions, analyzing the opportunity, and doing research.

Watch Out!
Never jump into any employment situation that seems too good to be true or that you haven't carefully evaluated.

Should you consider relocating?

Sometimes, you find the best job opportunities in other cities, which means you'll have to relocate. If you're single and have few family ties and few friends in your immediate area, then this probably won't be a major problem for you. However, if you have well-established roots in a city or community, along with plenty of family and friends in the immediate area, a spouse that's happily employed locally, and children in the local schools, the decision to relocate is much grander. Moving your entire family to another city or across the country becomes a major life-altering decision that doesn't just affect you personally.

While employers will most likely make your physical move extremely easy, by handling the details involved (such as packing your belongings, hiring a moving company, and even helping you sell your home and find a new one), there's a huge emotional toll that goes with moving. Consider your options extremely carefully, paying careful attention to the long term. If you accept the new job and move, how will this help you achieve your long-term career goals five or ten years down the road? How will the move impact your personal life, your marriage, and your children? What are the financial rewards? What are the risks involved? What are the downsides of making the move? What happens if the job doesn't work out in three or six months?

Things to consider before making a job/career change

Changing jobs is very different from changing careers or occupations. When you change jobs, you take your existing personal skill set and work experiences and instead of working for one employer, you land a job working for another, doing similar tasks or holding similar responsibilities. If you're a secretary, for example, who specializes in word processing and office management, you can easily work for the ABC Company or the DEF Company, if both of these employers require someone with your skills to perform word processing and office-management tasks.

The majority of your skills and work experiences are transferable. This means all you need to do in order to find a new job is locate an employer

Timesaver
Are you interested to learn which cities *Money* magazine discovered to be the best places in America to live and work? Check out the magazine's web site (http://pathfinder.com/money/bestplaces/col/compare.html). This site also offers a handy utility that allows you to compare the cost of living. If you're moving in order to land a new job that'll provide you with a 15 percent pay raise, but the cost of living in the new city is 20 percent higher, you might want to think twice about making the move and switching jobs.

looking to hire someone with your skill set and background, and then convince that employer to hire you (by submitting a resumé, participating in a job interview, etc.) If you want higher pay, you can acquire additional and related skills, and be willing to take on additional responsibilities. Your core skill set and previous (and related) work experience is what makes you marketable.

Changing occupations, however, is a much bigger deal and often requires returning to school or acquiring a substantial amount of additional training or retraining. Having an occupation, such as being an accountant, electrician, psychologist, teacher, doctor, lawyer, secretary, programmer, etc. suggests you have received specialized training and have acquired a specific set of skills. In many cases, it also means you've earned a license or degree that makes you qualified to hold the type of job you've trained for.

As long as you stay within the same field or industry, you can perform your work for any employer, because you're skills are transferable from one employer to the next. For example, if you're an accountant, you can go from working with a CPA firm to a different CPA firm, or choose to work in the accounting department of any company. You can also form your own accounting firm. As an accountant, however, you couldn't easily change occupations and instantly become a lawyer or psychologist without returning to school to pursue a law or psychology degree.

If you're an accountant who moves from one accounting firm to another, that's a job change. As an accountant, if you return to school, pursue a law degree, and then get a job working for a law firm, that's a career change. As you've probably guessed,

Watch out!
Anytime you decide to change jobs, it's always an excellent strategy to line up a new job before quitting your old one. Even if someone with your skills and experience is in hot demand, you could find yourself unemployed for several weeks or months before finding a new job if you quit too soon.

changing careers can be a time-consuming, costly, and life-changing endeavor, but if you make the change for the right reasons, it can also be financially and emotionally rewarding.

Before deciding to change jobs (and work for a different employer), ask yourself the following questions:

- Why do you want to change jobs?

- What will a different employer offer?

- How easy will it be to land a new job with a different employer?

- What is the current job market like in your geographic area for someone with your skills, education, and work experience?

- What will the benefits of working for a new employer be?

- What will be the drawbacks or potential pitfalls?

- Does changing employers increase your earning potential or open up new career opportunities in the future?

Changing careers or occupations is a much bigger deal. You may choose to do this because the occupation you originally went to school and trained for turns out to be one that you hate or find unfulfilling. Unless you plan on maintaining your full-time job and returning to school at night and/or on weekends, you must be prepared to support yourself financially while you return to school full-time. If you choose to do this, not only will you be living without a paycheck, you'll have to continue paying your living expenses and the cost of your education.

Before making the decision to change careers or occupations, ask yourself the following questions:

- Why do you want to change careers/occupations?

- What will be the biggest long-term benefit to you?

- Exactly what's involved in pursuing a new career/occupation?

- What training or additional education is required?

- How much of a time and financial investment is required?

- Will you be able to deal with a loss of income while you're back in school or receiving additional training?

- Once you complete your education/training, what will be your immediate and long-term earning potential? How does that earning potential compare to how much you're making now or could be making in several years down the road if you stay on your current career path?

- How easily will you be able to find a job once you've completed your education/training?

- What is the job market like in the industry in which you want to work?

- How will your career change impact your lifestyle? Your family?

- What are five or ten reasons for choosing the career/occupation you've decided to pursue?

- What are the five or ten of your biggest reasons for leaving your current career/occupation?

Be creative when looking for job opportunities

Being an independent thinker and creative are two traits sought after by many employers. When it comes to defining your own career goals and job search strategies, these are also traits that you'll find particularly useful. After determining what comprises your personal skill set and figuring out what your personal interests are, that's when to begin using your creativity to find ways to bring these two things together into one job opportunity.

For example, suppose you're a talented advertising professional. You've spent the last five years working for an ad agency that handles a handful of small, regional accounts, the majority of which you found to be boring and unchallenging. As you begin looking for a new job in advertising, you want to find one that'll be far more exciting. As you review your list of interests and hobbies, you know you love downhill skiing. In fact, you have a true passion for it, and know the sport inside out. Well, all of the ski slopes and resorts, ski equipment manufacturers, and athletic clothing manufacturers all have in-house advertising departments or work with ad agencies. Why not pursue an advertising job that involves having a ski slope, resort, ski equipment manufacturer, or winter clothing manufacturer as your client(s)?

This example can be applied to accountants, secretaries, managers, marketing people, product design engineers, or anyone with specialized talent that the downhill skiing industry (or a related industry) can take advantage of.

Unofficially...
As you evaluate job opportunities, don't just look at what you're being offered in the short term. Consider the long term, as well. When comparing job offers, you may discover one job that offers a lower up-front salary, but an excellent benefits package and a far greater opportunity for career advancement over a three- or five-year period. Assuming you meet the expectations of the employer and are able to advance your career, in three to five years, your income potential could be substantially higher than if you choose a job that pays more immediately, but offers fewer career advancement opportunities.

Once you decide to combine your interests and passions with your skills, you'll find the job possibilities are extremely diverse, now all you have to do is locate the available job opportunities that aren't necessary advertised. Be creative. Hunt down opportunities that aren't necessarily obvious or mainstream. Consider all of your options, including jobs opportunities with non-profit organizations and government agencies.

Yes, you can earn a living doing something that you love. Millions of people do it everyday and so can you!

The job opportunity you ultimately accept will impact your life dramatically. It will determine your lifestyle and take up a significant portion of your day, Monday through Friday (or whatever days you're hired to work). Knowing this, you'll definitely want to take some time and seek the best job opportunities for you personally.

Just the facts

- Find a job you'll love and prosper in.
- Accepting a job that combines your interests, skills, hobbies, and passions.
- Seek unusual job or career opportunities, keeping in mind that up to 80 percent of all job openings are never advertised.
- Tap your networking skills to gather information and learn about job opportunities.
- Use the resources available on the Internet to track down job/career opportunities.

GET THE SCOOP ON...
The risks and benefits associated with being
your own boss ▪ Starting your own business ▪
How to become a consultant or freelance
worker ▪ The benefits and drawbacks of being a
commission-based worker

Becoming Your Own Boss

B y the year 2006, the number of self-employed workers in America is projected to reach 11.6 million. Will you be among them? Some people go through life working for one or more employers and are content working for someone else and receiving a regular paycheck. This is a perfectly legitimate way to earn a living and one that offers little personal risk. Other people, however, have a strong desire for independence, and don't like having to answer to a boss. These people often go through life miserable (because they spend their career working for someone else), or they decide to work for themselves and be their own boss. This means starting a business, working as a consultant or freelancer, or possibly becoming a commission-based professional.

As you'll learn from this chapter, being your own boss can be a very rewarding experience, both emotionally and financially. To be successful, however, you must have the right personality type, the right

Chapter 7

Watch Out!
The biggest reason why start-up businesses fail is due to poor planning and a lack of research.

education, the right skill set, the ability to make decisions and manage people, and you must be willing to take risks that could impact your entire lifestyle and future. Being your own boss may be "the American dream" and your ultimate goal, but if you're coming from a background that involved working for others, you must be totally prepared for everything that's involved with working for yourself. Being unprepared or entering into this situation without the proper knowledge and skills, you could easily fail and find yourself in serious financial trouble.

Does the high failure rate of start-up companies mean you should not pursue a career working for yourself (starting your own company, becoming a consultant or a commission-based worker)? No way! Everyone needs to follow their own path, make their own career decisions, and pursue their own dreams. This chapter will help you understand what to expect if you choose to branch out on your own.

This book is all about earning what you deserve. When you're working for yourself, how much you earn, how hard you work, and what benefits you receive are entirely up to you. This chapter will help you direct your own career so that you'll have the greatest earning potential. When you're your own boss, however, nothing leads to success except hard work and having a sincere dedication to whatever it is you decide to pursue. If you ultimately pursue something that you truly love, not only will you find your career emotionally rewarding and fulfilling, chances are you'll also reap the financial benefits associated with true success.

Types of self-employment opportunities

You have many options. You can start your own business, invest in a franchise that you operate, start a home-based business, work as a consultant or free-lancer for other companies, or take on a 100-percent commission-based sales job. If you want to experience the independence of being self-employed, yet want the security of having an employer and receiving a regular paycheck, you might consider a job that involves telecommuting (working from home or a satellite office location).

Each of these self-employment opportunities offers its own set of benefits, drawbacks, and risks, yet success in each requires the same basic personality profile and skills. Being highly motivated, well organized, hardworking, and having the ability to make decisions are all critical for someone interested in working for themselves and being successful at it. After all, when you're self-employed, how much you earn, how successful you are, and how hard you work are all entirely up to you.

Starting your own business

The over 20 million small businesses in America are the true backbone of the country's economy. According to the U.S. Small Business Administration, "They create two of every three new jobs, produce 39 percent of the gross national product (51 percent of the private gross national product), and invent more than half of the nation's technological innovations. Small businesses employ 53 percent of the private non-farm work force."

By definition, a small business has fewer than 500 employees. The U.S. Department of Labor estimated that industries dominated by small businesses produced 64 percent of the 2.5 million new jobs created in 1996. The type of small business that you start can be anything from a home-based mail order business, to a retail store, a catering business or your very own accounting firm or law firm (assuming you're a CPA or have a law degree). Unless your business is mail-order based (or you'll be doing business on the net), the business you launch should cater to the needs of your local or regional area and allow you to take full advantage of your own knowledge and skills.

Since there are so many different types of business you can launch, and each one has different steps involved for getting it off the ground, this chapter will focus on the common steps involved in starting any business:

- Coming up with a brilliant business idea.

- Developing a detailed business plan.

- Performing the necessary research.

- Raising the required start-up capital.

- Seeking free guidance to make up for your lack of business experience.

Unofficially...
Choosing to invest in and operate a franchise, as opposed to an independently owned and operated business, is always a viable option, but one that has many additional considerations that will be explored later in this chapter.

Assuming you have the intelligence, personality type, motivation and financial backing to launch your own business, the first step is to determine what type of business to launch, based on your interests and skills. Ideally, you want to create a business opportunity for yourself that makes full use of your background, knowledge, and talents. Next, you want to determine what types of opportunities are available based on the resources at your disposal.

Having what you think is a great idea for a business is certainly a good first step, but before investing your time and money, create a detailed business plan that specifically defines your business, identifies the goals of the business, and includes a balance sheet and cash flow analysis.

Upon creating a business plan and after doing extensive research, as well as analyzing the demand for the services and/or products offered by your business in your geographic area or potential marketplace, you should be able to accurately project start-up costs, operating costs, revenues, and profits.

If you don't have a financial background, consider hiring an accountant or someone with financial knowledge who will be able to assist you in creating a financial model for your company (in advance), and help you set up the financial aspects of your business. Right from the start, be sure that you have an adequate accounting and record keeping system in place. Whether you plan on doing the necessary record keeping and accounting by hand or using an off-the-shelf computer software program is up to you. For small businesses, QuickBooks Pro by Intuit Software (http://www.intuit.com/quickbooks) is one of the top-selling accounting and bookkeeping software packages on the market.

Maintaining a current balance sheet and income statement (a.k.a. profit and loss statement), along with accurate banking records are important for keeping your business on track financially. This represents the bare minimum level of accounting work that'll need to be done.

Unless you're planning on getting a second or third mortgage on your home in order to finance your business venture, you'll either need to find investors or take out business loans in order to generate the start-up capital you require. No matter how you intend to raise your start-up capital, potential investors and/or financial institutions are going to look carefully at your business plan, projected

Bright Idea
Intuit designed QuickBooks to bring complete financial management capabilities to small business owners who do not want to deal with the hassle of trying to understand accounting jargon or debit/credit accounting. Users can quickly set up their entire business with QuickBooks, making it easy to create custom invoices, enter sales, perform electronic banking and bill payment, track customer contacts, track time, perform job costing, manage inventory, handle payroll and even prepare for tax time.

financial statements and at how much of your own funds you're investing in the business.

Unfortunately, no matter how strong your business concept is, there are absolutely no guarantees when it comes to launching a business. To greatly minimize your chances of failure, implement well-thought-out and well-defined management practices, ensure that you have as much industry expertise as possible and that you also have whatever technical support you'll need to properly manage and operate your business. Carefully planning every aspect of your business is also critical.

Creating a well-thought-out business plan is an important first step for any business owner. This document will help you determine whether or not your idea for a business is actually viable, and can later be used to attract potential investors, or help you obtain loans from financial institutions. The more detail your business plan offers, the better your long-term chances for success will be.

An accountant (or CPA) will be able to assist you with the financial aspects of a business plan, while someone who studied business in school (on the undergraduate or graduate level) should have the basic know-how to create a coherent business plan once the necessary research has been done. To help you format your business plan and compile the information you'll need, the SBA's web site offers several shareware and public domain software programs that can be downloaded (free of charge) that are designed to assist in the creation of a business plan. For a directory of these programs, point your web browser to http://www.sba.gov/shareware/starfile.html.

There are also a variety of commercially available, off-the-shelf software packages designed to assist in the creation of business plans for start-up companies. PLANMaker by POWERSolutions for Business (314-421 0670 or http://www.planmaker.com) helps create professional, well-documented business plans for the entrepreneur. Making no assumption of a user's expertise in constructing a plan, PLANMaker's tutorial system and on-screen resources make this a powerful program for both the beginner and the experienced business person. Extensive instructions, in-depth questionnaires, and three professionally written plans provide users with the resources needed to create a comprehensive plan that is both meaningful and persuasive. Totally self-supporting, the program needs no spreadsheet or word processor to operate. Priced at $129, this program is available for PC CD-ROM and operates under Windows 3.1/95/98. A Macintosh version is also available.

Business Plan Pro 3.0 by Palo Alto Software Products (888-PLAN-PRO or http://www.pasware.com) is another easy to use business plan package featuring context-sensitive audio help, 20 sample plans, a large database of venture capitalists, customizable business charts and professional-looking full-color printouts. Use the plan wizard to customize a plan to fit your business, then follow the program's seven simple steps to writing a business plan. Hundreds of thousands of entrepreneurs have used Business Plan Pro to obtain start-up funding or ongoing financing. A free demo version of this $89.95 program is available for download from the company's web site.

Watch Out!
According to a report issued by the Small Business Association (SBA), "One of the leading causes of business failure is insufficient start-up capital. Consequently, you should work closely with your accountant to estimate your cash flow needs. Once you have taken care of your building and equipment needs you also must have enough money on hand to cover operating expenses for at least a year. These expenses include your salary as the owner and money to repay your loans."

Using a specialized software package to develop a business plan is an excellent idea for someone who hasn't done this type of thing before. The majority of the available software packages will guide you through the process and help you determine what information needs to be incorporated into your business plan and how to best format this information. Basically, a business plan is a resumé for your business idea. This is a professional-looking document that combines text and graphics (charts, graphics, pictures, etc.) as well as spreadsheet/ projected financial information. Based on the type of business being created, a well-written business plan will probably include most, if not all of the following sections:

- The Company Name—The first line on the first page of any business plan.

- Executive Summary—A text-based overview of the business that can be anywhere from a few sentences to several pages long.

- Objectives—Using bulleted points or short paragraphs, this section describes what the goals of the business will be.

- Mission Statement—A one-paragraph description that explains the overall purpose of the company's existence.

- Keys to Success—What will the company offer that will make it successful? What will the company do differently?

- Risks—What risks, financial or otherwise, is the company facing?

- Company Summary—More detail about the company, including information about its products and/or services is described in this section.

- Company Ownership—Who are the executives/founders involved with the company?

- Start-Up Summary—What will be required to get this company launched? What costs are involved? Financial projections and a list of start-up costs/expenses should be included here.

- Start-Up Assets Needed—This is a listing of the assets the company must acquire prior to its launch. Depending on the type of company, what's included in this list will vary, as will the listed costs of the assets.

- Investment—Based on the total start-up costs, this section of the business plan should break up and describe where the initial start-up capital is coming from (loans, private investors, etc.)

- Company Locations and Facilities—This section of the business plan describes where the company will be located and what facilities the business will operate from. From a business standpoint, what are the benefits and drawbacks of these facilities and the company's location?

- Detailed Product/Service Descriptions—Use this section of the business plan to explain exactly (in detail) what the company will be offering.

- Competitive Comparison—Describe your company's key competitors. What will your company offer that sets it apart from the competition?

- Sourcing—Who will be your company's suppliers?

- Technology—How will technology be used as a tool within your company?

- Future Products/Services—What new types of products/services or specific products/services will your company launch in the future?

- Market Segmentation—How does your company fit within its industry? Will your company cater to a specific or niche market?

- Overall Industry Analysis—Provide a brief description of the industry in which your business will do business. Describe the state of the industry, who the key players are, whether or not the industry is expected to expand in the future, etc.

- Market Analysis—Describe the target customer/audience for your company's product(s)/service(s). Break down this information geographically, by demographics or however you can best demonstrate to the reader who would be interested in your company's product(s)/service(s). This is just one section of the business plan where charts and graphs can come in handy.

- Marketing Strategy—How will your company promote its products and services in order to capture the attention of its target audience? This section can be broken down into sections that describe your company's marketing, promotions, advertising, and public relations plans.

- Sales Strategy—How will your company sell and distribute its products/services?

- Service and Support—What type of service and support will your company offer?

- Strategic Alliances—How will your company benefit from developing and implementing strategic alliances with other companies in order to achieve its goals?

■ Organizational Structure of the Company—Using a chart or text, describe the hierarchy of the company from the founder/president/CEO down to the entry-level people. Include projected salary costs for at least the first three years of business.

■ Financial Plan—This section of the business plan should contain detailed financial statements and projections.

Once your business plan is complete, make sure that you have it reviewed and critiqued by your lawyer, accountant, and/or someone who is an expert in business, before submitting it to potential investors or financial institutions (to apply for a loan).

Even if you've graduated with a degree in business administration, you're an expert in your particular field, and you have a great idea for a business, if you've never run a business before, the one thing you lack is experience. To help make up for your own lack of experience in the business world, you can hire someone with experience as a partner or employee. You can also take advantage of the free resources available to small business owners from The U.S. Small Business Administration (SBA) and The Service Corps of Retired Executives (SCORE).

The SBA was created by Congress in 1953 to help America's entrepreneurs form successful small enterprises. Currently, the SBA (http://www.sba.org) has established offices in every state and offers financing, training, and advocacy services to small firms. The organization offers its services to any small business that is independently owned and operated, that's not dominant within its field, and that falls within the size standards set by the SBA.

Watch Out!
There are many con artists that advertise high-profits by participating in various home-based businesses. Before investing your money in any type of business opportunity, research it carefully. If you're concerned about fraud, contact the National Fraud Information Center (NFIC) at (800) 876-7060 or on the web at http://www.fraud.org. The NFIC is a private, non-profit organization that operates a consumer hotline to provide service and assistance in filing complaints. The NFIC helps the state Attorneys General by entering complaints into a computerized database to help track and identify fraud operators.

SCORE is a division of the SBA founded in 1964 that is dedicated to aiding in the formation, growth, and success of small businesses nationwide. This is a non-profit association comprised of over 12,400 volunteer business counselors throughout the U.S. and its territories. SCORE volunteers are trained to serve as counselors, advisors, and mentors to aspiring entrepreneurs and business owners. The organization's services are all offered free of charge, as a community service. To date, over 3.5 million Americans have utilized SCORE's services, which include offering general business advice and helping entrepreneurs create and write detailed business plans.

To reach SCORE volunteers in your area, call (800) 634-0245 or take advantage of the services offered on the SCORE web site (http://www.score.org).

American Express also offers information and services to small business owners on the World Wide Web. Promote your business for free using the Business-to-Business Directory on the service's Small Business Exchange. The site also provides business planning as well as answers from business experts to your questions.

Learn more about American Express' Small Business Services at their web site (http://www.americanexpress.com/smallbusiness). Visa has teamed up with *Entrepreneur* magazine to create Visa's SmallBiz Insider (http://www.entrepreneur-mag.com/visa/visa_smartbiz.hts), a weekly presentation of timely tips and information designed to help you better manage and grow your business in an increasingly competitive environment. Visa also offers its own web site targeted to small businesses that can be accessed at http://www.visa.com/cgi-bin/vee/fb/smbiz/main.html?2+0.

Raising start-up capital to launch your business

No matter what type of business you plan on launching, it's going to require start-up capital (probably more than you think). Starting a business has a lot of expenses associated with it. After those expenses (which vary based on the type of business) are taken into account, you still need enough operating capital at the start to keep your business going for at least one year. Very few businesses become profitable immediately and most of those that fail do so because there wasn't enough capital available.

Not every business has the same start-up expenses. Some of the start-up expenses you'll have to calculate into your budget when creating your business plan include:

- Accounting and consulting fees
- Advertising and public relations expenses
- Business travel expenses
- Communications equipment (telephones, telephone service, cellular service, pagers, etc.)
- Company cars and vehicles
- Computer equipment and office technology (copy machine, fax machine, etc.)
- Custom-printed stationary, business cards, envelopes, etc.
- Insurance
- Interest on loans
- Inventory
- Labor (salaries and payroll)
- Legal expenses

- Manufacturing or any specialized equipment
- Marketing expenses
- Office furniture and fixtures
- Office supplies
- Printing brochures, press kits, marketing materials
- Recruiting costs
- Rent
- Taxes
- Utility bills (water, electricity, sewerage, heat, etc.)

After you have figured out exactly what it will cost you to get your business up and running and fully operational for a least one year (although you'll eventually need projections for at least three to five years), you'll need to raise the necessary capital. Once again, you have many options available to you, including:

- Investing your own funds (using your savings, mortgaging your home, maxing out your credit cards, taking out a personal loan)
- Seeking independent partners and investors
- Obtaining one or more small business loans from a financial institution
- Applying for state, federal, or private grants
- Borrowing money from close relatives or friends
- Winning the lottery (which is probably not a viable option, so don't rely on it)

Obviously, if you have some money in your personal savings account and it's enough to launch your business, doing this provides you with the most freedom, but also opens you up for major risk if your business fails. Consult with an accountant and/or lawyer to explore the various pros and cons of each option before deciding how you'll fund your business.

Do you have what it takes to become your own boss?

So, you want to be your own boss. You want to be financially independent, have total freedom to make your own decisions and you want to take the best possible advantage of your personal skill set in order to earn a living. Wanting these things is necessary if you plan on being self-employed, but you also need the following ingredients to help guarantee your success:

Motivation

From deep within your heart, you must be willing to do whatever it takes to make your business a success. This includes working long hours, taking financial risks, making difficult business decisions, and always doing your absolute best to ensure the success of your business.

Desire

Creating and managing a successful business must be something you truly want to do, for the right reasons. To achieve long-term success, operating a business should not be something you have to do or are being forced to do.

Talent

Do you, your partners and/or employees have the skills, education, experience, and know-how to make your business a success? Do you know your product(s)/service(s) and industry inside out? Can you provide your clients and/or customers something your competition can't?

Watch Out!
As you form your business, you must decide if you want to incorporate (and what type of corporation you want to form), or if you'll establish your business as a sole proprietorship or partnership. Each of these options has different legal implications and can protect you from various types of risks associated with starting a company. Consult with an accountant and/or lawyer to help you decide how you want to establish your business from a legal standpoint. Making the wrong decision could lead to costly problems down the road, especially if your company fails or winds up being sued.

Timesaver
Looking for sources of venture capital? Save time when researching and narrowing your options. On the web, check out America's Business Funding Directory (http://www. businessfinance. com), an entrepreneurial database designed to match capital sources with people seeking funding. The service covers venture capital, equipment leasing, commercial real estate, accounts receivable factoring, purchase order financing, inventory floor planning, Small Business Administration (SBA) or SBIC loans, private investments, public offerings, and more.

Research

Prior to opening your doors for business, you must do extensive research on a variety of topics. You must plan exactly how your business will operate; thoroughly know your industry, products and/or services; understand the marketplace; know who your customers are (or will be); know who the competition is and how you plan to deal with it; understand exactly what costs are associated with operating your business (so there are no costly surprises); discover the best and cheapest sources for raising capital; and understand precisely how to operate a business and make the necessary decisions associated with being a business owner.

Planning

Poor planning is one of the major reasons why a start-up business fails. Developing a detailed and well-thought-out business plan will help you in this area, however, you must deal in advance with a variety of financial and business operations issues and know exactly how you plan to handle these issues once your business is operational. Inventory planning for many businesses is critical. Not having enough inventory on-hand at any given time could be a costly mistake, yet having too much inventory on-hand leads to extra storage costs and the need for a larger up-front investment. Thus, your research and planning efforts go hand-in-hand.

Here's a partial checklist of things you'll need to do in the planning stages of forming your business (listed in alphabetical order, not necessarily in the order you should complete these activities). These tasks should be completed prior to your business' official starting/opening date:

- Calculate your start-up costs.

- Choose a local banker (after meeting several representatives and comparing services and rates).

- Choose a reliable lawyer and accountant. Have the accountant prepare the necessary tax forms for establishing your business.

- Conduct market research. Who will your customers be? How big is the market? Who are your competitors?

- Create a well-defined and detailed business plan.

- Create a well-defined and detailed marketing plan.

- Determine your business' goals, mission statement, and objective.

- Determine your business' legal entity (sole proprietorship, partnership, or corporation).

- Determine your business' location and sign a lease (if necessary).

- Determine your financial resources.

- Establish your company's line of credit.

- Identify the risks (financial or otherwise).

- Identify your personal strengths and weaknesses (as they apply to operating a business), and then the strengths and weaknesses of your business idea.

- Join the local Chamber of Commerce and/or professional organizations/associations.

- Line up your suppliers for inventory, manufacturing supplies, etc. Open accounts with these vendors or suppliers and apply for credit terms.

- Obtain the necessary local, state, or federal licenses or permits (most towns or cities require that you obtain some form of local business license). If you'll have employees, you'll also need an employee identification number.

- Obtain financing and raise start-up capital.

- Purchase or lease office furniture, business equipment, and related fixtures.

- Select an insurance agent and purchase all of the insurance you'll need. Having the right insurance and enough of it is critical, for your own protection.

Discipline

Starting a new business venture will require that you stay totally focused on its mission statement and objectives. Likewise, it will become extremely necessary to maintain discipline over yourself and your employees and at the same time, keep a tight hand on all of the financial issues, making sure you don't overspend or get involved in excessive spending situations.

Hard work

Being your own boss and operating your own business isn't a job, it's a lifestyle, and one that will require an extensive time commitment, personal sacrifice, and an incredible amount of hard work. You must be prepared to work mornings, afternoons, and nights, on holidays and on weekends in order to keep your business running smoothly. (Of course, this might not always be necessary, but you will always have to be prepared to deal with emergencies that arise. No matter how hard you plan, they will arise.) At any given time you must be willing to step in and do the work of your employees or partners, always oversee everything, and never totally rely on someone else to handle important matters.

If you're not 100-percent convinced that you have what it takes to become successfully self-employed, you probably shouldn't take the risk.

Home-based business opportunities

Starting your own home-based business can be a lot easier and less of a time and financial commitment than a traditional small business, however, depending on the type of business you choose to start, the commitment and challenges involved can be equal. As the name implies, a home-based business is operated from your home and usually requires only a small number of employees, if any.

Many types of businesses can be run from a home. To do this successfully, you must create a positive work environment for yourself within your home (i.e., a fully equipped home office), which means you need to give up some of your valuable living space to make room for things like computers, copying machines, file cabinets, and desks. Chapter 15 offers tips for creating a home office and a good working environment where you live.

There are many benefits to operating a small business from your home. You can make your own schedule, be available to spend time with your spouse and children, avoid a frustrating commute, and you often don't have to dress up to go to work (in some cases a robe works just great). You also don't have to rent, lease, or purchase office space, which can save you a considerable amount of money, and you can get a home office deduction off your personal income taxes.

Watch Out!
Most people who start their own businesses don't realize until it's too late the time commitment involved in keeping their business running. Before starting your own business, speak with several small business owners. Also, discuss the sacrifices you'll have to make with your family members. While you may be able to earn substantially more money working for yourself, you will often have to sacrifice your free time, work late, and possibly forgo taking vacations (at least initially). This will take a toll on your entire family and is something that should be carefully considered in advance.

Watch Out!
Many residential areas prohibit home-based businesses that involve customers or clients coming into your home, however, other types of businesses work well anywhere. Check with your local government offices and the management office of your apartment complex or condo (or your homeowners' association) to determine what rules apply to you in terms of operating a business from your home.

Many people operate a small home business as a part-time project to supplement their income, while others use it as a way to grow a business cheaply before moving into traditional offices and hiring lots of employees.

Network marketing opportunities are similar in a way to multi-level marketing opportunities, but their business structures are different. According to the Home-Based Business Mall, "Network Marketing is an efficient method of distributing a product or service to the end consumer. It is a way of doing business, not a business itself. It is a marketing method, and each marketer is an independent distributor, not a company employee. Each has his or her own business. It is the perfect vehicle for home-based business. Traditionally, 80 percent of the cost of getting a product or service to the consumer is marketing and distribution. Network marketing companies eliminate the wholesalers, eliminate the high cost of centralized advertising, eliminate the high cost of having employees, and deliver the product or service directly to the consumer with the assistance of independent contractors; i.e. distributors. This greatly reduces the expense of getting the product or service sold, and the increased profits are shared with the distributor network."

The following are just a few home-based business ideas that people throughout the country have been successful with. By combining your imagination and creativity with your personal skill set, work experience, education, and knowledge, you'll be able to tap your own entrepreneurial spirit and discover a home business opportunity that's right for you, assuming you're interested in establishing a home business. (Some of these opportunities require special certification or a license.)

- Antique Locator
- Bed & Breakfast
- Bookkeeping
- Caterer
- Childcare Provider
- Cleaning Service
- Computer Consultant/ Instructor
- Database Designer
- Delivery Service/Messenger
- Fitness Instructor/Personal Trainer
- Freelance Programmer
- Freelance Writer, Author, Technical Writer
- Gift Basket Service
- Graphic Designer
- Headhunter/ Recruiting Service
- Home Improvement

- Specialist
- Information Broker
- Landscaping
- Mail Order Business (using U.S. Mail or the Internet)
- Massage Therapist
- Medical Billing
- Medical Transcriptions
- Party/Event Planner
- Personal Shopper
- Pet Sitting/ Grooming
- Public Relations/ Marketing/ Consulting
- Resumé Writing Service
- Tutoring Service
- Typing Service
- Web Page Designer
- Wedding (or Freelance) Photographer

Watch Out!
Beware of multi-level marketing opportunities. Some of these opportunities are perfectly legitimate and offer income opportunities for people who want to work from their home. Others are illegal pyramid schemes or scams that should be avoided. Before getting involved in any business opportunity, research it carefully! To access an online directory of multi-level marketing and home business opportunities, check out the Home-Based Business Mall web site at http:// homebusiness. mlm-mall.com.

Should you consider a franchise?

Unfortunately, in today's business environment, the failure rate for independent start-up businesses is almost eight out of ten. If you're considering going into business for yourself, consider purchasing a franchise to greatly improve your chances for success.

Unofficially...
As a home-business owner, you're responsible for providing your own benefits, such as health insurance. There are, however, many different organizations, including The Home Office Association of America (http://www.hoaa.com) established to help you gather the resources you need to operate your business successfully. The National Association of Home Based Businesses (http://www.usahomebusiness.com) offers another information-packed web site.

A franchise is a network of independent business relationships that allow multiple people to share brand identification, a successful and pre-determined method of doing business, and a proven marketing and distribution system. People who own and operate franchises are given ongoing support from the franchisor, and participate in national or regional marketing and advertising campaigns with other franchise operators.

Currently, there are over 4,000 franchise business opportunities available in America. While everyone has heard of successful franchises like McDonald's and Mail Boxes, Etc., there are many lesser known franchise opportunities that offer investors an opportunity to invest in a successful business. In general, people are brand-driven and purchase items or services from brands they know and trust. This is one of the biggest advantages of operating a well-known franchise. After all, people know that they can visit a McDonald's restaurant virtually anywhere and they'll be served a Big Mac and fries that looks and tastes the same as the Big Mac and fries served at the McDonald's in their hometown.

Based on your knowledge, experience, skills and financial status, chances are you can find a retail or service-oriented franchise opportunity that you're suited for and can afford. Some of the benefits of investing in a franchise are that the franchise owner/operator can open for business faster, experience success sooner, develop a loyal customer base in less time, and take less of an overall risk.

Investigate the franchisor's background and reputation carefully. Speak with several established franchisees to make sure they've been successful and that the franchisor has offered them the level of support that's being promised to you. Ask existing franchisees how quickly they recouped their initial investment, how much they're making now, and if they're happy working with the franchisor and other franchisees.

Make sure the franchise opportunity you're evaluating offers a top-notch product or service, and that the product or service that's offered isn't a passing fad. Since you'll probably be making a substantial financial investment in your franchise, make sure you will get your money's worth. Ask yourself what a franchise opportunity offers you that other business opportunities don't. Determine in advance what your financial and time commitment will be, and make sure that you understand that from a time standpoint, you'll most likely be married to your business, at least until it's fully established.

Whatever product or service the franchise offers should have broad appeal. The franchisor should be well capitalized and have a strong business plan that details a long-term plan for growth. The franchisor should also offer extensive training, management, marketing, and advertising support. This support could include help negotiating a lease agreement with a potential landlord and setting up credit with suppliers.

As a franchisee (someone who purchases a franchise), you are legally obligated to follow all of the established business practices set up and dictated by the parent company, the franchisor. Thus, many of the business decisions an independent business owner would have to make on a daily basis are made by the franchisor. For a business relationship to

Bright Idea
Before investing in any franchise opportunity, it's important to carefully study the industry you'll be getting into, evaluate the opportunity the franchise offers, and make sure that you're capable of managing the business.

Bright Idea
An excellent resource for someone interested in buying a franchise is The International Franchise Association, which can be reached by calling (202) 628-8000. On the Internet, Franchising.Org (http://www.franchising.org) offers an abundance of information of interest to anyone interested in learning more about franchising opportunities.

work, the franchise owner must be willing to follow the protocols and business practices set by the franchisor. If the relationship between the franchisor and the franchisee breaks down, the chances of the business failing increases dramatically.

Since purchasing a franchise involves a legal agreement as well as a financial investment, it's an excellent idea to consult with an independent franchise advisor, accountant, or lawyer who will look out for your interests. Depending on the type of franchise you're interested in purchasing, your initial investment could be anywhere from $15,000 up to $500,000 (or more.)

As a franchisee, you own the assets of your company. However, you are investing in someone else's brand and operating system. While investing in a franchise helps to ensure the success of your business, there are never any guarantees. Ultimately, the success of your franchise will depend heavily on your own knowledge and capabilities, as well as the support you receive from the franchisor.

Entrepreneur magazine (www.entrepreneurmag.com) offers regularly published articles of interest to those who are considering purchasing any type of franchise business opportunity. The magazine's editors have also published a highly informative book, called *Buying A Franchise* ($59/Product #1807/800-421-2300).

To help you evaluate whether owning a franchise is right for you, the Federal Trade Commission (202-326-2222/http://www.ftc.gov) has prepared a free report entitled, *A Consumer Guide To Buying A Franchise.* It's designed to help you understand your obligations as a franchise owner, how to shop for franchise opportunities, and how to ask the right questions before you invest. To request a copy of this report, write to: Public Reference, Federal Trade Commission, Washington, DC 20580, or download the report from the web at http://www. ftc.gov/bcp/conline/pubs/invest/buyfran.htm.

According to this report, "A franchise typically enables you, the investor or 'franchisee,' to operate a business. By paying a franchise fee, which may cost several thousand dollars, you are given a format or system developed by the company ('franchisor'), the right to use the franchisor's name for a limited time, and assistance. For example, the franchisor may help you find a location for your outlet; provide initial training and an operating manual; and advise you on management, marketing, or personnel. Some franchisors offer ongoing support such as monthly newsletters, a toll free telephone number for technical assistance, and periodic workshops or seminars."

The Federal Trade Commission's report goes on to state, "While buying a franchise may reduce your investment risk by enabling you to associate with an established company, it can be costly. You also may be required to relinquish significant control over your business, while taking on contractual obligations with the franchisor."

Before investing in any type of franchise opportunity, consider the following:

- The cost of the franchise, including the initial franchise fee and the continuing royalty payments.

- How the franchisor controls how franchisees conduct their business and what restrictions are placed on the franchisees' ability to make business decisions.

Watch Out!
The Federal Trade Commission recommends, "Before investing in any franchise system, be sure to get a copy of the franchisor's disclosure document. Sometimes this document is called a Franchise Offering Circular. Under the FTC's Franchise Rule, you must receive the document at least 10 business days before you are asked to sign any contract or pay any money to the franchisor. You should read the entire disclosure document. Make sure you understand all of the provisions. Get clarification or answers to your concerns before you invest."

Watch Out!
As you evaluate franchise opportunities, it's an excellent idea to consult with a lawyer and an accountant before making any type of financial investment. Also, contact the banks and/or financial institutions that the franchisor does business with, and the Better Business Bureau. Doing as much research as possible in advance will eliminate the potential for problems or misunderstandings down the road.

- The termination and renewal aspect of the franchise contract.

- Your abilities to operate a particular franchise.

- Your personal and career-oriented goals.

- The demand for the franchisor's product(s) or services(s).

- The competition (both nationally and in your geographic area).

- The name recognition of the franchise.

- The training and support services offered.

- The franchisor's experience.

- The growth potential and earning potential of the franchise and your individual business.

According to *Entrepreneur* magazine, the top ten fastest growing franchises in 1997 were:

1. McDonald's
2. Yogen Fruz/Bresler's Ice Cream
3. Subway
4. Jani-King
5. 7-Eleven Convenience Stores
6. Snap-On Tools
7. Novus Windshield Repair
8. Coverall Cleaning Concepts
9. Coldwell Banker Residential Affiliates, Inc.
10. Blimpie International Inc.

The 1998 top ten franchises overall include:

1. McDonald's
2. Burger King
3. Yogen Fruz/Bresler's Ice Cream / TCBY
4. Subway

5. 7-Eleven

6. Baskin-Robbins

7. GNC Franchising

8. Dairy Queen

9. Mail Boxes, Etc.

10. Taco Bell

According to the editors of *Entrepreneur* magazine, "In our ranking, we consider numerous factors, some of which are weighed more heavily than others. The most important ones include financial strength and stability, growth rate, and size of the system. We also consider the number of years the company has been in business and the length of time it's been franchising, start-up costs, litigation history, percentage of terminations, and whether the company provides financing. The financial data was audited by an independent CPA firm. These factors are objective, quantifiable measures of a franchise operation. We do not measure subjective elements, such as franchisee satisfaction or management style, since these are judgments only you can make based on your own needs and experiences. All companies, regardless of size, are judged by the same criteria."

Consulting/freelancing

If you're an expert if your field, you have a specialized set of skills and/or a unique understanding of a specific business type or industry, you could consider working for yourself as an independent consultant for a variety of clients. Consultants work in many different industries and can have many different areas of expertise, but the one thing you must have to be a consultant is expertise in a specific field.

Unofficially...
As a small business owner or franchise operator, three magazines that you should consider required reading are *Entrepreneur, Business Start Ups* and *Entrepreneur's Home Office*. These publications are available at newsstands, by subscription, or on the Internet (http://www. entrepreneurmag. com). To subscribe to these publications or learn about other resources available to small business owners and entrepreneurs, visit the SmallBizBooks web site at http://www. smallbizbooks. com/cgi-bin/ bookstore. storefront.

While your hourly or daily rate could go up dramatically if you're a consultant, it becomes your responsibly to line-up clients and find work for yourself. Since clients may hire you on a per-project or hourly basis, you'll have to find enough clients to keep yourself busy. After all, when you're not working, your not getting paid. As an independent consultant, you also receive no benefits (health insurance, etc.), so these expenses come out of your own pocket.

An alternative to being an independent consultant is to work for a consulting firm, such as Ernst and Young. A consulting firm will work as your representative and hire you out to clients. In return, you'll either be paid a salary by the consulting firm, or the consulting firm will take a percentage of the consulting fees you earn from the job you get placed in. Most consulting firms tend to hire well-educated people (with MBAs or other advanced degrees).

Companies tend to hire consultants for many reasons. For a company, it's often cheaper to hire a consultant, especially for seasonal or periodic work, than it is to hire a full-time or part-time employee (and they don't have to pay for benefits). Companies also turn to consultants to provide objectivity or because they require their special skills and knowledge for a specific project. Consultants are also hired to help train a company's employees or to fix problem areas within a company. Thus, as a consultant, you must be able to define the needs of your clients and have the knowledge and skills needed to meet those needs. The more specialized your skills and knowledge, the more you'll be able to charge your clients who are in need of your services. As a consultant, you must be able to deal with people, diagnose problems, be detail-oriented, well organized, and be able to develop solutions for your clients' problems (and help implement those solutions). Marketing, sales, management, and communication skills are also useful to many types of consultants.

As an independent consultant, in order to obtain clients, you'll need to network, market yourself, generate publicity for yourself, and seek potential clients that could use your services. This will require becoming a sales person and selling your professional services as a consultant, even if your background has nothing to do with selling. Thus, excellent communication, selling, and people skills are tools used by consultants to land new clients. At times, especially when you're first establishing yourself as a consultant, you may have to do some volunteer work in order to prove yourself to a client and develop a reputation for yourself.

After you establish yourself as a consultant, scheduling your time and balancing your responsibilities becomes a bit tricky. If you don't have enough clients, you won't earn enough money to maintain your standard of living. If you take on too many clients, you won't always be available to those clients when they need you, and you could wind up losing their business.

As a consultant, your primary job is to cater to your clients' needs and always be seeking new clients (until your time is totally booked and accounted for). You are responsible for yourself, your scheduling, bookkeeping, mistakes, successes, and everything else related to being a consultant. If you succeed and make a fortune, it's because of your hard work. If you fail to earn a living as a

Unofficially...
While anyone with a specialized set of skills, or unique and extensive knowledge about a company type or an industry can become a consultant, there's risk involved unless you can create a list of clients for yourself early on. While still employed with a company, you might consider working as a consultant part-time in the beginning, in order to establish yourself while you still have a regular paycheck coming in. Consulting work is excellent for recently retired professionals who no longer hold full-time jobs, but aren't ready to move into a retirement home or spend all of their newly found time fishing or hitting golf balls.

consultant, that too is your fault. (Possible reasons: Maybe you didn't work hard enough. Perhaps you didn't have the necessary skills or knowledge that potential clients were looking for.)

Being a consultant, you'll be expected to always be extremely knowledgeable about all of the latest developments in your industry, which means you'll need to spend time researching and analyzing trends, and making sure you're on the cutting-edge of what's happening.

Watch Out!
Your consulting contracts should be in writing, dated, and signed by the consultant and the company or individual hiring the consultant.

As you take on clients as a consultant, put together a consulting contract that outlines the terms and fees associated with your work. Work with a lawyer to develop a standard contract for yourself that you'll probably be able to use with most if not all of your clients. The contract should discuss the consultant's responsibilities and obligations, compensation, the length of employment, confidentiality issues, reimbursement of expenses, limitation of consultant liability, payment terms and other related issues. In a nutshell, the contract should spell out who, what, where, when, why, and how much as it relates to the work being done by the consultant for a client.

How much you can charge your clients will vary greatly, based on your area and level of expertise, the demand for your services, what industry you'll be serving, what you're actually being hired to do, and what type of time commitment will be required on your part. Even if you have a set hourly, daily, weekly, or monthly rate that you charge clients, as you solicit new clients, be prepared to negotiate your rates, but never settle for receiving less than what you're worth. Once you agree to work as a consultant for a client at a specific rate, it's often difficult to renegotiate a higher rate later on. Chapters 10 and 11 focus on how to improve your negotiating skills and can be used to help you earn the most money possible as an independent consultant.

If you choose to work for (or with) a consulting firm, your rates will be set by the firm, eliminating the need to handle your own negotiations, billing, etc.

Becoming a commission-based professional

This type of work usually applies to salespeople (a.k.a. sales reps or manufacturer's reps) who are independent, yet represent one or more companies' products or services. Sales representatives typically work for themselves and act as the middleman between a company and potential customers (wholesale or retail). They are paid solely on a commission basis, based on their sales. As a sales representative for one or more companies, someone working in this capacity needs to have excellent selling skills, relationships with key buyers, and the ability to maintain relationships with clients.

Since this is a commission-only job, someone working in this capacity must continue to make sales in order to take home a regular paycheck. How large that paycheck is will be based on how hard the salesperson works and how results-oriented their sales efforts turn out to be. This type of work is ideal for salespeople with experience and plenty of connections in their industry. Unlimited earning potential is possible, but the work is often highly competitive and challenging.

Telecommuting

"Telecommuting" allows people who work from home (or a satellite office), but usually refers to

Watch Out!
Being your own boss, whether you're a business owner, franchise operator, consultant, or commission-based professional, involves risks. To help minimize these risks, especially the financial and legal ones, planning and research is critical. Make sure you understand exactly what you're getting into, what's involved and what it's going to take to be successful. Not doing the necessary research and planning could easily lead to failure or serious problems that could otherwise be avoided.

someone who works for an employer, not for themselves. People who telecommute, however, have an incredible amount of independence when it comes to doing their jobs, just like someone who is self-employed or who operates their own business.

The telecommuting trend in America has become so popular, over 57 percent of the Fortune 1000 companies either have a telecommuting policy in place, or expect to initiate one within the next few years.

So, what exactly is telecommuting? Telecommuting allows people to work from home, or from virtually any off-site location, and communicate with coworkers and clients electronically, via computer, fax, and telephone. Many employers report that the overall productivity of employees who telecommute between one and three days per week increases dramatically, while the company reduces its need for office space and is able to cut expenses associated with having a full staff working from a traditional office. At the same time, employees experience reduced stress, improved morale, and are better able to balance their professional and personal lives.

Wouldn't it be great if you could simply roll out of bed and be at the office and on-the-job in minutes, without having to deal with a hectic rush hour commute or fight for a parking spot? In America, over 11 million people have discovered that telecommuting, at least one or two days per week, is an ideal way to increase productivity, relieve on-the-job stress, spend more time with family, and save valuable time.

Thanks to the vast communications capabilities of e-mail, fax, teleconferencing and video conferencing, it's no longer necessary for some types of workers to spend their entire week in an office environment. A growing number of employers, in many different industries, are starting to explore the benefits of allowing employees to telecommute one or more days each week.

Obviously, telecommuting is not the ideal solution for everyone, but for certain types of work, especially sales positions, marketing or public relations positions, or jobs that involve a lot of time spent on the telephone or working on a computer, telecommuting can be a viable option. Before an employer will adopt a telecommuter program, it's important to work out exactly how issues will be resolved on a daily basis, how an employee's time will be managed, formulate specific procedures for communicating with coworkers and customers, and to determine how workflow will be managed. Determining answers to these and other questions often becomes the responsibility of the potential telecommuter, who should submit a report to management outlining the financial and productivity benefits a telecommuting policy can have for the company and its employees.

AT&T School of Business and Technology currently provides its customers with on-site training programs designed to help employers and employees successfully launch telecommuting programs. Since AT&T provides many of the communications services required by a telecommuter, the company has already helped thousands of companies formulate the best possible telecommuting solutions. To learn about AT&T's Virtual Workplace Education Series, call (732) 302-3236/46 (http://www.att.com/telework).

Unofficially...
Telecommute America (www.telecommute.org), a public–private effort launched in 1995 to promote awareness and understanding of telecommuting and telework arrangements, projects that by the year 2000, there will be at least 14 million home-based workers in America. In addition, the group reports approximately 40 percent of today's workers could be telecommuting at least part of the time.

Timesaver
If you're looking for a job with an employer that already has a telecommuting program in place, one online resource to use as you kick off your job search efforts is Telecommuting Jobs (http://www. tjobs.com).

Becoming a successful telecommuter requires a high degree of organization and well-defined procedures for staying in touch with coworkers, superiors, and clients throughout the day when you're not physically working from your office. Carefully scheduling your week becomes extremely important, since in-person meetings need to be held during your time in the office, and your time spent working from home needs to be highly productive, without supervision or direct guidance from superiors.

A growing number of large corporations now have policies and procedures in place for people interested in working from outside of the office, at least for part of the work week. This involves having a direct and open line of communication established between the telecommuter and the employer. It's also necessary for the telecommuter to have a fully equipped home office, which includes having a laptop or desktop computer equipped with a modem and access to the Internet, along with the employer's Intranet or e-mail system. A fax machine, multi-line telephone, pager, and cellular phone are also tools used by most telecommuters.

If you're interested in participating in or helping to launch a telecommuting program with your employer, but you're not sure you have what it takes to be a successful telecommuter, a few questions to ask yourself:

- Do I have the experience and skills necessary to work on my own, without supervision?

- Are you disciplined enough to maintain good work habits when you're working from home?

- How important is it for you to have interaction with coworkers throughout the day?

- Is your home a good work environment? Is it quiet and comfortable? Do you have space to set up a dedicated home office?

- If you begin telecommuting one, two, or three days per week, what positive and negative impact would it have on you, your family, your employer, and your coworkers?

- Do you have the technical expertise to use a computer equipped with a modem, a fax machine, and any other office equipment needed to communicate with your office electronically while you're working from home?

- How much of your daily work could actually be completed from home?

While not everyone is cut out to operate their own business or be self-employed, working for an employer as a telecommuter, at least several days per week, is the next best thing for many people. When you're working outside of a traditional office environment, you're given greater freedom and have to deal with fewer interruptions. Successfully telecommuting, being self-employed and/or operating a home business all require similar skills and personality traits.

To learn more about telecommuting and the career opportunities available (or that will be available in the near future), the following organizations will provide useful information to employees or employers interested in launching a telecommuting program:

- American Telecommuting Association   (800) ATA-4-YOU

- The Home Office Association of America (212) 980-4622

- The National Association for the Self Employed (800) 232-6273

- International Telework Association (202) 547-6157

Being self-employed and working for yourself is "the American dream" and one that is attainable by most people through hard work and dedication. Before pursuing this type of career path, make sure you fully understand the risk and commitment involved, and that you're willing to make the necessary personal sacrifices in order to ensure the success of your endeavors.

Just the facts

- Planning and research is vital once you decide to work for yourself and/or launch your own business.

- Create a detailed business plan if you choose to launch your own business.

- Opportunities are available to consultants, commission-based salespeople, franchisers, and telecommuters.

- Telecommuting is an option for someone who wants or needs more independence, but doesn't want to work for themselves.

The Job Search Process

GET THE SCOOP ON...
Determining what information to include in
your resumé ▪ Choosing a resumé format ▪
Avoiding the most common resumé creation mistakes ▪ Understanding the difference between a
printed resumé and an electronic resumé

PART IV

Looking Valuable on Paper

Chapter 8

No matter what type of job you apply for, your resumé will ultimately be your primary sales tool for capturing the attention of an employer. If your resumé does its job, it will set you apart from the competition and result in your being invited for an in-person job interview. But first, it's critical that you do your part by creating a resumé that will grab the reader's attention.

Creating a resumé that works

When it comes to landing a job, your resumé is one of your most important sales and promotional tools. Using just one side of an 8.5" x 11" sheet of paper, you must convince a potential employer that you're the perfect candidate for the available job. Creating a resumé that conveys the information you need to get across quickly is a skill that every job seeker must master. Your resumé has to be powerful, positive, attention getting, yet truthful. It should shout out to the employer, "Hire me!" not "File me!"

Timesaver
To assist in for-
matting and
designing your
resumé, you
might consider
using specialized
resumé creation
software, but
more on that
later…

Spending extra time on your resumé is an excel-lent investment in your future. Pay careful attention to detail, and make sure that it promotes you in the best possible way.

What's so good about you anyway? Answer these questions and find out!

This is a question that many job applicants have a lot of trouble answering. The following questionnaire will assist you in determining pertinent information about yourself that should be included within your resumé. As you answer the following questions, don't worry about the wording you use. Once you know what information you want and need to include within your resumé, then spend the neces-sary time polishing the text.

Using a separate pad of paper, take as much time as necessary to write out answers to the following questions. Provide as much detail and as many spe-cific examples as you can think of. Later, you can narrow down the information when choosing what to actually include in your resumé. Information that doesn't get included in your resumé can still be brought up in a cover letter or during a job inter-view.

Resumé heading information
Your full name:
Permanent home street address:
City, state, zip:
Home telephone number:
Fax number (optional):
Pager number (optional):
E-mail address (optional, but recommended):
Personal web page URL (optional):

Address at school (optional):

Your telephone number at school (optional):

Current work address: (optional)

Current work phone number: (optional)

Current work fax number: (optional)

What's Your Job Search Objective?

In one or two sentences (maximum), write a description of the job you're seeking. Within this description, you want to incorporate something about how your skills can benefit a potential employer.

Summarizing Your Educational Background

Most Recent College/University You Attended:

City, State:

Year started:

Graduation year (or projected graduation date):

Your Major:

Degree(s) and/or award(s) earned:

Describe your accomplishments, extracurricular activities and whatever else you think will be of interest to an employer:

College/University you attended (If you attended graduate school, that should be listed above. Provide information about your under-graduate education or high school education here.):

City, State:

Year Started:

Watch Out!
If you're trying to keep your job search a secret from a current employer, do not include your current work address, work phone number, or work fax number within your resumé.

continues

Graduation Year:

Your Major:

Degree(s) and/or award(s) earned:

Describe your accomplishments, extracurricular activities and whatever else you think will be of Interest to an employer:

Showcasing Your Personal Skills

What do you believe to be your most marketable skill?

Provide five examples of how you have used this skill on the job in the past:

1.

2.

3.

4.

5.

What is your second most marketable skill?

Provide three examples of how you have used this skill on the job in the past:

1.

2.

3.

What are two or three of your other marketable skills that a potential employer will be interested in?

1.

2.

3.

Your Employment History

Most Recent Employer (Company Name):

    City, State:

    Year you started working:

    Month and year your employment ended:
(Write "Present" if you're currently
employed at this company.)

    Job Title:

    Job Description:

Describe your three biggest accomplishments at this job.

    1.

    2.

    3.

What skills were used to achieve these accomplishments?

Name of the person at this company you will be using as a reference:

    Reference person's phone number:

    Employer (Company Name):

    City, State:

    Year you started working:

    Month and year your employment ended:

    Job Title:

    Job Description:

Describe your three biggest accomplishments at this job.

    1.

    2.

    3.

continues

What skills were used to achieve these accomplishments?

Name of the person at this company you will be using as a reference:

Reference person's phone number:

(Complete this section for all of your previous employers.)

Military Service (Complete only if applicable)
Branch of service in which you served:
Years served:
Rank:
Decorations and/or awards earned:
Special Skills or Training you acquired:

Accreditation and Licenses
Describe any professional accreditations and/or licenses that you have earned.

Hobbies and Special Interests
Describe your hobbies, special interests, skills, or other information that makes you more marketable as an applicant, but that doesn't fit nicely into other sections of this questionnaire:

What are your long-term career ambitions? Where do you see yourself in one, three, five and ten years?

The anatomy of a resumé

No matter which resumé format you ultimately determine is best suited to showcase your skills, education, and employment history, the resumé itself will be divided into several unique sections. Before actually sitting down to create your resumé, think about what information you should provide about yourself within each of the resumé sections. The answers to the questions that you provided in the previous section of this chapter will be helpful in narrowing down what information is pertinent.

The sections of a resumé include:

Heading

At the very top of your resumé, you must list your full name, home address and phone number. You can also include a fax number, pager number, e-mail address, personal web page URL, work telephone number (as long as your job search isn't a secret), and/or your address/phone number while at school.

Make sure that the phone number you list on your resumé has an answering machine connected to it. It's critical that a potential employer be able reach you anytime.

The information in a resumé's Heading section can be centered at the top of the page, right justified, or can be formatted in several other ways.

Bright Idea
(If you don't have an answering machine, the telephone company offers a service called Call Answering that you can pay for as an option.)

Job objective (a.k.a. position objective, objective, goal, career objective)

This is a one sentence summary of the job you're applying for. The wording you use is critical. It should closely resemble the job description and job title provided by the potential employer in a "help wanted" ad or job opening description. If you plan on incorporating this section into your resumé, it should be specific. Don't include a generic job description, such as, "Seeking a challenging and rewarding opportunity." If you need the space, depending on how specific the job is you're applying for, you may choose to omit the objective.

Work and employment experience

Bright Idea
When describing employment information within your resumé, be conscientious and use as many action words as possible. A partial list of action words is included later in this chapter.

This section of your resumé should describe all of your internships, after-school jobs, summer jobs, part-time jobs, full-time jobs and volunteer or charitable work. You'll need to list the employer's name, specific dates of employment, your job title(s), specific job responsibilities, and your work-related accomplishments for each job listing.

In your resumé, never include information about your past salary or what your current salary requirements or expectations are. Also, avoid including specifics about why you stopped working for an employer, switched jobs, or why you're currently looking for a new job. In other words, if you were fired, you don't want to advertise this fact in your resumé. Information about why you no longer work with past employers can be brought up later, during a job interview, if necessary.

Education (a.k.a. training, schools, academic record)

Use this section of your resumé to describe your high school, college, and advanced degree educational background and training. Each item in this resumé section should include the name of the educational institution you attended, the date of completion (graduation), the degree(s) and/or certificate(s) you've earned, and the city and state where the institution is located. All of the items in this section should be listed in reverse chronological order, describing your most advanced (and most recent) degree earned (or that you're in the process of earning) first.

Within each item, you can include information about any specific courses or extracurricular programs that would be of direct interest to the potential employer.

Do not include information about your grade point average or class rank, unless you've graduated with a solid 4.0 (straight A) average or were at the very top of your graduating class.

Accreditation and licenses

If you've earned any special accreditation or license that directly relates to the job you're applying for, it should be included within this section of your resumé. You'll also want to mention if your are close to obtaining a specific accreditation or license, along with the projected date you plan on acquiring it.

Skills

What skills do you have that the potential employer would be interested in knowing about? What skills make you the perfect candidate to fill a specific job opening? Employers are extremely interested in your personal skill set and your ability to successfully do the job. The work experience you list in your resumé should support the specific skills you describe. As with all of the sections in your resumé, the wording you use to describe your skills is critical. Since many employers are looking for applicants with computer skills, be sure that you describe specifically what computer-related skills you have. If you're proficient using specific applications that are common in your field, make sure you list those programs (such as Microsoft Word, Excel, Lotus 1-2-3, PageMaker, etc.)

Professional affiliations

If you're a member of a professional organization or association that directly relates to the job you're apply for, you'll want to include this information within this portion of your resumé. Be sure to men-tion any leadership positions you've held and any special accomplishments you're directly responsible for.

Military service

Describing your military service helps to position you as a more marketable applicant. Virtually every employer knows that the military provides excellent training and teaches self-discipline, along with lead-ership skills that are in hot demand by employers. (Be sure to describe any specialized training you received during your military service within the "Education" section of your resumé.) Within this section, provide information about when and where you served, your rank, and the branch of the mili-tary in which you served. Be sure to list any special decorations you earned while serving.

References

Don't waste valuable space within your resumé listing the names and telephone numbers of per-sonal or professional references. In fact, it's not even necessary to include a line stating, "References available upon request" because this is pretty much a given, and there's no need to state the obvious.

Be sure to make copies of your letters of recom-mendation and any other documentation that will help demonstrate your accomplishments and capa-bilities, and present these documents to the employer during an initial in-person job interview.

It's also a good strategy to type out a list of pro-fessional references (past employers, etc.) that a potential employer can call to learn more about you. Be sure to include current work and/or home telephone numbers for your references. The list you provide during your initial job interview should not contain immediate family members.

Personal information

It is never necessary to reveal personal information about yourself to a potential employer. Personal information includes your age, sex, sexual orientation, race, religion, marital status, family size, physical handicaps, height, or weight. This section of a resumé is totally optional and can be used to include information about hobbies or special interests that somehow relate to the job you're applying for. This resumé section can also be used to include information about yourself that doesn't easily fit into other areas of your resumé, such as volunteer work.

Choosing the best resumé format

There are three main resumé formats, each of which can be personalized and stylized in order to promote you in the best possible light. These resumé formats are the Chronological, Functional and Targeted/Combination format.

The chronological format resumé

The most popular resumé format is a chronological resumé, which summarizes your educational background and work experience (in separate sections) in reverse chronological order. In the "Education" portion of your resumé, your most advanced (and most recent) educational experience is listed first. In the "Employment" section of your resumé, your most recent job is listed first. Each past employer is then described.

Bright Idea
Be sure to ask permission, in advance, from anyone you plan on listing as a personal or professional reference. Be sure to ask if it's okay to provide work and/or home telephone numbers of your references to potential employers. It's also an excellent idea to specifically describe to your references the type(s) of jobs you're applying for and review with them what you'd like them to convey to potential employers.

Unofficially...
In order to con-
serve space and
convey only rele-
vant information,
it's not necessary
to include each
one of the cate-
gories in your
resumé. However,
every resumé
must include a
heading, infor-
mation about
your educational
background,
along with a sec-
tion summarizing
your work and
employment
experience.

Following a chronological format makes it easy for a potential employer to quickly scan your resumé and see your entire professional history, from the time you graduated high school to the present. This format is ideal for someone with no major gaps in their employment history. Using this format, each job listing should demonstrate upward or lateral mobility and a well-defined career path.

The information actually included in each listing under the "Education" and "Employment" sections of your resumé is very similar to what you provided in the questionnaire earlier in this chapter. How this information is actually formatted and the wording you use is important, but will vary, based on the chronological resumé style you choose. Every word and sentence in your resumé should make a statement about your value to the potential employer. If your resumé depicts you as an extremely valuable asset to the reader, you'll be in a much better position when negotiating after receiving a job offer.

The functional resumé format

Using this resumé format, describe your past work experiences by placing them into categories in your resumé. Each category focuses on a specific skill or job function. This format uses virtually the same information that would be included in a chronological resumé, however, the placement and organization of the information is different.

This resumé format puts the focus on your past job responsibilities and accomplishments, not on your dates of employment or the actual employers. Thus, the functional resumé format is best used by job seekers with gaps in their employment history or who don't have a lot of real-world work experience (recent graduates). If you choose this format, focus on up to six of your most marketable and applicable skills and list them. Under each skill, using bulleted points, describe between one and three specific achievements that took advantage of that skill. Also, list where you worked when the skill was used.

The targeted or combination resumé format

Why are you the perfect candidate to fill a very specific job opening? That's the question this resumé format is designed to answer. The targeted format allows for the most personalization. It can be used when you're applying for a very specific job at a specific employer, and everything within the resumé is designed to promote yourself as the perfect person to fill a specific job opening.

Use a targeted resumé only when you know the exact responsibilities of the job for are, and you have the skills and work experience that you believe perfectly match these responsibilities. What's highlighted in the "Employment" section of a targeted resumé are past job titles, job responsibilities, and skills (listed in reverse chronological order). Specific dates of employment can be placed at the end of each employment listing, giving them less importance.

With this resumé format, the most important information are the skills you list and the specific examples you provide as to how each skill was used. The problem with this type of resumé is that if the employer doesn't believe you're the perfect person to fill the job opening the resumé is targeted for, you probably won't be considered for other available positions.

Bright Idea
Many books have been published that contain sample resumés. Check out any of these books to choose a chronological style that you're comfortable with. While it's okay to copy a sample resumé's formatting and style, your resumé should describe your own skills, accomplishments and experience, without stretching the truth or fabricating any information.

Selecting resumé paper: Presentation is critical

Watch Out!
Most employers prefer to receive chronological resumés, because it's easier for them to determine your work history. Using the functional or targeted resumé format can create a perception in the potential employer's mind that you're trying to hide something about your past. To compensate for this potential drawback, it's critical that the information you include in a functional or targeted resumé be extremely compelling and relevant to the reader, as well as to the job you're applying for.

As a job seeker, when it comes to creating your resumé and cover letter, how these documents look is as important as what they say. When applying for most jobs, you want your cover letter and resumé to convey a highly professional and somewhat conservative image. To achieve this, you'll have to choose the right paper, select the right resumé format, and decide whether or not to add a touch of color in order to make your resumé stand out. Those resumés that stand out in a positive way will be the ones that human resources professionals and those who make the hiring decisions read first.

When you visit an office supply store or print shop to purchase resumé paper, you'll be surprised at how many different shades of white there are from which to choose. You can also find paper stocks in several different weights. Some will contain watermarks and most will have at least some cotton content.

As for resumé paper color, the most traditional choices are "bright white," "ultra white," or "ivory." It's also acceptable to use a "slate" or "light gray" colored paper. Avoid using any bright-colored papers, which will cause your resumé to stand out, but for the wrong reasons. Expect to pay between 25¢ and $1 per sheet of quality resumé paper.

The ink color you choose for your resumé and cover letters should be standard black, however, navy or burgundy ink is also acceptable. Make sure that the paper color and ink color work together to maximize readability. Some people choose to use a small amount of colored text within their resumé to highlight specific items. This strategy can be effective, however, using multiple color inks is not considered traditional. Multi-color printing is also more expensive.

The type of job you're pursuing should also impact the look of your resumé. Someone applying for a job as an accountant, for example, should definitely stick with a traditional white paper and black ink. A graphic artist, on the other hand, should show more creativity through the use of color and design.

When choosing resumé paper, make sure you see and feel an actual sample of the paper stock, prior to purchasing a sealed package of that paper. Finally, if you'll be printing your resumés and cover letters on a laser or high-quality ink-jet printer, make sure the paper you choose was designed for this. Resumé paper can be purchased from office supply stores, local print shops, and from mail-order companies such as Paper Direct (800-272-7377 or http://www.paperdirect.com).

Resumé creation do's and don'ts

Creating a powerful resumé will take time and effort. Don't be afraid to write and then re-write your resumé multiple times until you're confident it has the impact needed to set you apart from the competition.

These 10 tips will help you create a resumé that contains the information employers are looking for.

1. Start by writing out answers to the following questions: What are your skills and qualifications? What work experience do you have that directly relates to the job you're applying for? Are you worth the salary you're asking for or that the job pays? What can you offer to the employer? Specifically, how will hiring you benefit the employer? Can you help solve problems

> 66
>
> Choosing paper for your resumé and cover letters is a personal decision; however, you want a paper with a high cotton content, and with a bond weight of 24 or 28 pounds. Watermarks aren't too important, but they do add to the overall high-quality image you're trying to convey.
> —Linda Ireland, directorof marketing at Paper Direct, a mail-order paper company
>
> 99

> 66
>
> You want your resumé to stand out, but you also want your documents to look professional, and sometimes that's a contradiction. No matter what type of paper and color ink you select, it's vital that your resumé, cover letters, thank-you notes and envelopes all match. Part of being professional is being coordinated.
> —Linda Ireland of Paper Direct
>
> 99

Watch Out!
Make sure that there's an answering machine connected to the telephone number that's listed on your resumé, so a potential employer can reach you anytime. Missing a message could result in a missed job opportunity.

or challenges that the employer is facing? What sets you apart from other people applying for the same job? Answering these questions will help you determine what information to include in your resumé. Also, use the information you provided in the questionnaire found earlier in this chapter.

2. The main sections of a resumé are the Heading, Job Objectives, Education, Accreditation and Licenses, Skills, Work and Employment Experience, Professional Affiliations, Military Service, References and Personal Information. Choose what information about yourself should be included under each of the headings. The actual wording for each resumé section can be modified. Also, only include the sections that apply to you.

3. In the Heading, include your full name, address, telephone number(s), fax number, pager number and e-mail address. If you're trying to keep your job search a secret from your current employer, don't list your work telephone or fax number.

4. When listing your education, don't include your grades, class rank or overall average unless this information is extremely impressive and will help to set you apart from other applicants. Obviously, graduating first in your class with a solid 4.0 (straight-A average) is worth mentioning. The first piece of information listed in the "Education" section of your resumé should describe the highest degree you've earned or that you're in the process of earning.

5. To decide what work experience to include on your resumé, start by listing all of your internships, after-school jobs, summer jobs, part-time jobs, full-time jobs, and your volunteer and charitable work. Be prepared to provide specific dates of employment, job titles, responsibilities, and accomplishments for each position. How you convey this information in your resumé will be critical. Ultimately, you may have to refrain from including some of the less pertinent information in order to conserve space.

6. As you sit down to write your resumé, use action words, which are usually verbs that make your accomplishments sound even better, without stretching the truth. What your resumé says about you, and more importantly, how it's said, is what will make your resumé a powerful job search tool.

7. Choose a resumé format that best organizes your information for an employer. Using a "Chronological" format is the most popular. Your employment experience is listed in reverse chronological order, with your most recent job listed first. The "Functional" format organizes your past work experience into categories based on actual job responsibilities or skills. This format downplays dates of employment and makes it easier to put a positive spin on large gaps in your employment history. The "Targeted/Combination" resumé format is designed to answer the question, "Why are you perfect for a specific job?"

8. Keep your resumé short and to the point. Make sure all of the information is well organized and

Unofficially...
Virtually all employers like to see applicants who can work well with others. Stress teamwork in your resumé, and focus on leadership or managerial positions you've had in order to demonstrate you can take charge of a situation or a group of people.

is stated as succinctly as possible. Your sentences should be under 20 words each, and all paragraphs should be 10 lines or less. Remove words and phrases the are redundant.

9. Print your resumé on good quality, white, off-white or cream-colored paper. Use 24- or 28-pound bond paper made of 100-percent cotton stock. Your finished resumé should look neat and well-balanced on the page. It should be inviting to the reader and not look cluttered.

Bright Idea
Have at least two other people proofread your resumé.

10. Before distributing your resumé to potential employers, proofread it carefully. Even the smallest spelling or grammatical error will not be tolerated and could result in your missing out on a job opportunity.

Successful job seekers spend many hours creating multiple drafts of their resumé, fine-tuning each sentence to make sure every word makes a positive statement. A resumé is a one-page composition designed to sell your skills, work experience, and educational background to a potential employer. Taking short cuts when creating this extremely important document can have disastrous results.

To ensure your resumé will be seriously considered by a potential employer, avoid making these common errors:

1. *Typos or grammatical errors.* Having these in a resumé is the worst mistake you can make. If you refuse to take the time necessary to proofread your resumé, why should an employer assume you'll take the time needed to do your job properly if you're hired?

2. *Stretching the truth.* A growing number of employers are verifying all resumé information. If you're caught lying, you won't be offered a job,

or you could be fired later if it's discovered that you weren't truthful.

3. *Incomplete information.* Forgetting to list your full name, address, and telephone number at the top of your resumé as part of the heading. A potential employer must be able to contact you easily.

4. *Too many typefaces.* Choose one easy-to-read, 12-point font, such as Times Roman or Courier. Don't use multiple fonts. Refrain from overusing bold or italic typestyles.

5. *Inappropriate embellishments.* If you're applying for a traditional job, don't include clip art or graphic images in your resumé. This is only appropriate if you're hoping to land a job as an artist, or plan to work in an industry, such as advertising, where employers are looking for creativity.

6. *Salary references.* Refrain from including within your resumé and cover letter any references to past salary or how much you're looking to earn—unless the advertisement specifically asked you to include this information. Many employers who ask for salary references will not call you if you do not supply it. If you must supply salary information, list a range, not a specific figure.

7. *Too much explanation.* Never include the reasons why you stopped working for an employer, switched jobs, or are currently looking for a new job. If necessary, this information can be brought up later, during an interview. Do not include a line in your resumé saying, "Unemployed" or "Out of Work" along with the corresponding dates in order to fill a time gap.

Watch Out!
One of the biggest complaints from human resources professionals is that applicants often apply for jobs they're not qualified to fill. Before submitting your resumé to a potential employer, read the job description carefully to ensure you have the skills, experience and educational background the employer is looking for.

8. *Clutter and jargon.* Instead of using long paragraphs of text to describe past work experiences, consider using a bulleted list. Most employers will spend less then one-minute initially reading a resumé, so it's critical that key information, such as work experience, is easy to find and described using descriptive and punchy action words and phrases. Avoid using too much technical jargon or industry buzzwords.

9. *Mismatched, low-quality paper.* It is vital that you print your resumé and cover letter on the same type of paper, and use matching envelopes to create synergy. You must avoid brightly colored paper or cheap 20-pound copy paper. Visit any stationary or office supply store to purchase quality resumé paper. Be prepared to spend between .25¢ and $1 per sheet of resumé paper (a bit less if you purchase packages of matching paper and envelopes.) The paper you use helps convey an image for yourself. Using quality resumé paper conveys a highly professional image and helps give you credibility.

10. *Photocopied resumé.* Never photocopy your resumé. Use a laser printer to generate resumés from your computer, or have it professionally typeset and printed.

Using action words

Your one-page resumé has to successfully convey your personality, skills, education, accomplishments, work experience, and at the same time, set you apart from the competition. Often, it will be your resumé that potential employers use to determine if you should be invited for an interview. Thus, what your resumé says about you, and more importantly, how

Watch Out!
It's an excellent strategy to customize your resumé for each job you apply for, however, padding your resumé so you can apply for jobs you're not qualified to fill will often be a waste of your time as well as the employer's.

it's said, is what can make your resumé a powerful job search tool.

As you create your resumé, you want to say as much as possible about yourself, using the fewest words possible. Your resumé has to profile you as the ideal person to fill the job you're applying for and answer the question, "Why should I hire you?"

Using short sentences containing carefully selected "action words" throughout your resumé is one way of adding impact. The words you incorporate into your resumé should relate back to the skill words listed in the ad or job description you're responding to, and demonstrate an action.

Someone applying for a financial analyst position, for example, should use phrases like, "Analyzed financial statements and created detailed cash flow projections for (company name)" or "Managed client relationships and coordinated investment banking projects with (company name)." Words like "analyzed," "created," "managed," and "coordinated" all demonstrate action and accomplishments that relate directly to the position the applicant is hoping to fill.

It's an excellent resumé creation strategy to use bulleted statements to highlight your work experience, accomplishments, and skills. Action words present themselves in a very bold fashion when used in bulleted points, as opposed to within paragraphs of text in a resumé. In today's market, someone will spend less then one minute looking at your resumé. If employers don't immediately like what they see you'll get passed over.

With each item of information you list in your resumé, choose one or two action words that make that piece of information jump off the page. Choose action words that relate directly to your job

Watch Out!
Never use words that you don't know the meaning of, just because you think they make you look smarter. Before sending out your resumé, always have someone proofread your work. Incorporating all of the right words into your resumé will be useless if they're spelled or used incorrectly.

objective and that help to quantify your skills and experience in tangible terms that can be applied to the job. Select action words that demonstrate efficiency and accomplishment, without stretching the truth.

Emphasize your skills and accomplishments in your resumé using "action words," such as:

Bright Idea
If you know the resumé you're sending to an employer will be scanned into an automated applicant tracking system and not initially be read by a human, it should be created as a keyword resumé. Instead of using action verbs, use nouns or adjectives to describe your skills, job responsibilities, and qualifications. For example, instead of using the action word "managed," use the word "manager" or "management." Also, be sure to use the keywords listed by the employer within the job description or help wanted ad.

TABLE 8.1. RESUMÉ ACTION WORDS

Accomplished	Achieved
Adapted	Administered
Advised	Allocated
Analyzed	Arbitrated
Assigned	Audited
Authorized	Awarded
Balanced	Broadened
Budgeted	Calculated
Centralized	Chaired
Collaborated	Collected
Compiled	Completed
Composed	Conceptualized
Conducted	Consolidated
Contributed	Coordinated
Counseled	Delegated
Demonstrated	Designed
Detected	Devised
Diagnosed	Directed
Downsized	Drafted
Eliminated	Enabled
Enforced	Engineered
Established	Expanded
Facilitated	Focused
Forecasted	Formulated
Fostered	Guided
Headed Up	Identified
Illustrated	Improved

Increased	Influenced
Initiated	Innovated
Installed	Instructed
Integrated	Interfaced
Invented	Launched
Lectured	Led
Maintained	Managed
Marketed	Merchandised
Moderated	Modernized
Monitored	Motivated
Negotiated	Networked
Nurtured	Optimized
Organized	Overhauled
Oversaw	Performed
Planned	Presented
Produced	Programmed
Projected	Proposed
Published	Reclaimed
Recommended	Reconciled
Recruited	Rectified
Reduced	Referred
Repaired	Researched
Reshaped	Restored
Routed	Scheduled
Screened	Settled
Shaped	Sold
Solved	Spearheaded
Stimulated	Streamlined
Strengthened	Supervised
Trained	Translated
Trimmed	Unified
Upgraded	Won
Wrote	

Putting your resumé together

This chapter is designed to help you determine what information should be included in your resumé, choose a resumé format that will best showcase you as an applicant, and help you actually write your resumé using the best possible wording.

Creating a tantalizing resumé that will get attention will take a lot of thought and a lot of time. You'll need to write, edit, and re-write your resumé, creating multiple drafts. Spend as much time as is necessary to produce a professional looking document that you truly believe highlights your most positive and marketable skills, accomplishments, and experience. If your resumé isn't a powerful marketing tool, you won't be given the opportunity to participate in job interviews.

If after submitting your resumé to multiple potential employers, you're not invited for job interviews, take a close look at your resumé and cover letters and ask yourself:

- Does this resumé fail to stress enough work experience?

- Does the resumé make you appear unqualified for the job(s)?

- Does the resumé fail to stress the right educational background for the job(s)?

- Are there any spelling or grammatical errors in your resumé?

- Does the resumé depict you as having the wrong skill set for the job(s)?

- Is the telephone number listed in the heading of your resumé incorrect? (Is there an answering machine connected to the phone line?)

- Does your resumé look too cluttered? Is it difficult to read?

If you've answered "yes" to any of these questions, you need to go back and spend additional time re-working your resumé. Also, if an employer sends you a rejection letter, give the person a call and try to determine exactly what their objections are. Consider making modifications to your resumé if you receive feedback that makes sense. You might need to add more focus to your resumé when applying for similar jobs with other companies.

Resumé writing is a difficult skill to master. If you don't have the time to spend creating a resumé for yourself, or you have trouble conveying your thoughts in writing, consider hiring a professional resumé writer to provide assistance.

Cover letters are important, too

Every resumé you submit to a potential employer should be accompanied by a cover letter on a separate sheet of paper. The purpose of the cover letter is to introduce yourself, and pique the potential employer's interest in you by getting them to read your resumé.

A cover letter should be relatively short and to the point (no longer than one page). It should be addressed to a specific individual by name and explain specifically what job opening you're applying for. This letter should be written in a business-letter format and should be custom-written for the employer to whom you're sending your resumé. It should be addressed to a specific individual, using their name. Never send a cover letter addressed to "To whom this may concern" or "Dear Sir or Madam."

Instead of repeating information provided in your resumé, use the cover letter to explain, in plain

Watch Out!
If you find yourself getting invited for job interviews but consistently not receiving job offers, your resumé could be well written, but misleading. Chances are you don't live up to the expectations created by your resumé. Assuming you didn't lie or stretch the truth in your resumé, the best remedy is to focus on perfecting your interviewing skills. Pay careful attention to feedback provided by the employers that choose not to hire you.

Unofficially...
The paper your cover letter is printed on should match your resumé paper and envelope.

English, what job you're applying for and why you're the perfect person to fill the job opening that's available. Whenever possible, it's always a good idea to use bullet points to focus attention on key points, skills, or your work history.

In the opening paragraph of your cover letter, explain who you are and why you're writing the letter. This paragraph should be no more than two or three sentences. For example, you could write, "I noticed your advertisement in the (insert date) edition of (insert newspaper/magazine name), and believe that I have the skills and work experience necessary to successfully fill the (insert job title) position that (insert company name) has available. Enclosed please find my resumé for your consideration."

Bright Idea
If you are responding to an advertisement and it contained a reference number, be sure to include that number in this paragraph, and on the envelope.

In the second and (if necessary) third paragraph of the cover letter, write about what sets you apart from the competition. Use this paragraph to sell yourself as the best person for the job. Be sure to address the employer's needs using very specific examples of how you can fill those needs. Stress your experience and accomplishments. Never include information about your earning history, salary requirements, or cover personal topics (such as your age, height, weight, hobbies, physical disabilities, health, etc.)

Answer the questions that are on the mind of the reader. Do you have the skills, education, and work experience necessary to fill the job's requirements? Are you knowledgeable about the industry and the company? Do you communicate well in writing? Do you have what it takes to succeed within the company? Will you be an asset to the company if you're hired? What sets you apart from other applicants?

Why should you be invited to come in for an interview?

The next paragraph in a cover letter should be used to kiss up. Discuss what specifically about the potential employer appeals to you. Use this opportunity to demonstrate in a few short sentences that you know something about the company.

The final paragraph of a cover letter should request that some type of action be taken. If you're hoping to schedule an in-person interview, ask for the opportunity to meet with someone from the company. Knowing that the person receiving your cover letter and resuméç is busy, conclude by stating that you'll give the person a call shortly to schedule an interview. You could write something like, "I look forward to speaking with you in greater detail about this job opportunity. I will give you a call early next week to schedule a convenient time for an interview. In the meantime, please feel free to give me a call at (insert your phone number)."

Conclude with a closing phrase, such as "Sincerely," followed by your signature with your name typed underneath.

Cover letter writing tips

Remember, spend time carefully considering the information you will include within this important document and pay attention to the wording you use. If necessary, create multiple drafts of a cover letter before sending it out. Your cover letter should nicely complement your resumé from both a content and visual standpoint.

The following are some useful tips for writing and formatting your cover letter:

- Use a formal business letter style when writing your cover letters.

- Keep your cover letters short and to the point.

- Personalize your cover letters, addressing them to specific people. Make sure the recipient's name is spelled correctly. If you don't know the name of the person to whom you should address your cover letter, call the potential employer and ask.

- As many recruiters are women, never begin a letter with "Dear Sirs." Try "Dear Employment Manager" instead.

- Use a standard text font, such as Times Roman or Courier. Use an easy-to-read font size, between 10 and 12 points. Avoid using too much bold and italic text, and never mix fonts.

- The font you use to print your cover letter should be identical to the font used to print your resumé. Also, use the same type of paper.

- Your cover letter should be visually appealing. Use a standard one-inch top and bottom margin and a 1.25 inch left and right margin. The cover letter (and resumé) should be printed using a laser printer or high-quality typewriter.

- Customize the cover letter to the job you're applying for.

- The cover letter should be no longer than one single spaced 8.5" x 11" page.

- All sentences should be short, less than 15 words. Keep paragraphs under five sentences in length. It is okay to have a one-sentence paragraph in a cover letter.

- Never lie or stretch the truth in a cover letter or resumé.

- Use bullet points whenever possible to get your ideas across to the reader quickly and easily.

- Avoid using clichés in your cover letter text.

- Make sure your cover letters contain no spelling or grammatical errors. Proofread your cover letters carefully before sending them. It's always a good idea to ask a friend or family member to also proofread them carefully.

- Keep the tone of your cover letters positive and up-beat. Avoid including negative information about yourself or your employment history.

- Avoid listing your personal or professional references in your cover letters. This information should be provided in writing to the employer during a first interview.

- When signing your cover letters, use a black or blue ballpoint pen.

- Make sure you keep a copy of each letter you send out.

Watch Out!
Never write "Confidential" or "Personal" on the envelope that contains your resumé or cover letter. This is highly unprofessional and makes you look foolish.

Printed resumés versus electronic resumés

Once a resumé is printed on a sheet of 8.5" x 11" paper and it's sent to a potential employer, a real-life person working in the human resources department or an executive representing the company the resumé was sent to will review it…right? Well, in many cases yes, but not always.

A growing number of companies are using specialized applicant tracking software. One feature of these software packages is that resumés submitted to a company are immediately scanned into a computerized database and then picked apart by the computer that searches for and analyzes keywords or phrases within the resumé. The software then spits out a list of applicants whose resumés contained a high number of keywords that match what the employer is looking for. In other words, a human doesn't actually read and review your resumé—a computer does.

One way to avoid missing out on a potential job opportunity because your resumé wasn't formatted correctly is to call the company and ask if your resumé will be scanned into an applicant tracking system or reviewed by a human.

If you know your resumé will be scanned, here are some basic guidelines to follow when creating and printing your resumé:

Watch Out!
Refrain from folding your resumé or stapling it.

- Your full name should be listed on the first line of the resumé, at the top of the page.

- Print your resumé on white paper using black ink.

- Use a basic 10 to 12 point font, such as Times Roman or Courier.

- Don't use italics or bold typestyles within your resumé.

- Avoid incorporating any type of graphics of fancy formatting into your resumé.

- Use a standard resumé format.

- Be sure to add "buzzwords" you think the employer is looking for when describing your skills, educational experience, and employment history. Take words or phrases directly from the help wanted ad or job description provided by the employer.

- Avoid abbreviating terms or industry jargon within your resumé.

- Ask the potential employer if a specific resumé format should be used or specific guidelines should be followed when submitting your resumé.

Many of these rules hold true when creating an electronic resumé, which is a resumé that will be sent to an employer via e-mail, posted on a web site, or added to an online resumé database. An electronic resumé should be keyword-based. Try to anticipate the keywords and phrases the applicant tracking software (used by a potential employer) will be looking for when trying to pinpoint the best applicants for a specific job opening.

Electronic resumés often need to be created using a very specific format. Career-related web sites, such as The Monster Board (www.monster.com), offers an online resumé creation form, allowing applicants to simply fill in the blanks in order to create an electronic resumé. It's an excellent strategy to first create a paper-based resumé and then adapt the information in your traditional resumé into the electronic resumé format.

Online resumé databases: Places to post your electronic resumé

Once you have created a resumé that you're proud of, take advantage of the resumé databases and services offered online. On the Internet's World Wide Web, you'll find literally dozens of career-related web sites that allow you to add your resumé to a database that is available to hundreds (and in some cases thousands) of potential employers worldwide. Including your resumé in these databases is often free of charge and very easy to do, even if you only have the most basic of computer skills.

If you're attempting to keep your job search a secret from a current employer, however, posting your resumé on the Internet probably isn't the safest move, since your resumé will be accessible by anyone, including your current employer.

Bright Idea
Since adding your resumé to multiple online databases is free, and it takes little time, part of your overall job search strategy (once you've created your resumé) should be to take advantage of these resumé databases as a way to market yourself to potential employers.

The following are some of the most popular career-related web sites on the Internet. You'll find that each of these sites offers a variety of complimentary services to job seekers.

TABLE 8.2. CAREER-RELATED WEB SITES

AltaVista Careers	http://www.altavista.digital.com
America's Job Bank	http://www.ajb.dni.us
Career Builder	http://www.careerbuilder.com
Career City	http://www.careercity.com
Career Exchange	http://www.careerexchange.com
Career Mosaic	http://www.careermosaic.com
CareerMart	http://www.careermart.com
CareerNet	http://www.careernet.com
CareerWeb	http://www.careerweb.com
E-Span	http://www.espan.com
Job Bank USA	http://www.jobbankusa.com
Jobfind.Com	http://www.jobfind.com
JobLynx	http://www.joblyunx.com
Net-Temps	http://www.net-temps.com
The Monster Board	http://www.monster.com
Yahoo Employment Classifieds	http://classifieds.yahoo.com/employment.html
ZD Net Job Database	http://www.zdnet.com/cc/jobs/jobs.html

Using resumé creation software and/or a professional resumé preparation service

Most career counselors and resumé preparation experts agree that one of the best ways to get attention when applying for virtually any job is to custom tailor your resumé for the position you want. Using your personal computer and some specially designed resumé creation software, developing and then customizing your resumé is fast and easy. The result is a professional quality resumé that you can print out on any laser or ink jet printer.

If you visit any computer software store, you'll find several PC- and Mac-based resumé creation software packages that sell for under $40. The best software packages in this category do a lot more than just print out resumés. Look for a software package that automatically formats your resumé information into a variety of different layouts and that allows you to easily customize your resumé for each job opportunity. This process becomes even easier when the software offers a spelling checker, "action word" glossary and thesaurus to help you add impact and accuracy to your resumé.

Your investment in a resumé creation software package will go further if the software also helps you write and format cover letters, and provides a large database of sample resumés and cover letters that you can use for reference. The best resumé creation software packages also have a built-in contact manager and appointment scheduler, allowing you to keep track of everyone you contact regarding a job opportunity.

These software packages are designed to walk you through the resumé creation process. At the appropriate on-screen prompts, you select a resumé format, and then type in the required information about yourself, your education, employment history, and skills. The software will often suggest ways of improving your resumé using action words or phrases, or by helping you to choose what type of information should be included.

Sure, it's possible to create a resumé using just your computer's word processor, however, you'll probably spend hours adjusting tabs, margins and type sizes trying to make your final resumé look professional and fit neatly onto one page. The biggest benefit of using resumé creation software is that it takes the hassle out of the process. These packages are far easier to use than most word processors, and when it comes to creating resumés, they're also more powerful. Why spend hundreds of dollars hiring a resumé preparation expert to create your resumé, and then have to pay extra each time you need to edit your resumé, when you can do it all yourself, easily, using any personal computer?

As powerful as these software packages are, they are primarily designed for formatting the *look* of your resumé—not the content. Thus, the output they create is only as good as the informational content you input. It's still necessary for you to choose what information will ultimately be included in your resumé and decide how that information will be conveyed.

To find the resumé software that best fits your needs, visit a local computer software store and read each software package's box for a list of features. These popular resumé creation software packages operate on any PC-based computer running Microsoft Windows 3.1, or Windows 95/98:

- The Perfect Resumé (Davidson & Associates, $34.95); Macintosh version also available.

- WinWay Resumé 4.0 (WinWay Corporation, $39.95)

- Adams JobBank Fast Resumé Suite (Adams Media Corp., $39.95)

- You're Hired! (DataTech Software, $19.95)

- Resumé Maker Deluxe (Individual Software, $39.95)

Unofficially...
One feature added to the latest editions of several popular resumé creation software packages is the ability to automatically post electronic resumés online to multiple career-related web sites. Look for a software package that's designed to work with the resources available on the Internet.

- Resumé Power 95 (DataTech Software, $39.95)

- Resumé Writer (Expert Software, $14.95)

While resumé creation software will automatically format your resumé using whatever format you choose, it's ultimately up to you to select the specific wording used in your resumé. Some of the more powerful resumé creation software packages will provide plenty of samples and suggestions for adding impact to your resumé, however, using specialized resumé software still requires that you know basic resumé writing skills.

If you truly believe you need help communicating your talents and accomplishments in writing, consider making a financial investment in your future by hiring a professional resumé writer. Someone who makes a living writing professional-quality resumés will be particularly useful helping job seekers with complicated backgrounds or problem areas in their employment history. People making major career changes or with lengthy absences from the workforce can also benefit from the experience and skills of a professional resumé writer.

A resumé writer can assist you in writing cover letters; targeting your resumé to specific job opportunities; creating electronic resumés; writing resignation letters; preparing reference letters and lists; choosing the best resumé format based on your personal situation; and determining what information should be included within your resumé.

If you choose to hire a professional resumé writer, be prepared to spend some time answering questions about yourself and provide them with much of the same detailed information that the questionnaire found earlier in this chapter requested.

Professional resumé writers can be found online or by checking a local telephone book. Using an Internet search engine, use the phrase "resumé creation" or "resumé writing services." When you make contact with a resumé writer, ask specifically how their service works and about their credentials.

How long have they been creating resumés? Do they specialize in creating resumés for people in your field? Do they use a "fill-in-the-blanks" computer program? (If so, go elsewhere.) Also, ask about the turn-around time for creating a resumé and exactly what their fees are. If you're not satisfied with the resumé writer's work, what happens?

A professional resumé writer should be willing to answer your questions and work closely with you to create your resumé. The person you hire should also be skilled in creating electronic (keyword-based) resumés and traditional resumés using a variety of different formats. It's important that you feel comfortable working with the resumé writer you hire, so shop around. Remember, you usually get what you pay for, so the cheapest resumé writer might not be the best.

Always send a "thank you" note

Unfortunately, the business world is a cut-throat environment. People often maintain a selfish, look-out-for-themselves attitude. As a job applicant this is not the attitude you want to adopt. Many applicants believe that when they go on a job interview, the interviewer is simply doing his or her job by trying to fill the position(s) their company has open. They believe that part of the interviewer's job is interviewing applicants, so the applicants offer no gratitude to the interviewer for their interest or for taking the time to meet with them. As a result of having this somewhat cynical attitude, many applicants never send a "thank-you" note after their interview—and that's a mistake.

The following are some basic steps to follow when writing and sending "thank-you" notes:

- Send individual and personalized "thank-you" notes within 24 hours of your interview, to everyone you met while visiting a potential employer. Send separate notes containing different messages to each person you met.

- Address your "thank-you" note using the recipient's full name and title. Make sure you spell the recipient's name correctly.

- A note can be typewritten on personal stationery. If you choose to type your note, follow a standard business letter format. A much more personal alternative is to hand-write your "thank-you" note on a professional looking note card that can be purchased at any stationery, greeting card, or office supply store. The personal touch will help you make a positive impression and separate you from your competition.

- In the note itself, address the interviewer as "Mr./Mrs./Ms./Dr. (insert last name)" in the salutation.

- Keep your message brief and to the point. Thank the interviewer for taking the time out of their busy schedule to meet with you, and for considering you for the job opening available. Make sure you include the exact job title or position you applied for. In one or two sentences, highlight the important details discussed in your interview. You want the

66

Sending a personal and well-thought-out note immediately after an interview is extremely beneficial. It will keep your name in the forefront of the hiring manager's mind. It will also show that you have good follow up skills and that you're genuinely interested in the job opportunity. —Sue Nowacki, a partner at 1st Impressions, a full-service resumé writing firm that operates on the Internet at http://www.1st-imp.com

99

interviewer to remember you. Finally, reaffirm your interest in the position and invite further contact.

- Make sure your full name and phone number is included in the note.

- The "thank-you" note is never the place to discuss issues under negotiation, such as salary, benefits, concerns, work schedule, etc.

- If possible, match the stationery or note card you use to your cover letter and resumé paper. This helps you convey a synergistic and well-thought-out image.

Just as your resumé and cover letters are valuable job search tools, think of the "thank-you" note as an extremely important follow-up tool that has the potential to help you to land the job you're interested in.

As a job applicant, it's important to show your gratitude to everyone who helps you find and land a job. This includes the people you interview with, as well as any networking contacts who helped you find job opportunities. If you demonstrate that you're grateful for someone's help, they're more apt to keep helping you in the future. A "thank-you" note is a perfect and professional way to show your appreciation.

> 66
> Even if an employer likes an applicant, I know that many human resources professionals actually wait to see if they receive a "thank-you" note from an applicant before making a job offer. They also check the postmark to see how quickly after the interview the note was sent.
> —Sue Nowacki of 1st Impressions
> 99

Just the facts

- Your resumé and cover letters are important sales tools. Spend whatever time is necessary to ensure that these documents showcase your skills, accomplishments, and experience in the best possible way.

- Every element of your resumé, including its content, appearance, and organization is equally important, so pay careful attention to the guidelines offered in this chapter.

- Once your resumé is complete, be sure to take advantage of the Internet as just one way of marketing yourself to potential employers. Take advantage of on-line resumé databases and career-related web sites.

- If you're having serious trouble creating your own resumé, consider hiring a professional resumé writer or using specialized resumé creation software.

- Make sure the impression you create with your resumé and cover letters is a highly positive one.

GET THE SCOOP ON...
Preparing for the interview ▪ Making a perfect
first impression ▪ Selling yourself during the
actual interview ▪ Ending the interview ▪
Negotiating a salary (if you're offered a job) ▪
Choosing whether or not to accept the job

Mastering the Job Interview

Chapter 9

From the day you begin sending out your resumés to potential employers, you'll probably find yourself periodically starring at the telephone waiting for it to ring. When it does ring, you'll find yourself hoping that it will be someone inviting you to come in for a job interview, and not a telemarketer trying to get you to switch your long distance telephone service.

The period between when you actually send out your resumés and start receiving calls from potential employers can be filled with anxious anticipation, which is totally normal. Instead of worrying about which potential employers will invite you for an interview, use the time to continue looking for new and exciting job opportunities and start planning for your eventual interviews.

The time it will take for an employer to actually respond after you submit a resume, cover letter and/or application will vary greatly, depending on the individual employer, the type of job you're applying for, and how desperate the employer is to fill its job opening(s).

What will ultimately determine whether or not you receive a job offer after one or more interviews will be your credentials, your appearance during the interview, and your ability to sell yourself as someone who is dependable with the potential of becoming an asset to the company. In a nutshell, it's necessary to exceed the employer's expectations.

What to do when that telephone rings

Eventually, unless you've applied for jobs you're clearly not qualified for, the telephone will ring and you'll be invited by a potential employer to come in for an interview. When this happens, don't panic. It's important that when a potential employer calls, you obtain some important information regarding the job interview. Thus, if you're in a noisy room, ask the person to hold while you change phones, turn down the television, or do whatever is necessary to create a quiet atmosphere where you can think clearly and hold an intelligent conversation.

For starters, immediately write down the name of the person who calls and what company they're calling from. When choosing a time and date for your interview, be sure to pull out your daily planner to ensure that you don't double-book appointments and that you're available when the employer wants to see you. Ideally, you'll want to accommodate the employer's schedule, however, if you're not available at the time the employer suggests, offer the employer several alternatives and make it clear that you're very excited about the opportunity.

As soon as you agree on a date and time for the interview, confirm the address and telephone number of the employer. Determine exactly whom you'll be meeting with (be sure to get their full name and title), and ask specifically where you should go and what you should do when you arrive at the employer's offices. Ask if there's a specific floor or office number you should report to, or if you should you check in with a receptionist.

Before ending this initial telephone conversation, confirm all of the details and thank the person for calling. Be sure to say something like, "I look forward to meeting with you on (insert date). This sounds like an excellent job opportunity." Of course, throughout the entire conversation, you want to be extremely friendly, outgoing, and professional. This initial telephone conversation is not the time to discuss the salary or benefits. You simply want to set up an in-person meeting.

If a job description hasn't been supplied in the "Help Wanted" ad you responded to and you need additional information from the employer, use the initial phone conversation to obtain a basic job description. This will help you prepare for the interview.

Now that you have a job interview lined up, you're well on your way to landing a job, but you still have some very important hurdles. Your resumé and cover letter served their purpose in getting a potential employer interested in you as an applicant, now it's your responsibility to use the in-person meeting to sell yourself to the employer and land the job. Achieving this objective will take preparation!

Preparation

Between the time you schedule a job interview and the actual date and time of your interview, you have a lot to accomplish. Thus, it's always a good strategy to give yourself at least 24 to 48 hours advance

Bright Idea
When an employer calls inviting you to come in for an interview, here's a quick checklist of information you need to obtain during the conversation:

■ The caller's name, title and telephone number

■ What company the caller is from

■ The name and title of the person you'll be meeting with

■ The time and date of the interview

■ Where you'll need to go for the interview (the address, including the floor number and office number)

■ What you should do when you arrive for your interview

■ Get directions to the interview location

notice when scheduling interview appointments. Also, never schedule more than two interviews in a single day (one in the morning and one in the afternoon).

Here are seven primary steps for preparing for an all-important job interview:

1. You must do some research to find out everything there is to know about a potential employer and the industry you hope to work in. If you walk into an interview situation uninformed, your chances of landing the job are practically zero.

2. Prepare a detailed list of questions to ask the interviewer.

3. Prepare answers to some of the common questions you'll most likely be asked during the interview.

4. Determine how you're going to sell yourself during the interview. Why will you be an asset to the company? What skills and experience do you offer? What sets you apart from other applicants? Why are you the perfect candidate for the job?

5. Select and prepare your interview outfit and gather your notes, research, and copies of your resumé.

6. Determine how you'll get to your interview, how long it will take (don't forget about traffic), and determine your route. If you need directions to the potential employer, obtain them in advance by calling the company's main telephone number and asking the receptionist.

7. Arrive at the interview location between 15 and 30 minutes early. Under no circumstances

should you be even one minute late for an interview—no matter what! Spend the waiting time composing yourself, reviewing your research, and psychologically preparing for the interview. This is also the ideal time to use the rest room, take a drink of water, and take a few deep breaths to relax.

Doing your homework—research

Unfortunately, there are no shortcuts when it comes to preparing for a job interview. Consider your preparation time and effort to be a worthwhile investment in your future. Obtaining up-to-date information is critical. Conducting research isn't as difficult as you might think, especially if you have access to the Internet and a local library. The first steps are to:

> **Gather information about the job.** This information is almost always listed in the help wanted ad you responded to, or can be obtained from the job description provided by the employer. Basically, you want to know: What position you're hoping to fill? What are the requirements for the position? What special skills and training are required?

> **Research the company you.** What is the company's history? What are the primary products or services offered by the company? What sets the company apart from its competition? Who are the company's clients or customers? What are the company's revenues? Is the company currently growing or facing financial problems? What are the biggest strengths and weaknesses of the company? Has the company received any media

Bright Idea
The very best way to dazzle a potential employer is to go into an interview situation fully prepared and totally confident. You'll find that the more qualified you are for the job you're applying for and the more prepared you are for the interview, the more confident you'll be.

attention recently? If so, was this media coverage favorable? What are some of the challenges the company is facing? If you get hired, think about what you'll be able to do to help the company face these challenges head-on and overcome them?

Find out as much as you possibly can about the industry.   Who are the key players in the industry? Who are the competitors of the company you're interviewing with? How big is the industry as a whole? What size market share does the potential employer hold? Is the industry growing? What issues are facing the industry as a whole? What major events have recently occurred within the industry?

Find out as much as possible about the person who will be interviewing you.   In addition to knowing about the company, one of the best ways to impress an interviewer is to know something about them. What is their exact title? What are his or her responsibilities? Where did he or she go to school? If you'll be meeting with an executive as opposed to a human resources person, what are the executive's biggest accomplishments?

Where to perform research

If you're applying for a job at a publicly held company, the first thing to do when you begin researching the company is to obtain its most recent annual report. Annual reports can often be obtained online, from a stockbroker, or from libraries. You can also contact the investor relations department at the company and ask that an annual report be mailed to you (but it might take a while for your request to get processed).

Another excellent source of company information is a corporate press kit, which you can often obtain from the company's public relations department. A growing number of companies also post all of their press releases on their corporate web site, so the first thing you should do when you connect to the Internet in order to conduct research on a company is to visit the company's web site.

If you don't know the URL (web site address) for the company you're researching, you can call the company or use one of the popular Internet search engines, such as Yahoo! (www.yahoo.com), Excite (www.excite.com) or AltaVista (www.altavista.digital.com). Using an Internet search engine, enter the name of the company as the keyword or search phrase.

Once you find a company's web site, spend time accessing as much information as you can, and be sure to visit the "Job Openings" or "Career Opportunities" section of the site. Here, you will probably be able to obtain a detailed job description for the position you're applying for.

Aside from using the Internet to visit a potential employer's web site, you can also access the online editions of many local and national newspapers and magazines in order to search for recently published articles about a company or industry.

Virtually any public library is also an abundant source of company and industry-oriented information. Most libraries have a selection of reference directories that can provide basic information about public and private companies.

Timesaver
PR Newswire (www.prnewswire.com) and BusinessWire (www.business-wire.com) are press release distribution services that are available online. You can often obtain extremely timely company and industry-oriented information from these services. PR Newswire also offers a free fax-on-demand service. If you have access to a fax machine or a computer that can accept faxes, call (800) 753-0352, and request extension #662 for information on how to obtain press releases issued by participating companies.

Timesaver
Standard & Poor's Reports-On-Demand is a service that will fax you up-to-date information about any of over 4,600 U.S. companies. There's a charge to receive each report, but one complementary sample report is available by calling (800) 642-2858. For additional information about this service, call (800) 292-0808.

Ask the librarian for assistance in finding publications such as *The Dun & Bradstreet Database, Thomas' Register of American Manufacturers, Ward's Business Directory, The Wall Street Journal Index, Occupational Outlook Handbook, The Adams Job Almanac, The Almanac of American Employers, Directory of Leading Private Companies, Encyclopedia of Associations, Hoover's Top 2,500 Employers* or *Hoover's MasterList of Major U.S. Corporations.*

While visiting the library, don't forget to check recent issues of popular business newspapers and magazines, like *BusinessWeek, Forbes, Fast Company, Crain's Small Business, Investor's Business Daily, The Wall Street Journal,* and any locally published business news journals. Back issues of many publications can be searched quickly using a CD-ROM called InfoTrac, which many libraries offer. You can also find these business-related publications online. Use these publications to learn about specific companies, industries, trends, and even gather profiles of top executives at the company you're researching.

Don't forget to visit the career services office at any high school, college, university, or vocational school. Even if you're not a student or alumnus, a school's career services office will often grant you access to their reference materials. If you are a graduate of the school you visit, ask what complementary career guidance services are available.

Other sources of research material are available from state employment agencies that you can find listed in your local telephone directory. Your town or city's local Chamber of Commerce is an ideal source of information about local companies. Employment agencies, temp agencies, and headhunters can also provide useful information about employers.

To get the real inside scoop on a company, speak with current employees. If you already know someone working for the company you're researching, give that person a call. You can also go to the company's offices and strike up conversations with people standing outside, in public smoking areas, or who are going to and from their cars.

Choosing an interview outfit

No matter what type of job you're applying for, when selecting an interview outfit, choose one that's conservative and professional looking. You'll be wearing this outfit when you make your incredibly important first impression. From the moment the interviewer sees you for the first time, the question that will be going through their mind is, do you look like someone who is capable of succeeding in the job that's available? Unfortunately, in the real world, looking like a top-notch employee is almost as important as actually being one. In other words, perception is everything, so don't let your appearance blow your chances of landing the job you want.

Choose an outfit that, at the very least, adheres to the company's established dress code. It's totally appropriate to dress in slightly more formal business attire than what the other employees wear to work. There are a few industries where what you wear simply doesn't matter, but as a general rule, wear something that would be classified as formal business attire.

Fashion advice for men

For men, the perfect interview outfit includes a nicely tailored, and recently dry-cleaned navy blue, charcoal or light gray two-piece suit. Darker colors provide a conservative and businesslike appearance,

Timesaver
To access searchable news stories online, use CNN Online (www.cnn.com), MSNBC (www. msnbc.com), *USA Today* Online (www.usatoday. com), or *The Wall Street Journal/* Dow Jones Online (www.djns.com).

Bright Idea
As you conduct your research, read up on the latest news, business, financial, and sports headlines. During the job interview, many interviewers will bring up topics in the news to see if you stay up-to-date on current events. The morning of your interview, it's an excellent strategy to read that day's edition of your city's newspaper and/or *The Wall Street Journal*.

Moneysaver
Here's a sampling of the major daily newspapers currently online:

▪ *Boston Herald* (www.bostonherald.com)

▪ *Chicago Tribune* (www.chicago.tribune.com)

▪ *Dallas Morning News* (www.dallasnews.com)

▪ *Detroit Free-Press* (www.freep.com)

▪ *Los Angeles Times* (www.latimes.com)

▪ *Miami Herald* (www.herald.com)

▪ *New York Times* (www.nytimes.com)

▪ *Philadelphia Inquirer* (www.phillynews.com)

▪ *Washington Post* (www.washingtonpost.com)

but you want to avoid wearing solid black. Brown, tan or beige fabrics are acceptable, but they're less conservative. It doesn't matter if the suit is made from solid or pinstripe fabric (as long as they're narrow).

Along with the two-piece suit, select a wrinkle-free white or light blue long-sleeved, cotton dress shirt. Complete the outfit with a silk (or silk-like) tie that coordinates well with your suit. Choose a leather belt that matches your dress shoes, and dark socks (that goes with the suit). Your leather dress shoes should be shined. Finally, bring along a nice briefcase or portfolio. Not only will this enhance your professional image, it will also give you a way to carry copies of your resumé, a pen, pad, and research materials to the interview.

If you're applying for a job in a business/corporate environment, your hairstyle should reflect your professional image. As a general rule, in the business world, men don't wear their hair long or in a ponytail. Some employers also frown upon facial hair (beards and mustaches). Choose a hairstyle that is conservative and that gives you a clean-cut appearance.

Fashion advice for women

In the business world, men are restricted to wearing suits, however, women are given a bit of additional freedom to express themselves with the clothes they wear although some employers require suits for women too. As an applicant, however, you want to choose an outfit that is businesslike and that fits within the company's dress code. Avoid plunging necklines, sheer blouses, and miniskirts. You also want to choose shoes that match the outfit you'll be wearing.

As for your make-up, hairstyle and fashion accessories, the natural look is always in style. You want to avoid anything overly flashy or that could be distracting to the interviewer, including perfume. If you wear jewelry, choose earrings and/or a necklace that complement your outfit but that aren't distracting or cheap-looking. Your nails should be nicely manicured. Nail polish is optional, but once again, it should complement the outfit as a whole.

The outfit that you choose should be tailored to fit you nicely. It should also be clean and wrinkle-free. Turn to the pages of the current women's fashion magazines to help you determine the latest fashion trends and styles for the business world. You can also solicit fashion advice from a sales clerk at a clothing boutique or department store. When seeking fashion advice, make it clear that you're looking for a conservative business outfit for a job interview.

It's always a safe approach from a fashion standpoint to choose an overall look that you're comfortable with and that creates the impression that you're a low-maintenance, but well-groomed professional.

As a woman, dressing in business attire doesn't necessarily mean having to spend an absolute fortune on designer clothing. It's much more important that your outfits fit perfectly and that you look clean, neat, and wrinkle-free than it is to wear a costly designer outfit. The day before your interview, try on your interview outfit at home. Put on all of the related accessories and style your hair the way you plan to for the interview. Make sure that every aspect of your interview outfit fits properly and helps to convey the right image.

Watch Out!
Men should avoid wearing a brightly colored tie or flashy jewelry. Also, avoid wearing any religious jewelry or anything that associates you with a political party, club, or organization.

Bright Idea
Let's face it, some guys just don't know how to put together an outfit that matches. If you fall into this category, seek help. Read a few issues of the various men's fashion magazines and ask for guidance from a sales associate or fashion consultant working in the men's department of a major department store. Your wife or girlfriend will also be able to provide fashion tips.

Fashion advice from a professional

Whether you're seeking employment at a company that enforces a strict dress code, or where employees are generally allowed to dress in casual business attire, what you wear to your job interview (and ultimately to work on a daily basis once you land the job), can and will impact your career, not to mention your self-esteem.

Mary Lou Andre is founder and president of Needham, Massachusetts-based Organization By Design (781-444-0140/www.dressingwell.com), a wardrobe management and fashion consulting firm that helps individuals and organizations understand the power of being appropriately dressed in a variety of situations. Through her extensive corporate and private client services, Andre has helped thousands of male and female business professionals identify and pull together a wardrobe that complements their professional and casual lifestyle.

Ninety percent of all companies in the country have adopted "dress down" policies. One-third of employers now allow casual business attire to be worn every day. What many consider to be casual attire for their weekend wardrobe, however, is often totally inappropriate for the workplace. "For some people, having to dress casually at the office presents a dilemma. Spring and summertime exacerbates the problem. People see open-toed shoes, sleeveless tops and shorts, and wonder whether these are suitable for the office," stated Andre. "They're not. Think of your casual work clothes as a slightly relaxed version of your formal business style."

When it comes to formulating a wardrobe that provides suitable casual business attire, leave your printed T-shirts at home, and save your sweat pants

Bright Idea
If you don't want to reveal your marital status, be sure to remove your engagement and/or wedding ring(s) before leaving for your interview.

for the gym. In addition, Andre believes it's important to always keep your shoes shined and scuff-free. Your belt should also always match your shoes.

She explained, "When choosing an outfit for a professional situation, such as a job interview, there are three words that you must remember: appropriateness, boundaries, and respect. In terms of appropriateness, very different fashion rules apply if you're working for a bank as opposed to an advertising agency or retail shop. It's important for your outfit to fit into the corporate atmosphere where you're applying to work."

For males, casual business attire might mean wearing a crisp pair of khakis, a belt, polished shoes, and an ironed oxford shirt. A tie and blazer are optional for daily work attire, but a two-piece business suit with a tie is an absolute must for a job interview situation. "Business is about communication, and you don't want to look sloppy or like you just rolled out of bed," added Andre. "People should always dress for the job they want, not the one they have."

Once you land a job, Andre believes that women who normally wear skirt suits as their formal business attire should consider a pants suit when they want to dress casually. "I believe women should wear jackets, because jackets are an authoritative garment. Males and females can replace a jacket with a vest or a cardigan sweater. I look at fashion as a business tool. It's important to represent yourself and your company well, and one place to start is with how you look. It's all about appropriateness and cleanliness. Nobody would send out a resumé with coffee spilled on it. Likewise, people should never wear an article of clothing that's stained, wrinkled, or that's not suitable for the workplace."

Bright Idea
Be prepared and plan for the unexpected! For example, if your interview outfit includes a pair of stockings, always take an extra pair along in your purse.

Andre stated that the workplace is not a forum for making a personal fashion statement. If you aren't totally clear about what your employer's dress code is, ask. If you're not sure whether or not an outfit or article of clothing is suitable, most of the time it's an excellent strategy to stick with what's conservative. "Women shouldn't be afraid to look feminine in the workplace. The best way to do this, however, is to wear a dark suit and accessorize with color. Also, avoid wearing too many different textures at once," she said. "For guys, monochromatic dressing is now in style. Simplified, clean lines are really in. Those big, wild ties that were in a few years ago are now pretty passé."

When it comes to buying a new wardrobe, pay attention to the difference between fads and trends. A trend is something that stays around for more than one season. Spend your money on key articles of clothing. Andre suggested, "Never take your fashion cues from fashion magazines. Instead, pay attention to fashion catalogs, ads, and in-store displays. Wearing designer clothing is not a prerequisite for looking good. If you're going to buy a designer suit, that's fine, but you can then buy non-designer shirts to go with it. Men and women can use shirts as an accessory to modify outfits. In a daily work environment, a men's blazer can be worn with an oxford shirt for one look and a mock turtleneck for a totally different look."

Spend your money on the key wardrobe pieces, like skirts, pants, jackets, suits, and dresses. Andre adds that everyone should have a trench coat with a removable lining, so it can be worn virtually all year. "You'll often meet people for the first time when you're still wearing your coat, and a nice trench coat will always help you make a good first impression," said Andre.

Anyone can redo their entire professional wardrobe for between $1,000 and $3,000, and it will last for several years if you buy key pieces that are of good quality. You can then maintain your wardrobe by spending just a few hundred dollars in subsequent years in order to add new shoes and accessories.

Shopping for a new wardrobe doesn't mean you have to spend a fortune in order to be stylish. Watch for sales, shop at discount retailers, and don't forget about vintage clothing shops. Before wearing a new outfit in public, preview it in the privacy of your home. Try on your new outfit along with all of the accessories you plan to wear with it. Check to see that shades and textures match and that the sleeves and hems are the correct length.

Finally, when investing in a new wardrobe, never skimp on alterations. There is no substitute for a good fit. Spending a fortune on a business suit is worthless unless it fits you properly and enhances your image. Form a good relationship with your tailor and dry cleaner in order to help ensure that your clothes will last longer, look better, and fit you properly.

Answering the interviewer's questions

As part of your job interview preparation, determine the types of questions the interviewer will ask. Next, spend some time developing well-thought-out, complete, and intelligent answers to these questions. Thinking about potential answers, or even writing out answers on paper will be helpful, but what will benefit you the most is actual practice answering interview questions out loud, and having someone you trust evaluate your responses honestly.

Bright Idea
Try to make the job interview a conversation where you and the interview both participate on a 50–50 basis. This means developing an open line of communication with the interviewer so that you can find out as much as possible about the available job, and the interviewer can discover as much as they can about you.

Most of the questions you'll be asked by potential employers will be pretty obvious, however, be prepared for an interviewer to ask you a few questions that are unexpected. By doing this, the interviewer wants to see how you react and how well you think on your feet.

How you answer questions during the job interview with have a major impact on your chances of getting hired. As you answer all of the interviewer's questions:

- Use complete sentences and proper English. "Yup," "Umm," "Nah," and "Huh?" ain't considered proper English.

- Don't be evasive, especially if you're asked about negative aspects of your employment history.

- Never imply that a question is "stupid."

- Don't lie or stretch the truth.

- Be prepared to answer the same questions multiple times, and never to restate your previous answer. Make sure your answers are consistent, and never reply, "You already asked me that."

- Never apologize for negative information regarding your past.

- Avoid talking down to an interviewer, or making them feel less intelligent than you are.

- Try to incorporate positive words and phrases into your answers. Think about how you can use the following words to describe yourself, your skills and your previous work experience: able, accurate, articulate, clever, creative, dependable, detail-oriented, driven, effective, efficient, flexible, fast, hardworking, honest, imaginative, motivated, organized, people-oriented, polite, reliable, self-reliant, stable, up-beat, well-organized and willing.

- Never be negative about your current job. Being negative about your current job might cost you the job you're interviewing for!

- Each answer you provide should somehow be used to sell yourself, your capabilities, your experiences, and your personality to a potential employer. Don't rely on your resume to inform the interviewer about your qualifications and capabilities.

- Use specific examples when answering an interviewer's questions Try to position yourself as a team player. For example, when answering a question about your proudest accomplishment while working for your previous employer, you could say something like, "When I was working for (insert company name), we did . . ." By using the word "we," you imply that you're a team player. Keep in mind, however, you want to clearly state your personal accomplishments.

- Don't babble! If you find yourself babbling, it's probably due to being nervous. Take a deep breath and formulate your responses before opening your mouth. It's okay if there is a pause between the interviewer asking a question and you answering it. Having a few moments of silence implies that you're thinking about your answer, which is a good thing.

- As you describe your work experiences, pretend you're telling a story. Make the interviewer interested in what you have to say. Never just respond to a question by nodding your head or using one word answers.

Unofficially...
As you answer an interviewer's questions, your responses should inform the potential employer that you're hardworking, honest, dedicated, and dependable. Show that you're a team player. Always provide examples by describing your accomplishments, specialized training, and related work experience. Remember, the interviewer's own job depends on his or her ability to hire the best applicants. Make the interviewer feel excited about hiring you.

- Periodically try to incorporate the interviewer's name into your conversation.

- Determine exactly what the employer is asking. Understanding what information the interviewer is looking for is the first step to being able to provide it.

The following are 15 common interview questions and suggestions on how you can best answer them:

1. What can you tell me about yourself?

   Potential response: Stress your skills and accomplishments. Avoid talking about your family, hobbies, or topics not relevant to your ability to do the job.

2. Why have you chosen to pursue your current career path?

   Potential response: Give specific reasons and examples.

3. In your personal or professional life, what has been your greatest failure? What did you learn from that experience?

   Potential response: Be open and honest. Everyone has had some type of failure. Focus on what you learned from the experience and how it helped you to grow as a person.

4. Why did you leave your previous job?

   Potential response: Try to put a positive spin on your answer, especially if you were fired for negative reasons. Company downsizing, a company going out of business, or some other reason that was out of your control is a perfectly acceptable answer. Remember, your answer will probably be verified.

5. What would you consider to be your biggest accomplishment at your last job?

   Potential response: Talk about what made you a productive employee and valuable asset to your previous employer. Stress that teamwork was involved in achieving your success, and that you work well with others.

6. In college, I see you were a (insert subject) major. Why did you choose (insert subject) as your major?

   Potential response: Explain your interest in the subject matter, where that interest comes from, and how it relates to your current career-related goals.

7. What are your long-term goals?

   Potential response: Talk about how you have been following a career path, and where you think this pre-planned career path will take you in the future. Describe how you believe this job is a logical step forward.

8. Why do you think you're the most qualified person to fill this job?

   Potential response: Focus on the positive things that set you apart from the competition. What's unique about you, your skill set, and past experiences? Describe what work-related experience you have that relates directly to the job you're applying for.

9. What have you heard about this company that was of interest to you?

   Potential response: Focus on the company's reputation. Refer to positive publicity, media attention, or published information that caught your attention. This shows you've done your research.

10. What else can you tell me about yourself that isn't listed in your resumé?

    Potential response: This is yet another opportunity for you to sell yourself to the employer. Take advantage of the opportunity.

11. What you do see as being your biggest strengths?

    Potential response: Discuss your specific skills, education, and provide examples of your on-the-job successes.

12. What do you see as your biggest weakness?

    Potential response: To answer this question, you'll want to turn any negatives into positives. If you're too specific about your weaknesses, you could blow your chances for landing the job. At the same time, you never want to lie. Just one possible response is that your spouse or past co-workers accuse you of being too dedicated to your work. For an answer like this to be believable, you must provide proof.

13. Tell me about your personal situation.

    Potential response: Watch out! This is a trick question that's designed to get applicants to volunteer information that the interviewer is legally not allowed to ask. The interviewer could be looking to determine your martial status, whether or not you have children, what your health is like, what you do during your free time, or whether or not you're in serious debt. When answering this question, avoid discussing any personal problems, no matter how trivial.

14. How does your previous work experience relate to the position you've applied for here?

Potential response: Once again, this is an opportunity to discuss your skills, interests, and past accomplishments.

15. What sort of salary, benefits or overall compensation package are you looking to receive?

Potential response: Make sure you're prepared for this question by knowing in advance what you're worth and what people in the position you're applying for are paid. Never provide an exact figure. A first interview is seldom the time to negotiate a salary. You can, however, say that in the past you've always been paid a very competitive wage, and that is what you'd be looking for at this job. If absolutely necessary, you can provide a range, but make sure that the figures you state aren't too low or too high. Since you don't want to discuss salary until after you've been offered the job, you can turn the question around by asking what the salary range is for others working for the company with similar skills and experience. Finally, you could answer this question by stating that the position seems extremely interesting to you and that your salary requirements are negotiable.

You ask the questions

One way to impress an interviewer is to ask intelligent and relevant questions. For some people this is extremely hard to do during a stressful interview situation, which is why you should create a list of five or ten questions in advance. Since you'll be bringing a portfolio containing a pad, pen, and extra copies of your resumé to the interview, you can also bring

Watch Out!
Avoid questions that relate to what the company can do for you (the potential employee.) Don't ask about vacation days, sick days, benefits, or salary until after you've received a job offer.

along a written list and refer to it during the interview. (Obviously, it's better to memorize this list.)

As you ask questions, listen carefully to the interviewer's response (and look interested) and try to ask intelligent follow-up questions when it's appropriate. While the interviewer is responding to your questions, feel free to jot down notes. This makes you come across as someone who is attentive and well organized, plus it allows you to keep a list of issues or topics you want to follow up or get clarified later.

By asking questions, you'll be able to create more of a conversation-style interview situation and avoid being interrogated by the interviewer.

The following is a list of general questions you can pose during an interview situation. You should, however, also ask questions that are directly related to the company and/or industry you hope to be working in.

- Could you please provide me with a detailed job description of the position? Could you describe a typical day on the job?

- Why is the position I'm applying for currently open? Is the division I'll be working in expanding? How many additional people do you plan to add to this division over the next six months? Was the last person promoted or did they leave the company? If they left, why did they leave?

- What would you expect someone working in my position to accomplish during their first six months on the job? What about during the first year?

- How would you describe the corporate culture (or the work environment) of this company?

How would you describe the company's management style?

- How big is the division I'll be working in? What are the overall goals of the division?

- What can you tell me about my potential supervisor and coworkers? While I'm here visiting the company, would it be possible to meet some of the people I'd be working with if you decide to offer me this job?

- Will the job I'm applying for require a lot of travel? If so, how much? Does the company pay all travel costs?

- What are the qualities that make a good employee in this organization?

- Can you describe a typical work day or week? What would be my job responsibilities on a daily basis? Specifically, what type of tasks would I be doing if I'm hired for this job?

- Are my hours flexible, or am I expected to work specific hours (9:00 a.m. to 5:00 p.m.)? How much overtime do you anticipate this job will require? This should be clear in the interview, but make sure that the interviewer does not feel that you are unwilling to work extra hours.

- How are employees at (insert company name) evaluated? How often do evaluations take place? Who does the evaluating?

- What type of on-the-job training is available? Does the company encourage employees to pursue additional education and training?

- If I were interested in moving up within the company, what opportunities would be available to me? When would I be considered for a

Watch Out!
Never ask the interviewer personal questions about themselves. Let them volunteer information, but try to discover things you have in common with the interviewer. Even if you develop an instant bond with the person interviewing you, remember you're still participating in a formal job interview and you both have specific objectives that need to be accomplished.

promotion? Theoretically, how high up the corporate ladder could someone starting at my level go?

- During the past few years, how as the company grown or evolved? What are your predications for the next year?

Making the perfect first impression

The moment you step through the front door of the company for your interview, consider the interview process started. Every person you meet, including the receptionist or secretary, may have input into whether or not you get hired. Smile, be friendly and act professionally with everyone you meet.

Many employers ask secretaries or receptionists their opinion of applicants based on how they acted when they arrived for their appointment and what they did in the waiting room. Thus, it's important to look and act composed, even if you're not. Control your nervous habits while sitting in the waiting room. Don't tap your foot, bite your nails, or play with your hair. Whatever you do, never start smoking a cigarette to calm yourself down. If you need something to do while sitting in the waiting room, read any company literature that's on display, review your research notes or your resumé, or flip through a magazine.

Making the perfect first impression means initially focusing on your appearance and general attitude. You should arrive to your interview early, looking calm and collected, and your body language (non-verbal communication) should communicate confidence. Your interview outfit, including your overcoat, should be clean, wrinkle-free, and convey professionalism.

While it's acceptable for the interviewer to be running late and keep you, the applicant, waiting, it's never acceptable for the applicant to be late for an interview or to keep the interviewer waiting.

When you're introduced to someone new, including a receptionist or secretary, introduce yourself by name, make direct eye contact, smile, and extend your hand. Interviewers look for a firm handshake, eye contact, and how you carry yourself when formulating their first impression of an applicant.

Body language, or your non-verbal communication, is an important element in conveying a positive first impression. You should be standing or sitting up straight, paying attention to your mannerisms. If you know you have specific nervous habits, it's important to be aware of them and control them during an interview situation. Learning to control these habits will probably take practice.

Before an actual interview begins you'll be brought into the office or room where it will take place. When you're introduced to the person interviewing you, refer to them formally, by saying something like, "It's a pleasure meeting you Mr./Mrs. (insert name)." At this point, if the interviewer asks you to call them by their first name, it's okay to do so. Otherwise, keep referring to them as Mr./Mrs. (insert name). Allow the interviewer to sit down either before you or at the same time as you. You want to avoid having the interviewer look down upon you while you're sitting and he or she is standing. As you sit down, don't slouch. Instead, lean slightly forward, toward the interviewer and make eye contact while smiling. Place your briefcase next to your chair and remove your portfolio (pad and pen).

Watch Out!
Avoid drinking coffee or caffeinated soda before an interview. If you're offered something to drink by the receptionist or interviewer, ask for water or nothing at all. Caffeine tends to make people more nervous or hyperactive. During a job interview or salary negotiation, you want to appear calm, cool, and collected.

During the interview, listen carefully to everything the interviewer says. Once again, be conscious of nervous habits and try to control them. Many people when they're nervous start saying "Umm" or "you know what I mean?" after every sentence. If you find yourself doing this, attempt to control it. Often, just being aware of these nervous habits while they're happening makes it easier to control them.

The best way to control your nervous habits and convey positive non-verbal communication is practice. Participate in mock interviews with friends or a career counselor, and apply for a few jobs you're not necessarily interested in just to gain some practice participating in actual interviews—and you never know, you might get an offer you like.

Once everyone is seated and the interview session is about to begin, be prepared to spend a few minutes chatting about unrelated topics. This is a technique used by many interviewers to relax the applicant. Since you have read the local newspaper before your interview, you should be prepared to discuss the weather, a recent sporting event, or current news headlines.

As your eyes scan the interviewer's office, if you notice that he or she has a hobby, such as boating, fishing, or golf, it's appropriate to ask a question or make a comment about their hobby, such as, "Where do you play golf? Are you a member of a nearby club?" (Avoid asking about the interviewer's skill level.) This is just one way you and the interviewer can share something in common. During this chatting period, try to make sincere compliments to the interviewer.

It's during the first one or two minutes of your interview that the interviewer will establish their

Watch Out!
It's never a good idea to look at your watch during an interview. If the interviewer perceives you're bored or have someplace better to be, it'll hurt your chances of landing the job.

first impression. Notice that at this point, there has been no discussion about the job opening, your skills, or qualifications. Within a few minutes after the initial chit–chat period, the actual interview should begin. Hopefully, the interviewer will segue into a topic that relates to the job opening or you as an applicant, but if after a few minutes this doesn't seem to be happening, you may have to take matters into your own hands. After all, depending on the job you're applying for, you may only have 15 or 30 minutes of the interviewer's time. If you spend most of that time discussing irrelevant topics, you'll have less time to sell yourself as the perfect applicant for the job.

Topics to avoid during the interview

During your first interview, there are a variety of topics you should avoid raising yourself, including questions about salary, benefits, paid sick days, or vacation time. Eventually, the employer will bring up these topics, or you can bring them up later, after you've received a job offer. Also, don't ask the interviewer personal questions or questions relating to his or her career (although this is sometimes okay— use your judgment).

There are interview questions that the employer is not legally allowed to ask you. Some of these illegal questions include:

- Are you a U.S. citizen?
- Where were you or your parents born?
- What is your "native tongue?"
- What is your religion?
- How old are you?
- When did you graduate from college?

Unofficially...
If the interviewer is an executive with the company and not a human resources person, chances are they're looking for applicants they consider similar to themselves in terms of personality, ethics, and values. The people the interviewer hires will be a reflection of them within the organization, and everyone always wants to look favorable in the eyes of their peers and superiors. Thus, it becomes increasingly more important to establish an open line of communication with the interviewer early on.

- What is your date of birth?
- Are you married?
- Do you have children?
- Do you plan on having children in the future?
- What are your child-care arrangements?
- What clubs or social organizations do you belong to?
- How tall are you?
- What do you weigh?
- Do you have any physical, emotional, or mental disabilities?
- Do you have any illnesses?
- Have you ever been arrested?

Instead of asking these specific questions, an interviewer can ask more general questions in hopes that you'll volunteer some personal information about yourself. Whether or not you reveal personal information when asked a general question is up to you, however, you should understand an interviewer's reasons for asking various questions. During an interview, if you're asked multiple questions that you're not comfortable with or that are illegal, seriously consider ending the interview and seeking employment elsewhere. (Most interviewers are totally ethical, so the chances that you'll be bombarded with illegal questions is slim.)

Tell your story...no matter what

During the interview process, it's important that you use every available opportunity to sell yourself as the perfect candidate for the job. As you answer each question, use your answer to describe at least one of your skills or accomplishments and provide specific examples of how you can help the company meet its goals and objectives.

Don't wait for the interviewer to ask you the right questions before you start selling yourself. Remember, the interviewer wants to be sure that you have the skills, experience, intelligence, and motivation necessary to be successful in the job. If the company hires you, will they be making a good investment? Will you be a positive asset to the company?

If the interview ends and you have failed to provide the interviewer with the information they need to make an intelligent hiring decision, that's your fault, not theirs.

Avoid jobs that are being misrepresented by the employer

All too often, applicants apply for what sounds like the ideal job, only to have their expectations shattered when they discover that how the job was advertised was misleading or misrepresented. No matter how well a job opening is described, it's your responsibility as the applicant to ask specific questions to avoid misunderstandings and to ensure that the job you accept is the one that you want and are qualified for.

When applying for a job, you have several opportunities to learn as much as you can about the expectations of the employer and the actual responsibilities of the position. If you're responding to a "help wanted" ad, one of the first things to ask a potential employer is to describe the job or to provide you with a detailed job description in writing.

Advertisements that sound too good to be true probably are. If an ad is looking for "management trainees," that's usually a come-on for an retail store

Unofficially... Employers are permitted to ask certain variations of the illegal questions if they relate directly to the job that's being offered. For example, an employer is allowed to ask if you're authorized to work in the United States. They can ask if you're over the age of 18, and if you'd be willing to relocate or be available for business-related travel An employer can also outline specific job responsibilities and ask if you'll be able to perform the essential functions of the job with or without reasonable accommodations.

assistant manager-type position, a commission-only sales job, or another low-paying sales position. "Marketing of financial services" usually refers to some type of insurance sales, and ads that state "no sales" usually means you'll be selling something, either directly or indirectly. Companies that are recruiting people with a wide range of backgrounds for a specific job are often looking for as many candidates as possible for a job that's not too exciting.

You have to be clear about what you expect from a job, and the employer has to be clear about what they're presenting. As an applicant, you have to take an active role during the interview process, and not always believe what people tell you. You have to ask questions. Having a slightly skeptical point of view can be helpful during the job search process, but you can't come off as cynical or as an untrusting person.

Most of the time, companies that misrepresent job openings do so unintentionally. When discussing a job opportunity with a potential employer, you can't stay on the abstract level. Early on, ask specifically what the responsibilities of the job are. If the employer uses descriptive phrases like, "work in a low stress environment" or "flexible work hours," have them define exactly what they mean. Often, how the employer defines terms in their job descriptions is different from how the applicant defines them. This is what leads to misunderstandings. As you ask questions, push the employer to provide complete answers about what will be expected of you.

Before accepting a job offer, ask to speak with someone at the company who will be your colleague. They should tell you what to expect. They might not be able to explain things in bold or

Watch Out
If a candidate is invited to participate in a group interview with other applicants, it's usually a commission-only sales position that's being offered. If the employer evades questions about its product or service, or refers to extremely high income potential, that should definitely raise a red flag in the applicant's mind.

straightforward terms, but they will provide you with valuable clues about what the job and the company are actually like. As you interact with potential co-workers, ask yourself if you would enjoy working with these people on a daily basis.

Plenty of great jobs are available, but to find the position that's right for you, it's your responsibility to ask questions about the company, before accepting a job offer. If you know what you're getting into, you can easily avoid unwanted surprises and dead-end, boring jobs.

Overcoming nervousness

Almost everyone gets nervous before a job interview, especially if they're applying for a job that they really, really want. This is totally normal, however, it's critical that you never let your nervousness take control of your actions.

Before an interview, think about what happens to you when you enter into a stressful situation. Do you sweat? Do you tap your foot? Play with your hair? Tap your pen on against a table? Do you have trouble thinking clearly? Do you become hyperactive? Perhaps you bite your fingernails or start saying "umm" between every sentence.

No matter what your nervous habits are, it's important to control them. One of the easiest ways to control nervous habits is to eliminate the reasons you have for being nervous. Are you afraid of failure? Are you afraid that you're not qualified for the job you're applying for? Are you totally unprepared for the interview you're about to participate in? If you answered "yes" to any of these questions, it's probably one of the main causes of your nervousness.

As you embark on the entire job search process, it's critical that you develop a strong (but not cocky) confidence in yourself, your personal skill set, and your accomplishments. It's also important that you do your research and enter into every interview situation totally prepared.

With the right mental attitude and preparation, you'll still probably be a bit nervous just before an interview, however, within minutes after the actual interview process begins, your fears and nervousness will melt away, allowing you to focus all of your energies on landing the job. To help boost your confidence, ask yourself what you have to lose if you don't get this job? The answer is nothing. There are always other jobs you can apply for. By not getting yourself over-anxious about each job opportunity, you'll be able to generate more confidence.

Just before an interview, while sitting in the waiting room, take a moment to close your eyes, take several deep breaths and picture yourself acing the interview. Visualize yourself answering all of the interviewers questions perfectly and developing a bond with the interviewer. Visualize every detail of the interview process and see yourself acting totally cool, calm, and collected. Say to yourself, "I have the right skills needed for this job. I've done my research and I know all about the company. I'm totally motivated and I know I'm the best applicant that the interviewer is going to meet."

Dealing with multiple interviewers

It's much more common to be faced with multiple interviewers during your second and/or third interview, but there are always exceptions. When faced with two or more interviewers, don't allow them to make you feel like you're being ganged up on.

Unofficially...
The job interview process is a game with no losers. If you receive a job offer, you've earned first prize, however, if you don't land the job, you've still gained valuable experience by participating in a job interview. You can now evaluate your mistakes and correct them in time for your next interview.

Pretend you're doing some public speaking. You'll still answer and ask questions in the same manner, except you should move your eye contact back and forth between each of the interviewers.

Dealing with negative info in your employment history

As potential employers evaluate your resumé and then conduct a job interview, one thing they'll be interested in is your employment history. Employers want to make sure that an applicant hasn't been "job hopping" and that he or she doesn't have too many large gaps in their employment history. An interviewer will want to know the reasons why you left your previous job(s), especially if you were fired. Interviewers will also want to know what you did while unemployed. Obtaining additional training or education is looked upon much more favorably than staying home watching soap operas.

An ideal employment record shows constant employment from right after your graduation to the present. As you moved from job to job, did you follow a carefully planned career path and take on more responsibilities with each new position? Did you stay within a specific industry and remain in each position for a good amount of time before getting promoted or moving on? Are there large gaps in your employment record? If so, why? Do you have excellent recommendations from each of their previous employers?

Unfortunately, very few applicants have perfect employment histories. This is okay as long as you deal with the negative information correctly as you apply for new jobs. Within your cover letter, never mention any negative information. Focus only on your positive accomplishments, skills, and what makes you an ideal candidate for the job you're applying for.

All of the information within your resumé should highlight your strengths, accomplishments, and skills. The time to bring up negative information is during your job interview, when you're face-to-face with the potential employer. Never volunteer any information, but when asked, be prepared to put a positive spin on any information you're not proud of. During your explanation, never apologize for negative information.

Pam Meyers, president of HRI, Inc., a South Bend, Indiana-based company that provides human resources-related services to small- and medium-sized companies, explained, "During the interview, you must be totally honest about your employment history, but you don't want to come right out and say that you were fired. Offer a very brief explanation of any negative information, and say what you learned from the experience. Keep in mind that most interviewers are going to check with your previous employers. If something you say somewhat contradicts what a previous employer or reference says, you're chances of getting hired become very slim. It's more common for an applicant to be denied employment because the interviewer discovers that the applicant lied about being fired, not because they were actually fired."

Myers stressed that being fired is very different from getting "downsized" or terminated from a job due to circumstances beyond your control. "If a previous employer goes out of business or closes a division, that's something the job seeker had no control over, so it will never be held against them," said Myers.

When to talk salary

Much of this book is dedicated to helping you negotiate the best possible salary and benefits package
for yourself. However, there's a right time and place
for discussing salary, and the first job interview is
not the correct time. Wait until you receive a job
offer before you begin the salary negotiation
process. If you're offered a job at the conclusion of
the first interview, congratulations! Don't however,
accept or reject the offer during this meeting.

Ending the interview

At some point, your initial job interview will come to
an end. You might receive a job offer right on the
spot, but it's more common for the interviewer to
explain that they'll be in touch. Before actually leaving the interview, you should determine exactly
what the next step is.

Is it necessary to supply the employer with additional information? Should you sit tight and wait for
an offer? Is it necessary to contact the interviewer
again? Will additional interviews be necessary
before a decision to hire you is made? If so, can you
schedule a second interview right on the spot?
When will the employer be making their hiring
decision?

If at the end of the interview you don't know the
answer to these questions, it's important that you
ask additional questions. Once you know exactly
what will happen next, look the interview in the
eye, smile, and thank him or her for their time and
interest. Reaffirm that you're extremely interested
in the job.

Evaluating your performance

Immediately after the interview, while everything is
still fresh in your mind, find a quite place to sit

Timesaver
Chapters 10 and
11 will provide
you with detailed
information on
how to deal with
the salary nego-
tiation process.

down and collect your thoughts. Using a pad, write down notes to yourself as you evaluate your overall interview performance. Be honest with yourself as you consider what you could have done better. Determine what mistakes you've made and develop a plan for avoiding those mistakes in the future. Think about what you learned from the interview. What didn't you learn? What questions do you still need answers to from the employer? You'll want to bring up these issues during the second interview.

Deep in your heart, do you believe that you did everything possible to sell yourself and your skills to the employer? Did you forget to provide a useful fact? Could you have answered any of the interviewer's questions more completely? Were there better examples you could have provided? How did you deal with your nervous habits?

Write down what actions you need to take. Do you need to follow up by sending additional information or documentation to the employer? Are you supposed to call the interviewer back? Within 24 hours after the interview, be sure to send a thank-you note to the interviewer and follow up on any promises you made regarding follow-up actions.

The pre-interview checklist

As you're preparing for each interview, use this checklist to help insure you're totally prepared. Knowing that you're prepared will provide you with additional confidence.

To ensure that you look well rested and appear alert, it's important to get a good night's sleep before an interview.

The morning of the interview, take a shower. Make sure your hair is clean, your fingernails are manicured (if you're female) and you shave. Brush your teeth and use a mouthwash or breath freshener. It's critical that you look and feel your best, both to enhance your own confidence and to create a positive first impression.

Apply deodorant and antiperspirant. Avoid using any perfume or cologne.

Put on your interview outfit. Make sure that it's clean and wrinkle-free, and that you haven't forgotten any accessories. Refrain from wearing any flashy jewelry.

Shine your shoes.

Make extra copies of your resumé and bring them with you.

Make copies of your letters of recommendation and your list of references. You'll want to provide these for the interviewer.

Pack up your briefcase or portfolio, making sure you bring a pen and pad to the interview. Also, don't forget to bring your personal planner/appointment book, in case you need to schedule a second interview. Within your briefcase/portfolio, insert your company research notes.

Write down the address and phone number of the potential employer, along with the name of the person you're supposed to meet. You'll also want to bring the written directions so you don't get lost on your way to the interview. Place this information safely within your portfolio so you don't forget it.

Plan your travel route to the interview, making sure you allow plenty of time for traffic or any other unexpected delays.

Refrain from drinking beverages containing caffeine before the interview. Also, avoid eating any foods that could cause bad breath.

Use the rest room before your interview.

The morning of the interview, read the local newspaper, watch a morning news program on television and/or read *The Wall Street Journal.* It's important to be familiar with current events.

Arrive to your interview location at least 15 minutes early. Use the time to review your research notes and visualize yourself succeeding in the interview.

Remember, the moment you step through the front door of the potential employer, the interview process has begun. Be friendly and smile at everyone.

Just the facts

- The job interview process consists of several steps, including preparation; making a perfect first impression; selling yourself during the actual interview; ending the interview; negotiating a salary (if you're offered a job); and choosing whether or not to accept the job.

- The trick to being successful in any job interview situation is preparation. Do your research and make sure you look your best.

- Making a positive first impression during an interview is critical.

- During the interview, answer all questions using complete sentences, and be prepared to ask intelligent and relevant questions.

- Avoid discussing salary or compensation during the first interview, or until you receive a firm job offer.

- During the interview process, make sure you tell your story and sell yourself by providing plenty of concrete examples that showcase your skills, experience, education, and enthusiasm. Sell yourself as the perfect person to fill the available job opening.

How to Negotiate a
Top Salary

GET THE SCOOP ON...
The best strategies to use during a salary negotiation ▪ How to avoid common mistakes made
during the negotiation process ▪ Why listening is
important ▪ How to make counter-offers and
use creativity ▪ When and how to end a
negotiation by accepting an offer ▪ Getting your
job offer in writing ▪ The steps to take after
accepting a new job offer

PART V

Bargaining Strategies

Whether you've applied for a new job with a new employer and are about to begin negotiating your compensation package, or are about to negotiate with your present employer to obtain a raise and/or promotion, your approach to the whole negotiation process will affect your success and determine what you actually receive.

Most people become very uncomfortable talking about financial issues, and absolutely hate the negotiation process. This is a perfectly normal reaction, but one that you'll have to overcome unless you plan on accepting whatever it is the employer offers you, with no questions asked. (Needless to say, this isn't the best strategy if you want to earn what you deserve.)

Ultimately, it will be your negotiation skills and willingness to participate in a negotiation that will guarantee that you get exactly what you deserve in terms of your overall compensation package, which includes your salary, benefits, and perks.

Everyone has to participate in negotiations at various times in their life, such as when they buy a new house, a car, or an expensive appliance. If you've visited a yard sale or flea market, perhaps a product caught your eye and you haggled down the price from $50 to $30. Maybe you and your spouse recently decided to see a movie. When you got to the theater, however, you each wanted to see a different movie. A discussion ensued and you eventually reached an agreement or compromise. This, too, can be considered a negotiation.

Some jobs and occupations require people to participate in negotiations on a daily basis, so when it comes time to negotiate a salary, it's no big deal for them. For others, however, negotiation is something that they've had little practice in, and as a result, they're very uncomfortable with the whole process.

This chapter will help you develop the basic negotiation skills needed when dealing with a new employer or your current employer. Just as with any new skill, to really get good at it will require a lot of practice. Once you've mastered these skills, they'll help you throughout your entire career, as well as in your personal life.

Be prepared to negotiate your compensation

Okay, so you've spent a considerable amount of time and effort participating in the whole job search process and your results thus far have been very positive—you've received at least one job offer. While you're currently experiencing a strong sense of relief that the whole process is over, in reality, there are a few additional steps you still need to take before you'll be happily and gainfully employed.

After receiving a job offer, you must evaluate the opportunity and do everything within your power to ensure that the job you're being offered is something you're qualified for and interested in. You also want to make sure that the job is not being misrepresented in any way by the employer. This will require asking a lot of questions about the responsibilities of the job, what expectations the employer has, and making sure that the commitment involved is one you're prepared to make. Before proceeding any further, you want to receive a detailed job description, in writing, and have an opportunity to speak directly with the people who will be your coworkers and superiors.

Once you've determined that the job being offered is one that you really want, it will be time for you and the employer to agree on a compensation package, which includes your salary, benefits, and perks. This is where your negotiation skills will come in handy, because what the employer will offer you initially isn't necessary the highest salary or the best compensation package they're actually willing to offer…so don't ever accept the first offer!

For every position that a company needs to fill, the people managing the company's finances have calculated a salary range. The employer's initial offer will typically be at the low end of this range. Your job is to prove that you deserve to be paid at the high end of the employer's pre-established range, which can often be between 10 and 30 percent higher than the initial offer. How much flexibility an employer has when negotiating a salary will vary greatly, based on the size of the company;

Bright Idea
The best time to begin discussing salary is after you receive a job offer from an employer. It's best to allow the employer to broach the compensation topic first. Try to refrain from discussing financial issues during your initial job interview, unless you're actually offered a job at the conclusion of the interview.

your skills, experience, and background; and how much the employer wants to recruit you.

As the salary/compensation package negotiation between you and your new (or potential) employer begins, the employer might ask you how much you're looking to earn. You might also be asked how much you've earned at your last job (allowing the employer to calculate their offer by adding between 10 and 30 percent, depending on the circumstances). The very first rule in negotiation is never be the first to bring up a financial figure. Let the employer make an initial offer and then negotiate from that point, but more on the specifics of negotiating a bit later.

Whether you're about to accept a new job, or you're hoping to receive a raise and/or promotion, plan on actively participating in a negotiation in order to ensure that you'll eventually be earning what you want and deserve. Unlike what you may envision, negotiating your salary and overall compensation package will most likely be little more than a face-to-face conversation with the person hiring you. There will be no shouting, no attempts at trickery, and no underhanded dealings.

By the time you reach the salary negotiation phase of the job search process, you have already received a job offer, you know what you want and need, and the employer knows what it wants and needs from you (and what it's willing to pay). Now, all you have to do is agree upon the specific financial figures that make both parties happy. This will mean:

- Explaining your point of view.
- Doing your best to understand the employer's point of view.

- Getting the employer to agree that you have skills that they're interested in (that you will be a tremendous asset to the company). Remember, value is a very subjective thing. What you consider valuable, in terms of your skills, education, accomplishments, or experience, your employer or potential employer might not hold in as high of a regard as you do. Thus, it's important to understand the employer's point of view and tailor your negotiation strategies to address the issues that the employer believes are important.

- Evaluating the offer made by the employer.

- Preparing counter-offers and discussing them.

- Reaching an agreement and accepting the job offer.

Of course, there are a lot of smaller steps that must transpire during the negotiation process. Remember, once you receive a job offer, this demonstrates that the employer wants to hire you. It's your job to determine how valuable you'll be to the employer and to make sure that your compensation package reflects that value.

Why negotiation is important

A small minority of employers will make you a job offer and at the same time offer you a firm salary offer, explaining that it is non-negotiable and that you can accept the job (and the salary offer), or seek employment elsewhere. This scenario if far more common in low paying, entry-level type positions, especially if you'll be working for a large company.

Unless you happen to come across an employment opportunity where the employer makes you a

Unofficially...
Prior to any negotiation, you must prepare for it. This means knowing about the company, the industry, and the job you're applying to fill. It also means having a good understanding of your own capabilities, skills, strengths, and weaknesses. In addition, you need to know how much you're actually worth. You need to know what people with your qualifications are currently being paid by the employer, within your industry as a whole, and within your geographic area. Finally, you need to know what you want and what you'll be willing to settle for. You'll still want to keep an open mind.

firm, non-negotiable offer, what you will receive from the employer in addition to a job offer is an initial offer for your compensation package. At this point you are expected to negotiate, since what the employer offered is typically between five and 20 percent lower than what they're actually willing to pay you.

Since your future raises will probably be based on a percentage of your salary, it's important that you negotiate the best possible starting salary for yourself—one that you deserve. To determine exactly how much higher than the employer's initial offer you might be able to negotiate your actual salary will require research, in advance. Failing to do this research will place you at a major disadvantage when it comes to negotiating your salary and compensation package.

Even if you're a shy person who feels uncomfortable holding a conversation with strangers, you dislike talking about financial issues, and you really hate negotiating, if you want to earn the highest salary possible based on your skills, experience, and education, participating in at least a simple negotiation session with your potential employer is necessary. Likewise, if you want to receive a raise and/or promotion, in order to actually get what you want (and—more importantly—deserve) from the employer, once again you'll need to tap your negotiating skills.

Negotiating strategies

The first step in any negotiation is to do thorough research before the negotiation actually begins. You need to know what you want, determine what the employer will be willing and able to offer, and calculate the salary range that's appropriate for the job you'll be filling. The more you know going into the negotiation—about yourself, the employer, the industry, and the issues that concern the employer—the better off you'll be.

The second step in the negotiating process involves creating a detailed negotiation plan for yourself and writing out an agenda describing the details of what issues have to be worked out (salary, benefits, perks, etc.). Anticipate everything that could possibly happen during the negotiation, and what the employer's needs and desires are. Be prepared to handle any situation.

Next, make sure that the person you plan on negotiating with actually has the power and authority to handle the negotiation and that you're not wasting your time. You can easily determine if you're dealing with the right person by coming right out and asking them if they're in a position to negotiate your salary, or if you're better off dealing with someone else.

There are five basic steps you'll need to incorporate into your negotiation style and strategies:

1. Preparation before the negotiation.

2. Careful and attentive listening; be an active listener, not a passive listener.

3. The ability to keep your emotions and body language under control, using them to your advantage.

4. The ability to communicate clearly, get your points across, and convince the employer to agree with and accept your arguments and terms.

5. Always work toward a win–win situation that both parties (you and the employer) will be happy with.

Unofficially...
Even if you develop air-tight arguments to support your position and you know deep in your heart that everything you're requesting is well deserved, don't expect the employer to simply agree with everything you have to say and immediately give you whatever it is you ask for.

Knowing that you want to accept the job that's being offered to you and that the employer actually wants to hire you is very positive. However, you never want to let on to the employer that you're desperate for the job or just how badly you want to work for them. You want to appear highly motivated, but not overly eager. If the employer perceives that you're desperate or extremely eager to reach an agreement so that you can begin working, they'll probably offer you a lower salary. If the employer believes you're considering multiple job offers, you'll be in a better negotiating position, because if the employer really want to hire you, they'll be more aggressive in their attempts at recruiting you.

Throughout the entire negotiation process as you discuss salary and compensation, the following are some of the basic strategies and skills you'll want to incorporate.

Dress for the job you want, not the one you have

Just as how your "look" played an important role in your job interview(s), it's equally important to look the part when you're involved in a salary negotiation or attempting to negotiate a raise and/or promotion.

Part of your preparation should involve choosing an outfit to wear to your in-person negotiation that makes you look professional and your absolute best. This will help you command respect from the employer. If you're negotiating for a job in middle management, for example, dress like you already have the job.

Keep the lines of communication open

Always participate actively in an open discussion. Ask questions, state your opinions, share your thoughts, and listen carefully to absolutely every-thing that's said. By carefully listening to what the employer has to say, you'll learn about their con-cerns and objections and be better able to address these issues. You'll also be able to gain insight into their position.

Select an environment where you and your employer are on equal ground

In sports, there's a belief that the home team has the advantage. This holds true in the business world as well, especially during a negotiation. When your (potential) boss is sitting behind his or her desk, in their own office, and you're sitting in a smaller chair opposite that desk, the person behind the desk has the psychological advantage. Ideally, you want to be sitting opposite the person you're negotiating with, at eye level with him. Neither person should be looking up or down at the other person.

Never be the first to bring up specific financial figures

During the initial stages of a salary negotiation, let the employer set the stage by making the first offer when it comes to compensation. If the employer isn't willing to come out with a specific offer, ask them to suggest the salary range they're interested or able to pay.

Let the employer offer you at least a ballpark fig-ure first. When you're given this figure, repeat it and then be quiet. If you're given a range, for exam-ple, and the employer says, "We typically offer some-one with your skills and experience between $35,000 and $45,000 per year as a starting salary," respond by saying something like, "So you'd be offering me somewhere between $40,000 and $45,000...." (Repeat the higher end of the range,

Bright Idea
During the nego-tiation, ideally you want to be listening as much as you're speak-ing, which means giving the other party plenty of opportunities to voice their opin-ions and concerns.

and then be quiet for a few moments.) Use the quiet time to evaluate the offer and use your body language to show if the range is acceptable or not. If the employer perceives you're unhappy with the offer, during that period of silence she may provide you with additional information by saying, "$45,000 is as high as we can go" or "Of course, those figures are flexible." Eventually, when you do open you're mouth, what you say should be honest and to the point. Indicate if the range is acceptable, too low, or totally unacceptable.

Always act professionally

While you may feel stressed out, scared, anxious, or angry during the negotiation process, avoid making your emotions obvious, and don't take anything that happens personally. What you are embarking on is a business transaction. It's not a reflection of what the employer thinks of you as a person, or how likable you are.

Maintain eye contact and pay attention to body language

People communicate a lot with their eyes and body language. One of the hardest negotiating skills to learn is being able to maintain eye contact, keeping a tight reign on your emotions, and controlling your body language. At the same time, you want to be studying the body language of the person (or people) you're negotiating with. (It's like using a "poker" face when playing cards with your pals and you're trying to bluff.)

By studying body language, you can often tell if someone is nervous, uptight, being dishonest, or if they're relaxed and confident, simply by how they sit, their facial expressions, and how they handle themselves. Things like excessive blinking, wincing, sighing, squirming, sloughing, or not making direct eye contact are typically negative reactions. If someone is being dishonest, for example, they'll seldom be able to look you in the eye.

Sitting upright (or leaning toward the other person in a friendly way), smiling, and maintaining eye contact tend to be positive reactions when it comes to body language. During any negotiation, you want to maintain a friendly, yet professional attitude and constantly smile.

Demonstrate confidence

When you think about the objectives of the negotiation, you'll realize that your goal is to sell your beliefs to someone else. If you're negotiating a salary, you should know how much you want and deserve to make. Your objective is to make the person you're negotiating with change their line of thinking so that it's more consistent with your line of thinking. The best way to do this is to portray a strong sense of confidence and to truly believe in everything you say.

If in your heart you don't believe you deserve more money or a better benefits package than what's been offered to you, you're not going to be able to convince your employer or potential employer.

Demonstrating confidence means not acting overly nervous, maintaining control over your body language, sitting up straight and leaning slightly toward the person you're negotiating with, as well as making plenty of eye contact and smiling. As you speak, you want to use full sentences, say what you must to get your points across, but not babble. Make a point to demonstrate that you have well-thought-out things to say and a well-defined objective.

Bright Idea
Pay careful attention to the body language of the person you're negotiating with, and also maintain control of your own body language. This includes your facial expressions, and the movement of your eyes, arms, hands, legs and feet, as well as your overall posture.

Through what you say, show that you have done your research and that you're not afraid to listen to and evaluate the other party's point of view or opinions.

If you're totally prepared, open, and honest with the person you're negotiating with, you will automatically develop the internal confidence you'll need to be successful. Confidence (and the ability to overcome nervousness) comes from preparation, practice, and truly believing whatever it is that you're saying.

Watch Out!
Never use a pen and paper to doodle during a negotiation or discussion with your (potential) employer or during an important meeting.

Take notes

Not only will taking notes help you keep track of important points as they're discussed, this action can also be used to create periodic pauses during the negotiation process, giving you short periods of time to consider what's being said or to formulate your next argument. Taking notes allows you to refer to them later and have important facts at your fingertips. As you take notes, only write down important facts and figures. Don't spend too much time taking notes, because it takes away from your opportunity to be making eye contact with the person you're negotiating with.

Tap your creativity

Participating in a successful negotiation means using your creativity. Don't be afraid to make counter-offers or creative suggestions that take a totally different approach to an issue both parties are having trouble agreeing upon.

Sometimes, the person you're negotiating with simply won't agree to give you what you're asking for, no matter how convincing your arguments might be. If you're requesting a five-percent pay raise, for example, this simply might not be in the employer's budget right now. This doesn't mean you should give up, however. Instead, use your negotiating skills to get the employer to agree that you're worth the extra five percent, even if they can't give it to you.

Once the employer agrees to your worth, now you can use your creativity to come up with a way that your employer can compensate you immediately, without having to pay money that's not in their budget. Just one possibility is that you could receive additional vacation days, or a higher commission rate (if part of your salary is commission based). You could also set a time period, say three or six months, at which time the employer agrees to give you the raise you're looking for, assuming your work stays up to par. During any negotiation, be prepared to make counteroffers that may be non-traditional, but that could result in you getting what you want, at least in part.

Before you consider making a counteroffer that's creative or non-traditional, make sure that the reason the employer is using to avoid giving you what you want is legitimate. For example, there really is no money in the budget to offer you a traditional raise at this time. If you know that the funds are available, but the employer simply doesn't want to give you a raise, you may need to do a better job selling yourself and demonstrating your value to the employer. Determine what their reservations are, and address them directly. After you have tried everything you can think of to obtain your initial objective, but the employer isn't agreeing to your requests, that's when to start being creative.

Agree on small things first

Work your way toward the bigger issues or the issues where you and the person you're negotiating with

Bright Idea
When you're suggesting a counteroffer or trying to convey a key concept or idea, avoid confusing the issue by using too much jargon or double speak. Speak honestly and openly, using plain English that the employer will easily understand. Using too much jargon, techno-babble or double speak may cause the person you're negotiating with to believe you're trying to hide something, confuse the situation, or that you're not being totally honest.

have the biggest disagreements. When it comes to making concessions, however, offer up something big first. This demonstrates you're willing to work toward an agreement that's mutually beneficial and that you're willing make compromises. If additional concessions are required on your part, make them smaller ones, and spread them out over the course of the negotiation process. Never cave in and give up multiple things (no matter how big or small) at once.

Always be flexible and open minded

A negotiation involves a lot of give and take. To get what you want, you'll probably have to make some concessions. Keep an open mind during your discussion and avoid agreeing to anything without carefully considering all of the ramifications first. Being flexible does not mean accepting an offer that's less than what you deserve, but it might mean considering alternatives to what you initially asked for.

If necessary, ask for help from the employer during your negotiation. If you reach a stalemate when discussing a specific issue, ask questions to determine what it'll take to get the employer to agree to what you're asking for. Asking something like, "What would be required of me in order to receive the additional $2,000 per year salary that I'm asking for?" The employer may respond by saying you'd have to take on additional responsibilities, work for the company for a period of time first, or obtain additional training before starting your job. You can then agree to these requirements and negotiate further.

As you negotiate a salary and overall compensation package for yourself, you may determine that initially what's being offered to you is less that what you could be earning elsewhere. This being the case, before you walk away from the opportunity, investigate what future potential the opportunity offers. Will you be given the opportunity to advance faster within the company? Is the benefits package far more attractive than what other employers are offering? If the employer is offering you less money up front, but guarantees a pay raise every six months, in two years what will your earning potential be if you accept this job? Will accepting less now lead to greater earning potential and a faster career track in the future? Being a good negotiator, especially when it comes to salary negotiations, means always looking at the big picture and how whatever is being offered to you will impact you in the future.

Don't be afraid of silence

You can use periods of silence to your advantage. If asked a question, always take a few moments to formulate a response in your head before opening your mouth. Likewise, if an employer makes some type of offer or counteroffer, or states an important piece of information, repeat or paraphrase what the other person said, then take a moment to consider it. You can use this time to jot down notes, or just consider what's been said.

Do your research!

When it comes to being a successful negotiator, there are two slogans to remember: "Knowledge Is Power!" and "Information Is Power!" Prior to a negotiation, you want to have both knowledge and information as tools in your arsenal.

As you're preparing for a negotiation session, ask yourself the following questions:

- What do you want to get out of the negotiation? What are your specific goals and objectives?

Unofficially...
One of the keys to being a successful negotiator is to anticipate in advance everything that's going to happen and be prepared to deal with it. Think about all of the possible objections and arguments the employer is going to use to justify paying you a lower salary, and be prepared to convince them that you're worth more. An employer isn't going to offer you a higher salary because he or she likes you. You must convince the employer that you're worth what you're asking for.

Bright Idea
If after partici-
pating in a
lengthy negotia-
tion, you and a
potential (or cur-
rent) employer
simply can't
reach a mutually
beneficial agree-
ment, consider
taking a break so
that both parties
can evaluate
where they
stand. At some
point, it might
become neces-
sary to walk
away from a job
offer if the
employer isn't
offering a salary
or compensation
package that you
find acceptable.
If you choose to
walk away from
the negotiation,
do so in a pro-
fessional and
positive way,
making it clear
that you'd be
willing to
re-open the
negotiation in
the future.

- Do you have a detailed job description for the position you'd be filling? What are the employer's expectations?

- What type of salary does someone with your skills, experience, and education typically receive from the company you're negotiating with? Within your industry? In your geographic area?

- What are the employer's policies regarding salary negotiations?

- What type of constraints will the person you're negotiating with have to deal with?

- How much negotiating authority does the person you're negotiating with actually have?

- Do you know anyone who has dealt directly with the person you'll be negotiating with? What can you learn from that person's experiences?

- How will the person you're negotiating with perceive you? How do you want them (or need them) to perceive you?

- How much money and what benefits do you want and need?

- How much money and what benefits do you deserve?

- What is the lowest salary you'd be willing to accept?

- What are the employer's needs (as they pertain to why you're being hired)?

- What are the employer's concerns (as they pertain to why you're being hired)?

- What are the challenges the employer is currently facing?

- Specifically, how can you use your skills, experience, and education to meet the needs of the employer? What can you offer that you know they want, need and are most interested in? What can you offer that sets you apart from others and that makes you particularly valuable to the employer?

- What can you say and do to alleviate the employer's concerns about hiring you and paying you what you deserve?

- What negative information about you, your skills, work history or your qualifications might the employer bring up during your negotiation as a way to justify offering you less than what you know you deserve? What will you say or do to counteract this negative information, put a positive spin on it, or make the employer believe that what they think is relevant really isn't?

- What are your biggest concerns as they relate to the job you're being offered?

- What information do you need from the employer in order to make an "educated" decision about whether or not to accept an offer?

Formulating answers to these questions will help you go into a negotiating session prepared. Having this information at your disposal, however, doesn't mean you necessarily want to share it with the person you're negotiating with. For example, if you're considering accepting a job offer with a new employer, and all that's left before you get hired is agreeing upon a compensation package, you should never, under any circumstances, mention what your bare minimum salary requirements are.

You need to know this figure for your own purposes (to ensure that if you accept the job, you'll be able to pay your bills and maintain your current lifestyle, if not improve upon it), but this is none of the employer's business. If the potential employer discovers the minimum salary you'd consider working for, that's what will be offered to you.

Likewise, you want to know (or have a general idea) of what the company currently pays people with your skills, education and experience. At the very least, you want to ensure that what you're being offered is similar to what others are being paid. You also want to ensure that the salary you're being offered is in-line with what you could be earning working for other employers in the same industry and/or within the same geographic area (especially if your skills are highly transferable).

For example, if you're a secretary, office manager, or executive assistant, you have highly transferable skills that can be used in multiple industries. You want to ensure that the compensation package being offered to you is at least equal to, if not more attractive than what you could be making working for an employer across town, in another industry. Knowing what you're worth in the job market is important because having this knowledge allows you to better evaluate specific job offers.

When to use these strategies

Use your negotiating strategies when it's appropriate to actually begin salary discussions (after receiving a job offer and once you've received a detailed job description). Unless you know that the employer is interested in hiring you and you know exactly what you'd be hired to do, there's no point in negotiating a compensation package.

Once you have received a job offer (preferably in writing), set up an appointment to discuss the details of the offer, including your salary. This might be after your initial job interview, or it might be after your second or third interview. When you make an appointment to negotiate your salary, make sure you'll be dealing with someone with the appropriate authority.

After you've done your preparation and it's time to actually sit down, face-to-face with an employer or potential employer, be prepared to begin with some light chit-chat. Try to get the employer to make the segue into the formal negotiations. It's common for the employer to attempt to put things in your lap by asking what you're looking for in terms of salary. They might come right out and ask, "So, what are your salary requirements?" or "What is your current compensation?" Since you don't want to be the first to bring up a figure (because you want to the employer to reveal what their willing to pay), respond by asking one of the following questions or using one of these phrases:

■ What do you typically pay someone with my skills, education, and experience to fill the type of job opening you have available?

■ I'm looking to be compensated fairly based on my skills, education, and experience.

■ What do you have budgeted to pay someone to fill the position I am being offered?

Once you get the employer to provide a ballpark figure for what they're willing to offer, the negotiation process can officially begin. You can accept the offer and become employed, you can state the offer is totally unacceptable and walk away, or you can

Bright Idea
Once the employer offers a salary, you should start at the upper-end of the employer's range and go slightly higher than what you actually expect to earn. Thus, if the employer says the range they're willing to offer is between $35,000 and $40,000, the range you should probably negotiate for is between $39,000 and $43,000.

negotiate to improve upon the offer. Now that you have a salary range from the employer, immediately put your focus toward negotiating a salary that's on the high end of the range, and use your negotiating skills to try to push that range a bit higher.

Assuming you plan to do some negotiating (which is usually what's expected of you for most non-entry level positions), now is when you need to start highlighting your skills and providing specific reasons why you're worth more to the employer. As you go through your sales pitch (remember, you're selling yourself, your skills, and your qualifications to your potential employer), get the person you're negotiating with to agree to the things you're explaining to them. For example, if you're describing your skills as a salesperson, ask "Do you agree that these skills will be useful in the job you're offering to me?" or "Can you see how my personal skill set and experience can be a benefit to your company?" Develop agreement between you and the employer. The answer you want from the employer to these questions is "yes."

To be successful, you must always negotiate from a position of strength, using your skills, experience, education and potential as your primary sales tool to establish your value to the employer. Throughout the negotiation process, never convey greed or desperation. When dealing with objections, such as, "The salary you're requesting isn't within our budget," focus on demonstrating your value using cost-benefit examples. By paying you more because you have the special skills, knowledge, and experience the employer needs, they'll receive higher productivity and/or the ability to boost revenues, improve sales, or whatever it is that you do best (that will help the company function better.)

At the start of the negotiating process, instead of asking what you're looking for in terms of salary, the employer might begin by stating, "We're offering $(insert amount) for this position. Does that seem reasonable to you?" You might receive a specific figure or a range from the employer as part of this statement. If you're given a specific figure, you'll need to mention that they're in the right ballpark, however, because of your specific experience, skills, etc., you're worth slightly more, and then provide specific example to help justify your response. If you're provided with a range, and the higher part of that range is somewhat acceptable, you can begin negotiating accordingly in an attempt to boost that range a bit higher, using your unique abilities, skill set, experience, etc. as justification for being paid more.

Bright Idea
Your actual salary negotiation is when you want to use most, if not all, of the negotiation tactics described earlier in this chapter.

Negotiating mistakes to avoid

There's no such thing as a typical negotiation session, because in addition to dealing with facts and figures, you're dealing with human beings that have unique personalities and emotions. Also, everyone faces a different set of circumstances that come into play. How you negotiate with your employer (or potential employer) will have a huge impact on your working relationship with that employer once you're hired, which is why it's important to keep things friendly and non-confrontational.

The following are some negotiating tactics that are best avoided:

Watch Out!
The primary purpose of a negotiation is to create a win–win situation between you and the person you're negotiating with. This can't be done if you develop a rivalry, if either party becomes overly emotional, or if either party isn't willing to make concessions and keep an open mind.

- Never give an ultimatum, such as "take it or leave it" or "give me the raise I want or I quit." Playing hardball creates a very tense situation that can easily be avoided. This approach will seldom lead to both parties getting what they want out of the negotiation.

▪ If for some reason the person you're negotiating with becomes overly emotional, don't mimic their behavior. For example, if the other party raises their voice or somehow acts unprofessional, don't drop down to their level. Some people try to use a bullying negotiating tactic. Determine if how the person is acting is part of their personal (and pre-determined) negotiating tactic or strategy, or if they've actually lost control of their emotions, in which case you might consider taking a break.

Unofficially...
If you're being hired by a government agency, or are entering an entry-level or unionized position, your negotiation opportunities in regards to salary will be limited. Instead of attempting to negotiate a higher salary, focus on expanding the job description to include additional responsibilities. Position your qualifications so that they apply to a higher level job. You may not receive this job (or the greater responsibility) right away, but your advancement opportunities could come a lot sooner, if you start positioning yourself for that job now.

▪ There are some phrases that you never want to use during your negotiation. These include: "Let me be honest with you" and "Trust me." When someone uses one of these phrases, it's almost always assumed that they're either lying now, or what they've been saying up until now is a lie.

▪ Keep in mind, a negotiation is a business transaction. Never start using personal attacks, insults, or any type of derogatory comments in an effort to get what you want or win an argument. This is particularly inappropriate if you're negotiating with someone who is or will be your superior.

▪ Several times in this chapter the importance of doing research, prior to the negotiation, has been brought up. Failing to do this research is one of the worst mistakes you can make.

Listen carefully during a negotiation

Listening is as important as speaking during any negotiation. By being an active listener, you will learn what the person you're negotiating with is thinking and be able to immediately address their concerns, making it easier for them to accept whatever it is you're negotiating for.

Being an active listener means paying careful attention to what's said, reading between the lines for information that's being conveyed but not spoken out loud, and taking the necessary time to consider what the other person is actually saying. Make the other person truly believe that what they have to say is important to you, that their ideas are of interest to you, and that it's a priority of yours that their concerns are addressed.

By listening and responding appropriately, you will make it clear that you're aware of and understand the importance of the other person's opinions and position, and that you're not simply looking out for yourself. By demonstrating that your goal is to create a win–win situation, not just a situation in which you get what you want (so that you win), you'll find that the other party will be far more interested in working with you. This will make it easier to ultimately get what you want and deserve.

To demonstrate that you're an active listener, when the other person is speaking, look directly at them, and when appropriate rehash what they tell you by paraphrasing or restating their key points. When the other party brings up a concern, for example, restate that concern, validate it by saying that you understand where they're coming from, and then address it. In doing this, bring up your point of view and propose possible solutions that address their concern(s).

Part of being an active listener means keeping control of your body language. If for example,

Unofficially...
During a typical negotiation, you should be actively listening about 50 percent of the time and speaking 50 percent of the time.

you're sitting with your arms crossed or not making eye contact, that's negative body language. When someone else is speaking, you want your body language to demonstrate that you're paying attention and that you're open to listening to their point of view. Even if you disagree with everything that's being said, don't cut the other person off in mid-sentence, or roll your eyes or in a way that imply what they're saying has little or no merit.

Always think about an offer before accepting it

Unfortunately, some employers aren't willing to negotiate when it comes to salary and/or benefits. Others will negotiate, but will only make small concessions, while others are totally open to compensating their employees with a salary and benefits package that's customized to address each employee's value to the employer.

Through your research and by dealing with an employer (or potential employer) directly, you'll quickly be able to determine which of the three categories of employers you're dealing with. Once you know this, you'll be in a better position to evaluate whatever offers are made to you.

Even after a heavy-duty negotiation session in which the employer basically offers you everything you asked for, never immediately accept an offer that's made to you. Ask that the offer be put in writing, and then take some time, preferably at least 24 hours, to consider the offer and evaluate it carefully. Never agree to anything on the spot, even if the employer pushes you for an immediate decision. Agree to get back to them by the end of that business day, the following day, or by the end of the week.

Unofficially...
Be confident, not arrogant! There's a big difference between having demonstrated confidence, and being arrogant or obnoxious. How people perceive you, especially the people you'll be negotiating with, will have a major impact in how hard they're willing to work with you to create that win–win situation that's so important in any negotiation.

The next section of this chapter explores how to evaluate a job offer and determine whether or not it's in your best interest to accept the offer. If you choose not to accept an offer, take the following steps after receiving and evaluating it:

1. Determine exactly why you have chosen not to accept the offer.

2. Outline your reasons providing details and spelling out your concerns and/or objections. Be open and honest. If you're not happy with the salary, benefits, job responsibilities, or the employer's expectations, bring up these issues.

3. Listen carefully to how the employer responds to your rejection of the offer. If they make it clear that the offer was final and you should take it or leave it, then unless you're willing to accept the offer, you should walk away. If the employer is, however, willing to address your concerns, listen carefully to their responses and try to develop an understanding for their point of view.

4. Make a counteroffer that takes into account what you need to make the deal work, and that also addresses the point of view of the employer.

5. Make it clear that you're open to continuing to negotiate or to consider a counteroffer from the employer.

6. Give the employer time to consider your counteroffer, consider the counteroffer made by the employer, or choose to walk away from the deal if it looks like no concessions will be made by you or the employer.

When to say "yes" to an offer

One of the final stages of the job search process is actually choosing which job you'll accept, especially if you receive multiple offers from different employers. To ensure that you choose the best job for you, ask yourself if the job will provide:

- Fair financial compensation and benefits.

- A work environment in which you can prosper.

- A chance to move your career forward (with future upward mobility and career advancement potential). Make sure it's not a dead-end job.

- An opportunity to work with people you will relate to and admire.

- A work experience that interests you and that you'll enjoy.

- A chance to learn new skills, expand upon your personal skill set, and make you a more marketable and valuable employee.

Ideally, you want a job that will allow you to exploit your talents and allow you to perform work you really enjoy doing, while minimizing the things you dislike or aren't as skilled in. Likewise, you want to ensure that you'll be excited to wake up every morning to go to work and that your job won't become a frustrating and depressing aspect of your life.

After receiving a firm job offer, evaluate it by asking yourself the following questions:

1. What type of lifestyle would you like for yourself five or ten years down the road? Will the job you're about to accept help you achieve that lifestyle?

2. What are the five qualities about yourself that you are the most proud of? Can these qualities be incorporated into your work?

Watch Out!
It's vitally important that you have a good understanding of what you can expect from the employer in the future. The worst mistake you can make is accepting a dead-end job with an employer that won't promote you or transfer you to a position that offers more interesting work.

3. What are your five work-related accomplishments that you're most proud of? Will you be able to achieve similar or greater accomplishments if you accept the job being offered to you?

4. What are your five most useful work-related skills or talents? Will you be able to use these skills and talents in your new job?

5. What skills do you lack or have difficulty performing? Will the job you're about to accept offer training or tuition reimbursement to help you develop your skills?

6. What are your five favorite and least favorite work-related tasks? How much of your job involves dealing with these tasks?

7. What would be the ideal work environment for you? (A small office environment, a large and crowded office, a common work area, a private office, etc.) Will you be able to reach your maximum potential working in the environment you'll be placed in if you accept the job offer you're considering?

8. What did you like and hate the most about your last job? Will the new job incorporate the elements you liked most about your past work experiences, but allow you to avoid the situations or circumstances that made you dislike your past job(s)?

9. What kind of coworkers and boss will you have in this new job? Are these the type of people you believe you'd work well with?

10. Describe the ideal work schedule for yourself. How does the work schedule outlined this new job description compare to what you consider

Watch Out!
As you answer these questions, do so based on facts. If you're desperate to land a job, don't let your desperation cloud your judgment, and don't allow friends or relatives to push you into an employment situation you know you won't be happy with.

ideal? Do the hours outlined in the job description mesh with what the employer's expectations appear to be?

11. In terms of financial compensation and benefits, what do you absolutely require to maintain your current lifestyle and improve upon it?

12. What hobbies, interests, or special skills do you have that could be incorporated into your job to make it more enjoyable? Does the job offer you're evaluating provide the opportunity to incorporate your hobbies, interests, and special skills?

13. If you could write a job description for your ultimate dream job, what would it be? How does this job description compare to the one provided by the potential employer? If there are major differences in what you'd consider to be your dream job and the job offer you're considering, can you live with and accept these differences on a long-term basis?

By answering these questions, you should be able to learn about yourself and determine the type of work-related activities and environment you're best suited to. Knowing what to expect from an employer once you accept an offer means doing plenty of research about the company and the industry you'll be working in, asking as many questions as you can think of during your job interview(s) and salary negotiation sessions, and getting introduced to as many of your potential coworkers as possible prior to accepting the job.

If you have trouble determining your likes and dislikes and pinpointing your work-related skills, consider meeting with a career counselor who can assist you in your career planning and help you pin-point suitable job opportunities.

The people who are the happiest in their careers are the ones who absolutely love what they're doing. While on the job, they're doing what they're good at and what they enjoy, plus they're constantly being challenged and improving themselves. If you can honestly say that the job you're about to accept offers these and other benefits, then chances are you've found a job in which you'll prosper.

Never settle for a job due to desperation. If you need income during your job search, consider accepting a temp position so you can take whatever time is necessary to pursue the right permanent career opportunity. Finding the right opportunity for you might take a bit of extra work on your part, and it might take some time. Very seldom are employees (especially new employees) able to alter the way a company does business or step in and change the work environment. Accepting a job offer with the hope of doing this will most often lead to frustration and disappointment.

Only accept a job offer if you fully understand the job's requirements and the employer's expecta-tions, if you're willing to meet these requirements and expectations, if you believe the job will offer you long-term career advancement opportunities, and if you're happy with the compensation package being offered to you. Most importantly, choose to accept the offer if the job is one you believe you'll be happy and prosper in.

Dealing with the tension

People feel uncomfortable participating in a nego-tiation session for a variety of reasons. In order to

Watch Out!
Never simply accept a job opportunity on faith, with the hope that you'll be able to turn it into something you'll enjoy and prosper in.

Bright Idea
Practice the individual skills and tactics described in this chapter, but also practice by participating in mock negotiating sessions with a friend, family member, or career counselor who has some experience with salary negotiation and can offer you constructive criticism. Knowing what you need to do is just part of the equation. Practicing and perfecting your negotiating skills is critical.

perform at your absolute best, you must determine for yourself where your weaknesses are. Are you afraid to confront others, particularly strangers or authority figures? Do you have trouble controlling your emotions and/or body language during stressful situations? Do you have trouble thinking on your feet or making decisions under pressure? Are you afraid of rejection? Do you have trouble communicating verbally?

It's perfectly normal to enter into a negotiation session feeling a bit nervous. Within a few minutes, for most people, that nervousness will simply vanish. In order to help alleviate the stress and tension that typically goes hand-in-hand with a negotiation, go into the meeting knowing that you're totally prepared. You also want to truly believe that you're the best person that the employer could possibly hire for the job and that you're worth every penny that you'll be asking to get paid. Being prepared, knowing you're worth what you're asking for, and dressing to look your best (in formal business attire, of course) will give you a tremendous confidence boost.

Put everything in writing

Let's face it, the business world is cutthroat, competitive, often bureaucratic and usually very difficult to understand. As an employee in today's business environment, you always need to be looking out for your own best interests and making sure nobody is trying to stab you in the back. Especially when a potential employee and an employer are discussing job opportunities and compensation packages, there is always too much room for misunderstandings and miscommunication. Knowing this, the best way to protect yourself is to put everything in writing and have both parties (you and the employer) agree to everything, from the definition of terms, to the job description, and the details of a compensation package.

As you engage in job search process, receive a job offer, and negotiate a compensation package, protect yourself by getting the following things in writing (and, if applicable, signed by the person hiring you or an executive within the company):

Your Resumé and Cover Letter   These documents are provided by you and given to the employer. They outline your skills, education, work experience, and anything else that makes you a potentially valuable asset to a company. The employer should be able to assume that everything listed in your resumé and cover letter is 100-percent truthful.

A Detailed Job Description   During your first job interview, it's okay to discuss the details of a job opening verbally. However, once it's made clear that you're a serious candidate for the job, and you're invited back for a second job interview or you're actually offered a job, you want to obtain a detailed job description in writing. The job description should outline:

- Your exact job title
- Your specific responsibilities
- The work hours/schedule (including overtime requirements)
- Who you'll be answering to
- How your position fits into the company's hierarchy

Bright Idea
To repeat: Never
accept a verbal
job offer.

- The employer's expectations of you if you accept the job

- What type of career advancement opportunities will be made available to you

- What type of training will be offered

- How you'll be evaluated as an employee

- Any other details that you need to know about the job prior to accepting an offer

The Job Offer   After you have submitted your resume and cover letter, completed an employment application (if applicable), and have gone through the job interview process, if the employer chooses to hire you, you will receive a job offer. This offer may be given to you verbally at the conclusion of a job interview or on the telephone after the job interview process is complete. *Never accept a verbal job offer!* If the job offer is reasonable, explain that you're very interested and would like to receive the offer in writing so that you can evaluate it properly. Make sure that this offer describes the details of the job (re-hashes the job description), includes details about your compensation package, and defines all terms so that there's no misunderstandings. For example, if the job description states that reasonable overtime work is expected of all employees, make sure that employer defines what "reasonable" means and lists how you'll be compensated for that additional work.

Acceptance Letter   Upon receiving a written job offer that you're willing to accept (one that describes the compensation package you'll receive), verbally accept the offer in-person or by telephone, and then follow up with a written acceptance letter. This letter (which must be signed and dated) should be written in a formal business letter style and should:

- State that you are accepting the offer (mention the exact job title as well as the division or branch of the company you'll be working for).

- Thank the person who hired you for their time and consideration.

- Briefly outline the key points of the job offer and/or the terms of employment.

- Enthusiastically state how excited you are about accepting the job and having an opportunity to work for the employer.

- Mention the starting date that you have agreed upon in advance.

Employment Contract For entry-level or even middle-management positions, it's not typical for you to have a formal employment contract, unless you're provided one by the employer (in which case you should have a lawyer evaluate it before signing it). Employment contracts are more important for people accepting executive-level positions or jobs that involve high salaries. An employment contract is a formal legal document that goes into far more detail than a written job offer and job acceptance letter, and is created to protect both parties (the employer and the employee). When an employment contract is created, lawyers representing both parties are typically involved.

Bright Idea
After your in-person job interviews, you should have followed them up with personalized "thank-you" notes, addressed to the person or people you met with. The job acceptance letter should once again thank the person hiring you for their interest and help.

It's become common practice for employers to require new employees to sign non-compete, non-disclosure and/or confidentiality agreements upon being hired. These are legal documents that are somewhat standard in many industries and usually protect the employer after an employee leaves their job.

Both non-disclosure and confidentiality agreements help to ensure that an employee or former employee won't divulge trade secrets, formulas, client lists, process secrets, business approaches, or product knowledge that could benefit the employer's competition. A non-compete agreement is most often used to keep an employee from leaving their position to work for an employer's competitor for a pre-defined period of time.

When signing any type of legal document related to employment, make sure that the document is reasonable on its face in terms of what it restricts. If an employee is about to sign a non-compete agreement, the period of time they are restricted from working in a similar job at a competing company must be reasonable for it to be enforced by the courts. Look at time limits, geographical restrictions, and what type of work is being restricted as you evaluate the reasonableness of the document. The term "reasonable" should be clearly defined in the document.

Employment contracts are also legal documents, but they are designed to protect both the employer and employee. These documents go well beyond post-employment restrictions. Employment contracts are usually used when someone is being hired for a middle management or executive level position. They govern the employment relationship and will outline what is expected of both the employee and employer.

Employment contracts will define a number of issues, such as compensation in all of its forms, job responsibilities, expectations of the employer, and the employee's severance package. There is always a pre-defined time period during which the employment contract will be in effect. Often, an employment contract will also outline special arrangements made between the employee and employer. There's a comfort in having an employment contract, because the work relationship is well defined and laid out.

One document that is not legally binding is a written or verbal job offer from an employer. A job-offer letter is a description of what the employer chooses to describe as the employment arrangement. These letters are written in loose terms and are far more general than an employment contract.

As an employee, any time you're asked to sign a legal document, it's vital that you have a good understanding of what the document entails. The moment you feel uncomfortable with a document because you don't understand it, you should seek the advice of an attorney. Never sign anything that you don't understand or that you haven't read. Always exercise caution when signing a legal document, because you could be creating a legal obligation that you'll be required to adhere to and that you may ultimately be disappointed with if you didn't understand what you were signing. In addition, if the document is created by the employer (or the employer's legal advisors), you can bet that it protects the employer, but it should also protect you as the employee.

Unofficially...
An employment contract should describe, in writing, the term (length) of employment; duties of the job; compensation; benefits; severance; perks; include a non-compete and/or non-disclosure clause; and spell out everything relating to the relationship between the employee and the employer. For example, if moving expenses are being covered by the employer, this should be listed in the contract as a benefit or perk, as should details related to a sign-on bonus, etc. If an arbitration clause is included in the contract, it should be consistent with what the American Arbitration Association recommends.

Unofficially...
The American Arbitration Association's web site (http://www.adr.org) offers useful information of interest to people dealing with contract negotiations and or who have an arbitration clause in their contract. The American Arbitration Association (AAA) is available to resolve a wide range of disputes through mediation, arbitration, elections, and other out-of-court settlement procedures. The 70-year history, mission and not-for-profit status of the AAA are unique within the ADR industry.

The best way to locate a qualified attorney is to solicit a referral from a friend, relative, or coworker who has used the services of an attorney. You can also contact the Bar Association in your state and request a free referral.

Upon accepting virtually any type of new job, expect that you'll be required to sign various legal documents. Sign these documents only after you read them carefully and have a complete understanding of what they say.

To cut down legal costs and to prevent frivolous lawsuits, many employment contracts and other legal documents related to employment issues contain arbitration clauses. This means that if a disagreement occurs between the two parties, instead of going to court, an arbitrator will be used. In some cases, arbitration is legally binding, while in other cases, arbitration that doesn't settle a matter can be appealed in a traditional courtroom. Before signing any legal document with an arbitration clause, make sure you understand what it means. Likewise, any legal wording that discusses how disagreements or legal issues will be dealt with should be examined carefully. Be careful about agreeing to a city or state where litigation will take place, or agreeing to cover the legal expenses of the other party if you lose the court case.

Giving notice to a current employer

There are countless reasons why someone leaves one job to pursue a career with another company, but to maintain a good reputation within an industry, it's important to act professionally when you actually quit a job. Getting into a fight with your boss, shouting, "I quit!" and then stomping out of the building forever is never the best way to handle things.

If you get into a major disagreement with your employer, never make a decision to quit impulsively. Spend a few days thinking about your decision, and if you decide it's time to move on, start looking for a new job before actually tendering your resignation with your current employer. As a general rule, even if you're not getting along with your boss or coworkers, it's never a good idea to quit your current job until you'll lined up a new one.

Once you've actually landed that new job, be prepared to give your current employer the traditional two weeks' notice. Some people give notice and then use their accumulated vacation or sick days to avoid showing up for work. This is not appropriate behavior. Even if your new employer wants you to start work immediately, they will almost always understand that as a matter of loyalty and professional courtesy, it is necessary for you to stay with your current employer for those two weeks after giving your notice.

During those last two weeks on the job, offer to do whatever you can to maintain a positive relationship with your coworkers and boss, such as offering to train your replacement. Make your exit from the company as smooth as possible. Purposely causing problems, stealing from the employer, or sabotaging business deals are all actions that are unethical and totally inappropriate. Some companies will request your immediate departure when you quit, and will cut off your computer access and escort you out of the building, especially if you're leaving on a negative note. Prior to quitting, try to determine how past coworkers were treated, so you'll know what to expect.

Watch Out!
Even if you think your boss is a incompetent jerk, in the heat of anger, never let your negative feelings cause you to act unprofessionally.

"
It's very impor-
tant to never
burn bridges.
Your actions with
your employers
will follow you
throughout your
career, especially
if you stay within
one city and
keep working in
a specific indus-
try. You'll find
that most people
within an indus-
try know each
other, and your
reputation will
follow you from
job to job.
—Lisa Elias,
branch opera-
tions manager,
Framingham,
Mass. office of
Kelly Services

"

As you actually leave the company for the last time, take with you only your personal belongings and nothing that is considered the company's property. Make a point to return, directly to your boss, your office keys and any company-owned equipment that was in your possession. If possible, for your protection, obtain a written memo stating that everything was returned promptly and in working order.

If you're planning on taking a copy of your personal client list, for example, make sure you have legal rights to take this information. All companies have different restrictions that their employees are legally bound to adhere to through non-compete agreements and employee contracts.

Down the road, you might need to use your current employer as a reference. Simply walking off the job and leaving them in a bind is not the best way to maintain positive relationships.

When you're actually ready to quit your current job, arrange a private meeting with your boss or with the appropriate person within the company, and offer your resignation in-person, following it up in writing with a friendly and professional letter. Whether you're leaving your full-time job or a temporary employment position, never simply walk off the job, and always try to give your current employer proper notice.

Starting your new job

Once you've accepted a new job, you have already come a very long way in the job search process. Now it's time to settle down into your new job. As your first day of work approaches, choose an outfit that fits well within the company's dress code and the corporate culture of the employer, but also that's a bit formal and that makes you look professional. Since you'll be meeting many of your coworkers and superiors for the first time, you want to make the best possible first impression, and how you look will have a major impact in how other people formulate their initial impression of you.

Prior to your first day of work, practice making the commute to work, determine the best route to take, analyze traffic patterns so you know how much time you'll need for your morning commute, and determine exactly where you'll park. Also, if you're working for a large company, determine in advance where your office, cubicle, or workspace will be (in which building and on what floor), and ask where you should report to on your first day.

Either before you start working, or during your first few days on the job, you'll have to deal with the details associated with your benefits package, such as making decisions about your health insurance, life insurance, stock option plan, retirement plan, etc. The decisions you make regarding these benefits and perks could be worth up to 30 or 40 percent of your overall salary, so it's important that you understand what you're being offered. Chapter 13 goes into far greater detail about evaluating and selecting benefits and perks as part of your compensation package.

The morning you're supposed to start work, make a point to arrive at least 15 minutes early, and report directly to whomever you've been assigned to work with or work for. Be prepared to be introduced to a lot of different people throughout the first few days on the job. While you're not expected to remember everyone's name immediately, you'll want to make a point of getting to know as many

Bright Idea
If you've been given a list if people who you'll be working with in advance, take time to memorize their names, as well as their job titles or functions within the organization.

Bright Idea
Be sure to bring a pad and pen to work with you so that you can take plenty of notes throughout your first few days on the job. Also, always have your personal planner/ calendar handy so that you can jot down appointments and write down your training schedule, etc.

Unofficially...
If you want to quickly fit in with your coworkers and be accepted by them, you're going to have to work at it initially. Make a point of being friendly and of conversing with people. It will take an active effort on your part to be social as you work toward fitting in.

people as you can as quickly as possible, especially your immediate superiors and the people you'll be directly working with on a daily basis.

During your first few days on the job, you may be put through formal training, or you might be assigned to a coworker or supervisor who will be responsible for showing you the ropes. Throughout this training period, be sure to ask lots of questions (but don't be annoying). Watch other people carefully to see how things are done, and use this time to learn as much as possible about your job and your responsibilities. It's also a good idea to start trying to figure out the office politics within your company.

As a new employee, you will be considered "the new person" by your coworkers, and might receive some resentment initially. Many people are afraid of changes or anything that's new, and become very defensive when forced to work with someone new. Any negative vibes you receive from your new coworkers are not a reflection on you personally, but are their response to a potential threat. Make a point to be friendly and considerate to everyone you meet, and show respect to your coworkers. Don't be afraid to solicit advice or information from your coworkers as a way of demonstrating that you respect their knowledge and opinions.

During breaks, if people congregate in an employee lounge or go out to lunch together, for example, make a point to mingle and strike up conversations. As soon as people get to know you and see you prove yourself on the job, you'll be accepted.

By the end of your first week or two on the job, chances are you'll feel totally comfortable in your new work environment and you'll settle into a daily routine. This is the time to start proving yourself to your superiors and start positioning yourself for a promotion or raise, by consistently working hard, meeting employer expectations, and making sure that your work is done correctly and completed in a timely manner.

Dealing with a difficult boss

Some people love 'em, some don't mind dealing with them, but many employees simply don't get along with their boss, manager or supervisor. A boss can be a dictator, hypocrite, con artist, office politician, bully, blamer, manipulator, know-it-all, a total wimp, or if you're lucky, a mentor, friend, and caring supervisor.

If you're in a situation where you simply don't see eye-to-eye with your boss, you have several options. You can do nothing, live with the situation, hope that it doesn't get worse, and not let your relationship with your boss impact you emotionally. Or you can quit your job and seek employment elsewhere. Either of these might appear to be the easiest solution to your problem, but neither will most likely lead to long-term career fulfillment.

Another option is to carefully evaluate your situation and choose to alter your attitude and behavior, and to do whatever it takes to develop a relationship with your boss that evolves around mutual respect. Developing this type of professional relationship doesn't mean you'll become best friends with your boss, but it does mean that you should find a way to work together so that you're both happy and productive.

Dealing with a difficult boss who acts unprofessionally or childishly and attacks or criticizes you in front of your peers can be extremely difficult. The worst mistake you can make in this situation is to allow yourself to drop to their level. This will only intensify the situation, creating a more stressful work environment. Developing a relationship with a boss that's based upon mutual respect is critical, which means it'll probably be necessary to confront your boss.

As you prepare to confront your boss, ask yourself if you're being singled out by his or her unprofessional behavior, or if your boss treats everyone poorly. Prior to an actual confrontation, try to determine the core reasons for your boss' behavior. Do your intelligence, capabilities and potential threaten him or her? Is your boss bullying you because he's filled with self-doubt and insecurity? Does your boss simply lack good management or communication skills? Is your boss such a control freak that anything anyone else does is wrong?

Bright Idea
Without being overly aggressive or rude, make it clear that you expect respect from your superior.

Once you understand the true reasons for your boss' actions and behavior, you'll be in a much better position to deal with it in a highly professional manner. If your boss is a bully, he or she expects subordinates to be spineless followers. Simply by standing up for yourself, making direct eye contact with your boss and standing or sitting up straight when in their presence, you will be in a much better position to earn their respect.

Bosses who are control freaks often lack the ability to trust others. Thus, to make your situation more bearable, your goal should be to build trust between yourself and your boss. This will require exceeding their expectations and performing with a high level of efficiency over time. Demonstrate that you respect your boss' opinion and knowledge, and take your time trying to build your own autonomy in the workplace.

One of the worst situations is when a boss is untrustworthy or unethical in the way they perform their job. In this case, watch your back carefully. Be sure that you document all of your work and accomplishments. When dealing directly with your boss, make sure that other people are present, and never agree to do anything that might jeopardize your reputation or job. If your boss' actions are illegal or highly unethical, it might be necessary to take drastic measures in order to protect yourself and your career.

When dealing with a difficult boss, never show fear. Use direct eye contact and confident body language to convey your professional attitude. Don't assume you can work hard to change someone else, because you can't. You'll wind up wasting your time and energy. If you choose to accept the situation, set boundaries and then make it clear if your boss goes beyond those boundaries. If a particular situation becomes too intense, take a break, walk away, and let yourself cool down. Often, if you can determine why your boss is acting the way he or she is, you'll be able to find easy ways to lighten the situation.

Quitting or getting transferred is always an option, but if you're willing to suggest some compromises, chances are you'll be able to find a way to work together. All it takes is the guts to face your boss and confront him or her in a friendly and professional manner. Prior to confronting your boss, make sure that your problems aren't a result of your own attitude or behavior.

Executives don't have to be smart from an emotional standpoint to succeed in the business world, thus many bosses don't have the emotional

Watch Out!
Sometimes it'll become necessary to confront your boss and explain how you feel about a situation. Never confront your boss in public or let your emotions get in the way of explaining how you feel in a professional manner.

intelligence to manage their employees properly. When applying for a job, the only way to avoid being hired by a bad boss is to speak with other people already working for that person and learn as much as possible about the boss before accepting the job.

Most people will learn everything there is to learn about a specific job after two years. Thus, if a bad situation between yourself and a boss doesn't improve and your potential career advancement with your currently employer looks grim after two years, despite your best efforts, it might be time to seek other employment opportunities.

Mustering enough courage and using tact when approaching your boss with a problem are the two ingredients that'll help lead to a positive solution. If you're a good worker and you have skills and capabilities that your employer needs, you'll have more leverage than you think when it comes to dealing with a difficult or uncomfortable situation that involves your boss.

Having an occasional disagreement with a superior is normal, but if your life is being ruined by the actions of a mean or difficult boss, it's up to you to take action and find a solution that you can be happy with.

Additional resources to help you polish your negotiation skills

The Negotiation Skills Company (978-927- 6775/ http://www.negotiationskills.com) has been established with the goal of helping people enhance their negotiation skills in order to increase their proficiency, efficiency, and satisfaction with the process of reaching agreements. The company provides consulting and in-house training for corporate clients worldwide. Their clients have come from more than 25 countries and a wide variety of business sectors ranging from healthcare and banking to utilities and defense manufacturing. A free subscription to an electronic newsletter that covers all aspects of negotiating is available from the company's web site.

The Negotiation Institute (212-715-0176/ http://www.negotiation.com) is another consulting company that offers training in negotiation skills through seminars and one-on-one instruction. According to the company, some of the topics covered in their seminars include: "how to prepare for any negotiation; how to isolate the facts; how to discover the vital common ground; how to ask questions that illuminate; how to interpret exactly what is being said—and not said; and how to read all the nonverbal conversation, the body language and the actions, of the other side."

In addition to the dozens of consulting and training companies you'll find by checking any telephone book or surfing the Internet, simply by visiting a major bookstore you'll find many books that focus specifically on developing and enhancing your negotiating skills. The National Association of Entrepreneurs (http://www.nae.org/illneg.htm) has developed a suggested reading list for anyone interested in improving their negotiating skills. Information about books on this list can be obtained from the organization's web site.

Throughout this book, you've been learning about all of the steps necessary to find job opportunities, apply for, and ultimately land the best jobs, and how to ensure that you'll be earning what you truly deserve. This book also explores how to seek

Timesaver
If you don't have time in your hectic schedule to visit a local bookstore, use the web to access Amazon.com (http://www. amazon.com) or Barnes & Noble online (http://www. barnesandnoble. com). Both of these services allow you to enter a keyword, such as "negotiating" or "salary negotiating" and then search through thousands of books in order to find appropriate titles. Books can then be ordered securely online and shipped directly to you, usually within 24 hours.

Unofficially...
Whether you're evaluating new job offers, seeking a promotion, or hoping to earn a raise, in order to get what you truly deserve (based on your qualifications, skills, experience, and education), it'll be necessary to negotiate with your employer or potential employer.

out and earn a raise and/or promotion, and discusses the opportunities available to you to reach higher levels of earning potential by becoming self-employed.

While few people enjoy the prospect of having to openly discuss financial issues and take part in an active negotiation, this is part of the job search process (or the career advancement process) that virtually everyone has to deal with. Knowing how to approach a negotiation and be successful at it will make the difference between earning the minimum salary that an employer is able to pay and earning the maximum salary an employer is willing to pay to employ someone with your qualifications, skills, experience, and education.

After all, if an employer has the flexibility to pay someone between $35,000 and $40,000 to fill a specific job, it's in the employer's best interest to hire you at $35,000. It's in your best interest, however, to convince the employer that you are worth $40,000 (or more) and that you deserve to be paid at the higher end of their pre-determined salary range.

Later, in Chapters 12 and 13, forms of monetary compensation, benefits, and perks will be discussed in detail, which will help you to better formulate the compensation package you want and evaluate the overall compensation package that's being offered to you.

Just the facts

- The best time to begin discussing salary is after you receive a job offer from an employer. It's best to allow the employer to broach the compensation topic first. Try to refrain from discussing financial issues during your initial job interview (unless you're actually offered a job at the conclusion of the interview).

- Prior to starting any negotiation, you absolutely must prepare to ensure that you have the ammunition you'll need to win the employer over. This means knowing about the company, the industry, and the job you're applying to fill. It also means having a good understanding of your own capabilities, skills, strengths, and weaknesses. In addition, you need to know how much you're actually worth (not what you think you're worth or how much you want to earn, but what you're actually worth as an employee.) You need to know what people with your skills and experience are currently being paid by the employer you're negotiating with, within your industry as a whole, and within your geographic area. Finally, you need to go into an a negotiation session with a good understanding of what you're hoping to get out of it, and what you'll be willing to settle for. Knowing this, you'll still want to keep a totally open mind throughout the negotiation process.

- Your negotiating style should include the following steps: preparation before the negotiation; being a careful and attentive listener; keeping control of your emotions and body language; using body language to your advantage; and using your ability to communicate clearly to get your points across and convince the employer to agree with and accept your arguments and terms. Your goal is to work toward a win–win situation that both parties (you and the employer) will be happy with.

- Anticipate in advance everything that's going to happen and be prepared to deal with it. Think about all of the possible objections and arguments the employer is going to use to justify paying you a lower salary than what you're looking for, and be prepared to convince them that you're worth more.

- While knowing what skills you'll need and doing the proper preparation is a huge part of being a successful negotiator, absolutely nothing replaces the need to practice negotiating skills in order to become improve them. Participate in mock negotiations with a career counselor, a friend, or a relative. Find someone who will be able to offer you constructive advice and criticism and also help you prepare for anything that might happen during a negotiation.

GET THE SCOOP ON...
Defining your needs and wants when it
comes to a compensation package ▪ The needs
and wants of your employer ▪ How far you
should go to get what you want ▪ When it's
appropriate to negotiate and when it's time
to walk away ▪ The right attitude in a salary
negotiation

Getting What You Want

W hen it comes to landing a new job and negotiating a compensation package for yourself, it's important to define what you want, what you need, and more importantly, what you deserve. You also must determine what your employer needs and wants, and then figure out a way to make everyone's wants, needs, and desires mesh so that you wind up happily employed (earning what you deserve), and your employer gets the benefits of having you as a valued employee.

Assuming you've done your homework and have realistic expectations regarding your earning potential, and your employer has done the same and is willing to offer a compensation package that's in line with industry standards for someone with your skills, experience, and education, your salary negotiation should be a fairly straightforward process, since both parties will be working within basically the same financial parameters.

Having unrealistic expectations, overvaluing yourself, or not having a good understanding of your employer's needs and wants virtually guarantees that your negotiations will fail or that you'll wind up with an unsatisfactory compensation package. Of course, there's absolutely no reason to accept a job offer (or compensation package) that's below your true earning potential, that is, unless there's a definite upside to the deal you're being offered. (A potential upside might be a guarantee that your career will be placed on the fast track and you can expect regular raises and/or promotions that will lead to far greater earning potential in the not-so-distant future. Another upside might be a very attractive stock option plan, especially if the company has plans to go public in the near future or there's something in the company's plans that will impact its stock price in the near future.)

Defining your needs

Watch Out!
Unless you have the qualifications to land a high-paying position right now, it's important that you set realistic expectations for yourself.

Having the desire for the better things that life (and money) has to offer is certainly a worthwhile goal. You can work toward, and achieve, your long-term goals by obtaining additional education and training and by working hard.

You want to earn what you deserve based on your current skills, education, and experience. Knowing your long-term wants will help you define your goals and choose career opportunities that will lead you toward achieving those goals.

Your needs should also be defined carefully so that as you negotiate your salary and overall compensation package, you'll be able to maintain your current standard of living, and hopefully improve upon it. The following worksheet should help you define your immediate salary needs.

TABLE 11.1. CALCULATING YOUR MONTHLY EXPENSES

Car Payment/Transportation	$_____
Child Care	$_____
Clothing	$_____
Credit Card Bills	$_____
Entertainment	$_____
Food	$_____
Health Club Membership	$_____
Insurance Payments (Auto, Health, Dental, Life, etc.)	$_____
Investments	$_____
Phone Bills	$_____
Rent/Mortgage	$_____
Retirement Investment, (e.g., 401(k), etc.)	$_____
Savings	$_____
Student Loans	$_____
Taxes	$_____
Utilities	$_____
Other Expenses	$_____
Total Monthly Expenses	$_____
(Multiply your total monthly expenses by 12 to determine your annual expenses.)	
Total Annual Expenses:	$_____

Based on your research, determine your market value as an employee. Based on your skills, experience, and education, how much can you expect to earn working for an employer? Instead of pinpointing a specific figure, determine a salary range for yourself. The low end of your range (the bare minimum regarding what you'd be willing to work for) should be slightly higher than the figure you determine to be your total annual expenses (unless you've been living beyond your means).

Bright Idea
Ideally, your total annual expenses should be slightly lower than what you can expect to earn assuming you receive a salary based on your fair market value. If this isn't the case, consider hiring a personal financial planner or accountant to help you and create a more realistic budget for yourself.

Obviously, if you have a spouse who works part-time or full-time, you should combine his or her salary with yours and calculate your joint annual expenses to determine how much you need to be earning in order to make ends meet (and be able to build up your savings).

By calculating your monthly and annual expenses and making sure that these figures jive with your earning potential, you'll be in a much better position to analyze job offers.

First, evaluate the job itself, the hours, overtime expectations, amount of travel required, responsibilities, required commute, work environment, who you'll be reporting to, how your work/performance will be evaluated, how often will your work be evaluated, etc.

Then evaluate the employer. How stable is the company? Is it growing/expanding? Who are the key competitors? Is the company able to deal with its competitors successfully? What are the company's biggest strengths and weaknesses? How will these strengths and weaknesses impact you personally if you accept the job and become an employee of the company?

Finally, evaluate the industry in which you'll be working. How large is the industry? Is it growing? What market share does your potential employer hold?

After considering these factors, analyze a job offer by taking into account the following parts of the offer:

- Base salary
- Incentives/bonus structure/stock participation plan

- Commissions (if applicable)

- Value of your benefits package

- Future earning potential (via raises, promotions, etc.)

- Medical benefits (the amount of the employer's contribution, the coverage being offered for you and your family, and any special perks of the medical plan, such as health club membership, etc.)

- Dental/eye care insurance benefits (the amount of the employer's contribution and the coverage being offered for your and your family)

- Retirement planning related benefits, including the 401(k) plan, profit-sharing, etc.

- Benefits that enhance your quality of life (child care, maternity/paternity leave, vacation days, personal/sick day allotments, etc.)

- The Employer's performance expectations

- Training/education opportunities (paid tuition, tuition reimbursement, etc.)

- Relocation benefits (moving expenses, sign-on bonus, career counseling for your spouse, etc.)

- How will the job help you to reach your long-term career goals and earning objectives?

- What impact will accepting the job have on you personally? Your spouse? Your children and/or parents? Your close friends?

Now that you know approximately how much you're looking to earn in salary terms, it's important to think about what benefits you need and want right now. Also, consider what benefits you will need

Watch Out!
You also need to think about the retirement plan offered by the employer. If the retirement plan isn't adequate, you may have to supplement it by investing a portion of your salary into your retirement plan, which means your monthly living expenses could be higher than you previously calculated.

in the future (based on changes in your personal life, such as getting married, having children, etc.) Chapters 13 and 14 will go into greater detail with regard to analyzing and choosing benefits, perks, and a retirement plan.

What does your employer need?

Becoming a successful negotiator means developing a true understanding of what your employer (or potential employer) needs and wants from you. If you've received a job offer, what was it about you that they were interested in? What special skill or value can you offer to the employer? How can you help the employer achieve its goals? What weaknesses does the employer have that you can help fix?

You'll be able to discover answers to many of these questions by researching the company (prior to your first job interview), and also through conversations with the human resources person or executive who is making the job offer to you. If possible, as part of your job interview(s), try to meet and hold conversations with as many employees as you can, including the person you'll be working under—your supervisor or immediate boss. During the interview process, try to discover answers to these questions as you attempt to learn as much about the company as possible.

Try to determine why the job you're being offered is currently available. How quickly does the employer need to fill the position? Are the other applicants who applied for the job as qualified as you, or are you able to offer something unique that helped you to stand out? Is the pool of applicants qualified to fill the position you're being offered large or small? How much in demand is someone with your skills, experience, and education?

If the employer is having trouble finding qualified candidates and is under pressure to quickly hire someone to fill a specific job opening for which you're qualified, then you'll have the upper hand when negotiating. To determine if you have the upper hand in a situation like this, simply listen for verbal clues from the person who is interviewing you or offering you a job.

You'll be able to determine pretty quickly how much the employer really wants you on their team based on the verbal clues that are offered during discussions and also by how quickly the person you're negotiating with is willing to make concessions in your favor when negotiating salary and benefits.

As your negotiations begin, focus on what you know to be of value to the employer. If you determine that high productivity, friendliness, and honesty are the qualities the employer is looking for in employees, make sure you clearly demonstrate these traits and qualities. Be sure to provide specific details, support materials, and examples whenever possible to strengthen your position.

Bright Idea
Chapters 6 and 9 discuss the best ways to research a company (a potential employer) prior to a job interview. Take full advantage of these resources as you do additional research in order to prepare for a salary negotiating session once you've received a job offer.

How far should you go to get what you want?

Negotiating is all about give and take, making concessions and getting the other party to see your point of view and give you whatever it is you want and are negotiating for. By now you should understand that preparation is critical prior to a negotiation, but to become a good negotiator you'll want to practice learning how to read people, based not just on what they say, but on their facial expressions, temperament, tone of voice, and body language. Throughout the negotiating process, look for non-verbal clues to help you determine how effective your negotiating tactics are and to help you better custom tailor your negotiation to the person you're dealing with.

Some people are much easier to read than others. People who show little emotion and have total control over their body language (and have a good "poker face") will be difficult to read, so you'll have to focus even more carefully on what they say, how they say it and their actions. If you're lucky enough to enter into a negotiation with someone who uses body language more freely and is more expressive with their tone of voice and facial expressions, you'll be able to use these factors as clues when trying to analyze where you stand during a negotiation.

Look for clues in how well your negotiations are going based on the language used by the employer. Pay attention to their actual language and the wording they use. Listen for positive comments like, "I know you're going to really enjoy working here once we reach an agreeable compensation package," "You have the perfect qualifications for this position. You're just the type of person we're looking to hire," or "I'm confident we'll be able to reach compensation terms that you'll find appealing." These statements indicate that the employer is eager to hire you or at least interested in negotiating with you to better explore what type of terms and compensation package you're looking for.

Comments like, "I've already offered you the maximum salary we're able and willing to pay someone with your qualifications" or "We're considering five other people who are equally qualified for the position, so I hope you'll accept the offer that's on the table" suggest that that employer is far less willing to negotiate or make the concessions you're asking for.

As long as you're receiving positive feedback in the form of verbal or nonverbal communication, keep the negotiation process going. Listen and evaluate whatever counteroffers are made, make your own counteroffers and keep the back and forth communication going until you reach terms that are agreeable to both parties.

It will most likely be clear when the employer is done negotiating, when you start hearing phrases like, "This is our final offer" or "We really can't do any better than what we've already offered you." Another clue that the other party is done negotiating is when you keep receiving the same offer (or counteroffer) repeatedly, with no significant modifications. At this point, don't push the employer too hard to continue the negotiating process. Either accept the offer and move on to the next point or choose to reject the offer and walk away (after spending time considering the offer).

When you're confident that you've received the final offer in terms of base salary, ask for a commitment from the employer that you'll be re-evaluated for a raise and/or promotion within a predetermined amount of time (three, six, or twelve months). Next, start discussing any improvements the employer can make to the benefits package that's being offered to you. Even if the base salary aspect of the offered compensation package is firm, you may be able to improve upon the vacation time, stock options, performance bonuses or other benefits that are being offered.

As you negotiate this portion of the compensation package, again look for verbal and nonverbal

Bright Idea
Never push an employer too hard for a commitment that they're simply unable or unwilling to make. Maintain a professional attitude and don't become obnoxious or overly emotional if the employer isn't willing to make concessions. Pushing too hard might turn off the employer and force them to reconsider their decision to hire you.

clues from the employer, and look for the clues from the employer that indicate the negotiation is over once they've given you their best and final offer.

Once you know that the offer you have in-hand is truly the employer's best and final offer, take at least 24 hours to consider and evaluate the offer before accepting or rejecting it.

When to negotiate and when to walk away

No matter what, once you receive a job offer, make an effort to negotiate the terms of your employment and your compensation package, even if it's made very clear that the employer isn't willing to negotiate. Once you've put forth your best effort, without alienating the employer or acting unprofessionally, take at least 24 hours to carefully evaluate the offer.

As part of your evaluation, consider everything you know about the job itself, the company, the industry, and what will be expected of you. Is the compensation plan that's been offered fair? Is it in line with industry standards for what someone with your qualifications should be earning? How does the offer compare to other offers you've received? If you keep up your job search, could you find a better paying or more suitable job within a reasonable amount of time? Does the compensation package allow you to maintain or improve upon your standard of living?

Only by carefully analyzing a job offer can you determine if it's right for you personally. If you have all of the facts you need about the job that's being offered and you determine that it's a good opportunity for you, then accept the job. Otherwise, if you determine the job itself or the compensation package doesn't fit with what you're looking for (even after you've been through a thorough negotiation), then you should seriously consider walking away and seeking employment elsewhere. One quick and easy way to ensure that you're making the right decision about accepting or rejecting a job offer is to list the ten things (in order of importance) that you most want out of a job. Every person will have a totally different list, so it's important that you create this list based on your own personal wants and needs. Next, compare your list to the job that's being offered to you. How many items from your list are incorporated into the job you're considering?

If you can match up at least seven or eight of the items from your list with the job that's being offered to you, then you should seriously consider accepting it. If only a few (under five) of the items from your list match up with the job you're considering, you either need more information about the position or you should seriously considering walking away from this opportunity, because it's probably not a good one for you personally.

After learning about the job opportunity that's being offered to you, if you know that the job isn't what you're looking for, even if you're being offered a generous compensation package, you should consider continuing your job search until you find a job that's better suited for you. It's important that you pursue career opportunities that offer you long-term rewards and that will help you achieve your long-term goals. Every job you accept during your career should be a stepping stone that leads you at least one step closer to achieving your ultimate professional, personal, and financial goals. If the job you're considering can't be classified as a positive stepping stone in your career, then it's stonewalling

Bright Idea
Until you've received the employer's absolute final job offer (and compensation package offer), keep an open mind and don't make any rash decisions regarding whether or not you should accept the job. Only when you have all of the facts should you decide whether or not to accept the offer.

your career and keeping you from achieving your goals.

Based on what you are looking for personally from your overall career and from your employment opportunities, only you can determine if an offer is worth considering and accepting. The important thing, however, is that you make well-educated decisions based upon your own knowledge and the facts available to you.

Attitude is everything

When it comes to landing a new job, earning a promotion, or obtaining a well-deserved raise, in addition to your aptitude, your attitude is important and is something that will be evaluated carefully by virtually all employers.

Throughout the job interview process and the salary negotiation process, an employer is going to be examining your personality traits to determine if you're motivated, dedicated, hardworking, honest, outgoing, creative, competent, intelligent, and friendly. They'll also want to ensure you have the other traits they believe are important in order to be successful working for their company. These traits are different from having the specific skills needed to successfully meet the requirements of a job, such as being able to type, use a computer, or having bookkeeping skills.

By the time you're actually given a job offer, the employer will probably have determined that you have most, if not all, of the personality traits that they're seeking. However, they're still going to evaluate your attitude throughout the salary negotiation process, paying particular attention to what motivates you. The employer will be looking for signs that you're interested in the company's point of view and overall prosperity, and not just looking to earn the most money you possible can for purely selfish reasons. They'll also want to know that if they decide to pay you what you're asking for that you'll be a hard worker who will make every effort to provide additional value to them as an employee.

Will you work toward achieving the company's short- and long-term goals, as well as your own? How excited are you at the prospect of being hired by the employer? Assuming you have the aptitude for the job you're being offered, demonstrating the right attitude will give you a definite edge in the salary negotiation process. By demonstrating the right attitude, the employer will be far more willing to negotiate a compensation package you can both agree upon, especially if they believe their investment in you will pay off, not just in the short-term, but in the long-term as well.

Don't be afraid to show your enthusiasm and interest in working with an employer, however, when actually involved in a negotiation session, you want to take on the attitude that you can offer the employer a lot. If you have multiple job offers, you might also want to bring this to the attention of the employer that you're negotiating with and use this as a bargaining tool, especially if you know the employer is very interested in hiring you.

Avoid ultimatums

Keeping the entire negotiation process cordial and professional should be rather easy, especially if both parties have similar goals and objectives and are entering into the negotiation process well informed. If the salary and overall compensation package you're looking for is in line with industry standards and what the employer typically pays someone with your qualifications, and the employer knows what those industry standards are and

Bright Idea
Demonstrating that you have a true desire to work for a particular employer (and that you're not just trying to land a job because you need a paycheck) is part of what having the right attitude is all about.

compensates its employees fairly, you're in excellent shape. All you need to do is work out the fine points of your compensation package so that you wind up receiving the highest salary possible.

Problems or obstacles arise during negotiations when there are misunderstandings, miscommunications, or the participants don't have all of the information they need to negotiate intelligently. When these problems arise, it's important to stay calm and continue acting professionally, keeping the lines of communication open. You're far better off taking a break so that you and/or the employer can spend some additional time doing research, than you are continuing with a negotiation when tensions are high and there is little chance of reaching a positive outcome.

It's during these periods of disagreement when tensions are high and people become uncomfortable participating in the negotiation process. Try using an ultimatum to bring the discussion to a quick end. Unless you're absolutely willing to follow through on your ultimatum, avoid using this negotiation tactic, because the chances are great that it will backfire or increase the hostility between the two parties.

Giving an ultimatum that you're not willing to back up with action is a poor negotiating tactic because it will actually hurt your chances of ultimately getting what you want. Backing down on a threat or ultimatum will cause you to lose the respect of the other party, and whatever sense of honesty and trust you've built up will be gone. Rejecting a job offer if the employer doesn't offer you the compensation package you're requesting is always an option, however, there is no need to advertise your intentions in a negative way.

Watch Out!
Avoid using statements like, "Give me the salary I'm asking for or I'll seek employment elsewhere." Ninety-five percent of the time, the employer will send you on your way, simply because they don't like your attitude. If you had taken a more subtle approach, you might very well have gotten what you were looking for.

In Chapter 10, you discovered some of the negotiating tactics available to you to help you get what you want from an employer. This chapter focused on helping you determine what exactly it is you want and need, so that you know what to negotiate for.

Just the facts

- Determine, in advance, what is most important to you, so that you know what you should be negotiating for.

- It's important to develop a true understanding of the employer's wants and needs in order to customize your negotiation techniques.

- In any negotiation, there's an appropriate time to stop negotiating and seriously consider the employer's offer. Being able to identify this time is an important skill to develop in order to be a successful negotiator.

- As you're evaluating a job offer, make sure that it incorporates what you're looking for in an employment opportunity and that it will be a stepping stone to help your career move forward (so that you can eventually achieve your long-term career, personal, and financial goals). If a potential job won't help your career move forward, than it probably isn't the best opportunity for you to pursue.

- Throughout the job search process, as well as during the salary negotiation process, you always want to convey the right attitude, since this is something that all employers will be evaluating carefully. Your use of words, eye contact, body language, and tone of voice all help convey your personality and reveal your attitude.

It's Not Only Your Paycheck That Matters

PART VI

GET THE SCOOP ON...
How to calculate your take-home pay ▪ How
and why bonuses are important ▪ How your
commission structure will work if your job
involves commissions ▪ Profit-sharing plans ▪
Stock option plans ▪ Negotiating and taking
advantage of a sign-on bonus ▪ How overtime
impacts the value of your salary

Monetary Compensation

Chapter 12

A fter receiving a job offer and negotiating your best possible compensation plan, it will become necessary for you to understand exactly what your getting. This means calculating your actual take home pay (once taxes and your contribution to benefits, such as your health plan or retirement plan, have been deducted from your base salary), and determining what you're getting in terms of perks and benefits (and calculating their value).

Since every perk and benefit has a financial value, it's important to calculate all of these values to determine the overall value of your compensation package. For example, if the employer is offering you free parking near where you'll be working, and the parking rate is $300 per month, for example, that benefit alone is worth $3,600 per year ($300 × 12 months).

Typically, your perks and benefits will be worth around 30 to 40 percent of your base salary, however, this will vary greatly based on your employer and what perks and benefits you'll be receiving, so use this as a ballpark figure only.

The next chapter will go into greater detail regarding specific perks and benefits, helping you to understand what they are, determine which ones you need, and calculate their value to you. This chapter, however, focuses mainly on the salary aspect of your compensation package.

How much will you really earn?

From each of your paychecks, the employer will be deducting local, state, and federal income taxes, along with your contribution to such things as your health insurance, life insurance, retirement plan, etc. After these deductions are made, whatever remains is what will be your take-home pay, and that figure will be significantly lower than the base salary figure that originally looked so impressive. The question you need to answer now is whether or not your take-home pay will be enough to cover cost of living expenses (food, clothing, rent, car payments, car insurance, debts, etc.). Once your expenses are covered, will you be able to put some of your take-home pay into savings? Will you have money left over to deal with unexpected expenses or emergencies, like your car needing new brakes or your washing machine needing repair?

For now, to calculate your take-home pay, forget about the value of your benefits package. Consider only the salary aspect of your benefits. Next, determine what will be deduced from each paycheck, and fill in the blanks below.

Watch Out!
When you look at your base salary (once you receive an offer from an employer), it might look impressive, but until you've done some calculations, it's difficult to determine how much money you'll be able to take home each pay period.

TABLE 12.2. CALCULATING YOUR TAKE-HOME PAY

Base salary:	$_____
Costs/expenses deducted from your paycheck:	
State and local income taxes (if applicable)	$_____
Federal income taxes	$_____
Employee contribution to benefits (to be deducted from your paycheck)	$_____
(*Note:* not all of these benefits will be applicable to you, and some will be optional.)	
Health insurance	$_____
Health insurance for dependants	$_____
Dental insurance	$_____
Dental insurance for dependants	$_____
Short-term disability insurance	$_____
Long-term disability insurance	$_____
Life insurance	$_____
Dependant life insurance	$_____
Retirement plan	$_____
Stock participation plan	$_____
Dependant care assistance program	$_____

Add up the deductions that will be taken from your paycheck each pay period and then subtract that total from your base salary in order to determine your take-home pay. Once you have calculated your take-home pay, you'll be in a better position to create a personal budget for yourself.

As you'll discover in the next chapter, your contribution to such things as your health insurance plan and other benefits are almost always negotiable with your employer. How much your contribution to each of these benefits is will impact your take-home pay. In some instances, your contribution to such things as health insurance will be determined by law.

Bright Idea
Figure into your calculations your sign-on bonus and any other guaranteed bonuses offered as part of your compensation plan but remember that you can't depend on your bonus if it changes every year.

Watch Out!
If paychecks are
issued twice
each month, you
receive 24
checks per year.
If paychecks are
issued every two
weeks, you
receive 26
checks each year.

How often are paychecks issued?

Knowing how much you'll receive with each paycheck is one thing, but you also need to know how often and when you can expect to receive your paycheck. Some employers issue paychecks weekly, other are on a biweekly or monthly schedule. Once you know the frequency that paychecks are issued, determine exactly when they're issued. If the employer cuts payroll checks twice each month, does this happen on the first and fifteenth of every month or some other variation?

How will you receive your paycheck and how long will it take after it's issued to land in your bank account? Some employers distribute paychecks to employees in-person during lunch hour or at the end of the business day on "paydays." Some employers also offer a direct deposit option that allows your paycheck to be automatically deposited in your personal checking or savings account, while another option is for the employer to mail your paycheck to your home address. Depending on which distribution method is used, how long it takes for your paycheck to actually get deposited into your bank account will vary.

For example, if you're given a paycheck at the end of the business day on the first of the month, chances are you won't be able to deposit it until the following day. Thus, the money won't be available in your account until the second of the month at the absolute earliest. If your paycheck is transferred directly to your checking accounting using a direct deposit option, it should go immediately to your account (but check with your bank, because electronic deposits may be delayed one or two days). Finally, if the check is cut on the first of the month and mailed to your home, it might be two or three days before it arrives in your mailbox. Since you won't get home from work until the end of the day in order to retrieve your mail, the check won't be deposited until the following day, and then it might take an additional 24 hours to be posted to your account.

It might take upwards of five or six days for your paycheck to be available to you. This will impact your ability to pay bills and meet your financial obligations, especially if your rent/mortgage is due on the first of the month, but your paycheck won't be posted to your checking account until the fifth of the month. Being in this situation may require that you stay one month ahead in your rent/mortgage payments.

How do bonuses come into play?

Some employers offer special bonuses to employees one or more times throughout the year. Sometimes these bonuses are automatic, while in other cases whether they are offered depends on the employee's ability to meet specific goals or objectives, or they are determined by the overall profitability of the company during a predetermined period.

If your employer does offer bonuses, they're usually paid as lump sums. A bonus is different from a raise, because a raise is something that increases your paycheck indefinitely, while a bonus is often a one-shot deal, a reward for a job well done, or used by the employer as some type of employee incentive.

When negotiating your compensation package with your employer (or potential employer) discuss whether or not the company issues bonuses, and what criteria are used to award them. If you know

Bright Idea
Some employers offer automatic deposit, which means your paycheck is sent electronically to your bank account. Another alternative to having your paycheck handed to you (in-person) is to have your check mailed directly to your home address or whatever address you specify. If you're considering this option, take into account the number of days it'll take for the U.S. Mail system to deliver your check.

you'll receive an end-of-year bonus each year, for example, you can count on that money when calculating and planning your personal budget. If bonuses are awarded based on your achieving specific objectives or the overall performance of the company, it's probably safer to not calculate this money into your personal budget until it's actually received.

When it comes to compensation, knowledge is power

Understanding benefits packages can be a bit confusing, however, it's in your best interest to know what options are available to you in terms of perks and benefits. Doing research is one way to learn what types of options are available. This research should include determining what several employers in your industry offer as benefits packages to their employees. If you'll be filling a middle-management or executive-level position, the options available to you, and your ability to negotiate your compensation package, will be much greater. Making the right decisions can have a large impact on the overall value of your compensation package.

To help you understand the current trends in employee compensation, and help you negotiate the best possible package for yourself, consider subscribing to the *Executive Compensation Report* newsletter. This biweekly newsletter is devoted to reporting on compensation practices at over 1,000 corporations. The publication has been in existence since 1980 and is often quoted in the *Wall Street Journal,* the *Washington Post,* the *Los Angeles Times, Forbes,* and many other publications.

The purpose of this newsletter is to provide executives with accurate, inside intelligence about compensation programs in use at corporations of all sizes, in many different industries, and throughout the country. In addition to offering information about compensation programs offered by specific corporations, this newsletter also offers feature articles that evaluate trends, and help executives understand those trends and perform comparative analyses of compensation in a specific industry.

In addition to publishing the *Executive Compensation Report* newsletter, Executive Compensation Advisor Services (ECAS), a division of Harcourt Brace Professional Publishing, offers personalized consulting services and customized reports to executives (for an additional fee). For more information about these services, call (800) 291-0045.

An annual subscription to the *Executive Compensation Report* (24 issues) is priced at $525 per year (anywhere in North America) and is available by calling (703) 913-7198. In addition to the newsletter, subscribers receive a copy of *Executive Compensation Report's Annual Golden Parachute Report* and a disk containing copies of 50 bonus plans. Subscribers also receive discounts on books and analytical reports published by ECAS.

A free three-month trial subscription to *Executive Compensation Report* is available. If you can't afford to subscribe to this informative newsletter, you'll probably be able to review recent issues by visiting a large public or college library or by visiting an executive recruiter/headhunter.

Whether or not you're a subscriber, you'll find useful information about executive compensation packages at the ECAS web site, which can be accessed by pointing your browser to http://www.ecronline.com.

Bright Idea
One way to discover if the compensation plan being offered to you is competitive with what's being offered by other companies in your industry is to research what these other companies offer. Contact the human resources department of other companies in your industry and request a copy of their employee orientation manual or employee policy manual. This will tell you about the types of benefits and perks you should be looking for.

Understanding commission structures

Getting paid in whole or in part on a commission basis means that your performance and success on the job will have a direct impact on your paycheck. Being paid using a commission structure gives you, the employee, control over how much you earn during a specific period, and in many cases offers you unlimited earning potential based on how good you are at what you do (and how successful you are). Commission pay structures usually come into play when you're hired in some sort of sales-oriented job.

There are many different types of commissions and many different ways commissions can be calculated. Coming up with a commission plan that suits your needs will involve careful negotiation with your employer and having a good understanding of the specific terms used to outline how you'll be compensated for your work. The following are some of the terms you'll need to understand when evaluating a commission-based job opportunity:

Base plus commission   For salespeople, this is a common compensation method. It involves receiving a pre-determined base salary plus some type of commission on the sales you actually make. The commission rate you'll be paid will probably be lower than you were on straight commission, but whether your sales are high or low in a given period, you're guaranteed to receive at least your base pay, which is yours to keep.

Draw against commission   This type of compensation plan is totally commission based, however, at the beginning of each pay period, you're given a pre-determined draw, a specific amount of money in advance. This draw is deducted from your commissions at the end of a pay period. If you don't cover your draw during a pay period, you will owe money to the employer, which can often be paid back later when you have a more prosperous period, however, if you have several poor performance periods, you could run into problems.

Residual commissions   Earning residual commissions is a salesperson's dream, because as long as their accounts are generating revenue for the employer, the salesperson continues to receive a commission. For example, many insurance salespeople receive residual commissions for all of their clients, as long as their clients continue paying their premiums, which could be for many years after the initial sale is made. Through negotiation, you may be able to continue receiving residual commissions owed to you, even after you leave the company. Many employers are reluctant to offer this type of compensation deal.

Salary plus bonus   If this is the method of compensation you agree upon, you'll receive a pre-determined salary each pay period that is not impacted by your performance. At the end of a year (or pre-set amount of time), you'd also receive an added bonus if your performance meets or exceeds specific goals.

Salary plus commission   This is the same as a "base plus commission" compensation structure.

Watch Out!
Suppose you are given a $2,000 draw at the start of a month, and by the end of the month you've earned $3,000 in commissions. You receive an additional $1,000 commission check. If, however, you only earn $1,500 in commissions, you'll owe the employer $500.

Straight commission   You earn a percentage of your sales. Unless you have proven sales skills and you're positive you'll have immediate success selling a specific product or service, this type of compensation can be a bit risky, since you only get paid based on how much you sell. If you make no sales, you take home no paycheck, even if you put in a 40+ hour work week. For talented sales people, this is an attractive compensation deal, since their income potential is entirely in their control.

Straight salary   As a salesperson, you'll earn a straight salary that is in no way impacted positively or negatively by your sales performance. For a salesperson who is developing their skills, this is a very safe compensation method, although there is no real incentive to excel. Poor performers, however, tend to get fired, since most companies won't continue to carry salespeople or salary-based workers that aren't performing up to expectations.

Variable commission   This type of commission structure is similar to a straight commission, however, the commission rate you're paid goes up or down based on predetermined circumstances. Some salespeople try to negotiate a higher sales commission if they reach or exceed specific monthly goals in order to incorporate an incentive plan into their commission-based compensation package.

Profit-sharing plans

By participating in a profit-sharing plan, you will directly benefit from how profitable your employer is. If the company earns a profit, you get a piece of it. Companies offer different types of profit-sharing plans, and some offer spin-offs of this concept, like "gain-sharing" plans in which employees are rewarded for increases in productivity. Thus, it's important to understand exactly what you're being offered and how the plan can benefit you. For example, some employers' profit-sharing plans don't kick in until the company achieves a specific level of profit, while some plans kick in once the first dollar of profit is earned by the company. Ultimately, when an employer offers a profit-sharing plan, it's designed to motivate employees to become more involved in the organization and to work harder toward reaching a common goal—making money. The law limits an employee's contribution to up 15% of pre-tax earnings.

Stock participation plans

If you'll be working for a publicly owned company or one that's planning to issue an IPO (Initial Public Offering) in the near future, as an employee you may be invited to enroll in a stock participation plan. This type of program gives you the opportunity to purchase your company's stock at a discounted rate determined by its fair market value during a specific period of time.

Over a pre-determined period, your contributions accumulate and will eventually be used to purchase stock at a discounted rate. Once you own the actual stock, you can keep it in within your personal investment portfolio or you can often sell it through your stock broker. Some employers restrict you from

Profit sharing extends a company's financial success to the employees who helped to achieve it. Profit-sharing and 401(k) plans are the most common type of defined-contribution plans, meaning that the benefit depends on the specific contributions made to the plan. In contrast, a defined-benefit plan provides a pre-determined benefit based on years of service and the employee's salary.
—The Profit Sharing/401(k) Council of America (312-441-8550/http://www.psca.org)

Timesaver
More information about profit sharing plans is covered in Chapter 14.

Unofficially...
Typically, participation in this type of plan involves setting aside anywhere from two percent to 10 percent (or more) of each paycheck. The deductions are usually made by the employer, on an after-tax basis.

selling all of your stock at once or within a specific period of time.

For details about your company's stock option or stock participation plan, contact the human resources department. Information about this type of benefit will also often be included in a company's employee orientation manual or employee policy manual. For the millions of people in America who are invited to participate in a stock participation plan as part of their overall compensation package, this aspect of their compensation is extremely valuable, especially when it comes to long-term savings and retirement planning.

What exactly is a **stock?** According to Fidelity Investments, "When you own a company's stock, you own part of the company. How much you own depends on how many shares of stock you have. Holders of common stock are the last to be paid any profits from the company but are likely to profit most from the company's growth. When people talk about a company's stock, they usually mean **common stock.** When you own common stock in a company, you share in its success or failure. As part owner, you vote on important policy issues, such as picking the board of directors. If the company prospers, you may get part of the profits, called a **dividend.** Also, the value of your share of the company many go up; common stock generally has the most potential for growth. However, that value also can drop if the company does poorly, and if it goes bankrupt, common stockholders are the last to receive any payment. The amount of each share's dividend depends on how well the company does."

Sign-on bonuses

As the name suggests, a sign-on bonus is an amount of money (negotiated as part of your compensation package) that's paid to you as a one-time fee when you sign an employment contract with a company or accept a job offer. A sign-on bonus is something an employer uses to attract qualified employees, especially when they're having trouble filling positions due to shortages in the applicant pool.

Sign-on bonuses are most commonly offered to people in the technology or high-tech field, in sales and marketing, financial services, middle management, people filling executive-level positions, and people who have an advanced degree, such as an MBA.

However, while sign-on bonuses are becoming more common in the above listed types of jobs, they are still relatively uncommon in non-technical positions and in jobs with salaries under $55,000. Sign-on bonuses average around five percent of the base salary. Keep in mind that most employers do not offer sign-on bonuses and that the availability of bonuses depends upon the industry you're in. As we keep saying, do your research to find out if you should be able to negotiate a sign-on bonus for yourself! How much of a sign-on bonus you're offered will depend on how eager the employer is to hire you, however, an average sign-on bonus is approximately five to ten percent of your agreed upon salary. So, if you'll be earned a $100,000 per year salary, a reasonable sign-on bonus would be $10,000. It's not uncommon, however, for someone filling an executive level position or someone who is in hot demand among multiple employers to receive a one-time sign-on bonus in excess of 25 percent of their annual salary.

Why do you deserve a sign-on bonus? Think about what costs are associated with you changing jobs. What lost income will you (or have you)

Unofficially...
The best time to bring up the concept of a sign-on bonus is after you have successfully negotiated your salary. Once you and your employer agree on a salary, ask what the employer offers as a sign-on bonus for the position. Encourage the employer to make the first offer when it comes time to discuss the amount of a sign-on bonus, and keep in mind that some employers simply don't offer this type of incentive.

experienced while you're in between jobs? A sign-on bonus is one way an employer can help you cover the cost of changing jobs. A sign-on bonus, however, is different from an employer covering your relocation expenses, which is another type of benefit that will be explored in greater detail in the next chapter.

If you legitimately have multiple job offers from several employers, all offering similar compensation packages, you should bring this up with each employer during your negotiations to encourage them to offer an attractive sign-on bonus in order to help you make your decision about which job offer to accept.

Considering overtime (paid versus unpaid)

Overtime work is something that's expected of most employees in virtually all industries, since companies are trying to maximize profits while streamlining their staff, giving each employee more work to do and less time to do it. Whether you need more time to get your personal work on the job done, your employer simply gives you too much work to complete during your normal work hours, or you're working on a major project under a tight deadline, overtime work will probably be required.

As you're evaluating a job offer, you need to determine the amount of overtime work you'll be expected to do, and whether it will be paid or unpaid. If it's paid, will you receive your hourly wage, time-and-a-half or double time? In addition, you must determine how much overtime work the employer expects you to put in, especially if this will be unpaid work. Are you willing to make the time commitment necessary to do your job properly and meet expectations, even if it means putting in overtime on a regular basis? Keep in mind, overtime is paid only to non-exempt or hourly employees. Exempt or professional salaried employees do not get paid extra for working extra long hours.

On paper, your job description may require you to work 9:00 a.m. to 5:00 p.m., Monday through Friday, and include one hour for lunch, however, you need to determine the reality of the situation. Do the other employees working in your department typically work until 6:00 p.m. (or later) virtually every night? Is it "expected" that you'll show up for work on Saturdays and/or Sundays in order to meet project deadlines or prepare for important meetings?

In addition to discussing this issue with your potential employer, before accepting a job offer, try to discuss this topic with your potential coworkers once you're introduced to them during your job interview process. If your employer doesn't pay overtime, but you discover you'll be expected to put in at five, 10 or 15 hours of overtime virtually every week or month, this is something you need to take into consideration when evaluating the salary aspect of your job offer.

What are you being offered in addition to salary?

Aside from your actual salary, the perks and benefits that also comprise your overall compensation package are extremely valuable. Depending on your individual needs, what benefits you'll want will vary greatly. If you have a family, for example, you'll require an excellent health insurance/health care program for yourself, your spouse, and your children. You'll want to ensure that your employer (or potential employer) offers a program with excellent

Bright Idea
After receiving a detailed job description from your employer, ask to have specific terms within the description defined. For example, if the job description talks about the employer's expectations for an employee to work a "reasonable" amount of unpaid overtime, determine what exactly the employer means by "reasonable." Understanding the terms of your employment now will eliminate misunderstandings and potential bad situations later that make you dissatisfied with your job.

benefits, but also one that you can afford in terms of your financial contribution toward this benefit.

In addition to health insurance, another major concern for many people is retirement. To ensure that you'll have the necessary funds available to you upon your retirement, you'll need to examine what options are available to you and start your retirement planning as early in your career as possible.

The next chapter will examine the various types of benefits and perks available and help you choose the ones you most need and want, based on what your employer (or potential employer) offers.

Of interest to working mothers and others

Every year, *Working Mother* magazine evaluates the benefits offered by companies in all industries throughout the country, and determines the best companies for working mothers, based on the benefits offered that cater to their needs, such as child care, flexible hours, and advancement opportunities for women.

The 1998 edition of the *Working Mother 100* list (an annual survey of the 100 best companies for women to work for based on benefits and perks offered) features companies ranging in size from 70 employees to more than 231,233, representing a variety of industries from banking and insurance to health care and technology.

TABLE 12.2. TOP 10 COMPANIES FOR WORKING MOTHERS

The 1998 10 best employers for working mothers, according to a study conducted by *Working Mother* magazine
1.   Citicorp/Citibank
2.   Glaxo Wellcome
3.   IBM
4.   Johnson & Johnson

5.	Eli Lilly
6.	MBNA America Bank
7.	Merck
8.	Nation's Bank
9.	SAS Institute
10.	Xerox

The 1998 edition of the *Working Mother 100* (WM 100) list also welcomed 17 new companies to the list, including: Acacia Life Insurance Co.; American Home Products Corp.; Autodesk; Bristol-Myers Squibb; Commercial Financial Services; Donaldson, Lufkin & Jenrette; GTE; Imation; JFK Medical Center; Lucent Technologies; Pfizer; Principal Financial Group; St. Luke's Hospital of Kansas City; SNET; Turner Broadcasting; Union Pacific Resources Group; and The Vanguard Group.

The October 1998 issue of *Working Mother* rates companies on six criteria: pay, opportunity for women to advance, childcare assistance, flexible work arrangements, work/life supports such as counseling and support groups for employees, and other family-friendly benefits such as extended maternity and parental leave, as well as adoption aid and elder care.

The 1998 survey reports that companies continue to look beyond on-site childcare to meet workers' dependent care needs. For example, 77 of the WM 100 now offer backup care, up from 67 last year (1997). Initiatives to increase the use of flexible schedules and encourage supervisors to mentor and advance women are also on the rise. In addition, the survey indicates that companies are going out of their way to streamline workers' lives by offering such amenities as concierge services, on-site cafeterias, and fitness centers. A handful of companies

> **"**
> Despite a tight labor market, an increasing number of companies report that their family-friendly policies enhance recruitment, lower turnover, and translate into a more loyal, focused workforce. According to *Working Mother* magazine's 13th annual ranking of the 100 Best Companies for Working Mothers.
> **"**

subsidize employee vacations to keep morale high, and some companies even allow pets in the office.

Additional trends that helped shape this year's list include:

Women Moving Up   Five of the WM 100 companies now have female CEOs (nearly double the number of just two years ago). An increasing number of women are breaking into the upper echelons of traditionally male-dominated fields.

Family Leave Continues to Expand   Merck and Merrill Lynch have the best-paid mater-nity-leave benefits on the list, with 13 weeks off at full pay. In terms of the total amount of job-protected time a new mom can take off, numerous companies on the list offer gener-ous unpaid leaves beyond the 12 weeks required under the Family and Medical Leave Act by businesses with 50 or more employees. IBM tops the list, offering a total of 156 weeks, and Eli Lilly offers 68 weeks of job-protected leave. Thirty-one companies on the WM 100 now provide paid leaves to new fathers, up from 27 last year. Donaldson, Lufkin & Jenrette and Ridgeview extend the same 12 weeks paid leave they give to new mothers to new fathers, as well. More dads are taking time off (paid or unpaid) to bond with their babies than ever before; nearly half of all leaves at MBNA America Bank were taken by men: 300 of 650. Roughly 75 percent of the WM 100 companies offer financial aid for adoption, up from 70 percent in 1997.

Focus on Flexibility   All of the WM 100 offer flextime, whether it's traditional, daily, or midday. It's clearly a popular benefit; 36 firms say more than half of their employees flex their hours. At First Tennessee Bank, 91 percent of employees work flextime. The vast majority of the WM 100 also offer compressed workweeks, work from home, and job sharing.

Exceptional Childcare   Twenty-one companies are in the process of opening new on- or near-site childcare centers or expanding existing facilities, while 67 companies operate an on-or near-site center. More than three-quarters (77) of the WM 100 recognize the wisdom of providing backup care (sometimes known as emergency or short-term care) to employees, whether at company centers or via subsidies for other care options. Forty-three of the WM 100 offer childcare options for mildly ill kids to ease the difficulties that come when a kid's sniffles coincide with a parent's tight deadline or critical meeting.

Amenities on the Rise   Firms on this year's WM 100 are finding increasingly innovative ways to make life better for their workforce. Ernst & Young and Texas Instruments provide a corporate concierge, who for a nominal fee will take care of those pesky chores such as picking up dry cleaning, bringing ailing cars to the shop, and even addressing holiday cards. Autodesk allows employees to bring their pets to work. S.C. Johnson & Son subsidizes employees' vacations, providing discounted lodging at a lakeside resort in northern Wisconsin or a portion of the hotel charges for field employees who choose to go

Bright Idea
To learn more about employee benefits, visit the *Employee Benefit News* web site at http://www. benefitnews.com. *Employee Benefit News* is a publication targeted to employee benefits managers, however, the information will be of interest to people negotiating their compensation package or trying to evaluate a job offer. Call Enterprise Communications, Inc. at (800) 966-3976 for more information.

someplace else. BP Exploration, located in
Alaska, offers an $800 travel allowance per
family member for visits to the lower 48.

Just the facts

- Your take-home pay is very different from your
  base salary. From your base salary, the employer
  will be deducting state and federal income taxes
  along with your contribution to such things as
  your health insurance, life insurance, your
  retirement plan, etc. After these deductions are
  made, whatever remains will be your take-home
  pay, and that amount will be significantly lower
  than your base salary.

- In order to properly plan your personal budget,
  you'll need to determine how often and exactly
  when your paychecks will be issued, and how the
  paychecks are actually distributed.

- Bonuses have the potential to boost your annual
  salary significantly. In order to calculate these
  into your job offer, you need to know what types
  of bonuses your (potential) employer offers,
  when they're awarded and what criteria are used
  to determine who receives a bonus and how
  large it will be.

- Other things that impact the dollar value of
  your compensation package are the profit-
  sharing plans and/or the stock participation
  plans that your employer may or may not offer.

- In some industries, such as high-tech jobs, sign-
  on bonuses have become standard. This is a
  one-time, lump sum of money used by the
  employer to lure you to their company.
  Depending on how eager an employer is to hire

you, a sign-on bonus can represent between five percent and 25 percent (or more) of your base salary.

■ As you evaluate a job offer, in addition to evaluating the salary, it's important to consider the benefits package and perks that are offered. This chapter began to examine some of the more important perks and benefits available to employees. This topic will be covered in greater detail in the next chapter.

GET THE SCOOP ON...
Choosing which benefits you want and need ▪
The most common types of benefits and perks
offered by employers ▪ The most common types
of benefits and perks offered by employers

Benefits and Perks

Besides a salary, your employer will probably offer you a selection of benefits and perks. When these benefits and perks are combined with your salary, your total compensation package will be complete. Keep in mind, however, that while some companies use perks (such as having casual Fridays or flexible work hours) as a way of attracting and/or keeping employees, they are not required to offer them. Thus, employees are not automatically entitled to receive perks.

Most employers typically offer a pre-determined assortment of perks and benefits, some of which will automatically be offered to you, and others that will require you to do a bit of negotiation in order to receive. Perks and benefits fall into two main categories: Those that are paid for entirely by the employer, and those that employees can contribute to (or pay for outright) in order to receive.

A benefit can be an incentive to employees, such as a stock option plan, cafeteria/meal plan, profit-sharing plan, free parking or a bonus plan. A benefit can also improve the overall quality of life and morale of employees, such as the option to work flexible hours or participate in a telecommuting program.

To meet legal obligations, some benefits must be offered by employers, at least to full-time employees. Finally, some benefits are offered because the employer is able to provide significant discounts on services or types of insurance that employees want and/or need, such as dental, life or vision care.

If you were to deal directly with an insurance agent as an individual to obtain health/medical insurance for yourself and/or your family, the cost of that insurance would be extremely high. Since your employer is purchasing health care insurance on behalf of many employees, this lowers the premiums and the overall costs of the insurance. While an employer may not be required to pay for the entire cost of offering you a particular benefit, they may choose to do so. Otherwise, you may be required to contribute financially to a particular benefit in order to receive it. In this case, your contribution to the benefits you sign up for will automatically be deducted from your paycheck (after taxes are deducted).

Since there are as many different benefits as there are employees, the purpose of this chapter is to familiarize you with some of the most popular benefits and perks offered by employers. This chapter will also point out some of the things to look out for (and the questions to ask) when evaluating a benefits package and deciding whether or not to accept a job offer.

If you're self-employed...

If you have decided to work for yourself and/or start your own small business (with less than five

Unofficially...
You'll find that every company offers a different overall benefits package. Some employers offer pre-defined benefits packages, with little room for negotiation in order to improve upon them; and some offer extremely flexible benefits packages that allow you to pick and choose (and in some cases pay for) only those benefits you most want and need.

additional employees), you may find that it's extremely costly to offer yourself the same benefits that a Fortune 500 company would offer to its employees. One way to enhance your own benefits package   and to make the benefits you need, such as health insurance, more affordable, is to take advantage of special programs offered by small business organizations and professional associations.

Timesaver
Chapter 16 offers additional information on obtaining the best deals in benefits when you're self-employed.

The Small Business Benefit Association (888-886-SBBA or http://www.sbba.com) is just one source of discounted benefits and services. According to the web site, "With national headquarters in Salt Lake City, Utah, we are a dynamic national organization created for the." With over 50 years experience, it was founded by management and marketing personnel who are committed to helping members succeed...All too often, small business owners are faced with competing with larger businesses. They sometimes feel isolated and don't know where to turn for help. For many small business owners, starting out on their own is a challenging experience because they are faced with the overwhelming responsibility of 'doing it all' or 'wearing many hats.' For this reason, SBBA was formed to help small business owners succeed."

What benefits and perks do you want and need?

Aside from heath insurance (or a health care plan), which is pretty much a given, what benefits and perks do you most need or want in order to ensure your quality of life? As you read this chapter, carefully consider your personal needs and the needs of your immediate family. Even after negotiating the best possible benefits package for yourself, you'll still have to decide what optional benefits you want. These additional benefits may cost you money, but in the long run, some of them can make you money, while others have the potential to save you substantial money.

For example, you could decide to allocate a portion of your paycheck each month toward your company's stock participation plan. Assuming your company does well over time, this can represent a wonderful (and easy) way to enhance your income, expand your portfolio, and even help you prepare for retirement. The drawback is, whatever money you subtract from your take-home pay to invest in your company's stock participation plan takes away from your available funds to cover your regular cost-of-living expenses.

Likewise, you might choose to spend a few extra dollars per month so that you and your family will be covered by a dental insurance plan, for example. The cost of this plan will most likely cost more than the price of semi-annual check-ups and cleanings, but should you require a root canal, oral surgery, or another costly dental procedure, this type of insurance can become very worthwhile and save you a fortune in dentist bills.

Take some time to carefully analyze your personal budget (the one you created in the last chapter), and then analyze what benefits are being offered by your employer. Now, choose which of these benefits are most important to you. Whenever possible, try to negotiate it so that your employer pays for as many of these benefits as possible, and then decide which ones you need to invest your own money in, in order to meet your needs.

Many people believe that it's important to be prepared for anything, including emergencies, and one way to do this is to be well insured. For some, paying a bit extra in insurance premiums brings them a tremendous amount of peace of mind, knowing that if they should suddenly die, for example, their life insurance will take care of their family's financial needs. Ultimately, how much insurance coverage you receive through your benefits package will be up to you (and what you receive from your employer).

Understanding benefits and perks offered by employers

The following is a list (in alphabetical order) of popular benefits and perks offered by many employers. Which benefits your employer offers, and the details of the individual benefits vary greatly, so this chapter deals in general terms when describing each benefit, its cost and/or value, and why the benefit might appeal to you. You'll want to consult with your employer (or potential employer) to learn the specific details of the benefits and perks that they offer, and well as the costs associated with receiving them. Be sure to ask a lot of questions, and carefully read whatever printed material your employer supplies that describes available benefits. This literature may be in the form of an employee orientation or employee policy manual.

In terms of insurance-related benefits, it's in your best interest to consult with one or more independent insurance agents (or insurance companies) to help you better evaluate what your employer is offering and determine your needs.

Cafeteria/meal plan

Every work day, you'll probably find yourself stopping at the local fast food establishment or diner and paying for your breakfast and/or lunch, or grabbing some food for dinner near where you work if you happen to be working late. Some companies offer special meal plans that provide employees with food allowances to pay for meals consumed while on the job. This might require you to submit restaurant receipts, or your employer might arrange (and pay) for meals to be delivered to your office. Finally, if you're working for a large company that has a cafeteria or dining room in-house, as an employee you may be offered highly discounted or free meals. If your employer offers some type of cafeteria or meal plan, it's to provide added convenience and cost savings to employees.

Casual Fridays or half-day Fridays

In order to boost employee morale and lighten up the office environment, at least on Fridays, many companies have initiated a dress-down policy, allowing employees to wear casual business attire, when they'd typically wear formal business attire the remainder of the week. Another trend for companies is to allow employees to go home early on Fridays, at least during the summer months. In some cases, these perks are mandated by unions.

Unofficially... While being allowed to wear casual clothing to work doesn't qualify as a financial benefit, it can make for a better place to work, which will make you a happier person on the job, so it's certainly a benefit that has merit and shouldn't be written off as frivolous.

As you evaluate a job offer, consider the dress code at the company. If you won't be dealing directly (in-person) with clients or customers, and the majority of your day will involve working in your cubical or office, you might opt to work for a company with a less formal dress code, so that you can be comfortable while doing your work. From a financial standpoint, what will be the out-of-pocket cost associated with maintaining a wardrobe of formal business attire clothing? Don't forget to include tailoring and dry cleaning costs when creating a wardrobe budget for yourself.

Childcare

If you have young children (kindergarten age or younger), one of the biggest child-related expenses you're going to incur is childcare if you and your spouse both hold full-time or part-time jobs. A growing number of companies that want to be considered "family friendly" offer some type of childcare program as a benefit to employees.

This might mean paying some or all of your childcare expenses (to place your child in day care or hire a home baby-sitter). Some larger employers have a childcare facility in-house, so you can spend free time with your child while on the job or at least have an emergency back-up in case your regular childcare provider is unavailable). It's also becoming more common for employers to offer various types of summer programs for children and pre-teens, allowing parents to maintain their full-time jobs while there children aren't in school.

Company car

Buying or leasing a car (and having to deal with monthly payments) and keeping that car in full working order can be one of your higher monthly expenses, especially if you drive an expensive car. As a benefit, some companies provide cars to employees. These vehicles usually remain the property of the employer (or the lease is held by the employer), but as long as you remain employed, all payments and repair costs are covered by the employer, allowing you to save the out-of-pocket expenses associated with buying, leasing, and maintaining a vehicle.

Typically, companies offer cars as an incentive to attract middle management or executive-level employees who are in hot demand. This type of

Bright Idea
At the end of a lease, some employers allow you to purchase the car directly from the dealer at whatever terms are spelled out in the lease.

incentive similar to a sign-on bonus. If the employer offers a company car as a benefit, you'll want to negotiate the type of car you'll receive, whether or not you'll be able to take ownership of the car after a certain period, and what happens if you leave the company during your car's lease period.

Dental and/or eye care insurance

Aside from regular health insurance, two benefits offered by some employers include dental and eye care insurance. If these two benefits aren't included in your compensation package, they may be available at an additional fee, and depending on your personal situation, may be a good investment.

Dental insurance, for example, usually includes semi-annual exams, X-rays, cleanings, and covers the cost of dental work. Without this type of insurance, if you happen to need a root canal, it could cost you (as an out of pocket expense) anywhere from $1,500 to $2,000, and braces for your child could run significantly higher. With dental insurance, you might have to pay only $50 to $150 for that same root canal. Obtaining dental insurance on your own is a costly proposition. It becomes far more affordable, however, if it's a benefit offered by your employer.

Eye care insurance works much like dental insurance. Regular eye exams are covered, as is the cost of prescription contact lenses and/or eyeglasses. (You'll typically have to pay for your own fancy designer eyeglass frames, however.)

If a dental plan or eye care plan isn't totally paid for by your employer, but is offered to you as an additional benefit or upgrade to your health care plan, investigate your options before signing up for these benefits through your employer (and having the premiums deducted from your paycheck).

Watch Out!
When choosing a dental plan, make sure that you can visit any dentist or oral surgeon and that the plan will cover their reasonable and customary fees. The plan should also cover all major orthodontic services. You'll want to pay attention to the plan's annual maximum benefit, your deductible amount, and what fees are associated with the plan.

Dependent Care Assistance Program (DCAP)

Dependent Care Spending Account (DCSA) is a voluntary payroll deduction that allows you to deposit up to $5,000 from your annual earnings into a DCSA. These deposits are made before federal and state taxes are deducted. You may withdraw money from this account in order to reimburse yourself for the care of your dependents. The amount you choose to contribute each month or pay period to your DCAP account is entirely up to you (as long as the total isn't more than $5,000 per year). The amount you decide upon, if you choose to accept this benefit, will be deducted from each paycheck.

Timesaver
DCSA offers an alternative to filing a tax credit for dependent care expenses.

Employee discounts

Working for a company that manufactures any type of product used by consumers, or that offers a service used by people like you, might mean that you'll receive employee discounts so that you can purchase the products or services offered by your employer, sometimes at extremely discounted prices.

Employee discounts are typically one of the most attractive benefits for jobs in retail or other entry-level jobs. If you work for a consumer electronics or computer company, such as Sony, you'll also most likely be offered very attractive discounts on the employer's computers, stereos, TVs, and other products. Employers offer these discounts as an incentive for employees, but also because they want the employees to be totally familiar with the company's products/services, and the best way for someone to learn about a product/service is to use it firsthand.

A few things to consider when evaluating the employee discounts offered by an employer are:

Unofficially...
Offering employee discounts on products usually costs a company little, since they tend to offer the products to employees at the same wholesale prices they typically earn by selling to their distributors. So, the employer still makes money selling its products at a discount to employees, and the employees are happy to receive the cost savings offered by the employer.

- How much the discount is (what percentage off of the suggested retail price). Remember, a suggested retail price is typically higher than what retail stores or dealers actually sell a product for. How generous is the employee discount if you take into account the actual street price of the product(s) or service(s)?

- How often can employees take advantage of the discount? Are you offered discounts year-round or just during specific times of the year? Does the discount apply to all products and/or services or just overruns, over-stocked items or discontinued items?

- Is there a limit to how much of a product/service an employee can purchase at the discounted prices within any given time period?

Flexible scheduling

A fast-growing number of employers want to be considered "family friendly" companies, which means they're offering perks and benefits that working mothers (and working fathers) will find particularly attractive. One of these benefits is flexible scheduling. Working a full-time, 40 hour work week, typically means showing up for work at 9:00 a.m. and leaving work at 5:00 p.m., Monday through Friday.

Flexible scheduling allows people to work that same 40-hour week, but choose which 40 hours they want to work. This sometimes means giving employees total control over their schedule on an ongoing basis (allowing them to modify it as the need arises), or at the very least, allowing them to set and adhere to a personalized schedule.

As a working mother, you may choose to arrive at work at 8:00 a.m. (when your children leave for school in the morning), and be able to leave work by 4:00 p.m. instead of 5:00 p.m., so that you can be home shortly after your kids get home from school. Another alternative may be to work longer hours on Monday through Thursday, so that you can take Fridays off from work altogether.

Exactly how "flexible" an employer is when allowing you to set your own schedule will vary greatly based on the employer, the job you're hired to fill, and your industry.

Health club membership

Some health care providers have determined that maintaining a physically fit body increases your mental and physical health. As a result, some health care programs automatically include membership to a health club or fitness facility. When a company's health care plan doesn't offer this benefit, some employers have decided to provide it to employees, allowing them to workout before work, during lunch, or after work at the company's expense. By having all of a company's employees join one health club or fitness facility, this encourages personal friendships outside of the workplace, which makes employees happier on the job, thus improving productivity and profits. Likewise, when employees are physically fit, they tend to be healthier, which means that they take fewer sick days, once again improving productivity.

If you've already looked into membership to a health club or fitness facility, you know this can get pretty expensive. So, if you enjoy working out and socializing with others, this is a benefit that you'll probably find extremely appealing, and one that a growing number of employers are starting to offer.

Timesaver
In addition to working flexible hours, some "family friendly" employers also have established job-sharing programs, as well as telecommuting programs. Both of these concepts are explored elsewhere in this chapter.

Bright Idea
As you know, networking is one of the most important skills for your career. Taking advantage of a health club or fitness facility membership that's offered to you as a benefit provides you with an excellent social opportunity ideal for networking. Even if you're not into working out, it's a great idea to take advantage of this benefit once in a while to improve your networking skills.

Health insurance/health care

Whether you need a routine physical examination or you're faced with a serious medical emergency, the cost of receiving health care continues to sky-rocket. Without having adequate medical coverage for yourself and your immediate family, you could easily find yourself faced with huge medical bills should you or a loved one experience a medical problem or emergency.

Most employers offer some form of health insurance or health care coverage to full-time and sometimes to long-term part-time employees. While you won't usually be able to select the company that will provide your health insurance or administer your health care program, you may have some choices in terms of the coverage you receive. Every health care plan is totally different. Four of the basic types of plans are:

1. **Indemnity (fee-for-service) Plan** This type of plan typically involves paying a pre-set deductible, plus 20 percent of the medical charges you incur.

2. **Health Maintenance Organization Plan (HMOs)** Through this type of plan, you select one primary health care physician who handles all of your medical problems, and when necessary, refers you to other experts or specialist within the HMO's network. It's usually required that you seek medical services exclusively from providers within the HMO network in order to receive full coverage. Instead of paying for each medical service you receive, as a member of an HMO, all of your medical costs are covered for one flat fee, as long as you use medical professionals and facilities that are associated the plan. With this type of plan, you never have to fill out

insurance forms, or wait to get reimbursed by the insurance company.

3. **Point of Service Plan (POS)** Like an HMO, you are provided with a directory of medical service providers within the network from which you can select a primary care physician. Depending on the specific plan, you can have one primary care physician, however, you're also permitted to use medical experts and specialists from outside of your network for an additional fee (that you must pay). This is considered a "managed care" plan.

4. **Preferred Provider Organization Plan (PPOs)** This type of plan offers you access to a group of medical professionals who have agreed to offer their services at discounted rates to members of your PPO. This is considered a "managed care" plan, because you're not supposed to go out side of the network to seek medical treatment, but unlike an HMO, a PPO does not require you to have one primary care physician.

When evaluating what's offered by your employer, some of the things to consider include the cost of the plan, what coverage is offered, and how much choice you have in terms of what doctors and/or medical facilities you use. You'll want to know:

- Whether you're allowed to use the services of any doctor and/or hospital, or only those affiliated with your plan's network.

- What your "out-of-area" or "out-of-network" coverage includes.

- Is there a limit to how long you can stay in a hospital?

- What percentage of the monthly premiums your employer will pay (and what you'll have to pay) for the coverage. If you pay a bit extra, will your benefits improve dramatically? If so, consider the potential advantages of making this additional investment. Not having adequate coverage can quickly deplete your savings and put you in debt if you experience a medical emergency.

- If you're forced to use one primary care physician or a doctor that's associated with your particular plan, how long do you typically have to wait to get a non-emergency-related appointment?

- What type of prescription drug plan is offered? For some prescription plans, you pay a flat fee ($5 or $10) for every prescription filled. In other types of plans, you pay a pre-determined percentage of the prescription's cost. Sometimes, a plan will only fill prescriptions using "generic" drugs.

- Can you be dropped from the health care plan if you need to use what the health care company considers too many services or rack up too many medical bills?

To determine what your options are in terms of coverage, you should receive a "Summary of Benefits" booklet published by the health care provider or health insurance company. This listing of services will describe what's included in your plan, and how much (in addition to your monthly premiums), you'll need to pay in order to receive each type of service.

Keep in mind that most heath care programs will *not* cover the following: general dental services (unless you have separate dental insurance); eye-glasses or contact lenses (unless you have separate vision care insurance); hearing aids; experimental medical procedures; cosmetic or non-medically necessary reconstructive surgery; custodial care or rest care; non-medically necessary routine foot care; personal comfort and convenience items; and other services that are not considered medically necessary.

When an employer offers employees some type of health insurance or health care coverage, this can cost the employer upwards of $1,500 per year or more per employee, or up to $8,000 per year to cover each employee's entire family. These costs are higher if your employer also offers dental and/or vision care benefits. The cost of these benefits is part of the overall value of your compensation package. The more that's covered by your health care plan, the fewer medical expenses you'll pay.

The Family and Medical Leave Act (FMLA) provides certain employees with up to 12 work weeks of unpaid, job-protected leave a year, and requires full group health benefits to be maintained during the leave.

FMLA coverage applies to all public agencies, including State, local and Federal employers, and local education agencies (schools); and private-sector employers who employ 50 or more employees for at least 20 work weeks in the current or preceding calendar year, including joint employers and successors of covered employers.

To be eligible for FMLA leave, an employee must work for a covered employer and have: 1) worked for that employer for at least 12 months; and 2) worked at least 1,250 hours during the 12 months prior to the start of the FMLA leave; and, 3) worked

Bright Idea
As you evaluate your health insurance coverage, determine if the policy has an annual deductible (the dollar amount of medical bills that you must pay for yourself each year) or maximum benefit (limit to what the policy will pay). These limitations will typically apply only if you go outside of your plan's "network" or "area," and they can result in you having to pay substantial fees for medical services.

Moneysaver
If you're paying some or all of your premiums, pay them annually instead of monthly. Check with your employer or insurance agent about how much money you can save if you pay premiums once per year. You can typically avoid the monthly service fee and receive a discount for pre-payment.

at a location where at least 50 employees are employed at the location or within 75 miles of the location.

A covered employer must grant an eligible employee up to a total of 12 work weeks of unpaid leave in a 12 month period for one or more of the following reasons: the birth of a son or daughter, and to care for the newborn child; the placement with the employee of a child for adoption or foster care, and to care for the newly placed child; to care for an immediate family member (spouse, child, or parent, but not a parent in-law) with a serious health condition; and when the employee is unable to work because of a serious health condition. This is called "leave entitlement."

Not long ago, group health coverage was available only to full-time workers and their families. That changed in 1985 with the passage of health benefit provisions in the Consolidated Omnibus Budget Reconciliation Act (COBRA).

Now, terminated employees or those who lose coverage because of reduced work hours may be able to buy group coverage for themselves and their families for limited periods of time (18 to 36 months, depending on the circumstances). If you are entitled to COBRA benefits, your health plan must give you a notice stating your right to choose to continue benefits provided by the plan. You have 60 days to accept coverage or lose all rights to benefits. Once COBRA coverage is chosen, you are required to pay for the coverage. Life insurance is not covered by COBRA. Under COBRA, spouses of deceased employees (and their children) can continue receiving health care benefits for a period of time after the benefit-receiving employee dies.

Consult with your employer (or former employer) for more details on how COBRA impacts you and your personal situation.

On the Internet, you can access an informative report about COBRA, published by U.S. Department of Labor Pension and Welfare Benefits Administration. Point your web browser to http://www.pueblo.gsa.gov/cic_text/employ/cobra/cobra.txt to access this report.

The biggest benefit of enrolling yourself (and your family) in your employer's group health program is that the coverage typically available in a group plan is usually more comprehensive and cheaper than what you can purchase on your own.

Job sharing

In a time when people are forced to work longer hours in order to make ends meet, and two income families have become the norm, many companies are now developing job-sharing plans so people can also enjoy a family life. From an employer's standpoint, job sharing can be used to keep top performing employees on the job when they'd ordinarily leave the workforce to raise a family, deal with an chronic illness, or retire.

Job sharing is a system of work where two employees take on the responsibilities of one full-time position, usually involving some level of management. Work, pay, benefits, and holidays are divided between the two employees, who in the eyes of the employer perform the work of one full-time person in a specific position. This allows working mothers to spend more time at home with their children, yet continue to pursue a career.

In a job sharing situation, two people share one job title, one office, and all work-related tasks. Each

Moneysaver
When given a choice, consider choosing a higher deductible to save money. If you and your family have experienced good health over the past several years, you may want to switch to a higher deductible—perhaps $500 or $1,000. This will result in you having to pay considerably lower monthly premiums.

job sharer is able to take over where the other left off. Job sharers can divide their schedules in a variety of ways, such as working alternate days or half-days everyday.

Companies like Merrill Lynch, Hewlett Packard, MetLife, 3M Corporation, Gannett, AllState Insurance, Hallmark Cards, Marriott and Ford Motor Company all have existing job sharing programs in place. If your employer doesn't yet offer this type of employment plan, there are ways of starting one, if you're willing to pioneer a pilot program for your employer.

Job sharing situations can go on for years, or it can be an interim type situation where a mother wants to spend more time at home with a newborn child, but doesn't want to give up her career totally. Job sharing programs often work exceptionally well, in virtually every industry, but it's often difficult to convince an employer to initiate this type of program.

If you're interested in pursuing a job-sharing plan, but it's not something your employer offers, do all of the research and planning before approaching your employer. Job sharers need to figure out what they want, how the job sharing will work, who their partner will be, and how the salary and benefits will be divided. All of this should be put in a detailed proposal and presented to the employer. The people who have the best results trying to launch a job-sharing program are the ones with a proven track record with their employer. Employees who the employer doesn't want to lose are in the best position to propose this type of work plan.

For job sharing to work successfully, employees have to overcome many logistical obstacles. Work

> 66
> Job sharing has been in existence in America since 1975, and the popularity of this type of work plan is growing quickly among Fortune 500 companies. A study conducted several years ago showed that 35 percent of Fortune 500 companies have a job-sharing plan in place. This statistic is now much higher.
> —Susan Smith, co-author of *The Job Sharing Handbook*
> 99

partners need to have common work habits and be able to work very well together. They must have a similar attitude about their work, be able to communicate extremely well, and be extremely organized. Workloads need to be divided equally, scheduling and compensation issues need to be resolved, and a close relationship with the supervisor or employer needs to be developed. All of this must be worked out in advance so that it all jives with company policy.

The people involved in a job-sharing program must develop a plan with their employer that works for everyone involved in terms of salary, benefits, and scheduling. In some cases, the full-time salary, benefits, and work hours are simply divided in half. Each employee then pays for half of their own health insurance benefits, for example. Most companies aren't willing to pay the added expense of providing full benefits to two employees responsible for one job.

Each year, *Working Mother* magazine publishes a list of the top 100 best employers for mothers, and this lists mentions which companies offer job sharing plans.

Life insurance

As part of your overall compensation package, your employer might offer you a life insurance policy that's worth one, two, or three times your annual earnings. For an additional fee (that you pay), you can enhance the value of this policy to be worth any value ($50,000, $100,000, $250,000 or more). When you're hired and initially receive this benefit, you'll be required to determine who the policy's beneficiaries will be (who will get paid if you die). You may also be given the option to purchase additional life

❝

The best advice I can offer is that if you want to participate in job sharing, you should seek out your own work partner. The best partner is someone you know well, and already has similar responsibilities. Job sharing only works when two people are doing one specific full-time job. The biggest obstacle is developing a communication system that works for the two people sharing the job.
—Susan Smith, co-author of *The Job Sharing Handbook*

insurance policies covering your spouse and/or children. Depending on the size and value of the policy, you may choose to consult your own insurance agent and purchase an additional policy outside of what your employer offers.

Just as with any type of insurance, there are several types of life insurance (whole life and term life being the two major categories.) The price you'll pay for a policy will be based on your age, the value of the policy, whether or not you smoke, and other related criteria. The younger and healthier you are, the cheaper a life insurance policy will be.

According to The American Council on Life Insurance, "Life insurance is an essential part of financial planning. One reason most people buy life insurance is to replace income that would be lost with the death of a wage earner. The cash provided by life insurance also can help ensure that your dependents are not burdened with significant debt when you die. Life insurance proceeds could mean that your dependents won't have to sell assets to pay outstanding bills or taxes. An important feature of life insurance is that there is no federal income tax on proceeds paid to beneficiaries."

Bright Idea
One rule of thumb when determining how much life insurance you need is to buy a policy with a value that is equal to five to seven times your annual gross income.

When determining how much life insurance you need, The American Council on Life Insurance suggests, "Before buying life insurance, you should assemble personal financial information and review your family's needs. There are a number of factors to consider when determining how much protection you should have. These include: any immediate needs at the time of death, such as final illness expenses, burial costs, and estate taxes; funds for a re-adjustment period, to finance a move or to provide time for family members to find jobs; and ongoing financial needs, such as monthly bills and expenses, day-care costs, college tuition or retirement."

Term life insurance provides protection for a specific period of time. It pays a benefit only if you die during the term. Some term insurance policies can be renewed when you reach the end of a specific period, which can be from one to 20 years.

According to The American Council on Life Insurance, "Permanent insurance provides lifelong protection and is known by a variety of names. As long as you pay the necessary premiums, the death benefit will be there. These policies are designed and priced for you to keep over a long period of time. If you don't intend to keep the policy for the long term, it could be the wrong type of insurance for you.

"Most permanent policies—including whole, ordinary, universal, adjustable, and variable life—have a feature known as 'cash value' or 'cash surrender value.' This feature is not found in most term insurance policies. Keep in mind that with all types of permanent policies, the cash value of a policy is different from the policy face amount. Cash value is the amount available when you surrender a policy before its maturity or your death. The face amount is the money that will be paid at death or at policy maturity."

For specific tips on how to buy a life insurance policy that best meets your needs, The American Council on Life Insurance (a trade association of more than 600 life insurance companies. Collectively, these companies provide about 90 percent of the life insurance in force in the United States) offers a web site (http://www.pueblo.gsa.gov/acli/

Unofficially...
Need more information? Contact the National Insurance Consumer Helpline (NICH) at (800) 942-4242. NICH is a toll-free consumer information telephone service sponsored by insurance industry trade associations.

index.htm) designed to provide a wealth of useful information.

Long-term disability

Unlike life insurance, to receive the benefit from a long-term disability plan, you need to get very sick and be unable to work due to medical reasons, but you don't have to die (which in the scheme of things is a good thing).

As a person with a job, your most valuable asset is yourself and your ability to earn an income. If that ability is taken away from you for one month, two months, six months, two years, or longer, you won't receive a paycheck. Thus, you could easily run into serious financial difficulties.

Moneysaver
Avoid purchasing multiple insurance plans that offer overlaps in coverage. Determine exactly what coverage you already have and then seek only the additional coverage you believe you need.

Assuming you're unable to work due to medical reasons, on top of not receiving a paycheck to cover your living expenses, you could be responsible for hefty medical bills that aren't covered by traditional health insurance. To protect yourself against the possibility of losing your income should you be forced to stop working (due to medical reasons), consider a long-term disability insurance policy.

Once you experience some type of medical problem, the criteria you'll need to meet before a long-term disability insurance policy kicks in will vary greatly based on the policy, as will the amount of the benefit you receive. For example, some policies don't go into affect until you've been out of work for one or two full months.

Whether or not you qualify to receive long-term disability insurance will depend on your age, income, health condition, and your occupation. The premiums for this type of policy can run anywhere from $500 to $6,000 per year, depending on your circumstances, and if you want the policy to fully replace your current salary or just a portion of it. Things to evaluate with regards to this type of insurance policy are the "daily benefit," the "benefit period," the "elimination period," and whether or not the policy offers "inflation protection." Any insurance agent will be able to explain these terms and how they apply to your needs.

Also, you want to make sure that the insurance provider has an excellent reputation and is rated at least an "A" by sources like Standard & Poor's which evaluate insurance companies. A few questions to ask about long term disability insurance policies are:

- Does the policy cover nursing home care and/or at home care? For how long?

- Does the policy cover long-term custodial care (someone to help you bathe, eat or perform other tasks if you become disabled)?

- Does the policy cover mental disorders as well as physical disabilities or problems?

Not all employers offer this type of insurance as part of their benefits package, mainly because it's costly and it's not suitable for every type of person. If this type of insurance isn't provided as part of your compensation package, contact an insurance agent to determine if this coverage would be in your best interest to have (and pay for yourself).

Low-interest rate loans

In order to help employees improve their quality of life, some employers (especially larger companies) will offer low-interest or no-interest loans to employers. These loans typically offer more competitive

Watch Out!
When purchasing any type of insurance, no matter what your insurance agent suggests, you must be totally honest about your medical history and pre-existing medical conditions if you're asked about them. Failure to provide this type of information can result in the insurance company not paying a claim or canceling your policy.

rates than a bank or financial institution would offer, and for the employee, they're easier to apply for and obtain.

Unofficially...
Some employers will take care of every detail of a new employee's move, including hiring, scheduling, and paying for people to pack up your belongings and unpack them in your new home or apartment. They'll also cover the cost to have your car(s) transported, and for your airfare.

Moving/relocation expenses

When it comes time to discussing your sign-on bonus, if you'll be moving to a new town or city in order to accept a new job, you should also inquire about whether your new employer will cover moving and/or relocation expenses. Most employers (especially medium- and large-sized companies) will pay an employee's moving expenses and even help the new employee find housing in the new city.

What moving-related services your employer covers is something that you'll want to negotiate prior to accepting your job. If possible, this should be kept separate from a sign-on bonus, which you'd negotiate to receive in exchange for accepting the job offer from the company.

On-the-job training

Most companies have their own way of doing things and offer on-the-job training and new-employee orientation programs designed to bring you up to speed once you're hired. Typically, you're paid your full salary while participating in these training and orientation programs, which in addition to helping you prepare for your job, will help you improve upon your personal skill set.

In addition to the on-the-job training the employer will determine if you'll be entitled to participate in additional training programs over time that will help you become qualified to fill more advanced (and higher paying) positions within the company. If the only way to move up the corporate ladder within your company is to obtain additional education and/or training, you want to ensure, in advance, that this training will be made available to you, preferably free of charge.

Paid sick days

No matter what size company you'll be working for, when you're hired, you will be awarded a pre-determined number of paid vacation days and paid sick days that you can use each year. If you're given five sick days as an employee first starting out with a company, but you catch a very bad case of the flu six months into your job, and you're sick for seven business days, those two extra sick days could be deducted from your vacation days. As an alternative, the employer could withhold pay for those two days when you weren't on the job, or may choose to be flexible and give you the additional vacation days if you provide a note from your doctor verifying your illness.

An employer's policy regarding sick days will be outlined in your employee policy manual, and should also be discussed prior to your accepting a job offer. As you're negotiating your overall compensation package, one of your final negotiating points before accepting an offer might be to request additional paid sick days. You're better off, however, negotiating for additional paid vacation days.

Paid vacation days

One of the benefits that people tend to pay a lot of attention to relates directly to how much time they *won't* have to spend on the job. Paid vacation days (outside of federal and/or state holidays) are usually awarded to employees based on the amount of time they've been with the company. Typically, a new employee will be given 10 days' (two weeks)

paid vacation per year, however, this is often negotiable, especially if you'll be accepting a non-entry-
level position.

In addition to considering how many paid vacation days you're entitled to, make sure you determine what the company's policy is for taking those
days. Can you take your vacation days all at once, or
do you have to break them up? How much notice do
you have to give your employer before taking one or
more of your vacation days? Is it possible to take only
a portion of a vacation day (such as a morning or
afternoon off), and have it not count as a full day?
Some employers measure time off in as little as six
minute increments, so if you need to take a few
hours off to take care of personal errands, you can
do so, but it will count as a portion of a used vacation day.

If, during your compensation package negotiation, you can get your employer to agree that you're
worth more than the salary you're being offered
(but the employer doesn't have it in their budget to
pay you more), one of the things you could negotiate for additional paid vacation days. You can also
negotiate to receive additional paid vacation days
as a reward for performance or for reaching pre-
determined objectives or goals while on the job.

Parking

No, this doesn't refer to what you did with your
boyfriend or girlfriend in the backseat of your car in
high school, and in this case, it has nothing to do
with the board game *Monopoly*. If you work in a
major city (like New York, Los Angeles, Chicago, or
San Francisco), where finding a parking spot on the
street is difficult at best, you'll appreciate that some
employers pay an employee's parking expenses

Unofficially...
In addition to
offering paid
vacation days,
some companies
also provide
employees with
an annual vaca-
tion allowance,
meaning that
they'll actually
pay for your
vacation up to a
pre-determined
limit. This is a
fast-growing
trend, and some-
thing that
employers are
using to boost
employee morale
and dedication.

while they're at work. This often saves the employee upwards of several hundred dollars per month and helps protect their car from theft.

Obviously, this isn't a need that everyone has, since some people prefer to take advantage of public transportation or company-organized carpools to get to work. If, however, you drive to work and have to worry about where you're going to park each day, having your employer pick up the tab for a spot in a parking lot is a nice benefit.

Profit-sharing plans

By participating in a profit-sharing plan, you will directly benefit from how profitable your employer is. If the company earns a profit, you get a piece of it. Simply by working hard and doing your job (without having to invest money), you have the opportunity to benefit financially from the growth and prosperity of your employer, if you're able to take part in a profit-sharing program.

Typically, at the end of each year, an employer places a portion of its profits for the year into the profit-sharing fund. This fund is then divided up among the employees who are eligible to participate in the program. The division of the profits is often calculated as a proportion of an employee's base salary and their years of employment. The longer you stay with a particular company, the larger this financial benefit becomes.

Since a profit-sharing plan is often part of what a company offers as its retirement benefits, the money you earn through profit sharing is automatically added to your individual retirement fund. If you leave your employer before retirement, typically only a portion of the funds earned will be available to you, however, this varies by employer.

A company often initiates a profit-sharing plan in an effort to keep employees motivated to continuously be profit motivated and to keep operating costs down. (After all, any money spent on expenses by the company reduces the amount of profit a company earns and ultimately contributes to the profit-sharing plan.)

Retirement plans

Bright Idea
To learn more about your available retirement plan options, visit the web sites or actual offices of Fidelity Investments (http://www. fidelity.com) and/or Charles Schwab (http:// www.schwab.com) —two popular discount brokerage services that offer retirement planning services and investment options.

The salary you get paid to do your job will help you cover your cost of living expenses, but in addition, your compensation package should help you plan for the future, at least in terms of your finances. The next chapter focuses on various types of retirement plans available, and will help you begin planning for your future retirement. Even if you've just graduated and you're about to enter the work force for the first time, it's important to start planning for your retirement.

Severance pay (or severance package)

As you negotiate with your employer how much money you'll earn while on the job and what benefits and perks you'll receive for doing your work, you'll also need to discuss what happens if your employment experience simply doesn't work out. If you're working for a small company, or you're a low-level employee with any company, chances are there won't be any fancy severance package associated with leaving the company. You may be paid until the end of the week or the end of the month, but if you leave, your paychecks (at least from this employer) will stop, and you'll once again find yourself embarking on a job search.

Severance packages are sometimes offered to all employees involved in downsizing or job elimination (for reasons such as mergers). If you're fired due to incompetence, or for not meeting the requirements of your job, you're not going to be rewarded by your employer.

A severance package, especially for a high-level executive, can be extremely elaborate and highly detailed. It will often become necessary to involve an attorney when developing this type of package, since what's offered by the employer will differ depending on the situation surrounding your departure, and virtually every possible scenario needs to be considered and spelled out in order for it to be binding.

Assuming you're being terminated from your job (due to downsizing, etc.), an employer will sometimes offer a severance package to help you cover your living expenses while you're unemployed and the costs associated with finding a new job. How quickly you'll be able to find a new job will vary, based on your salary requirements, your qualifications, the demand for people with your qualifications, and how much time and effort you put into your job search. Low-level employees will often receive no more than three months' pay as part of their severance package, while mid-level employees can expect up to 26 weeks of salary. Top-level executives can negotiate to receive all sorts of bonuses and benefits, in addition to upwards of one year's salary (or more).

Some companies measure how much severance pay they offer someone based not only on their position with the company, but also on how long they've been employed. For example, for a middle manager, one week's salary for every year of employment will be offered as severance pay. After the

Bright Idea
According to the Charles Schwab web site, when it comes to retirement, "It's important to determine how much you'll need to enjoy a comfortable retirement. The sooner you start saving, the more time your money has to grow. If you're a new investor, you should first develop a plan to identify your tolerance for risk and investing timeline." Another option is to hire a certified personal financial planner or accountant to assist you in planning for your future.

employee leaves the company, part of their severance package may include fully paid health care coverage for a pre-defined period, and career counseling to assist in creating a resumé or fine-tuning your job search skills.

Like all other types of benefits, the severance package offered by your employer will typically be either somewhat negotiable or extremely negotiable based on your position. When evaluating a severance package, think carefully about what it will take you to land a new job, and the cost associated with that experience. Figure into the equation the lost salary and the lost value of the benefits and perks you'll no longer receive.

Sign-on bonus (and other types of bonuses)

Aside from your salary, bonuses are used as incentives and rewards for employees. Information about sign-on bonuses and other types of bonuses offered by employers are described in Chapter 12.

Timesaver
More information on stock participation plans is offered in Chapter 12.

Stock participation plans (stock options)

This type of program gives you the opportunity to purchase your company's stock at a discount from its fair market value during a specific period of time. Typically, participation in this type of plan involves setting aside anywhere from two percent to ten percent (or more) of each paycheck. The deductions are usually made by your employer, on an after-tax basis. Also, consult with the employee orientation manual or employee policy manual issued by your employer to determine if this benefit is offered and what you need to do in order to participate.

Telecommuting

Wouldn't it be great if you could simply roll out of bed and be at the office and on the job in minutes, without having to deal with a hectic rush hour commute or fight for a parking spot? In America, over 11 million people have discovered that telecommuting at least one or two days per week is an ideal way to increase productivity, relieve on-the-job stress, spend more time with family, and save valuable time.

Thanks to the vast communications capabilities of e-mail, fax, teleconferencing, and video conferencing, it's no longer necessary for some types of workers to spend their entire week in an office environment. A growing number of employers, in many different industries, are starting to explore the benefits of allowing employees to "telecommute" one or more days each week.

Telecommuting allows people to work from home, or from virtually any off-site location, and communicate with coworkers and clients electronically, via computer, fax, and telephone. Many employers report that the overall productivity of employees who telecommute between one and three days per week increases dramatically, while the company reduces its need for office space. At the same time, employees experience reduced stress, improved morale, and are better able to balance their professional and personal lives.

Obviously, telecommuting is not the ideal solution for everyone, but for certain types of work, especially sales positions or jobs that involve a lot of time spent on the telephone or working on a computer, telecommuting can be a viable option. Before an employer will adopt a telecommuter program, it's important to work out exactly how issues will be resolved on a daily basis, how an employee's time will be managed, formulate specific procedures for

❝

Telecommute America (www.telecommute.org) projects that by the year 2000, there will be at least 14 million home-based workers, and that about 40 percent of today's workers could be telecommuting at least part of the time.

Unofficially...
If you're looking
for a job with an
employer that
already has a
telecommuting
program in place,
one on-line
resource to use
as you kick off
your job search
efforts is
Telecommuting
Jobs
(www.tjobs.com).

communicating with coworkers and customers, and to determine how work flow will be managed. Determining answers to these and other questions often becomes the responsibility of the potential telecommuter, who should submit a report to management outlining the financial and productivity benefits a telecommuting policy can have for the company and its employees.

Becoming a successful telecommuter requires a high degree of organization and well-defined procedures for staying in touch with co-workers, superiors, and clients throughout the day when you're not physically working from your office. Carefully scheduling your week becomes extremely important, since in-person meetings need to be held during your time in the office, and your time spent working from home needs to be highly productive, without supervision or direct guidance from superiors.

A growing number of large corporations now have policies and procedures in place for people interested in working outside of the office, at least for part of the work week. This involves having a direct and open line of communication between the telecommuter and the employer. It's also necessary for the telecommuter to have a fully equipped home office, which includes having a laptop or desktop computer that's equipped with a modem and access to the Internet along with the employer's intranet or e-mail system. A fax machine, multi-line telephone, pager, and cellular phone are also tools used by most telecommuters.

If you're interested in participating in or helping to launch a telecommuting program with your employer, but you're not sure you have what it takes

Timesaver
More information
about setting up
a home office is
provided in
Chapter 15.

to be a successful telecommuter, a few questions to ask yourself are:

- Do I have the experience and skills necessary to work on my own, without supervision?

- Am I disciplined enough to maintain good work habits when I'm working from home?

- How important is it for me to have interaction with coworkers throughout the day?

- Is my home a good work environment? Is it quiet and comfortable? Do I have space to set up a home office?

- If I begin telecommuting one, two, or three days per week, what positive and negative impact would it have on me, my family, my employer, and my coworkers?

- Do I have the technical expertise to use a computer equipped with a modem, a fax machine and any other office equipment needed to communicate with my office electronically while I'm working from home?

- How much of my daily work could actually be completed from home?

Tuition reimbursement

Throughout this book, the concept of working hard to constantly improve upon your personal skill set has been repeated several times—because it's important! Continuing your education so that you stay on the cutting-edge in terms of new developments in your field and keep up with technology in the workplace is critical. By constantly working to enhance your knowledge and skills, you'll remain a valuable asset (and increase your value) to your current employer over time and open up opportunities for career advancement. At the same time, if you choose to seek other employment opportunities (with other employers), you'll make yourself highly marketable during a job search.

Being able to take advantage of on-the-job training offered by your employer (in order to improve your knowledge and improve your chances of earning a promotion) is one thing, but pursuing additional formal education requires a much larger time and financial commitment on your part. Some employers realize the importance of helping their employees grow and are willing to pay for certain types of formal education that the employee pursues on a part-time or full-time basis.

Employers often require that the type of education you'll be pursuing be somehow related to your current occupation in order for it to qualify for reimbursement. In addition, you'll be required to maintain a pre-determined grade point average and attend an accredited college or university. Employers are sometimes also willing to pay for tuition associated with seminars taught by experts and sponsored by industry associations or other recognized organizations.

How much reimbursement you receive will vary, based on the program established by your employer. One common method used to ensure that employees put forth their best effort when pursuing additional education is to reward the employee for receiving good grades. For example, earning an "A" will result in 100-percent tuition reimbursement, a "B" is worth 80-percent tuition reimbursement, a "C" is worth 50-percent reimbursement, and anything lower than a "C" receives no reimbursement. Of course, you can expect employers to place a limit on the amount of tuition reimbursement you qualify for during a specific period.

If you're thinking of pursuing some form of an advanced degree, such as an MBA, attending graduate school full-time, without any form of tuition reimbursement, will be a costly endeavor. Plus, while you're in school, you probably won't be able to work full-time or even part-time, so your earning potential will drop dramatically until you graduate.

Most companies that offer a tuition reimbursement program want to see their employees reach their maximum potential, because the employer believes that this type of program will ultimately help the company by building employee loyalty and enhancing the value of its employees at the same time. By choosing a company that offers this benefit, as you plan out your long-term career plans, you can make pursing additional education part of those plans, yet be able to count on job security and support from your employer while you're in school. Once you obtain your advanced degree, your value as an employee will be greater and so will your earning potential.

Beyond formal benefits and perks

Your salary, along with benefits and perks, will add to the value of your overall compensation package. Even if you're offered a stellar deal from a financial standpoint, it's critical that you consider other things before accepting a job, such as whether or not you'll be emotionally happy, challenged, and fulfilled if you accept the job being offered. If you're receiving a fair and competitive benefits package, your health care coverage will allow you to receive counseling for stress management and depression that are job related.

Bright Idea
If you're concerned about starting a job with no career advancement potential, an employer's tuition reimbursement program can alleviate your fears. With further education, you'll enhance your earning potential, prove to your employer that you're looking for career advancement, and open up greater employment opportunities for yourself without having to make a large financial investment in your education. (A significant time commitment on your part will, however, be required.)

Unofficially...
The best benefit or job-related perk isn't something you can negotiate with your employer. This ultimate benefit is a job you love. The best way to get this, something too few Americans in the work force get to experience, is by making careful and well-thought-out career decisions. You also need to put in the time and effort for research prior to accepting any job offer.

By making well-thought-out career decisions now, you'll not only ensure your happiness, but you'll help to guarantee you won't ever need to take advantage of these mental health-related healthcare services, at least as a result of problems in your life caused by your job. Consider these questions:

- Does the job offer you long-term security and peace of mind, or will you constantly be worrying about losing your job for reasons beyond your control?

- Is the daily work environment conducive to your personal productivity?

- Are your coworkers and superiors people you'll enjoy spending time with and getting to know on a professional and personal level?

- Will you find the work stimulating?

- Will you be encouraged to strive toward achieving your true potential and have the opportunity to obtain the additional training and education you'll need to advance your career?

- Will you be truly excited to wake up every morning and go to work as the days, months, and years go by?

Just the facts

- Before you're able to successfully and accurately evaluate a benefits package, you must first determine what benefits you need and want, and develop a true understanding of what you actually deserve.

- Out of all the benefits and perks you'll be offered, the two most important ones for most people are health care and the ability to plan for retirement.

- Figuring out all of the lingo, restrictions, and fees associated with a health care program can require an advanced degree in several subjects, plus the ability to translate bureaucratic double-speak into something that actually makes sense. Under-standing the intricacies of the health care plan may require that you seek guidance from an independent insurance agent and take the time to carefully read whatever printed materials are supplied by your employer.

- Especially if you have a family (or relatives who depend on you for financial support), having a life insurance policy as part of your benefits package is also important. There are several different types of life insurance policies available to you, and the premiums for these policies will vary, based on your age, health and other criteria. If the benefits package doesn't offer you adequate life insurance, consider purchasing additional life insurance either through your employer or from an independent insurance agent.

- As you evaluate a job offer, consider the benefits and perks that have a direct financial value (such as your salary, the stock-participation plan, profit-sharing plan, the sign-on bonus, etc.). Also, take into account benefits like the employer's attitude toward telecommuting, childcare, and tuition reimbursement, which will directly improve the quality of life for you and your family.

GET THE SCOOP ON...
Why it's important to plan for your future ▪
Determining your future financial needs ▪
Where to go to seek investment and/or retire-
ment planning advice ▪ Various retirement plan
options that may be available to you

Retirement Plans

P art of the responsibility associated with earning what you deserve now, means being
responsible enough to plan carefully for the
future. Let's face it, with every passing day, you're
getting older. Right now, you work hard at your job
and perhaps you're struggling to make ends meet.
You're faced with a growing number of bills each
month, yet you're forced to work harder just to keep
your job.

In addition to dealing with your current financial issues and making ends meet today, it's critical
that you start thinking about your plans for retirement. Where will the money come from that you'll
need to live on, once you no longer have a steady
paycheck coming from an employer?

No matter how old you are, it's never too late or
too early to start planning for your retirement.
Unfortunately, retirement is an expensive proposition. Most financial planners agree that each year of
retirement will require between 70 and 90 percent
of your current annual income just to cover your
cost of living expenses and maintain your standard

Unofficially...
Now that people are living longer, current statistics show that the average American spends 18 years in retirement.

of living once you stop working. So, if you're earning $100,000 per year at your current job, you'll need anywhere from $70,000 to $90,000 per year (or more) to live once you retire.

So, where is this money going to come from? Hopefully, a significant portion of it will come from whatever retirement plan you set up for yourself, because only a portion of it (no more than 40 percent) will come from Social Security.

If you haven't yet established a retirement plan for yourself, you're not alone. The U.S. Department of Labor reports that less than half of all Americans have put aside money specifically for retirement. In addition, back in 1993, of those who had 401(k) coverage available, one third didn't participate by making an annual contribution.

While this chapter will *not* offer you investment advice, it will provide you with information about the retirement planning options you may have available, and will help you begin planning for your eventual retirement.

Planning for your future

Your retirement may be decades away, but by investing in a retirement fund starting now, you'll give that money plenty of time to grow, which is what must happen in order for you to have sufficient funds available when it actually comes time for retirement.

If you start at age 30 by investing $2,000 per year into an Individual Retirement Account (IRA), for example, and that investment earns just four percent per year, the following chart demonstrates what your retirement fund will be worth at ages 40, 50 and 60. By making this type of investment into an IRA, you can take a tax deduction for each year's contribution and delay paying taxes on investment earnings until you reach retirement age.

TABLE 14.1. RETIREMENT SAVINGS

Age	Your Retirement Plan's Value
30	$2,000
40	$24,012
50	$59,556
60	$112,170

For most people, simply putting $2,000 per year into an IRA isn't going to provide adequate funds for retirement. Thus, you must also take full advantage of Social Security benefits, participate in your employer's pension plan (which might include participation in a profit-sharing plan or your company's stock-participation plan), avoid dipping into your investment savings until retirement, and develop a basic understanding of investing.

If you're a homeowner, by the time you retire, your mortgage will most likely be paid off, which means you'll be able to live relatively rent free (you'll still have to maintain your home, plus pay utilities bills, home owner's insurance premiums, and property taxes, etc.) At least one of your largest monthly expenses right now (your mortgage payment) won't be an issue once you retire. To generate additional money for your retirement, you may choose to sell your home upon retiring and move into a smaller (and cheaper) residence.

Unfortunately, thanks to inflation, the basic cost of living will probably be substantially higher, so this is something you need to take into consideration when planning your retirement needs and calculating future expenses.

> " As a rule of thumb, for every five years you wait, you may need to double your monthly investing amount to reach the same goal.
> —Charles R. Schwab (800-435-4000 or www.schwab.com). "

Making decisions now that will meet your needs in the future

No matter how well you're doing financially right now, unless you plan for your future, you might not be able to maintain (or improve upon) your quality of life once you retire. The very first step in planning for your retirement is to determine your retirement needs. You'll need to consider:

- At what age you plan to retire.

- Your estimated life expectancy.

- Taking into account inflation, what is your annual retirement income goal (how much will you need for each year of retirement)?

- How much do you expect to receive from Social Security each year as a retirement benefit?

- Upon your retirement, how much will you receive each year from your pension?

- Do you plan to have a part-time or full-time job after your formal retirement? If so, what do you anticipate your income from that job to be? How many years after your formal retirement do you plan to continue working?

- Upon retirement, will you have any large assets (homes, etc.) that you'll want to sell?

- How much money are you currently able to invest in your retirement plan each year? Is this investment tax exempt, tax deferred or fully taxable?

With this information, you can meet with a financial planner or accountant, who will be able to assist you in creating an investment strategy in preparation for your retirement. The Fidelity Investments web site offers a Retirement Planning

Calculator designed to help you determine your needs and plan accordingly. To take advantage of this free service, point your web browser to http://personal421.fidelity.com/retirement/buildassets.

According to this web site, "The Retirement Planning Calculator makes it easier for you to develop your long-range savings strategy by helping you address four basic issues: When do you plan to retire, and how long do you expect your retirement income will need to last? How much money do you estimate you'll need to support your lifestyle after you've left the workforce? From which sources will you receive income during retirement? How much should you start saving now to help you meet your retirement goals?

Using this calculator, you'll be asked to enter information about your current income and savings as well as your long-range goals. Each piece of information will help you estimate your retirement savings goal and how much more you may need to save to help get you there. The calculator does not take into account income-reducing factors, such as taxes. Therefore, all results are rough estimates that are meant for informational purposes only. Also, keep in mind that as your income rises each year, you should increase how much you are saving for retirement as well."

Charles Schwab's web site offers a similar Retirement Savings Planner calculator which can be accessed by pointing your web browser to http://www.schwab.com/SchwabNOW/SNLibrary/SNLib090/SN090.html.

Part of your retirement planning strategy must involve determining how much risk you're willing to

Bright Idea
Typically, no matter what investments you choose, the more time you spend learning how to manage your retirement investments, the better return you'll receive. Of course, for a fee you can hire a certified financial planner, stockbroker, or accountant to manage your retirement investments for you.

take when investing the money you put aside for retirement. The more risk you take, the greater your potential gain (and the greater chance you have of losing some or all of your investment). As a general rule, young people should consider taking on higher than average investment risk, since they have more time to recoup their loses or benefit from their gains. As you get older, and you get closer to the time when you'll actually need your retirement money, it's usually a good idea to use less risky investments.

What types of investment you choose will depend on a number of factors, such as:

- What investments are available to you through your employer.
- Whether or not you want investments in addition to what your employer offers.
- How much money you have to invest.
- How much risk you're willing to accept.
- How much time you have before your retirement.
- How much money you'll actually need to retire.

Your computer can be a powerful investment management tool. Using the World Wide Web and/or specialized investment tracking software, you can easily learn how to track and/or manage your own retirement portfolio.

Using a certified financial planner

Financial planning is the process of meeting your life goals through the proper management of your finances. Life goals can include buying a home, saving for your child's education, or planning for retirement. The financial planning process consists of the following steps that will help you determine where you are financially:

- Gathering relevant financial information
- Setting life goals
- Examining your current financial status
- Coming up with a strategy or plan for how to achieve your goals

If you'd like to seek the advice of a financial planner, make sure the person you hire is a "certified financial planner" (CFP). According to The Institute of Certified Financial Planners, "While many people can call themselves 'financial planners,' CFP licensees must adhere to a rigorous code of ethics that requires them to put their client's interest first. The CFP mark is an indication of competence in financial planning. To earn the designation, individuals must pass a comprehensive examination and continue to meet the education, experience, and ethics standards established by the CFP Board. Financial planners are compensated in a variety of ways, including fee-only, commission, a fee/commission blend and salaried. Each method of compensation has its merits, depending on a consumer's age, lifestyle, and financial situation. As long as a planner's method and source of compensation is fully disclosed, the Institute of Certified Financial Planners believes that consumers should form a relationship with their planner based primarily on his or her competence."

A CFP, accountant, or a retirement specialist working for a company, like Fidelity Investments or Charles Schwab, will be able to help you plan for your retirement and help you develop an understanding of what retirement programs are available through your employer.

Timesaver
To find a CFP in your area, contact ICFP by calling (800) 282-PLAN or by visiting the organization's web site at http://www.icfp. org. You can also call the International Association of Financial Planning at (800) 930-4511.

Bright Idea
Some larger companies have a Benefits Office staffed by people who can assist employees with their retirement planning.

Consider your retirement when leaving or changing jobs

When changing jobs, be sure to protect your retirement nest egg by making smart investment decisions. While changing jobs for whatever reason is common, if you're involved in an employer-sponsored retirement plan, such as a 401(k), then there are some things to consider before actually leaving your current job in order to avoid paying large amounts of taxes and penalties unnecessarily.

Watch Out!
To avoid paying taxes and penalties, seriously consider reinvesting your 401(k) money immediately using what's called a "rollover IRA." An IRA is an Individual Retirement Account that you can create quickly and easily by working with a financial planner or consulting an investment institution, such as Fidelity Investments or Charles Schwab.

Upon leaving a job, you usually have two main choices regarding your retirement plan. You can have the employer issue a distribution check directly to you (and spend the money now), or you can reinvest the money elsewhere and have it continue to accumulate until your retirement. Requesting to receive your employer-sponsored 401(k) distribution now will result in at least 20 percent of that money being automatically withheld for federal taxes. Depending on your current tax bracket, this figure could increase. In addition, there will be a 10-percent early withdrawal penalty if you're under 59 years of age. Finally, both state and local taxes will be withheld from your check prior to you receiving any money. Thus, the retirement money you have accumulated will instantly be cut almost in half if you choose not to reinvest your money into another retirement plan.

Before leaving your current place of employment, you must instruct your employer to transfer your retirement money directly into some other retirement plan, such as the employer-sponsored 401(k) program operated by your new employer or into an IRA that you create for yourself through an investment institution. By reinvesting all of your retirement plan money into a "rollover IRA" or another employer-sponsored 401(k), you will not have to pay any taxes or penalties, so your money will continue to grow on a tax-deferred basis.

Upon choosing to reinvest your employer-sponsored 401(k) money, you have four primary options regarding where to invest the money. These options include:

1. **Reinvest in your new employer's retirement plan** Contact your new employer to ensure that it's possible to immediately transfer your retirement plan money into your new employer's employer-sponsored retirement plan, and find out what the exact procedure is for doing this.

   Before leaving your current employer, choose which financial institution you want your retirement money transferred into (such as Fidelity Investments or Charles Schwab). Choose how you want the money invested (mutual funds, annuities, CDs, stocks, bonds, etc.), and then tell your employer exactly where to send the funds. The money should go directly to the investment institution that will be managing your IRA. If your current employer issues a check directly to you, you'll automatically lose 20 percent of the money, which will go toward federal taxes.

2. **A rollover annuity** There are two types of annuities—fixed and variable. The difference between a rollover IRA and a rollover annuity is that the latter will guarantee your principal and pay a fixed interest rate, or a variable rate of return on your investment. Annuities will pay you an income for the rest of your life (once

Watch Out!
In addition to whatever money you're putting aside for retirement in an employee-sponsored 401(k) or IRA, upon retirement you'll also receive money from Social Security. Most financial planners agree, however, that Social Security will only provide you with a percentage of the money you'll need.

you retire), and offer a guaranteed minimum death benefit. A rollover Annuity can be purchased through an insurance company, such as MetLife (http://www.lifeadvice.com).

3. **Keep your money in your current plan**   Some companies will allow you to keep your money in your current employer-sponsored 401(k) or employer-sponsored retirement plan, even after you leave the company and pursue another job elsewhere. The main drawback to this is that once you leave the company, you must wait until your retirement before obtaining any control over the money you have invested, and your investment options could be limited.

No matter what you choose to do with your retirement money, before doing anything, consult a financial planner, accountant, or retirement investment specialist.

Upon retirement you want to have as much money as possible available to you, and the way to insure this is to make educated and well-thought-out decisions about your investments. By doing some simple research, you'll discover that there are many investment opportunities available to you, some of which offer you a lot of control over your invested funds, while others are managed on your behalf.

To learn more about rollover IRAs, contact an investment institution, such as Fidelity Investments, by dropping into any branch office or by calling (800) 544-4774 (http://www.fidelity.com). A Charles Schwab office can be reached by calling (800) 435-4000 (http://www.schwab.com).

To learn more about annuities, read the Consumer Information Center's free booklet, *About Annuities,* (http://www.pueblo.gsa.gov/press/

Bright Idea
Check with the Benefits Office at your current place of employment and have them review all of your options. The Benefits Office at your new place of employment is also an excellent source of information. Don't be afraid to do some research and ask plenty of questions.

nfcpubs/annuity.txt or write to: Consumer Information Center, Pueblo, CO, 81009).

What does "defined contribution" mean to you?

It was back in the 1920s that the U.S. Government
first introduced the concept of pensions to government workers. This practice was soon adopted by
public and private companies as a way for employers
to provide for employees after a lifetime of service.
Back then, people spent their entire career working
for a single employer, and when they retired, they
received a pension that was classified as a "defined
benefit plan." Under this type of pension plan,
retired people received a pre-determined, but regular, income for the rest of their lives. This income
was paid for by their former employer.

Needless to say, times have changed. These days,
while defined benefit plans are still offered by some
employers, it's more common for employees to have
the opportunity to participate in a "defined contribution plan," which means that money is taken from
an employee's paycheck and this contribution is
added to by the employer. (One common scenario
is that the employer will match 50 percent of the
employee's contribution, up to six percent of their
annual salary.) The total contribution goes into an
employee's pension fund. The employer, however,
does not guarantee how much of a retirement benefit the employee will ultimately receive. How these
plans are managed, where the contributions come
from, and how the money is invested determines
the size of the benefit that the recipient ultimately
receives upon retirement.

Unofficially...
In 1984, over 84 percent of all company-sponsored retirement plans were "defined contribution plans." This figure is believed to be higher today.

An employee's contribution to a defined contribution plan can come from a number of sources, such as a profit-sharing plan, stock-participation plan, 401(k) plan, 403(b) plan, Section 457 plan, or money-purchase plan.

In many cases, an employee has the option whether or not to participate in an employer's defined contribution plan. Deciding not to participate in this program usually means that you give up your company pension plan, which means you're on your own to plan for your retirement.

In addition to what your employer offers as a basic retirement plan, you may be eligible to participate in a Supplemental Executive Retirement Plan (SERP), a way for people with higher incomes to set aside additional funds for their retirement.

Unofficially...
A 403(b) is similar to a 401(k), however, it applies to people working for the educational system (a school system, college or university) and non-profit organizations. Under a 403(b) plan you can usually invest a larger portion of your salary than you can for a 401(k), up to a pre-determined annual cap.

401(k) plans

According to Fidelity Investments, "A 401(k) is a type of retirement plan that allows employees of corporations and private companies to save and invest for their own retirement. Through a 401(k), you can authorize your employer to deduct a certain amount of money from your paycheck before taxes are calculated, and invest it in a 401(k) plan. Your money is invested through your company's plan, which you choose. The federal government established the 401(k) in 1981, with special tax advantages to encourage people to prepare for retirement."

"You decide how much money you want deducted from your paycheck and invested during each pay period, up to the legal maximum (the IRS sets an annual dollar limit each year). You also decide how to invest that money, choosing from your plan's different investment options. The money you contribute to your 401(k) account is deducted from your pay before income taxes are taken out. This means that by contributing to a 401(k), you can actually lower the amount you pay each pay period in current taxes. For example, if you earn $1,000 each paycheck, and you contribute, say 5 percent ($50), you are only taxed on $950. You don't owe income taxes on the money you invest in a 401(k) plan until you withdraw it, when you could be in a lower tax bracket."

IRAs

According to Fidelity Investments, "An IRA, or Individual Retirement Account, is an account established with funds earmarked for retirement. Saving for retirement in an IRA instead of another type of account has tax advantages, which is one of its primary benefits. To encourage people to save for retirement, recent legislation has given IRAs features that make them an even smarter choice for every eligible retirement investor. This legislation not only enhanced the traditional IRA, but also created a new option, the Roth IRA. Under current law, you can contribute a maximum of 100 percent of compensation or $2,000, whichever is less, to all your IRAs for each tax year. Married couples who file jointly can contribute up to $2,000 to each spouse's IRA for any tax year for a total of $4,000 annually, even if one is a non-working spouse, provided combined contributions do not exceed combined compensation."

"Although you wouldn't want to rely on an IRA as your sole source of retirement income, it does provide an effective way to supplement your other long-term savings vehicles. Once you've contributed the maximum you can to an employer-sponsored retirement plan, such as a 401(k) plan, you'll want

> **❝**
> The total U.S. 401(k) asset base grew from $300 billion in 1991 to $700 billion in 1996, passing traditional pension funds. Twenty-two million people are doing it, and you probably should be, too.
> —The InvestorGuide web site (http://www. investorguide. com).
> **❞**

Unofficially...
The Vanguard Group's web site offers a comprehensive FAQ (frequently asked questions) document pertaining to IRAs. This document can be accessed by pointing your web browser to http://www.vanguard.com/educ/lib/retire/faqira.html or the company's home page at http://www.vanguard.com.

to consider an IRA as the next building block toward a more comfortable retirement. An IRA puts you in control of your retirement investments. You can invest your IRA contribution in almost any type of investment vehicle."

IRAs were created 20 years ago to help people save for their retirement. IRA holders receive two types of tax breaks. You can put $2,000 a year into an IRA ($4,000 a year if married) for as many years as you want, up until age 70. And you won't pay any tax on the IRA earnings until you begin taking the money out.

Many people can also deduct their IRA contributions from their current income. When you retire or leave a job, an IRA can also be used to hold a "rollover" of investments from a pension or profit-sharing plan, such as a 401(k) plan.

Keoghs and SEP-IRAs

A Keogh is ideal for self-employed individuals and small business owners, because it offers higher contribution limits than most other retirement plans available. You can contribute as much as 25 percent of your annual salary each year to a Keogh, up to the annual maximum of $30,000 per participant. Opening and administering a Keogh is more complex, because there are many ways this type of plan can be structured. One potential drawback is that you're required to make a minimum contribution each year. This minimum is determined by the amount with which you open the Keogh plan. With proper financial planning, a Keogh can reduce your income taxes, since you're permitted to deduct the entire amount of your contribution(s) from your taxable income each year.

A SEP-IRA (Simplified Employee Pension Plan) is a type of retirement plan designed for self-employed people and small-business owners. You're eligible to contribute to a SEP-IRA if you're a sole proprietor, in a partnership, or you're a small business owner. You're also eligible if you derive income from being self-employed (as a consultant or freelance worker, for example). If you qualify to participate in this type of retirement plan, you can invest between zero and 15 percent of your annual income (up to $24,000 per year) on a tax-deferred basis. This type of retirement plan is far easier to administer than a Keogh. However, it does have some limitations that you should investigate by discussing your options with an accountant or certified financial planner.

Social Security

Social Security is part of almost everyone's life. It protects more than 142 million workers and pays benefits to 43 million people. You and your family are probably protected by Social Security, because you pay taxes that help make the system work. There are three primary types of benefits that Social Security offers:

- Survivor benefits
- Disability protection
- Retirement benefits

According to the Social Security Administration, "Social Security is a foundation for building a comfortable retirement. A recent national poll found that three in four workers worry that they won't have enough money to live comfortably in retirement. Often the difference between retirees who enjoy retirement and those who struggle is financial

Unofficially...
The Vanguard Group is one of America's largest mutual fund organizations. It is also widely recognized as a premier provider of financial services. The company was ranked #1 in shareholder service for 1996, according to a national survey of nearly 4,000 mutual fund investors conducted by Financial World magazine, the sixth consecutive year that Vanguard received top honors in the survey.

Unofficially...
To learn about
what Social
Security benefits
exist and what
you'll be entitled
to, call the
Social Security
Administration at
(800) 772-1213
and request a
free *Personal
Earnings and
Benefit Estimate
Statement.* You
can also visit the
Social Security
Administration's
web site at
http://www.ssa.
gov.

planning. Social Security is part of a 'three-legged stool' that could solidly support a comfortable retirement. The other two legs of the stool are pension income and savings/investments. Financial advisers often tell people that, when they quit work, they'll need about 70 percent of pre-retirement income to live comfortably. By itself, Social Security replaces only about 42 percent of an average wage earner's salary."

The Social Security system provides a minimum "floor of protection" for retired workers, and for workers and their families who face a loss of income due to disability or the death of a family wage earner.

The Social Security Administration reports, "Social Security payments are based on two underlying philosophies. First, the system is designed so that there is a clear link between how much a worker pays into the system and how much he or she will get in benefits. Basically, high wage earners get more, low wage earners get less. At the same time, the Social Security benefits formula is weighted in favor of low wage earners, who have fewer resources to save or invest during their working years. Social Security retirement benefits replace approximately 60 percent of the pre-retirement earnings of a low wage earner, 42 percent of an average wage earner, and 26 percent of a high wage earner."

By calling a toll-free number (800-772-1213) anytime, you can request free publications offered by the Social Security Administration. These publications are designed to help people understand the benefits available to them.

The available publications include: *Understanding Social Security* (publication No. 05-10024),

Retirement Benefits (publication No. 05-10035), *Survivors Benefits* (publication No. 05-10084), *Disability Benefits* (publication No. 05-10029), *Medicare* (publication No. 05-10043), *Your Taxes... What They're Paying For...Where The Money Goes* (publication No. 05-10010) and *Your Number* (publication No. 05-10002).

Just the facts

- Begin planning for your retirement as early in your career as possible.

- A variety of retirement plans and options might be available to you.

- You can find a certified financial planner who is qualified to help you make intelligent retirement planning decisions. The services of an accountant can also be used.

Watch Out!
Companies like Fidelity Investments, Charles Schwab and the others listed as resources in this chapter all offer products and services designed to help people plan for their retirement. Neither author of this book or the publisher endorse these companies over any other. They're simply provided as a resource for readers interested in seeking out more information.

Tips for the Self-Employed

PART VII

GET THE SCOOP ON...
Defining your business and making sure that
it's viable before making a commitment ▪
Setting your rates to ensure profit while
remaining competitive ▪ Advertising, marketing,
and promotions ▪ Setting up a home office ▪
Juggling your personal and professional
commitments

Taking Care of Business from a Home Office

Chapter 15

Not everyone is cut out to work for someone else, or to take on a straight 9-to-5 job in which they have a specific job description and aren't encouraged to take on additional responsibilities. If you're one of these people, or you're looking for new challenges in your professional life, starting your own small business and becoming your own boss might be a viable option that will allow you to reach your true earning potential.

Becoming self-employed may sound extremely glamorous, especially if you're coming from an unfulfilling career working for others. But before pursuing this type of career opportunity, it's important to understand exactly what you're getting into. After all, if you're the boss, it becomes your responsibility to ensure that your business is successful. This will mean putting in long hours, wearing many hats, and taking on an incredible amount of responsibility. Being self-employed also means you need to be self-motivated, well organized, detail-oriented,

Watch Out!
Most apartment buildings, co-ops, and residentially zoned areas don't permit people to operate home-based businesses that involve having a steady stream of customers/clients coming and going to and from your home. If this is your plan, consult your local government, landlord, and/or tenant's association to determine what home business restrictions, if any, apply to you.

and able to stay focused when there's nobody looking over your shoulder to ensure you meet deadlines or maintain a certain quality of work.

Working from home, your options include starting a home-based business where you're selling a product (possibly via mail order) or service, working as a consultant, or as a freelancer.

Certain occupations and professions, such as a psychologist/therapist, lawyer, marketing/PR expert, writer, accountant, telemarketer, independent sales representative, graphic artist, or various other types of occupations are extremely conducive to working from a home office, provided you have the personality traits and desire to work for yourself.

The thing to understand about going from a traditional job to being self-employed and working from home is that this transition involves taking on a new type of lifestyle. Your work becomes an part of your life—not just during business hours, but in the evenings, at night, on weekends, and during holidays, as well. Having your office located just a few yards from your bedroom, living room, and kitchen has both its advantages and disadvantages. If you have children, this offers some wonderful benefits and potential drawbacks in a home office situation.

This chapter is written for someone interested in working from home and/or establishing a home-based business (with under five employees). It provides additional information to what was offered in Chapter 7. No matter what type of business or profession you're interested in pursuing, if it involves being a home worker, this chapter will help you.

What it means to be a home business owner or home office worker

Aside from the obvious perks of being able to control your own professional destiny and have total control over your income potential, working from home has its advantages, for example:

- You won't have a boss or supervisor constantly looking over your shoulder.

- You can work at your own pace.

- Your work hours are flexible.

- There's no dress code. (Yes, you can work in your underwear, and nobody will know!)

- You can be there for your children when you're needed.

- It's usually easier to juggle your personal and professional life.

- You'll save money on office space rent and additional utility bills.

- You won't have to deal with any type of commute or traffic. Just roll out of bed, walk into the next room, and you're at work.

If you've been stuck in an office job up until now in your career, working from home might sound like absolute paradise, which is why so many people are taking advantage of this type of opportunity. There are, however, a few things to consider before making this transition in your professional life.

Are you motivated and focused enough to do all of your work, in a timely manner, when you could be watching television, listening to the radio, catching up on your housework or errands, or just enjoying the weather if it happens to be a nice day?

Unofficially...
As someone who is self-employed working from home, if you choose to slack off and not work, you don't get paid. This may seem obvious, but it's something that many people don't realize until it's too late.

Do you live in an environment that's conducive to working from home?

Do you have a separate room in your home that can be transformed into a home office? Does this area have a way to shut it off from the rest of the house, so that you can have your privacy and quiet when you're hard at work and need to concentrate?

Do you have the type of job or profession that's compatible with a home-office lifestyle?

In the evenings, at night, and on weekends, once your work day is complete (and you have no pressing deadlines to meet), will you be able to focus on your personal life, instead of spending extra time in your office catching up on paperwork or checking your e-mail? It's extremely common for people working from home to get the urge to put in extra hours whenever they have free time, which is very important to a certain extent, but after a while this blurs the line between having a personal and professional life. If you're married and/or have children, spending too much time working can have a negative impact on your loved ones.

Working from home, no matter what type of work you do or type of business you operate, requires that you be extremely organized and detail oriented, because there's nobody to pick up the slack for you, or cover for your mistakes.

Define your business

Okay, so you've decided to work from home, either practicing your profession, working as a consultant, doing some type of freelance work, or operating your own business. The trick to being successful is learning how to carefully budget your time and money, and to keep setting goals for yourself. You'll also find it extremely useful, and in some cases 100

Watch Out!
Can you deal with the isolation involved with working from home? If you're a people person, will you enjoy spending so much time working alone, without the hustle and bustle of coworkers around you?

percent necessary, to formulate a detailed business plan (as described in Chapter 7).

You need to determine who your potential customers/clients will be, how you'll find them, and what service(s) or product(s) you'll provide. You also need to determine how much work you can handle yourself (and/or if you hire employees), what you can charge for your products/services, and what will be required for you to earn a profit.

If you'll be practicing some type of profession, consulting, or doing freelance work from your home, you'll need to spend time developing a niche for yourself and creating a reputation as an "expert" in a particular area or field. People and companies alike are willing to pay top dollar to hire someone who has an excellent reputation and who is extremely knowledgeable and considered an "expert" in their field. This applies to you whether you're working from home, or if you're using your home office as a base of operations and going out to see clients/customers in-person.

In order to obtain new clients/customers and keep them (or get repeat business), you must be able to work well with people, have excellent all-around communications skills, and be able to quickly develop a rapport or even a professional friendship with the people who hire you. This requires having an outgoing personality, always being up-beat and friendly, having a willingness to demonstrate to your clients/customers that they are a priority for you, and the ability to perform whatever service (or provide whatever product) your client/customer needs from you.

Marketing, advertising and promoting your business

If you're starting out as a home-based business operator or as a professional, consultant, or freelancer working from home, in order to establish yourself and attract a base of clientele, you'll need to do some marketing, advertising, and/or public relations to promote yourself and your work.

The very first step is to create a one- or two-page brochure, press release, and/or written document that you can distribute and use as your primary marketing tool. This document should:

- Tell who you are.

- Outline your qualifications and specialties.

- Detail the types of unique services/products you offer.

- Convey your marketing message.

- List your name, address, phone number (including a toll-free number, if you have one), e-mail address, pager number, or any other way a potential client/customer can reach you.

This document can be created on your computer, using a high-end word processor or desktop publishing package, or you can have a commercial printer design, typeset, and print the document so that it looks professional.

In addition to creating professional-looking marketing materials for yourself, you'll need business cards and a letterhead. Once you have business cards in-hand, you'll want to start distributing them wherever possible in order to solicit new clients/customers.

After you have created your marketing materials, there are a variety of ways you can use them.

Bright Idea
If your writing skills aren't up to par, you might consider hiring a freelance writer, public relations specialist, or marketing expert to write the document (brochure, press release, or marketing materials) on your behalf.

Through public relations efforts, you can contact the media (local newspapers, magazines, or radio stations that produce talk shows, and television news and talk shows) and try to obtain some free media coverage. If you're not familiar with how public relations works, or you don't know the correct format to use when creating a press release, you have several options. Read books that teach basic public relations skills, take a few public relations classes at a local college, or hire a PR consultant to help you get started.

Joining a local chamber of commerce and attending meetings in your area is another excellent networking opportunity, as is attending other local or regional events or conventions where potential customers/clients might be found. Another option is to become active in one or more professional associations and/or organizations, or attend industry trade shows. (You might even consider having a small booth at a trade show or event in your area.) If possible, offer yourself as an "expert" speaker or presenter at professional gatherings, such as a chamber of commerce meeting. Networking can almost always help you generate business. As you tap your networking skills, make sure you have your marketing materials with you so you can distribute them to potential customers/clients.

If you have any type of e-mail account, you probably receive anywhere from two or three to several dozen spam (i.e., junk mail) e-mail messages per day, hawking everything from phone/cyber sex to a method of earning unlimited income from your home without doing any work. Sending out unsolicited e-mail is one very cheap way you can attempt to generate clients/customers, but as much as you

Watch Out!
Your Internet service provider may cancel your account if you send large quantities of unsolicited e-mail messages (known as "spam") to people or companies.

hate receiving Spam in your e-mail inbox, so do others. Another way to tap the power of the Internet as a marketing tool is to create a web site for yourself that promotes your products/services. After your site is created, promote it by listing it with all of the Internet search engines and also listing the site's URL (web address) in all of your marketing and advertising materials.

If you're computer literate, creating a basic web site is extremely easy and can be done in a matter of hours, even if you have little artistic ability. There are many different software packages available, such as Symantec Visual Page (for Windows 95/98; http://www.symantec.com) and Microsoft Front-Page (for Windows 95/98; www.microsoft.com) that allow you to create your own web page with ease. Once the web page, or web site, is created, you need to hire an Internet service provider (ISP) that will actually host your site on the Internet, and you must register your domain name (which is something your Internet service provider can help with). Hiring a company to host your web site should cost anywhere from $20 to $100 per month. You can find these services in any Yellow Pages, using an Internet search engine, or by asking for a referral from someone you know who already has a web site.

Using your marketing materials, you can also create a mailing list and send out direct mailings to potential clients/customers, and then attempt to set up sales appointments with them in order to solicit business.

Telemarketing is yet another sales tool you can use to market yourself and your business. This can be as simple as opening a telephone book, pinpointing potential clients/customers and then

Bright Idea
Looking for design ideas for your web page? Many web page development software packages come with several pre-created templates. All you need to do is stick in your text and artwork, and you're done.

making cold calls to them. You can also purchase highly specialized lists of companies and/or individuals that meet virtually any criteria. Direct Channel, Inc. (781-986-1100 or http://www.directchannel.com) and Nationwide Data Services (800-579-5478; http://www.nationwidedata.com) are two mailing list brokerage firms providing "qualified" names for all of your prospecting needs. These companies specialize in target marketing and have access to millions of names in which you can cross reference different types of criteria to pinpoint your specific audience. The lists you choose to purchase can be supplied to you as a hard copy printout, in electronic form, or as mailing labels.

Paid advertising is perhaps one of the most costly methods to promote your business, products, or services, but it's a method that will usually provide the quickest results, providing you have the right advertising messages and you advertise somewhere that reaches the right target audience. If you determine that newspaper, radio, or television advertising is a viable option (and you can afford it), pinpoint what form of media you want to use and specifically which media outlets will help you reach your target customer/client. Contact those media outlets and speak with someone in the advertising sales department, who can answer your questions and provide you with a rate card.

Understand that advertising rates are almost always negotiable, and that the more advertising you're willing to commit to with each media outlet, the better rates you'll receive. If you're not familiar with how to create an advertising message or the best ways to use advertising to promote your business, read up on the topic, take advertising classes or hire an ad agency to work on your behalf.

Bright Idea
You can also surf the web looking for sites that you like, and borrow design ideas from those sites. (Avoid stealing copyrighted artwork or materials from other sites.) The C/Net web site (http://www.cnet.com) offers a selection of web site design software, artwork, and other materials that you can download, free of charge.

Unofficially...
Word-of-mouth and direct referrals are the best way to land new clients. Work hard to gain satisfied clients who will share your name with their friends, coworkers, and acquaintances. Developing an excellent reputation takes extra effort, but the benefits will be tremendous.

No matter how you decide to promote yourself and/or your business, the trick is to come up with a clear and concise advertising and marketing message that explains who you are, what you offer, and why someone should use your products/services. Be sure to clearly state your qualifications or what makes you stand out from the competition. Avoid making grand statements that mean little or that you cannot back up with hard facts.

Over time, you'll want to modify or fine-tune this sales pitch or advertising message to make it better, once you start determining how potential clients/customers react to it.

Determine the competition and build your reputation

From the moment you decide to start your own business and/or work from home, you'll need to determine who your competition is. Clearly define what sets you apart from them, and then work toward promoting and constantly building your reputation in your field, in your industry, and/or in your local (geographic) area. Try to differentiate your products/services from your competition (in terms of price, quality, or usefulness), and strive to offer the very best quality of product or service you can, at a fair price that people are willing to pay.

Setting up a home office

For someone who is motivated, focused, and disciplined, working from a home office can be a rewarding experience. But running a home office—whether you're self-employed or a telecommuter—requires an investment in supplies and equipment. This section describes some of the basics you'll need to run a home-based business.

A core business tool needed in virtually any home office is a powerful desktop or laptop computer equipped with a 28K or 56K modem to be used for surfing the Internet, accessing on-line services, and sending and receiving e-mail. The computer should also have an assortment of applications installed, including a word processor, spreadsheet, database, contact manager, scheduler, and, depending on your needs, any specialized programs such as accounting, computer-aided design (CAD), web page design, credit card processing software, or desktop publishing software.

Microsoft Office Professional Edition for Windows 95/98 (www.microsoft.com) is a popular and relatively inexpensive suite of business-related applications on one CD-ROM, soon to be replaced with Microsoft Office 2000. The software bundle includes Microsoft Word, Excel, Access, Outlook, and PowerPoint.

Other applications, such as FedEx Ship (800-238-5355), can be used to make sending FedEx packages an easy and automated process, while software packages provided by major airlines can be used for making your own travel reservations. For travel reservation, also take a look at Microsoft's Expedia on the web, at www.expedia.com.

You should also have a laser printer and some form of data backup device (such as a removable hard drive, Zip disk, or external hard drive) connected to your computer. Another important tool is a plain-paper fax machine. The Ricoh Aficio FX10 is an example of a fax machine that also works as a plain paper copier, high resolution scanner and laser printer for a computer. In a home-office situation where space is an issue, purchasing office

Bright Idea
To obtain free publicity, create a press release and send it to local media and industry-specific publications. Address your press release (and cover letter) to the specific person who covers your area of expertise. You can discover the names of the people you need to contact by calling the receptionist at each media outlet you want to target. Maintain a database of media contacts and send out periodic press releases.

Bright Idea
There are many magazines and newsletters that target small business owners and those who work from home. Three of these monthly publications include *Business@Home* —(800) 995-3590, *HomeOffice Computing* — (800) 288-7812 and *Entrepreneur's Home Office* — (800) 274-6229.

equipment with multiple uses will save both space and money.

You may also need between two and four telephone lines to accommodate a personal phone number, a work/business phone number, a fax line and a data line. To save money, the fax machine and computer can usually share a single phone line.

Your actual telephone should be capable of handling two phone lines and should have a hold feature, along with an auto dialer that can store your most frequently dialed numbers. Depending on the size of your home, consider connecting a 900 MHz digital cordless telephone to give you added convenience and mobility.

When ordering telephone service, consider adding call waiting, three-way calling, caller ID with name, call forwarding, and call answering to your plan. All are optional services offered for an additional monthly fee from your local phone company. Call answering will replace the need for an answering machine or voice mail system. Having the ability to retrieve messages remotely from a touch-tone phone is an absolute must.

Also, when ordering phone service, request a free copy of your city's Yellow Pages, and the Business-To-Business directory published by your phone company. You'll also want copies of your local phone directories (White and Yellow Pages).

For people who travel a lot or spend time on the road, a cellular telephone and/or pager is a critical tool for staying in touch with business associates and clients.

If you have the money, a desktop copy machine is also a valuable business tool in any home office. There are many desktop copiers to choose from,

from companies like Sharp, Xerox and Canon. Prices start at around $300.00, and go up considerably, based on the features you need. The Xerox XC-1255, for example, fits on a desktop and makes up to 12 copies per minute and it offers a zoom reduction and enlargement feature.

Another optional business tool is a personal digital assistant (PDA), which is a hand-held computer capable of storing hundreds or thousands of names, phone numbers, addresses, and appointments. All of these devices can easily transfer data between your PDA and desktop computer, usually with the touch of a single button.

You'll also need basic supplies, such as a business letterhead, envelopes, business cards and everything from pads of paper to paper clips. (For basic office supplies, visit your local office supply superstore, such as OfficeMax or Staples).

Once you have all of the tools necessary for a home office, it's important to choose a room or area of your home that's separate from your main living area. Your work area should be well lit with non-fluorescent light bulbs, and have at least one window to allow natural sunlight and fresh air into the area.

If you have the space, set up two desks, one desk for your computer and another for your other work. The desk used for your computer should have a built-in keyboard drawer or keyboard arm. This ensures that you'll have ample desk space and will help you avoid clutter. Make sure the desk chair you select is comfortable and provides adequate back support.

Other furniture and home-office equipment you should consider purchasing:

- A desk set (deskpad, business card holder, letter tray, etc.)
- Bookshelves
- Briefcase and pad/paper folio (for when you go out on appointments)
- Calculator
- Cassette (or microcassette) recorder for dictation or keeping track of ideas
- Credit card processing equipment (if your business will be accepting credit cards as payment for your products and/or services)
- File cabinets
- Floor lamps and desk lamps
- Office supply storage cabinet
- Plenty of AC outlets and phone jacks
- Postage machine and postage scale
- Printer stand
- Television and VCR
- Telephone answering machine (if you don't have call answering from your telephone company)
- Waste paper basket and paper shredder (if you deal with confidential documents)

As you set up your home office, visit furniture showrooms and office supply superstores (such as Staples and OfficeMax) to help you choose the right office furniture to meet your needs. Also, request the following mail-order catalogs or visit the web sites of the following companies that cater to home office operators:

BackSaver Products Company; (800) 251-2225   This company offers an assortment of chairs, desks, and products designed to protect your back from pain and stress in a home office environment.

Day-Timer; (800) 225-5005; http://www.daytimer.com   Offers a catalog of time management and organizational products useful to business professionals and home office operators.

Hello Direct; (800) 520-3311; http://www.hellodirect.com   A complete catalog of telephone equipment, including traditional telephones, multi-line phones, cordless phones, cellular phones, and all sorts of telephone accessories.

Home Office Direct; (888) 599-2112; http://www.homeofficedirect.com   An online source of office furniture (including desks, chairs, computer carts and cabinets) designed for a home office.

Home Office Furniture System; http://www.hofs.com   An on-line home office furniture showroom.

Levenger; (800) 544-0880; http://www.levenger.com   A catalog of fancy pens, home office furniture and other home office equipment.

Lizell; (800) 718-8800   This catalog is also filled with home office furniture, small business equipment and other products useful to people who work from home.

Reliable Home Office; (800) 869-6000   This catalog is filled with home office furniture, small business equipment, telephone equipment, and other products useful to people who work from home.

Bright Idea
To stay up-to-date on the latest developments in home office technology, visit the Home Office Computing forum on America Online (keyword: Home Office), or visit http://www.smalloffice.com.

Look professional

Working from a home office means you don't have to obey a dress code. In fact, you may often find yourself getting out of bed, throwing on a comfortable robe and slippers and working for a few hours before actually getting dressed. When you deal with clients, you'll need to dress professionally and convey an overall professional "look" and "attitude" in order to help boost a customer/client's confidence in you.

One way to enhance your professional image is to carry a nice briefcase or attaché case when attending sales calls, business meetings or in-person appointments. Spending between $100 and $500 (or more) on a fancy briefcase is an investment and there are many things to consider when making this type of purchase. Virtually everyone working in the business world uses some type of briefcase to carry work-related papers, files, a laptop computer, or other items in an organized manner.

Ultimately, the style of briefcase or attaché case you choose has an impact on your overall professional image. When it comes to purchasing a briefcase the things to consider are functionality, style, design, craftsmanship, warrantee and price.

When you purchase a good-quality briefcase, it should be designed to last many years. Thus, the style you choose should be timeless, yet the design should meet your individual needs perfectly. Briefcases come in all shapes, colors, and sizes, and are designed for many different uses. Many are made from leather, ballistic nylon, aluminum, or other durable yet visually attractive materials. Some convey a highly sophisticated image, while others are designed for more casual work environments.

There are also cases made to meet the needs of people with specific occupations, like pilots, lawyers, accountants, and salespeople.

A briefcase or attaché case that's used on a daily basis and will consistently be filled with lots of papers, files, a cellular phone, calculator, and other items, must be durable and able to withstand a lot of wear and tear. Look for a briefcase that's backed by a long-term warranty and that's manufactured by a company that will repair or replace the product.

In the business world, you only get one chance to make a positive first impression. The briefcase you carry, along with your wardrobe and how you handle yourself, all contribute to your image. Investing in a top-quality briefcase will cost several hundred dollars or more, but the investment should last for years.

Managing your finances

One of the keys to business success will be learning how to carefully manage your personal and company finances. As you set up your home business, one of the first steps should be developing an accounting and bookkeeping system, either on paper or using a personal computer.

If your accounting skills aren't up to par, consider hiring an accountant or bookkeeper to manage your company's finances and bookkeeping, or take college-level courses to bring you up to speed on basic accounting skills. In addition to ensuring that your business doesn't run into financial problems, having a well-thought-out accounting/bookkeeping system in place will cut down on the time and effort needed to prepare your company and personal tax returns.

Unofficially...
Ten Popular Briefcase Manufacturers

Coach (888) 262-6224; www.coach.com

Hartmann Luggage Company (800) 331-0613; www.hartmann. com

Jack Georges, Inc. (973) 777-6999; www.jackgeorges. com

Kenneth Cole (800) KEN-COLE; www.kencole.com

Michael Scott/Carlo Franzini (201) 525-0888

T.Z. Case International (888) 227-3393; www.tz-case.com

Targus (800) 998-8020; www.targus.com

The Leather Specialty Company (888) 771-0200

Tumi Luggage (800) 322-TUMI; www.tumi.com

ZERO Halliburton (800) 728-2530; http://www. zerocorp.com/ hal/zhindex.htm

Below are some of the financial issues you'll need to deal with as a home-based business owner.

Making sure you have enough start-up capital

One of the main reasons why small businesses and start-ups fail is because the person (or people) launching the business didn't properly evaluate their financial needs or raise enough start-up capital before opening for business. After carefully projecting your costs and expenses, as well as potential profits for the first year or two of business, set aside at least one year's worth of operating capital as your start-up capital. This will give you ample time to establish your business and build clientele (if applicable), while ensuring that you'll be able to pay your bills and continue earning a salary that supports your current standard of living.

Setting your rates/prices

In addition to having enough start-up capital, in order to maintain profitability and ensure the success of your business you'll need to carefully set your rates or prices so that you can earn a profit, yet be competitive in the marketplace. Knowing what you can charge will require you to do research so that you become intimately aware of what people are willing to pay for your products/services. You'll also need to determine who your competition is and be able to differentiate your product/service and ensure that what you're offering is competitive within your industry and/or geographic area.

As you set your rates, understand that people will pay more if they know they're getting their money's worth. If you have proven skills, knowledge, abilities, or products your customers need, and you offer these things at a fair (not necessarily a cheap) price,

Watch Out!
Chapter 7 discusses the need to develop a detailed business plan. Part of your business plan should include financial statements and projections that will help you plan and operate your business.

you'll find that people will want to hire you or buy from you.

You need to develop a sense of trust with your clients. Obviously, when someone hires you or decides to buy your products/services, they'll be willing to pay, however, in order to keep each client/customer happy, it's important that you don't nickel and dime them, pad your bills, or charge them unexpected fees just to earn more money. It's also critical that you provide your products/services in a timely manner and do whatever it takes to meet their expectations, which should be defined before you begin doing any work.

Knowing what your competition charges for similar products or services is important. Unless you're actually providing added value or additional services, especially if you're starting out, make sure your prices are comparable with your competition. If you determine there's a range that your competition is charging, your fees/prices can certainly be on the high end of that range, providing it becomes obvious to your (potential) clients/customers that you're worth what you're charging.

Making bids and estimates/writing proposals

If you'll be providing a professional service to a client or customer or selling high-priced items, once you get that potential client/customer interested in hiring you or buying from you, it will often be necessary to provide a bid or estimate, and/or submit a written proposal. A proposal must outline who you are, your qualifications, what you can do for the company, your time frame for doing the proposed work, and your rates. It will be from this proposal that someone will ultimately make their hiring or

Watch Out!
One common mistake people make when they're opening a home office, doing consulting, or freelancing, is that they charge too little, causing people to think that they are inferior to the competition. Make sure your rates are in line with what your competition charges or with what your clients/customers will be expecting to pay for your products/services based on the going rates within your industry or field.

Watch Out!
To land new cus-
tomers and
clients, you must
impress them,
make them feel
confident in your
abilities (or your
products), and
you must avoid
any and all typo-
graphical errors,
misspellings, or
anything that
will take away
from the profes-
sional look of
what you submit.

purchasing decision, so the document you submit must look professional, be written clearly, and answer the potential client/customer's questions honestly. This document should describe specific reasons to hire you or buy from you.

Your proposal will help your client/customer adjust their expectations regarding what they can expect from you, so it should spell out exactly what services/products you'll provide, at what price, in what time frame, etc. In your proposal, use facts, figures, statistics, and whatever documentation you can provide to back up your promises and marketing messages. If you're an expert in your field, for example, prove it. If your products are better than the competition, state specifically why.

If you'll be creating estimates, bids, or proposals on an ongoing basis, you might consider creating a template for yourself within your word processor to make the document creation process easier and faster. The content of your estimate, bid, or proposal, however, should be 100 percent customized for the potential client/customer and clearly address their particular needs and concerns.

Prior to creating an estimate, bid, or proposal, spend some time (this usually won't be billable time) with your prospective client/customer and analyze particular needs, problems, or issues that you can address, fix, or improve upon. Only by obtaining a first-hand understanding of your potential client/customer's needs can you provide a detailed and accurate estimate, bid, or proposal that demonstrates clearly what you can offer.

Many different specialized software packages are available that can help automate the estimate, bid, and proposal creation process. Visit any software retailer that sells business software for additional information on these products. QuickBooks Pro (from Intuit Software), for example, offers special modules designed for this purpose. This program is described in greater detail within Chapter 7.

Cutting costs

If you're starting out and you're attempting to attract clients/customers, you'll be tempted to spend a lot of money in order to buy the best furniture and office equipment, create the fanciest marketing materials, and spend top dollar on advertising and marketing. Focus on conveying the best possible image through your marketing materials, but be extremely careful choosing your advertising outlets. Take advantage of as much free publicity as you can generate, and don't buy things you don't need (at least right away).

Bright Idea
As your own boss, it's particularly important that you stay focused on the bottom line. The more profit you earn and the less money you spend, the higher your income will be.

Start off by taking a grass roots effort and developing a detailed budget and plan for yourself, based on your available funds, and stick to it. Start off by buying (or leasing) only what you need to get started, and as you achieve success, buy additional equipment. For example, when buying office furniture, choose desks and a chair that are functional (and a chair that's comfortable), but don't overspend to get the top-of-the-line model if you can't afford it. You can upgrade later once the money starts flowing in. The more money you save initially, the better your chances of long-term success. In addition, you'll get into the habit of carefully analyzing your expenses, so even when you have money, you'll carefully consider the purchases you make and buy only what you need.

Contract negotiations

As you solicit new clients or customers and submit estimates, bids or proposals, the potential

Bright Idea
Take full advantage of the negotiating skills and strategies outlined in Chapter 10, and go into every negotiation having done your research.

client/customer is going to haggle for a lower price. Thus, be prepared to negotiate. Never undersell your abilities or accept a fee that's significantly below what you, your product(s) and/or services are actually worth. If you quote a low price, even to get some initial work, it will be hard to increase your rates later if you do ongoing or repeat work for that same client. Even if you become desperate, never act overly anxious or eager, and never make too many costly compromises or concessions.

As you discovered in Chapter 10, becoming a good negotiator takes lots of practice, research, and a strong understanding of the other party's needs, wants, and desires. At the same time, you must also be keenly aware of your own needs, wants, and desires, and negotiate accordingly, always keeping an eye on your bottom line in order to protect your profits.

As a self-employed person, you too need insurance benefits and more

Deciding to forgo the safety and job security of working for someone else by choosing to work for yourself is a huge decision. This decision should be weighed carefully. Even if you have a spectacular idea for your own business or you're confident you'll be able to succeed as a consultant or freelance worker, make sure that you carefully weigh the pros and cons involved with becoming self-employed.

Consider the impact your decision will have on your life, as well as the lives of your immediate family members, and think about the dollars and cents involved. Will your earning potential improve dramatically if you become self-employed? Will your increase in earnings cover the added costs involved with being self-employed (such as having to pay for your own benefits)?

What are the financial risks involved in working for yourself and/or starting your own business? Upon leaving your job and making this major career transition, how quickly will you be able to generate enough income to support your current lifestyle? How long will it take you to build up your business or practice so that it's profitable? Do you have enough money in your savings to support yourself while you get your new career (as someone who is self-employed) off the ground? If applicable, do you have adequate start-up capital?

Typically, when you work for a company (other than your own), you automatically receive various benefits, such as health insurance, life insurance, long-term disability insurance and some type of retirement plan (or pension) from your employer. What benefits and perks will you be giving up once you quit your job? What will it cost to replace those benefits (since you'll now have to pay for them yourself)?

These are just a few of the many issues you'll have to consider if you choose to launch your own business or work as a self-employed professional. Chapter 7 discusses many of the issues you'll be faced with, so the remainder of this chapter focuses mainly on financial issues.

Create your own benefits plan and compensation package

Perhaps the biggest drawback of working for yourself is that you'll be giving up all of the benefits and perks that an employer would typically provide. This means that in addition to your homeowner's or renter's insurance and auto insurance (that everyone typically has to pay for), you'll now have to acquire and pay for your own:

- Health insurance (along with dental and/or eye care insurance)
- Life insurance
- Long-term disability insurance
- Umbrella insurance policy (if applicable)
- Various types of business-related insurance (if applicable, including fire insurance, worker's compensation insurance, business interruption insurance, etc.)
- Malpractice insurance (if applicable)
- Liability insurance (if applicable)

As a self-employed person who is adequately insured against various types of disaster, your monthly premiums alone can easily be anywhere from $1,000 to $3,000, depending on your level of coverage and the types of insurance you acquire for yourself, your business, and your family.

In addition to having to pay for insurance coverage, you also have to personally deal with insurance agents, shop around for the best available policies, and then maintain all of the paperwork associated with having each type of policy. No longer will your contribution to your insurance premiums simply be automatically deducted from your paycheck, while someone in the benefits office at your employer deals with administering the various policies and works with the insurance agents on your behalf.

Since paying for your own benefits (insurance in particular) will be expensive, it's an excellent idea to sit down with a personal financial planner, accountant, or some other impartial person who can help you define your needs. Since insurance agents are typically paid on commission, what they offer you might not always be the best policy, so knowing what you want and need in advance, and then shopping around by speaking with several insurance agents, is an excellent money-saving strategy.

Try to find an insurance agent whom you can trust and feel comfortable developing a long-term relationship with. Make sure the agent(s) you choose to work with represent only the top insurance providers and that they're familiar with the types of insurance policies are looking to purchase.

As you review all of the different types of insurance policies that are available, try to avoid too much overlap, so you don't wind up paying multiple times for the same coverage. Likewise, pay careful attention to the premiums, deductibles, and benefits offered by each policy. You can often save money on monthly premiums by choosing a policy with a higher deductible. The drawback to this is that with a $1,000 deductible, for example, you pay the first $1,000 of an insurance claim out of your pocket, before the insurance benefits kick in.

With life insurance, for example, the lower the benefit you desire, the lower the premiums will be. (What you'll actual pay for life insurance will also depend on several factors, including your age and current health.)

Health insurance

This will probably be your most expensive monthly insurance expenditure and also your most important one. As an individual, trying to get a health insurance plan that's equivalent to what a medium- or large-sized company would offer to its employees will be difficult to find and costly. If you form a company or corporation, finding a good health insurance plan will be a bit easier.

Bright Idea
The best way to find a reliable insurance agent is through a referral from someone you know, who already has a positive business relationship with their insurance agent. At the same time, you can also research what the best (or highest-rated) insurance companies are for the types of insurance you want to receive, and then call those insurance companies directly for the names of their authorized agents.

Timesaver
Chapter 13 explores some of the issues you'll need to concern yourself with when choosing a health care program or health insurance plan.

To save money and get the best benefits, consider contacting the various small business organizations and associations, many of which offer the ability to obtain insurance benefits at discounted rates. Some of the organizations and associations you can contact include:

National Small Business United; (202-293-8830; http://www.nsbu.org/benefits.htm) This organization has been an advocate for small businesses since 1937. With 65,000+ U.S. members through its chapters and affiliate organizations, NSBU not only keeps small-business owners in touch with legislative and regulatory issues that affect them, but also encourages the small business community to take action. NSBU constructively engages its members in legislative and regulatory initiatives that affect the small-business community's livelihood. The organization isn't a special-interest group, but sees itself as working for the common interest of all small businesses.

United States Association for Small Business and Entrepreneurship (USASBE); (1-608-262-9982; http://www.usasbe.org/about/index.htm)   The International Council for Small Business (ICSB) was founded in 1957 in the United States as a comprehensive organization of outstanding researchers, scholars, teachers, administrators, and public policy makers interested in entrepreneurship and small business. As the organization grew, members decided to form national affiliates, and the U.S. Affiliate of the ICSB was established in 1981. In 1985, the name was changed to the United States Association for Small Business and Entrepreneurship (USASBE).

USASBE is a non-profit organization made up of an eclectic group of government officials, directors of small business development centers, and academics in fields like finance, marketing, management, and economics united by their common interest in entrepreneurship and small business.

As leaders in their fields, they have an impact on government policy and on the development of small business and entrepreneurship. USASBE's forward-looking members are determined to remain on the cutting edge of research; they are extending the field of knowledge and shaping entrepreneurial thinking for the 1990s.

The Small Business Benefit Association (SBBA); (888-886-SBBA http://www.sbba. com)   SBBA is a national association for small- and home-based business owners. Members operate a wide variety of businesses and all have unique experiences and needs. Whether you're just beginning, or if you're a seasoned business professional, their goal is to help you succeed!

SBBA offers discounted benefits and resources, ongoing publications, valuable information, education, training, support, and membership materials.

Members enjoy discounts and access to benefits and services they probably couldn't get on their own. In most cases, the benefits and services exceed even those provided by many of the America's largest corporations.

Upon joining, members receive an 80-page Small Business Guidebook binder, which contains detailed information about each benefit and helpful small business tips. Members also receive the Small Business Update, an ongoing newsletter containing power-packed information to help you succeed. The organization is continually expanding and improving its benefits.

The National Business Association (NBA); (http://www.nationalbusiness.org) The National Business Association **(NBA)** was established in 1982 with the sole purpose of supporting and educating small-business owners, entrepreneurs, and professionals. As a nonprofit organization, the NBA uses its group buying power to provide members with vital support programs, cost- and time-saving products, services, and valuable small-business resource materials. The NBA represents the small-business sector in Washington, D.C., monitors legislation, and voices concerns to key government representatives.

Small Office/Home Office Association International; (http://www.sohoa.com)   This organization offers a range of discounted business services, insurance benefits, and travel discounts to small business owners.

The National Association of Private Enterprise (NAPE); (1-800-223-NAPE; http://www.nape.org)   This organization has been providing entrepreneurs with the direction, guidance, and support needed to effectively face the challenges of business ownership since 1983. NAPE recognizes the importance of small businesses—those with 10 or fewer employees—to the U.S. economy. Statistics show that small businesses contribute up to two-thirds of first-time jobs and produce more than 50 percent of the nation's goods and services.

By becoming a NAPE member, you will join a partner offering you business services, educational benefits, and the health care services that you need as a small business owner.

The American Association of Home-Based Businesses (AAHBB); (800) 447-9710 This is a nonprofit organization that provides information and resources to home-based business operators.

Home Office Association of America (HOAA); (800) 809-4622   Discover and benefit from a wide range of resources available to home-office workers by becoming a member of this organization.

Long-term disability insurance

Statistics from the Department of Housing and Urban Development (HUD) show that upwards of 48 percent of all mortgage foreclosures are a direct result of someone losing their income due to some form of disabling medical condition that prevented them from working. In addition, the number of people under age 65 who will lose their ability to work due to a disability lasting more than three months is staggering. Thanks to medical advancements, some conditions that were once considered fatal are not any longer. Instead, these conditions often cause long-term disability.

What would happen if you suddenly lost your ability to work and earn an income? If you experienced some type of medical disaster, would you want insurance to pick up your mortgage or rent payments, utility bills, food, car expenses, clothing expenses, taxes, and other expenses? Health insurance doesn't cover these basic living expenses, which means you'll need disability insurance if you want this type of protection. Disability insurance premiums are paid using after-tax dollars, but if you need to collect benefits from this type of policy, you'll receive those benefits as tax-free income during the time you're unable to work.

Depending on how much coverage you need, the monthly premium for this type of insurance will begin around $100 per month and can go up considerably, depending on your age, occupation, deductible, and the benefit(s) you desire.

Umbrella insurance policies

An umbrella policy works in conjunction with your other auto, home, or boat insurance policies and picks up where they leave off. If someone gets seriously injured while visiting your home and wins a one-million dollar settlement against you, but your homeowner's insurance policy only covers you up to $250,000, your umbrella policy will typically cover the remaining portion of the settlement. Thus, having this type of insurance keeps you from having to sell your assets or go into serious debt in order to pay the settlement. Umbrella insurance policies usually have coverage limits of one, two, or three million dollars, and some policies, depending on your profession, may also offer limited coverage for work-related issues where legal settlements are involved. Discuss your options regarding this type of insurance with your insurance agent, making sure you understand what it will and won't cover.

Planning for your retirement

Being self-employed, you have several different retirement plan options. Each option offers a variety of different benefits, such as the amount of money (or the percentage of your income) you can invest, tax-free, each year. The most popular retirement plan options for self-employed people are: IRAs, SEP-IRAs, Keoghs, and Simple-IRAs. To determine which of these might best fit your needs, contact a financial planning advisor or accountant who specialized in retirement planning.

A Keogh, for example, "offers higher contribution limits than most other retirement plans available to small business owners and self-employed individuals. In fact, you can contribute as much as 25 percent of your compensation each year to a Keogh, up to the annual maximum of $30,000 per participant. You also have a wide range of investment choices through a Keogh plan, ranging from mutual funds to stocks, bonds, CDs, and U.S. Treasuries," reports Fidelity Investments.

Hiring employees

One of the biggest expenses associated with operating a small business is hiring full-time or part-time employees. Once your business reaches a certain size, you'll need to expand, which means finding, hiring, and managing honest, hardworking, and dedicated people to work for you. While you may be

Watch Out!
As you learned from Chapter 14, you can't count on Social Security to take care of you once you're ready to retire. Being self-employed, you have no corporate pension plan to rely on either, which means that your retirement planning must be established and managed by you—it's totally your responsibility.

Timesaver
See Chapter 14 for more information on retirement planning.

Unofficially...
One excellent information resource when it comes to retirement planning is Fidelity Investments. You can call a Fidelity Retirement Specialist at (800-544-5373) from 8 a.m. to 9 p.m. Eastern Time, seven days a week or visit the company's web site at http://www. fidelity.com.

hiring additional people to help reduce your personal workload, the extra responsibilities of hiring those people could easily require an even bigger time commitment on your part.

If the business you launch grows large enough that you need to hire additional employees on a full-time (or permanent part-time) basis, you'll probably have to offer these employees benefits, plus have the appropriate worker's compensation insurance to protect yourself if they're working from your home (or from your office). You'll also have begin withholding federal income tax payments and Social Security taxes from their paychecks, and establish employee policies and procedures, which should be well thought out and offered in writing to the people you hire. Your level of responsibility also increases, because you'll now have people looking to you for ongoing guidance, and who rely on the success of your company for their paycheck.

So, in addition to all of the other personal qualities listed in this book, you'll also need to develop excellent managerial skills if you plan on running a business with employees.

Should you incorporate?

A corporation is a legal entity that is separate from its owners. While establishing and maintaining a corporation requires a substantial amount of paper work, and requires additional tax forms to be filed on a regular basis, the biggest benefit of incorporating is that your personal liability will be limited to your investment in the business. Operating a corporation also offers other types of financial and legal protections, plus has other benefits that make it worth considering.

There are several different types of corporations that you can form, depending on the type of business you'll be operating. An S Corporation, for example, is usually better suited to a small business operator, but this type of corporation limits the number of shareholders to 10 or fewer, plus there are limitations as to what the business can do.

To learn more about how incorporating can benefit you financially and legally, contact both an accountant and a lawyer. Also, while there are many "kits" that allow you to form your own corporation, your best strategy is to seek the guidance of a lawyer to help you with this process.

Juggling your personal and professional life

One of the tricks to making your new life as a home office worker or home-based business operator work is learning how to juggle your personal and professional life. At times, there will be little separation between the two.

Here are some scenarios to consider:

After working all day, you decide to have a relaxing dinner with your spouse. It's around 7:30 p.m., and your business telephone line rings. Do you answer it?

During your children's summer vacation, on one afternoon it rains, so your children are confined indoors. Due to their boredom, they go out of their way to get your attention. Meanwhile, you're in your home office trying to get work done. What do you do?

Your best friend decides to take the day off from work and calls you to make plans for the entire afternoon. Sure, you have work to do, but being your own boss, you have the ability to push things back, do some work at night and maybe catch up during the following day. What do you do?

These are just a few common scenarios that a home-based business owner, home-office worker, or telecommuter will no doubt encounter. When you're facing tight deadlines, your work will often have to come first, just as, if there's an emergency involving one of your children, you'll drop whatever you're doing to deal with that situation. Not everything will be so cut and dried, however, and the decisions you make on how to allocate your time will impact the success of your career (or business), and also impact the lives of your family or the people close to you.

While scheduling your time carefully will always play a vital role in your day-to-day business operations, for the first several weeks or months that you begin working from home, take meticulous notes regarding how you spend every minute of your day (and night). After several weeks, analyze how you spend your time and determine ways that you can be more productive during the time you spend working, so that you can more easily make the most out of your non-working hours and maximize those hours without jeopardizing your income or earning potential.

No matter how busy you are with your work (and you can expect to be pretty busy, especially as you get your business off the ground), the following are a few ideas designed to help you maintain some balance in your life.

Take breaks   During the work day, plan on taking one, two, or three breaks (no more than 15 or 30 minutes each) to relax, get some fresh air, have a snack, read a book,

Unofficially...
Just as you allocate time in your schedule to do your work on a day-to-day basis, make an effort to schedule quality time for yourself, your family, and your friends. There's a saying that many entrepreneurs like to use, and it's that they work hard and then they play hard. You should be able to find time in your week to get your work done properly, but also have time to relax and/or have some fun.

watch TV, or do some personal errands. During a break, leave your work area, don't accept any business calls, and focus your mind on something other than work.

Go out for lunch   If you spend your days working from home and your evenings at home with your spouse and children (or living alone), make a point to take time everyday for lunch and leave your home. Go pick up a sandwich at a local deli, take a walk or do some errands, but take between 30 and 60 minutes for lunch each day and get out of your home.

Make evening plans   Just as people who work in traditional offices wouldn't want to spend all day and night at their desk or in their work area, this is something you should avoid as a home-office worker (or home-based business operator). If you spend all day working from your home office, and don't have time during the day to take a real lunch break, make a point to make dinner plans (outside of your home) with friends or family. Obviously, this doesn't need to be done everyday, but ensuring that you have ample social opportunities at least once or twice during the week (and on weekends) will help you develop a more balanced life.

Set rewards for yourself   Let's face it, if you're working from home, you might decide to take an hour to watch a soap opera, game show, or talk show during the afternoon. Unless you're able to maintain a high level of productivity and continue working with the television or radio playing in the background,

Watch Out!
If you're spending long hours working and then evenings and nights at home, without taking sufficient breaks to leave your home, you could wind up feeling cooped up or trapped. If your work doesn't involve dealing in-person with clients or customers, spending all day at home working (and not having in-person interaction with others) can also lead to loneliness.

plan on setting up a reward system for yourself. For example, if during a particular day you have five individual tasks that must be accomplished, decide that after completing two of those tasks, you'll reward yourself with an hour break to watch television or do whatever it is you like to do. By planning the tasks you need to accomplish each day, determining how long each task will take, and then working hard to accomplish those tasks, you'll become a highly productive person. Using a personal reward system for yourself will help keep you motivated and focused, but keep you from burning yourself out.

Discovering the profit potential of a home-based mail-order business

Everyone dreams about working part-time from home and becoming a millionaire. Occasionally, this does happen, but it's very rare. What most people find is that starting a mail-order business requires a great idea, an entrepreneurial spirit, time, hard work, lots of planning, an initial financial investment, and the willingness to take risks. Keeping this in mind, it is possible to launch a profitable mail-order business from your home.

In 1996, mail-order businesses generated over $1.2 trillion dollars in revenue, thanks to over 50 percent of the U.S. population who made at least one mail-order purchase during the year. While this may sound like a perfect opportunity to get rich quick, starting any type of business involves taking financial risks and making a financial and time investment in your business idea.

The mail-order industry is extremely competitive. Those who achieve success are the people who

Watch Out!
Beware of multi-level marketing offers that sound too good to be true, and research this type of mail-order business opportunity carefully before becoming affiliated with it, no matter what profit potential is being offered.

avoid the many "get rich quick" schemes. Other keys to starting a successful mail-order business include having a unique idea or approach to marketing a product or service, and having a product or service that is extremely marketable, of the highest quality, and that is also in demand. A successful mail-order business often targets a specific audience with its products or services, and uses niche advertising and marketing to reach a potential customer base.

Finding the perfect product or service to sell via mail order is a challenge onto itself and requires extensive research. Upon finding a product or service that you'd be interested in selling, make sure that you'll be able to manufacture or purchase it at a wholesale price that allows you to earn a profit once you take all of your business-related costs into account. Until you know that your idea will be successful, you don't want to invest in a large inventory, so negotiation with your suppliers will be critical.

Once you've found the ideal product or service, determine if there's a market for it, and what the very best way to reach that potential market is. It will be necessary to invest money in advertising, so it's important to create an effective advertising message and then determine the perfect media outlets to advertise in. If used correctly, the Internet can be a powerful, yet extremely cost-effective marketing and advertising tool and shouldn't be overlooked. Many mail-order experts agree, however, that one of the best ways to test market a mail-order product or service is to use classified ads in newspapers, magazines, and newsletters.

Prior to selling any product or service, you must first establish the infrastructure for operating your mail-order business. If you'll be running this business from your home, this requires establishing a home office, filing the necessary legal documents to establish yourself as a business, and determining how incoming orders will be taken and processed.

Just a few of the questions you'll need to answer are:

> Will you need a toll-free phone number for incoming orders?
>
> Who will answer the phone?
>
> Is it necessary to hire an independent order taking or order fulfillment house?
>
> Will it be necessary to accept credit cards as payment?
>
> How will your orders be shipped to customers?

Once a mail-order business is established, there are specialized software packages for use on PC-based computers that are designed to automate such tasks as order entry and processing, inventory control, credit card authorization, advertising, bookkeeping, customer database management, and sales lead management. These software packages, such as Mail Order Manager (Dydacomp Development Corporation/800-858-3666 / www.dydacomp.com), cost several thousand dollars, but can make the daily operation of a home-based mail order business easier.

Starting a mail-order business from your home will require you to take on many responsibilities. The best way to prepare yourself for success is to do research about the mail-order industry, about the product or service you plan to offer, and about the buying habits of the customer base you're hoping to reach. Ultimately, it's be the persuasiveness of your advertising and marketing materials that will determine your level of success, so learn as much as

Bright Idea
To learn more about the mail-order industry, join The National Mail Order Association (612-788-1673; www.nmoa.org). The on-line edition of Direct Marketing News (www.dmnews.com) also provides information and resources for mail-order entrepreneurs.

possible about effective advertising and direct mail techniques.

One of the most appealing things about mail-order business opportunities is that they're open to anyone with a great idea or a product to sell. Unlike opening a retail store, the start-up costs are often low, yet the potential for growth and profits can be unlimited.

Just the facts

- Are you motivated and focused enough to do all of your work, in a timely manner, when you could be watching television, listening to the radio, catching up on your housework or errands, or just enjoying the weather if it happens to be a nice day?

- Set up a comfortable home office from which you can be productive.

- It's important to carefully define your business and offer a product or service that fills a specific need, targets a specific niche, and that people will want.

- Establish your business, consulting practice, or freelance practice using public relations, advertising and various types of marketing.

- You'll need to protect yourself by purchasing various types of insurance, most importantly health insurance.

Chapter 16

Learn from the Experience of Others

This chapter offers interviews with several individuals. Each is in a different profession and has found success working from home, either as a consultant, home-based business operator, sales professional, writer/author, or as a telecommuter working for a large company. Each of these people talks about their personal experiences working from a home office and discusses the pros and cons of this type of work environment.

You're about to read interviews with:

- A home-based entrepreneur who is a successful computer consultant and home mail-order business operator.

- A sales professional who works full-time from her home office.

- A nationally known author, newspaper/magazine columnist who works from home.

- A public relations executive who is employed by one of the country's leading PR firms, but works full-time from her home office.

473

Mark Giordani, home-based entrepreneur

Based in Wareham, Massachusetts, Mark Giordani is the president of The Portfolio Group, Inc. He's in his early-thirties, and for the past decade has worked as a computer consultant, offering his expertise to businesses in the Boston area. Until recently, most of his time was actually spent on-site at his various clients' offices, installing and maintaining computer networks. After growing his client base, Giordani began using sub-contractors and part-time employees to perform some of his company's computer consulting work. This consulting business continues to operate from Giordani's home office.

In addition to working as a successful computer consultant, Giordani is the president of LefKey International (888-59-LEFKEY; http://www.lefkey.com), a home-based company that markets and sells specially designed computer keyboards for left-handed computer users. LefKey is primarily a mail-order business that also does business via the Internet.

From his small but highly functional home office, Giordani shared his thoughts on operating a home-based business and working as a consultant.

What made you want to work for yourself?

"My father is a successful business owner. While I was given the opportunity to work for him, and did so for a few years after graduating from college, I was excited by the challenge of establishing my own company and being my own boss, especially after pursuing entrepreneurial studies at Babson College. I was interested in exploring my own ideas and creativity. The concept of working from a formal office was never appealing to me."

Why did you choose to work from a home office?

"I didn't want to be tied to a desk or be tucked away in an office day after day. The concept of working from home was an appealing one, and something I chose to pursue early on. In addition to the luxury of working from home, when I'm not out on an appointment, I'm able to save a fortune each month not having to pay for office space or the expenses involved in maintaining a traditional office. This is money that goes right to the bottom line."

How did you get started?

"I was always fascinated by computers and technology. When I was a teenager, I was given my first personal computer, and I taught myself how to use it. Computers were my hobby growing up, and something that I really enjoyed. Over the years, I continued enhancing my computer skills, and in college, supplemented my self-taught knowledge with formal computer training. When I decided to start my own business, computer consulting allowed me to earn an income doing something that I loved. I started by placing ads in a small weekly shopper publication, called *The Shopper's Guide*, that gets distributed to all homes in the South Shore area outside of Boston. From that ad, I generated my first handful of clients. My computer consulting business grew considerably when I began generating new clients through word-of-mouth."

What's the biggest benefit of working from a home office?

"I'd have to say that it's the convenience of being able to roll out of bed and be on-the-job, literally. Not being married or having children, I have total freedom to make my own hours. If I choose, I can take a day off, I can work late into the night, or at anytime, take a break to make myself a snack. If I choose to work at night, I have all of my business documents and resources right there, and don't have to travel back and forth to an office. I personally do my best work in a casual environment, when I'm surrounded by windows, natural light, and fresh air."

What's the biggest drawback?

"It's sometimes very hard to be at home in the evening trying to relax, knowing that just a few feet away, I have paperwork to do, bills to pay, letters to write, and financial records that need to be kept up to date. While I don't maintain any type of normal business hours or the same daily routine each day, I am sometimes drawn to my desk to get work done at very odd hours."

What is your most useful business tool?

"My desktop computer is by far my most useful business tool. From my PC, I create all of my correspondence, maintain my company's web site, manage my company's finances, handle virtually all of the details associated with my mail-order business (using a program called Mail Order Manager), process my client's credit card payments, maintain my daily schedule, and keep a database of all my business-related contacts using a powerful program called *Act!*. I also have separate telephone lines and a fax machine for my business, and I use a pager and cellular phone so that my clients can reach me in an emergency. These days, computers and home-office automation technology are extremely powerful and make operating a home-based business or consulting practice much easier."

What advice can you offer to someone interested in working from a home office?

"Don't get involved in anything without doing the proper research first. Also, make sure that you get involved in a business or profession that you really enjoy and have an interest in. I started LefKey International because I started to get burned out running around Boston catering to the needs of my clients as a computer consultant, and I needed a change in my daily routine. Starting a mail-order business requires a lot of planning, and having the financial resources available to you to do things properly. Maintaining inventory, for example, can be a costly endeavor, even if you're able to cut other business-related costs using a grass roots marketing approach. Be prepared to work hard, but take the time to enjoy the fruits of your labors. Anyone who starts a consulting business should make sure that they are an expert in their field and have something of value to offer to their clients. To launch a successful mail-order business, you need a product or idea that's unique, fills a definite need, and that's relatively easy to market and promote. You also need to have a product with enough margin that you can earn a profit even after covering all of your business expenses."

Ellen Bromfield, home-based sales professional

Ellen Bromfield is the president of The Innovations Group, Inc. She is in her early thirties, and for over 10 years she has consulted to a variety of small businesses on marketing and sales strategies and issues. In addition to helping other companies, Bromfield actively markets unique and innovative advertising vehicles to help increase company sales and brand awareness.

What made you want to work for yourself?

"After graduating from college, I was employed as the vice president of a New England-based television production company. I was responsible for all facets of the business' operation, including the supervision and guidance of a regional sales force, as well as making sure the business was profitable. The two owners of the company were absentee, enjoying the benefits of having someone else run their company. After doing this for three years, I realized that I was already running a company, but for someone else. I didn't have the total control involved with being self-employed and operating my own business, so I decided to make it official and do just that. It is important to me that I'm in control of my own destiny. I thrive on the challenge and responsibility of running my own business."

Why did you choose to work from a home office?

"I was tired of commuting almost three hours per day. By virtue of having an office in my home, I have the flexibility to work whenever I like, and I have all of my records and business equipment at my fingertips. Running a home office also saves the money of renting an outside office. I had a traditional office, outside my home, at one point, and found that I was using it as a glorified telephone booth for when I happened to be in the area. As a sales professional, most of my time is spent on the road or on the telephone. When on the road, I meet directly with my clients at their locations, and my paperwork and phone work I find much more comfortable and convenient to do at home. Since I don't have employees, I do not need the extra space."

What's the biggest benefit to a home office?

"I always have everything I need at my fingertips. I can work whenever I like, in a comfortable and pleasant environment. Since I don't have to commute, I have extra time to spend either working or doing something for myself. The flexibility to create my own schedule is attractive to me. A home office also affords me tax benefits in addition to saving money renting an office."

What's the biggest drawback?

"There is no socialization. If you are used to getting into the office, talking around the water cooler, and taking breaks with coworkers, you may start to feel lonely working from home. You may want to plan eating lunch out of the office a couple times a week if you miss this aspect. At home, your work is always staring you in the face, and you sometimes feel like you should be working 24 hours a day. It is easy to get distracted with household activities such as laundry, yard work, and other things on your to-do list. Because your clients are calling into your business lines located in your home, you may always feel on-call. It may also be difficult to stay focused."

What is your most useful business tool?

"The telephone. It is my primary communication vehicle with the outside world. In my business, I am constantly on the telephone cultivating new clients, and working with existing clients. I use current technology to help make me more efficient when using the telephone. For example, I use a computer to organize my ever-growing client database and schedule activities. It's also used for record keeping. I use a telephone headset and occasionally a speakerphone to avoid neck and shoulder fatigue.

Bright Idea
Speak to your accountant about the tax advantages of operating from a home office.

As part of my phone service, I have caller ID, three-way calling, and call answering, which make my daily tasks easier."

What advice can you offer to someone interested in working from a home office?

"Set up in an area which will be fun for you to work. Take your career seriously. Get up at a preset time, get dressed, and put yourself in a working environment that will be the most productive for you. If you feel you convey a more professional image when dressed in business attire, make sure you get up each morning and get dressed that way. If you are more comfortable in casual clothing, go with that."

"Set goals for yourself. Without a boss letting you know what is expected of you and monitoring your progress and growth, you must do this for yourself on a regular basis in order to succeed. You should pick a profession or business that combines your interests and skills and research how others who are successful in other related businesses are doing it. Spend some time talking to and, if possible, spend time with someone that runs their own home business and see how you feel about it. "

"Make sure you write a business plan which is viable and looks like it will be profitable. Make sure you can work well independently and can take the pressure of not having a consistent paycheck unless you've earned it on their own."

Steven Kent, author/writer/newspaper and magazine columnist

As a freelance writer and video game historian, Steven Kent is regularly published in numerous national magazines and some of the country's leading newspapers. He writes a column for *The Los*

Angeles Times Syndicate that is circulated to 120 news-papers, and also for *MSNBC, Next Generation, USA Today, React, Parade,* and *Family PC.* In addition to writing about technology, he explains, "I will also gladly write my perspectives on religion, govern-ment, and life, but people pay me to write about video and computer games. Go figure. My dad always thought that I should be a lawyer and my in-laws expected me to be a wealthy businessman."

Based on the West Coast, Kent lives with his wife and two children, and works full-time from his home office.

What made you want to work for yourself?

"I graduated with a master's degree in commu-nications, with an emphasis on public relations in 1990, and got a good job with a pressure washer manufacturer. (Pressure washers are machines that make water squirt really hard.) My company's aver-age pressure washer could wash graffiti from walls. I was on that job for three months, then released as part of a massive lay-off.

"Over the next two years I sold pens at an office supply store, drew graphics in the head office of a West Coast retailer, sold fax machines at exorbitant prices for an office automation company, and han-dled small accounts for a public relations agency. One thing that stood out in all of my jobs was that I do not do well in an office setting.

"I have no talent for office politics, and I piss off my superiors. After years of upsetting the people who signed my paycheck, I discovered the only way I would ever have job security would be by becoming my own boss. Now I work harder than ever before, work longer hours than I had ever imagined, and have a boss who puts up with my shortcomings...me."

Why did you choose to work from a home office?

"I can't afford an office. Well, maybe I could afford an office, I don't want to pay the money. I could also afford a secretary, if she were really cheap, but all of that would come out of my profits. By working out of my house, I keep my expenses down. People talk about writing expenses off on their taxes, but the government isn't in the business of buying my office equipment. I would still have out-of-pocket expenses, and I would rather use that money for other things."

What's the biggest benefit to a home office?

"It is very easy and convenient to work out of the house. I don't have a commute, so traffic is never a problem. I never have to rush home to get things. The biggest benefit, however, is my wife. She worked as a proofreader in college, correcting professors' manuscripts before they sent them to publishers. Spelling and grammar are her middle name, and they're not even in my vocabulary. As a writer, I have editors for clients. Editors are always looking for the easiest solution to any challenge, and by turning in clean articles and stories that have been proofed by my wife, I become very easy to work with."

What's the biggest drawback?

"The problem with working out of the house is my family. I have two young children who have no respect for my office door. They often come in and want to play or talk, and I am not good at saying no. By some odd coincidence, the closer my deadlines come, the more my children want to play. It can be very distracting.

"I am not, however, distracted by television or socializing. The majority of people who work out of their house complain that they have trouble concentrating on their jobs. For some reason, possibly the fear of going back to an office, I do not suffer from that problem."

What is your most useful business tool?

"My wife is my all-around best business tool. She cleans my copy, tells me when my articles are dull, gives me pleasant interruptions when there is interesting news, and makes sure that I eat when I am really busy. I highly recommend wives (or husbands)!

"After my wife, my next most important tool is my PC. I use it to test computer games and capture screens from games for use in magazines. I use it to submit my stories to editors over the Internet, and I also use it to fax information. It's also a great pedestal for displaying knick-knacks."

What advice can you offer to someone interested in working from a home office?

"Marry well, and I am not joking. Loneliness often wears people down when they work alone. If you and your spouse are good friends, you will be able to work together, and that will help you concentrate on your business.

"I also recommend keeping an eye on the bottom line. It's hard to concentrate on your work if you are distracted, and nothing distracts and stresses people more than worrying about finances. By keeping your expenses down and your productivity up, you will be able to concentrate on your work.

"Finally, do not be too tight with your money. Get a comfortable chair and a serviceable desk. If you need a computer, make sure to get a good one that won't need replacing in three months. Do not be extravagant, and don't buy the top-of-the-line equipment if you don't need it. Arrange your office so that you have the things that you really need available to you."

Eileen Tanner, public relations executive

Eileen Tanner is a Media Supervisor at Golin/Harris Communications, a public relations agency. She primarily works on the Nintendo of America account and her primary responsibility is to strategize and implement all aspects of media outreach for Nintendo. "I'm motivated, driven, organized, and a huge people person. All of these elements are important for me to work successfully from home," she says. While Tanner isn't self-employed, she's not really considered a "telecommuter" either, because she works full-time from her home office located outside of Seattle.

What made you want to work for your employer?

"I've been working at Golin/Harris–LA for over nine years. At the time it was a small PR agency with solid accounts but has since become an international communications and marketing company with some of the largest accounts in the world, including McDonald's and Nintendo. The people that work at G/H–LA are smart, fun, forward thinking and creative. The kind of people I want to work with."

Why did you choose to work from a home office?

"Working from my home office was actually a need more than a desire. After moving to Seattle from Los Angeles to work in G/H's new office designed to service Nintendo, my husband accepted an excellent job offer in a small community 200 miles southeast of Seattle. I didn't want to quit my job so I suggested to Golin/Harris that I work from home. My boss had been doing it for several years, albeit she only lived 10 minutes from our L.A. office, and I was confident I could be successful at it as well. Golin/Harris agreed and Nintendo, somewhat reluctantly, agreed as well. I've been working from home for over two years and it as been viewed as successful by all involved."

What's the biggest benefit to a home office?

"The biggest benefit to a home office is the lack of commute! The biggest benefit for my company and my client is that I work more efficiently, with fewer interruptions, and they can reach me nearly 24 hours a day."

What's the biggest drawback?

"The biggest drawback to a home office is that I tend to work a lot more because my office is right there. However, when I do put in the long hours I still get to see my husband in the evenings, eat dinner at home, usually in my office, and take breaks to walk the dogs."

What is your most useful business tool?

"The most useful business tool is my computer modem. E-mail has become a primary form of communication with my office, my client, and the media. When I've been out of town for three days, I'll come back to 350 or more e-mails. Plus, the Internet has become a useful tool for research and for monitoring what's going on in the media."

What advice can you offer to someone interested in working from a home office?

"My advice to someone who wants to work from home is to stay motivated. Avoid distractions. Don't ever turn the TV on when you've got work to do! Say to your spouse or pet or just out loud to yourself that you are going to work now to get yourself in that frame of mind. I actually leave the house every morning to get a latte knowing that when I return, I'm at work. Finally, when you "go home for the day" shut the ringer off on your office phone and close the door!

"Working from home is not all good. There is guilt to deal with as others working at the office envy you. There is loneliness because there is no physical person to talk to. There is the feeling that you never get out of the house (because you don't!). It's harder to be recognized for the good work you do and get promotions when you're a home office worker employed by someone other than yourself. Finally, the folks in the office tend to forget about you. They don't always remember to e-mail you important documents, or connect you into the staff meeting, and when there's an office party to celebrate a big win, it's hard to be included. However, if you stay motivated, organized, and in regular contact with the office, working from home has many rewards and benefits. For the right people working from home can be a successful and rewarding experience for the employer and its employee."

Just the facts

- The people interviewed in this chapter all chose to pursue careers that didn't involve working from a traditional office. As you learned from Chapters 7 and 15, there are many different types of jobs and professions than can be practiced from home, and the people interviewed within this chapter provide just a few examples.

- People have many different reasons for wanting to work from home, such as: they enjoy the freedom of not being stuck behind a desk all day within a highly corporate atmosphere, or they want more time to spend with their family. Some people don't want to deal with a commute to and from an office, or be stuck in traffic during rush hour.

- No matter what type of home business you plan to launch or profession you plan to practice, to be successful, you'll need to be extremely motivated, self-driven, hardworking, well organized and self-sufficient. While you're at home, there are many temptations to take extended breaks, watch television, or do non-work-related activities during the business day. Giving in to these temptations and not working can be a hazard, because when you're self-employed, if you're not working, you're not making money.

- One of the tricks home-office workers must discover is learning how to balance their personal and professional lives. Working from home is not a job, it's a lifestyle, and one that can easily consume you if you're not careful. Those who are the happiest and most successful in the long-term manage to find a nice balance that allows them to work hard, but enjoy a personal life.

- Working from a home office is certainly not for everyone, including many people who choose to be self-employed. After all, it is possible to launch your own small business, but have an office or retail shop, or even operate one of those cart-based businesses at the mall.

Resource Guide

Information about careers

When researching a career, always talk to people who are doing what you'd like to be doing.Here are some publications that could also help you, but the best information will come from people.

- *Adams Jobs Almanac*   Describes over 7,000 U.S. employers, is broken down by industry. It is published annually by Adams Media Corporation ($15.95) and is available from bookstores.

- *American Salaries & Wages Survey*   Published by Gale Research, this directory describes over 42,000 job titles and lists salary ranges for each.

- *National Association of Older Workers Employment Services* (The National Council on the Aging) Career services and information for older members of the work force (202-479-1200).

- *The American Almanac of Jobs and Salaries* Published by Avon Books.

- *The Directory of Occupational Titles (DOT)*   This online directory (http://www.wave.net/upg/

immigration/dot_index.html) offers de-scriptions of over 12,000 occupations and career opportunities.

- *The President's Committee on Employment of People with Disabilities*   Learn about job opportunities and career paths for people with physical or mental disabilities (202-376-6200).

- *The Salary Survey*   Published annually by the National Association of Colleges and Employers (800-544-5272 / www.jobweb.org) offers salary ranges for hundreds of entry-level positions.

- *The U.S. Industrial Outlook*   Published by the U.S. Department of Commerce, this directory offers descriptions of 350 industries and offers information about current and future (projected) trends within each industry (http://www.owt.com/jobsinfo/outlook.htm).

- National Internships (http://www.internships.com)   Publishes a series of directories that list hundreds of internship opportunities in specific U.S. cities.

- Veteran's Employment and Training Service (VETS)   Free career services and employment information for military veterans (202-219-9116).

Information about jobs

The place you live in will have it's own job network, whether a major newspaper or a bulleting board in a bookshop. Here are some other sources:

- National Internships (http://www.internships.com) publishes directories that list hundreds of internship opportunities in specific U.S. cities.

- Vault Report: The Job Seekers Secret Weapon (888-JOB-VAULT / http://www.vaultreports.

com/previews/internships.html) is one of many companies that offer online as well as printed directories of internship opportunities.

- AltaVista Careers, http://www.altavista.digital.com

- America's Job Bank, http://www.ajb.dni.us

- Career Builder, http://www.careerbuilder.com

- Career City, http://www.careercity.com

- Career Exchange, http://www.careerexchange.com

- Career Mosaic, http://www.careermosaic.com

- CareerMart, http://www.careermart.com

- CareerNet, http://www.careernet.com

- CareerPro, http://www.career-pro.com

- CareerWeb, http://www.careerweb.com

- E-Span, http://www.espan.com

- Job Bank USA, http://www.jobbankusa.com

- Jobfind.Com, http://www.jobfind.com

- JobLynx, http://www.joblyunx.com

- Net-Temps, http://www.net-temps.com

- The Monster Board, http://www.monster.com

- Yahoo Employment Classifieds, http://classifieds.yahoo.com/employment.html (also see www.yahoo.com)

- ZD Net Job Database, http://www.zdnet.com/cc/jobs/jobs.html

Information about companies

Here are some sources you can use when researching companies:

- Fortune 500 List, http://www.pathfinder.com/fortune/fortune500/500list.html

- Fortune 500 Homepage Directory at, http://www.sas.upenn.edu/~alizaidi/directory.html

- PR Newswire (www.prnewswire.com) and BusinessWire (www.businesswire.com) are press release distribution. PR Newswire also offers a free fax-on-demand service. Call (800) 753-0352, and request extension #662 for information on how to obtain press releases.

- Standard & Poor's Reports-On-Demand will fax you up-to-date information about any of over 4,600 U.S. companies. There's a charge to receive each report, but one complementary sample report is available by calling (800) 642-2858. For additional information about this service, call (800) 292-0808.

- If you don't know the URL (web site address) for a company you're researching, you can use one of the popular Internet search engines, such as Yahoo! (www.yahoo.com), Excite (www.excite.com) or AltaVista (www.altavista.digital.com) or call the company.

- Boston Herald (www.bostonherald.com)

- Chicago Tribune (www.chicago.tribune.com)

- Dallas Morning News (www.dallasnews.com)

- Detroit Free Press (www.freep.com)

- Los Angeles Times (www.latimes.com)

- Miami Herald (www.herald.com)

- New York Times (www.nytimes.com)

- Philadelphia Inquirer (www.phillynews.com)

- Washington Post (www.washingtonpost.com)

The 1998 ten best employers for working mothers, according to a study conducted by *Working Mother* magazine are:

1. Citicorp/Citibank
2. Glaxo Wellcome
3. IBM
4. Johnson & Johnson
5. Eli Lilly
6. MBNA America Bank
7. Merck
8. NationsBank
9. SAS Institute
10. Xerox

Information about salaries

- The *Executive Compensation Report* newsletter's web site, which can be accessed by pointing your browser to http://www.ecronline.com

- JobSmart, www.Jobsmart.org

- Wageweb, www.wageweb.com (not a free service)

- Exec-U-Net, www.execunet.com (not a free service)

- Pinpoint Salary Service (for AOL members, is not a free service)

- Futurestep, www.futurestep.com (free, but your information may be sent to recruiters)

- To learn about employee benefits from a trade paper for benefits professionals, visit the *Employee Benefit News* web site at http://www.benefitnews.com or call Enterprise Communications, Inc. at (800) 966-3976.

Financial information

Intuit Software (http://www.quicken.com) has created a web site (http://www.quicken. com/retirement) designed to help people use their computer and the Quicken software to plan their retirement. This site also offers an extensive glossary of financial and investment terms (http://www.quicken.com/glossary).

The Vanguard Group's web site offers a comprehensive FAQ (frequently asked questions) document pertaining to IRAs at www. vanguard.com/educ/lib/retire/faqira.html (or go to www.vanguard.com).

Call (800) 772-1213 to request free publications from the Social Security Administration, or visit www.ssa.gov.

One highly informative site, called Investor-Guide, can be found at http://www. investorguide.com/Retirement.htm.

The pre-interview checklist

As you're preparing for each interview, use this checklist to help you prepare. Knowing that you're prepared will make you more confident.

___ To ensure that you look well rested and appear alert, it's important to get a good night's sleep before an interview.

___ The morning of the interview, take a shower. Make sure your hair is clean, your fingernails are manicured and you shave. Brush your teeth and use a mouthwash or breath freshener. It's critical that you look and feel your best, both to enhance your own confidence and to create a positive first impression.

__ Apply deodorant and antiperspirant. Avoid using any perfume or cologne.

__ Put on your interview outfit. Make sure that it's clean and wrinkle-free, and that you haven't forgotten any accessories. Refrain from wearing any flashy jewelry.

__ Shine your shoes.

__ Make extra copies of your resume and bring them with you.

__ Make copies of your letters of recommendation and your list of references. You'll want to provide these to the interviewer.

__ Pack up your briefcase or portfolio, making sure you bring a pen and pad to the interview. Also, don't forget to bring your personal planner/appointment book, in case you need to schedule a second interview. Within your briefcase/portfolio, insert your company research notes.

__ Write down the address and phone number of the potential employer, along with the name of the person you're supposed to meet. You'll also want to being the written directions so you don't get lost on your way to the interview. Place this information safely within your portfolio so you don't forget it.

__ Plan your travel route to the interview, making sure you allow plenty of time for traffic or any other unexpected delays.

__ Refrain from drinking beverages containing caffeine before the interview. Also, avoid eating any foods that could cause bad breath.

__ Use the rest room before your interview.

___ The morning of the interview, read the local newspaper, watch a morning news program on television and/or read the *Wall Street Journal.* It's important to be familiar with current events.

___ Arrive to your interview location at least 15 minutes early. Use the time to review your research notes and visualize yourself succeeding in the interview.

___ Remember, the moment you step through the front door of the potential employer, the interview process has begun. Be friendly and smile at everyone.

Suggested Reading List

1998 Knock'em Dead: The Ultimate Job Seekers Handbook, by Martin Yate (Adams Media Corporation)

Adams Jobs Almanac 1998, The Editors of Adams Media Corporation (Adams Media Corporation)

Career Guide To Industries (U.S. Department of Labor, Bureau of Labor Statistics)

Diamond In The Rough, by Barry J. Farber (Berkley Publishing)

Employment Outlook Projections (U.S. Department of Labor, Bureau of Labor Statistics)

First Job, Great Job: America's Hottest Business Leaders Share Their Secrets, by Jason R. Rich (Macmillan)

How To Make It Big As A Consultant, by William Cohen (Amacom)

Job Hunting for the Utterly Confused, by Jason R. Rich (McGraw-Hill)

Mark H. McCormack On Negotiating, by Mark H. McCormack (Dove Books)

Negotiating For Dummies, by Michael Donaldson and Mimi Donaldson (IDG Books)

Resumes For Dummies, by Joyce Lain Kennedy (IDG Books)

Resumes That Knock'em Dead, by Martin Yate, (Adams Media Corporation)

Six Figure Consulting, by Dr. Gary Scott Goodman (Amacom)

The 1998 What Color Is Your Parachute, by Richard Nelson Bolles (Ten Speed Press)

The Occupational Outlook Handbook (U.S. Department of Labor, Bureau of Labor Statistics)

The Princeton Review: Negotiate Smart, by Nicholas Reid Schaffzin (The Princeton Review)

The Wall Street Journal Guide To Planning Your Financial Future, by Kenneth M. Morris (Lightbulb Press)

You Can Negotiate Anything, by Herb Cohen (Bantam Books)

Important Statistics

Career choices

According to the Bureau of Labor Statistics, the ten general industries with the fastest employment growth, between 1996 and 2006 are:

ESTIMATED GROWTH BETWEEN 1996 AND 2006

Computer and data processing services	108%
Health services	68%
Management and public relations	60%
Miscellaneous transportation services	60%
Residential care	59%
Personnel supply services	53%
Water and sanitation	51%
Individual and miscellaneous social services	50%
Offices of health practitioners	47%
Amusement and recreation services	41%

The Bureau of Labor Statistics also reports that the ten occupations with the largest job growth between 1996 and 2006 are projected to be:

ESTIMATED GROWTH BETWEEN 1996 AND 2006

Cashiers	17%
Systems analysts	103%
General managers and top executives	15%
Registered nurses	21%
Salespeople (retail)	10%
Truck drivers	15%
Home health aides	76%
Teacher aides and educational assistants	38%
Nursing aides, orderlies and attendants	25%
Receptionists and information clerks	30%

The ten occupations with the fastest employment growth between 1996 and 2006 include:

ESTIMATED GROWTH BETWEEN 1996 AND 2006

Database administrators, computer support specialists and all other computer scientists	118%
Computer engineers	109%
Systems analysts	103%
Personal and home care aides	85%
Physical and corrective therapy assistants and aides	79%
Home health aides	76%
Medical assistants	74%
Desktop publishing specialists	74%
Physical therapists	71%
Occupational therapy assistants and aides	69%

The *Unofficial Guide*™ Reader Questionnaire

If you would like to express your opinion about ace-ing the interview or this guide, please complete this questionnaire and mail it to:

The *Unofficial Guide*™ Reader Questionnaire
Macmillan Lifestyle Group
1633 Broadway, floor 7
New York, NY 10019-6785

Gender: ___ M ___ F

Age: ___ Under 30 ___ 31–40 ___ 41–50 ___ Over 50

Education: ___ High school ___ College ___ Graduate/Professional

What is your occupation?

_____

How did you hear about this guide?
___ Friend or relative
___ Newspaper, magazine, or Internet
___ Radio or TV
___ Recommended at bookstore
___ Recommended by librarian
___ Picked it up on my own
___ Familiar with the *Unofficial Guide*™ travel series

Did you go to the bookstore specifically for a book on earning what you deserve? Yes ___ No ___

Have you used any other *Unofficial Guides*™?
Yes ___ No ___

If Yes, which ones?

_____
_____
_____

What other book(s) on earning have you purchased?

_____

_____

_____

Was this book:
___ more helpful than other(s)
___ less helpful than other(s)

Do you think this book was worth its price?
Yes ___ No ___

Did this book cover all topics related to earning what you deserve adequately? Yes ___ No ___

Please explain your answer:

_____

_____

_____

Were there any specific sections in this book that were of particular help to you? Yes ___ No ___

Please explain your answer:

_____

_____

_____

On a scale of 1 to 10, with 10 being the best rating, how would you rate this guide? ___

What other titles would you like to see published in the _Unofficial Guide_™ series?

_____

_____

Are _Unofficial Guides_™ readily available in your area? Yes ___ No ___

Other comments:

_____

_____

_____

_____

Get the inside scoop...with the *Unofficial Guides*™!

The Unofficial Guide to Alternative Medicine
   ISBN: 0-02-862526-9   Price: $15.95

The Unofficial Guide to Buying a Home
   ISBN: 0-02-862461-0   Price: $15.95

The Unofficial Guide to Buying or Leasing a Car
   ISBN: 0-02-862524-2   Price: $15.95

The Unofficial Guide to Childcare
   ISBN: 0-02-862457-2   Price: $15.95

The Unofficial Guide to Cosmetic Surgery
   ISBN: 0-02-862522-6   Price: $15.95

The Unofficial Guide to Dieting Safely
   ISBN: 0-02-862521-8   Price: $15.95

The Unofficial Guide to Eldercare
   ISBN: 0-02-862456-4   Price: $15.95

The Unofficial Guide to Hiring Contractors
   ISBN: 0-02-862460-2   Price: $15.95

The Unofficial Guide to Investing
   ISBN: 0-02-862458-0   Price: $15.95

The Unofficial Guide to Planning Your Wedding
   ISBN: 0-02-862459-9   Price: $15.95

All books in the *Unofficial Guide*™ series are available at your local bookseller, or by calling 1-800-428-5331.

About the Author

Jason R. Rich can tell you everything you need to know about earning what you deserve. He is the author of several career-related books, including *Job Hunting for the Utterly Confused* (McGraw-Hill) and *First Job, Great Job* (Macmillan). He's also a weekly columnist for *The Boston Herald*'s Sunday 'Careers' section and continues to contribute articles to publications such as *The Wall Street Journal's Managing Your Career* and *National Business Employment Weekly*. *Visit his Web site at* http://www.jasonrich.com.